Elderly Clients – A Precedent Manual

GW00544374

Elderly Clients –
A Precedent Manual

Denzil Lush BA, MA, LLM

Solicitor
Master of the Court of Protection

JORDANS
1996

Published by
Jordan Publishing Limited
21 St Thomas Street
Bristol BS1 6JS

British Library Cataloguing-in-Publication Data
A catalogue record for this book is available from the British Library.

ISBN 0 85308 309 6

Typeset by ISL, Gloucester
Printed by Hobbs the Printers of Southampton

Neither to son nor wife, brother nor friend,
   give power over yourself during your own lifetime.
And do not give your property to anyone else,
   in case you regret it and have to ask for it back.
As long as you live and there is breath in your body,
   do not yield power over yourself to anyone;
since it is better for your children to be your suppliants,
   than for you to have to look to the generosity of your sons.
In all you do be the master,
   and do not spoil the honour that is rightly yours.
The day your life draws to a close,
   when death is approaching;
      that is the time to distribute your inheritance.

Ecclesiasticus 30: 20–24

PREFACE

The opening words come from Ecclesiasticus, an apocryphal book which was never accepted as part of the Old Testament – not to be confused with Ecclesiastes, which was. They were written more than two thousand years ago and are still probably the best advice for most elderly clients. Of course, in those days there was no such thing as retirement, advanced medical technology, enduring powers of attorney, inheritance tax, or means-testing for long-term care. So, although I would generally endorse those words of wisdom, this book is mainly about the circumstances in which it may be wiser to reject that advice and give power over yourself during your lifetime or give your property to somebody else.

I am conscious that anyone casually browsing through this book could jump to the conclusion that the majority of elderly people, however one defines 'elderly', are living in residential care, heavily subsidised by the State, and in the advanced stages of dementia; or that they are in need of protection from over-zealous social workers, rapacious care-home proprietors, and – perhaps worst of all – relatives who are prepared to go to any lengths to preserve their prospects of inheritance. It would be equally true to say that anyone who skimmed through a volume on child law would assume that most children come from broken homes, are inadequately maintained, and are the victims of physical, psychological and sexual abuse. Such conclusions are completely unfounded. As the statistics in the chapter on the elderly population reveal, most older people live in their own homes, have additional sources of income to supplement their State pension, and are likely never to become senile.

The same casual browser might also think that somewhere along the line the balance has gone adrift. For example, the chapters on living wills and statutory wills are almost as long as the one on conventional wills. I make no apologies for the emphasis. My primary aim has been to provide legal advisers and others with a selection of forms, precedents and materials that are not available or readily accessible elsewhere. A secondary aim has been to disseminate ideas and stimulate debate.

The author and publishers are grateful to the Benefits Agency for giving their kind permission to reproduce the social security forms in Chapter 7.

I would like to thank a number of people – in particular, Henry Anstey, Gordon Ashton, Luke Clements, Chris Docker, Penny Letts, Julia Lomas, Biddy Macfarlane, Alison Matthews, John Prioleau, Ian Purvis, Brian Sandy, Lydia Sinclair, Michael Smith, Ann Sommerville, and Martin West – for the good ideas or useful snippets of information they have given me from time to time. I must also thank my former clients in private practice, to whom this book is dedicated. Protocol prohibits me from mentioning their names, but their personalities and the problems they have encountered are portrayed in many of the precedents.

The law is stated as at 1 January 1996.

Denzil Lush
March 1996

CONTENTS

CHAPTER 14: STATUTORY WILLS

TABLE OF CASES

Bold type denotes cases summarised in the text.

TABLE OF STATUTES

References in the right-hand column are to page numbers.

TABLE OF STATUTORY INSTRUMENTS

References in the right-hand column are to page numbers.

CHAPTER 1: ELDERLY PEOPLE

INDEX

Text

ELDERLY PEOPLE

TEXT

Introduction

The ageing of the population has enormous implications for the future structure of society, the family, the work-force and public spending, and is likely to be the central social issue arising during the first half of the twenty-first century.[1] This chapter briefly considers why the population is ageing, and examines some of the demographic characteristics of the elderly population.[2]

---

1 Paul Paillat, 'Recent and Predictable Population Trends in Developed Countries', in John Eekelaar and David Pearl (eds), *An Aging World: Dilemmas and Challenges for Law and Social Policy* (Clarendon Press, Oxford, 1989), pp 25–35, at p 35.
2 The tables in this chapter may appear to be inconsistent. Sometimes the statistics relate solely to England and Wales. More often they relate to Great Britain (England, Wales and Scotland), and occasionally to the whole of the United Kingdom (Great Britain and Northern Ireland). Similarly, the ages stated often refer to people aged 60 and over, sometimes to people aged 65 and over, and occasionally to people of pensionable age (men aged 65 and over, and women aged 60 and over).

The population structure

Regardless of the age chosen as a starting point for defining *old* or *elderly*, the proportion of older people has increased in relation to the population as a whole. Whereas in 1891, only 7.5% of the population of Great Britain were aged 60 and over, by 1991, that percentage had almost trebled to 21%. And whereas in 1891, 45% of the population were under 20, in 1991, only 25% were under that age. (See Table 1 below.)

The proportion of *young elderly* people (say, the 65–79 age group) will decline slightly during the next two decades because of the low fertility rate until the end of the Second World War, but the proportion of *old elderly* (those aged 80 and over) has doubled during the last thirty years and is expected almost to double again in the next forty years. (See Table 2 below.) In 1961, there were 1,026,000 people aged 80 and over in Great Britain. In 1991, there were 2,046,555, and it is estimated that in 2031 there will be approximately 3,725,000.

Table 1. Population aged 60 or over: Great Britain, 1891–1991[1]

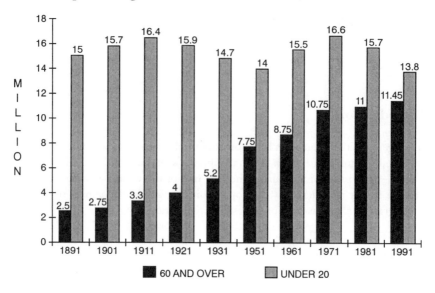

Table 2. Young and old elderly: United Kingdom, 1961–2031[2]

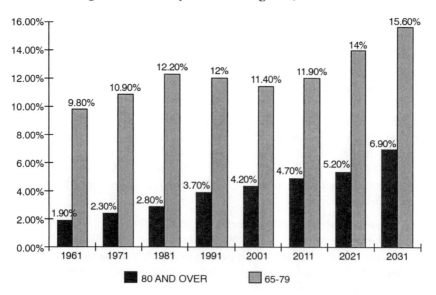

There are two main reasons why the population is ageing. The first is a decline in the mortality rate. People are living longer. The second is a decline in the fertility rate. Fewer children are being born. Migration is also an important factor, although its impact is felt more on a local than a national level.[3]

---

1 Source: Office of Population Censuses and Surveys, *1991 Census: Historical Tables, Great Britain* (CEN 91 HT: HMSO, 1993), Table 5, Age and Marital Status 1891–1991.
2 Source: Central Statistical Office, *Social Trends 1994* (HMSO, 1994), p 23, Table 4, Age and Structure of the Population.
3 See 'Geographical variations' at p 9 below.

Longer life expectancy

A century ago, a newly born male had a life expectancy of just over forty-four years. A baby boy born today can reasonably expect to live to celebrate his seventy-third birthday. This increase in life expectancy is the result of social, economic and medical advances during the twentieth century – improved housing, sanitation, diet, health care and the welfare state. (See Table 3 below.)

Table 3. Life expectancy at birth: England and Wales, 1891–1991[1]

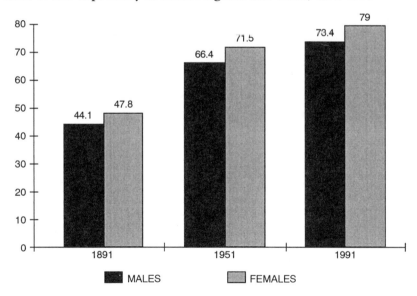

Women live longer than men. At birth, a female can expect to outlive a male by about five and a half years. The difference gradually diminishes with age. At 60, it is down to four years; at 70, three years; at 80, two years; and at 85 and over, one year. (See Table 4 below.)

Table 4. Life expectancy at age 55–85: England and Wales, 1991[2]

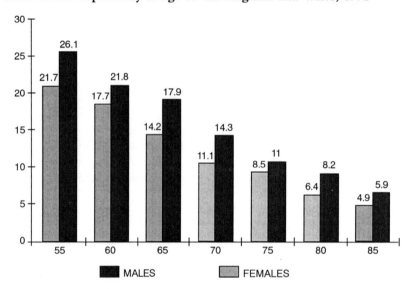

---

1 Source: Department of Health, *Health and Personal Social Services Statistics for England* (Government Statistical Service, 1994), p 20, Fig 3.3.

2 Source: Central Statistical Office, *Annual Abstract of Statistics 1994* (HMSO, 1994), p 41, Table 2.23, Interim Life Table for England and Wales 1989–91.

Lower fertility

To keep the population stable, every woman of child-bearing age should on average produce 2.1 children. This is known as the *replacement level*. When fertility exceeds the replacement level, the population increases and becomes proportionately younger. When fertility is lower than the replacement level, the population decreases and becomes proportionately older.

Table 5 below shows the fertility rate in Great Britain from 1860 to the projected figure for 2000. During the depression and Second World War, it sank below the replacement level, but after the war there was a baby boom, with fertility peaking at 2.95 in 1964. Since then it has again fallen below the replacement level, and currently stands at 1.8. Great Britain's fertility rate is the fourth highest in western Europe after Ireland, Sweden and Norway. The lowest, in Germany, is 1.3.

Table 5. Fertility rate: Great Britain, 1860–2000[1]

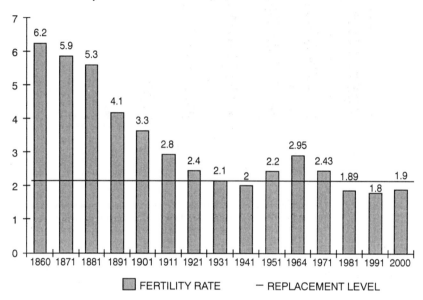

1 Sources: John Hobcraft and Philip Rees (eds), *Regional Demographic Development* (Croom Helm, 1977), Table 5.1, p 118, and Central Statistical Office, *Social Trends 1994* (HMSO, 1994), p 27.

Gender

There are more elderly women than elderly men. Until the age of 20, boys outnumber girls by roughly 51% to 49%. From 20 onwards, this ratio is reversed and, from the age of 60, the proportion of females to males steadily increases. At 90 and over, women outnumber men by 4 to 1. (See Table 6 below.)

Table 6. Gender of persons aged 60 and over: Great Britain, 1991[1]

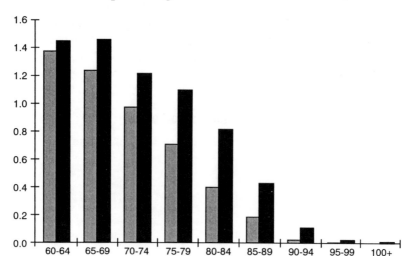

1 Source: Office of Population Censuses and Surveys, *1991 Census: Sex, Age and Marital Status, Great Britain* (Cen 91 SAM: HMSO, 1993), p 130, Table 4, Sex and year of birth.

Marital status

One of the effects of the longer life expectancy of women is that there are more elderly widows than widowers. The average age at which widowed people outnumber their married contemporaries is 72.5 years for women and 86.5 years for men.[1] 23,238 people aged 55 or over got married in the United Kingdom in 1991: 14,922 (64%) males, and 8,406 (36%) females.[2] The main reason for the disparity is that men tend to marry younger women. (See Table 7 below.)

Table 7. Marital status of people aged 60 and over: Great Britain, 1991[3]

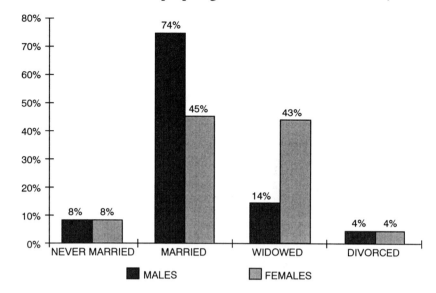

1 In the 1991 Census, there were 97,289 married women and 93,007 widows aged 72, and 85,132 married women and 91,921 widows aged 73. In 1991, there were 18,804 married men and 17,167 widowers aged 86, and 14,159 married men and 14,402 widowers aged 87.
2 Central Statistical Office, *Annual Abstract of Statistics 1994* (HMSO, 1994), p 21.
3 Source: Office of Population Censuses and Surveys, *1991 Census: Persons aged 60 and over* (Cen 91 Pen: HMSO, 1993), p 11, Table 1, Age and Marital Status.

Geographical variations

In the 1991 Census of Great Britain, 18.78% of the population were of pensionable age (ie 60 and over for women, and 65 and over for men). As Map 1 below reveals, the pensioner population is unevenly distributed over the country, with particularly high clusters in the traditional retirement resorts along the south coast of England. The extremes range from over 34% in the Christchurch and Rother districts to 11% in Tamworth, Milton Keynes and Wokingham.[1]

At first sight, this disproportionate spread would appear to have serious implications for the local authorities who are responsible for funding care in the community. However, the counties with the highest percentage of pensioners, namely the Isle of Wight (26.38%), East Sussex (26.38%) and Dorset (25.93%), are also those with the lowest percentage of children under 16 and, presumably, any savings on the education budget may partly compensate for increased expenditure on social services for the elderly.

1 See Office of Population Censuses and Surveys, *1991 Census: Key Statistics for Local Authorities: Great Britain* (Cen 91 KSLA: HMSO, 1994), pp 50–64, Table 3, Age Structure.

Map 1. Residents of pensionable age

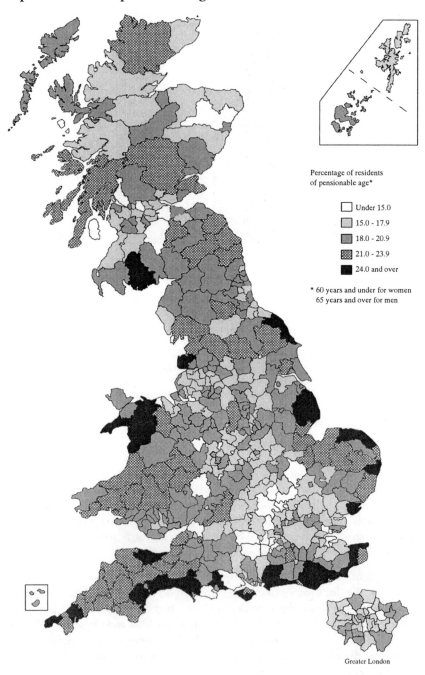

Percentage of residents
of pensionable age*

☐ Under 15.0
▨ 15.0 - 17.9
▨ 18.0 - 20.9
▨ 21.0 - 23.9
■ 24.0 and over

* 60 years and under for women
  65 years and over for men

Greater London

Crown copyright. Reproduced with permission from *1991 Census: Key Statistics for Local Authorities: Great Britain* (Cen 91 KSLA, HMSO, 1994), p 18.

Employment

The current trend is towards increasingly earlier retirement, especially for men. In 1975, 93% of men in their fifties were economically active. By 1991, that figure had dropped to 76%, although during the same period, the percentage of working women aged 50–59 remained constant at 59%.[1]

Early retirement is even more noticeable in the 60–64 age range. In 1975, 81% of men and 29% of women of that age were in work, but by 1991, those percentages had dropped to 45% and 22% respectively.[2]

People are retiring early partly because of the pressure on the job market exerted by the post-war baby boomers. This is likely to continue until the second decade of the twenty-first century when the trend could reverse; the technical skills and vocational experience of particularly the young elderly could acquire an enhanced value; and older people might even be encouraged to stay at work longer or take up new employment.[3]

No matter how attractive the incentives to retire may seem, people who are economically inactive generally have a lower standard of living than those in full-time or even part-time employment. A survey conducted in 1994 by *O50*, a magazine for the over 50s, asked the question 'If you are retired, how does your standard of living compare to when you were working?' Forty-one percent of those who replied considered that their standard of living was more or less the same, 34% were slightly worse off, and 24% were substantially worse off.[4] The same respondents also revealed that they had to economise most on motoring. Whereas 82% were able to run a car when they were working, only 32% could afford to do so in retirement.

---

1 Source: Margaret Thomas, Eileen Goddard, May Hickman and Paul Hunter, *1992 General Household Survey* (OPCS Social Survey Division: Series GHS No 23, HMSO, 1994), Tables 7.3(a) and (b).

2 *Ibid.*

3 *Ageing: A Report from the General Synod Board for Social Responsibility* (Church House Publishing, 1990), p 19.

4 *O50*, Autumn 1994, Issue 24, p 57.

Home ownership

The present elderly generation has participated substantially, although not fully, in the post-war growth of owner-occupation. Sixty-six per cent of people aged 60–64 own their own home, as do 61% of those aged 65–69, 54% in their 70s, and 53% aged 80 and over. (See Table 8 below.)

Table 8. Owner-occupation by head of household: Great Britain, 1991[1]

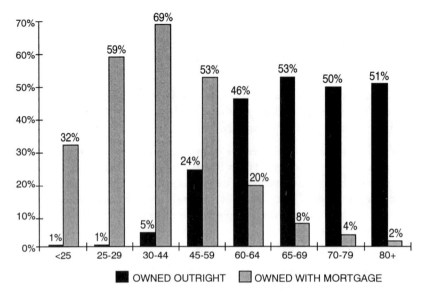

Approximately 35% of homes in which the head of the household is over 65 are rented from a local authority, 8% are privately rented, and 4% are rented from a housing association or co-operative.[2]

---

1 Source: Malcolm Smyth and Fiona Browne, *General Household Survey 1990* (OPCS Social Survey Division, HMSO, 1992), Tables 3.29(b) and 3.34(b).
2 Elizabeth Breeze, Gill Trevor and Amanda Wilmott, *General Household Survey 1989* (HMSO, 1991), Table No 8.61(b).

Income

Although more than half of the pensioners in Britain own their own home outright, and a growing number are retiring with the benefit of an occupational or personal pension, a considerable number are heavily dependent on state benefits. In 1992, when the average weekly income of all households was £302.50,[1] the average weekly income of a pensioner who had not recently retired was £150, more than half of which represented contributory or non-contributory benefits. (See Table 9 below.)

By contrast, in 1992 the average income of recently retired pensioners was £225 per week: 25% from an occupational pension; 19% from investment income; 15% from employment income; and 41% from social security. In this context, *recently retired* means men aged 65–69; women aged 60–64; and couples where the husband is aged between 65 and 69.[2]

Table 9. Income of pensioners by source: United Kingdom, 1992³

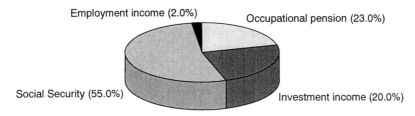

The financial position of older people often reflects their prior socio-economic circumstances, gender and marital status. Inequalities which existed throughout their working life can be perpetuated and amplified in retirement. Married couples are generally better off than single people. Men are generally better off than women. The young elderly are better off than the old elderly, and spinsters are better off than widows.⁴ (See Table 10 below.)

Table 10. Gross weekly income in retired households: United Kingdom, 1991⁵

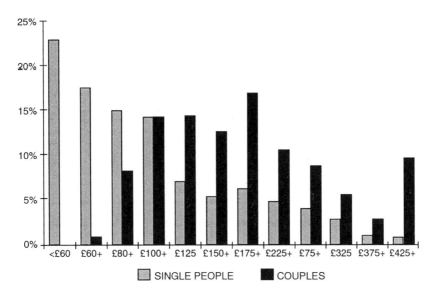

1 Central Statistical Office, *Annual Abstract of Statistics 1994* (HMSO, 1994), p 256.

2 Source: Central Statistical Office, *Social Trends 25, 1995 Edition* (HMSO, 1995), p 88, Chart 5.9.

3 *Ibid.*

4 Malcolm Wicks and Melanie Henwood, 'The Demographic and Social Circumstances of Elderly People', in Brian Gearing, Malcolm Johnson and Tom Heller (eds), *Mental Health Problems in Old Age* (Open University, 1988).

5 Source: Central Statistical Office, *Family Spending*, Report on the 1991 Family Expenditure Survey (HMSO, 1992).

Retirement pensions

The Old Age Pensions Act 1908 introduced a means-tested pension of a maximum of five shillings (25p) per week for anyone aged 70 and over with an annual income of less than £21. There was a reduced pension on a sliding scale for people whose income was less than £31 per year.[1] In 1925, the means test was abolished, contributory pensions were introduced, and the pensionable age was reduced to 65.[2] The pensionable age for women was further lowered to 60 in 1940.[3]

When the current flat-rate system was introduced in 1946,[4] it was envisaged that the pension would be adequate for subsistence in most cases, and that augmentation from other sources would be unnecessary. However, although the basic pension has kept roughly in pace with prices, it has never been sufficient to remove the dependence of a large number of pensioners on means-tested benefits. 1,765,000 people aged 60 or over were in receipt of income support in 1994,[5] and it is estimated that 33% of pensioners who are entitled to receive income support do not actually claim it.[6] For example, the basic retirement pension for a single person is £58.85 per week. The single personal allowance for income support is currently £46.50 and the single pensioner premium is £18.60. A single person who had no income other than the basic retirement pension could, if otherwise entitled, receive an additional £6.25 per week by way of income support.

The total expenditure on benefits in Great Britain in 1993–94 was £80.9 billion, of which £36.8 billion (45.5%) was spent on the elderly.[7] Table 11 below shows how expenditure on retirement pensions has doubled during the last ten years.

The pensionable age is to be equalised at 65 for both men and women, and will be phased in over a ten-year period from 2010.

Table 11. National Insurance: Retirement pensions: annualised expenditure, 1984–1992[8]

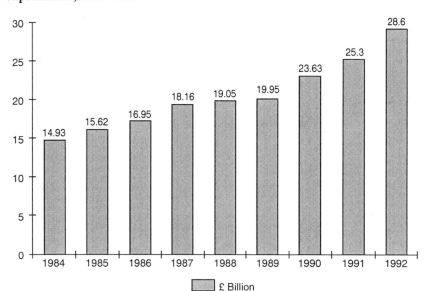

£ Billion

---

1 For the history of retirement pensions, see A.I. Ogus, E.M. Barendt and N.J. Wikeley, *The Law of Social Security* (4th edition, Butterworths, 1995), Chapter 5.
2 Widows', Orphans' and Old Age Contributory Pensions Act 1925
3 Old Age and Widows' Pensions Act 1940, s 1(1).
4 National Insurance Act 1946.
5 *Social Security Statistics 1995* (HMSO, 1995), Table A2.04.
6 Income-related benefits: estimate of take-up, 1989.
7 Central Statistical Office, *Social Trends 25, 1995 Edition* (HMSO, 1995), p 149, Table 8.28.
8 Source: Central Statistical Office, *Annual Abstract of Statistics 1994*, Table 3.11, National Insurance Fund.

Residential and nursing care

The number of people living in residential care or nursing homes is relatively small: about 425,000 in the whole of Great Britain which represents only 4% of the population over the age of 65.

Until the 1960s, most elderly people were looked after either at home by their families, or in long-stay geriatric wards in an NHS hospital. During the 1970s, the public sector provision of residential places (known as *Part III Accommodation*) gradually expanded until the spending cuts imposed on local authorities in the 1980s resulted in a contraction of the programme. The private sector then moved in to meet the increasing demand. (See Table 12 below.)

Table 12. Residential and nursing home places: Great Britain, 1970–1992[1]

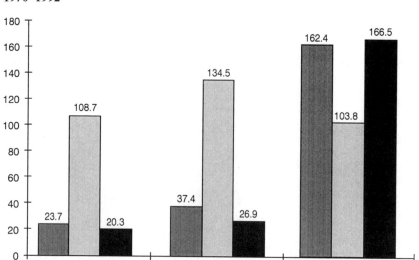

There are several reasons for the surge in the number of private residential and nursing homes during the 1980s:

- the reduction in public sector provision of residential accommodation;
- the closure of NHS mental hospitals and long-stay geriatric wards;
- increased longevity; and
- availability of State aid for residents and patients unable to fund themselves.

Means-tested benefits first became available for financing accommodation charges in 1981 and the Department of Social Security (DSS) found itself increasingly funding places in private residential and nursing homes through supplementary benefit and subsequently income support. (See Table 13 below.)

Table 13. DSS funding of residential care: Great Britain, 1980–1992

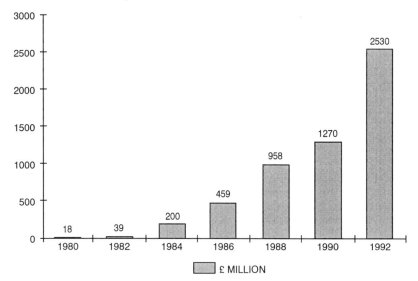

£ MILLION

The National Health Service and Community Care Act 1990, which came into force on 1 April 1993, will gradually transfer the burden of funding residential and nursing care from central to local government.

The effects of the funding changes are likely to be:[2]

- a levelling-off of State payment for long-term care, as the new cash-limited system replaces the more open-ended income support funding;
- an eventual shift from public to private payment, particularly as higher levels of owner-occupation filter through to the very elderly;
- bed-blocking in NHS hospitals as long-stay patients refuse to be discharged into the community and subjected to a means test by their local social services;
- increased artificial pauperisation, whereby people attempt to divest themselves of assets in order to avoid paying charges for long-term care;
- tougher measures to combat bed-blocking and artificial pauperisation;
- a decline in occupancy levels in private sector care homes;
- diversification, whereby residential care homes increase the range of services they offer: for example, by providing domiciliary respite or day care;
- the closure of homes of borderline financial viability, and the closure of substandard homes which, although they are able to meet the registration requirements, cannot comply with the quality standards now imposed in most social services' specifications;
- the problem of finding suitable alternative accommodation when substandard or non-viable care homes are forced to close down.

---

1 Source: *CCH Business Profiles* (CCH Editions Ltd, looseleaf), p 361, para 204 (Nursing Homes etc). In 1992, the occupancy level in nursing homes was 94%, and in residential homes 91%: *ibid*, p 361, para 451.

2 See *Laing's Review of Private Healthcare 1993*, p 166.

Dementia

Dementia is 'an acquired global impairment of intellect, memory and personality but without impairment of consciousness'.[1] *Amnesia*, or loss of short-term memory, is a universal symptom. Other signs or symptoms include some or all of the following: *aphasia* (the inability to express thoughts in words); *apraxia* (the inability to perform voluntary movements of the body); *agnosia* (the inability to recognise people or common objects); aggression; wandering; delusions; depression; and incontinence.

The causes of dementia are unknown, but recent studies suggest that a variant of the gene coding for the protein apolipoprotein E (*apo-E*) has been tied to a substantially increased risk of acquiring Alzheimer's Disease, which accounts for approximately two-thirds of the dementias in old age. People who inherit two *E4* genes (one from each parent) have an eight times greater risk of developing the disease than the general population, and display symptoms at an average age of 68. Patients with two *E3* genes demonstrate symptoms of the disease somewhat later, at about 75.[2]

The course of the disease is usually slowly progressive,[3] but may develop more rapidly in some people than others. There is currently little in the way of effective treatment. Death can occur at any time between a few months and twenty years from onset, although the average life expectancy is within the range of five to seven years from when the condition is first diagnosed.[4]

Table 14 below is, to some extent, conjecture, because estimates of the incidence of dementia vary considerably within the range of 20% to 40% of people aged 85 and over. The risk of acquiring dementia increases with age, and is greater for women, regardless of the higher ratio of females to males in any age group in later life. The drop in the percentage of men suffering from dementia in their late 90s represents the remaining survivors, and would probably be repeated in respect of women aged 100 and over because of the longer life expectancy of females.

The commonest psychiatric disorder in old age is not dementia but *depression*. In the elderly, it tends to assume a different form from depression in younger life. An older person who is clinically depressed is more likely to be increasingly agitated or irritable, sleep badly, become hypochondriacal and lose interest in life. It often occurs as a result of physical illness, loneliness or bereavement, and it is estimated that between 10% and 15% of people over 65 will suffer from clinical depression at some time in old age.[5]

Table 14. Estimated incidence of dementia by age and gender: England, 1988[6]

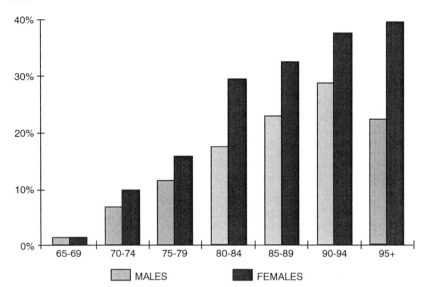

1 W.A. Lishman, *Organic Psychiatry* (Oxford, 1978).
2 Thomas T. Perls, 'The Oldest Old', *Scientific American*, January 1995, pp 50–55.
3 Although dementia is often considered to be an irreversible condition, recent studies have shown that about 10% of patients with dementia have conditions for which treatment can reverse the otherwise inexorable decline of mental function: Moyra Williams in the contribution on dementia in *The Oxford Companion to the Mind* (Oxford, 1987), p 185.
4 *Health Services Management*, April 1993, p 21.
5 *Health Services Management*, April 1993, p 20.
6 This table is based in part on Alastair Gray and Paul Fenn, 'Alzheimer's Disease: The burden of the illness in England', *Health Trends* (1993) vol 25, no 1, pp 31–37, Figs 1 and 2.

Elderly clients and the legal profession

On 26 June 1985, the Enduring Powers of Attorney Act received the Royal Assent. In November that year, the College of Law ran a couple of half-day courses entitled *Law and the Elderly: The Home, Finance and Taxation*: one in Bournemouth and the other in Brighton. In 1986, the College produced its lecture notes in booklet form, and, at roughly the same time, Age Concern published *The Law and Vulnerable Elderly People*. Since then, handling the problems of the elderly has become a discrete specialisation within private practice. The incidence of dementia and diminishing capacity in an increasing number of older people and the spiralling costs of residential and nursing care highlight the need for advance planning in all areas – legal, financial, personal and even medical – for possible incapacity in later life.

As the title of the College of Law's lectures back in 1985 suggests, advising elderly clients embraces a wide range of legal topics: land law, equity, succession, mental health law, welfare law, housing, medical law, tax planning, local government law, and even litigation. In addition to having a knowledge of the relevant aspects of these areas of the law, a specialist adviser needs to be sensitive to the ageing process; streetwise on all the community services and resources available; alert to possible conflicts of interest, undue influence or coercion; and prepared, if necessary, to act as a whistleblower.

The emergence of the law relating to elderly people as a speciality in its own right is comparable to the devolution of childcare from family law a decade ago. Within the next few years, there will almost certainly be a new professional organisation, interest group or panel – like The Academy of Elder Law Specialists formed in the USA in 1987[1] – which will provide continuing education for practitioners, its own diplomas, regulatory mechanisms, and greater opportunities for its members to become actively involved in policy and law reform.[2]

---

1 See, generally, Nancy Coleman, 'The Delivery of Legal Assistance to the Elderly in the United States', in John Eekelaar and David Pearl (eds), *An Aging World: Dilemmas and Challenges for Law and Social Policy* (Clarendon Press, Oxford, 1989), pp 463–477.

2 A community care practitioners group was formed in February 1995.

CHAPTER 2: WHO IS THE CLIENT?

INDEX

Text

Precedents

WHO IS THE CLIENT?

TEXT

Statutory definition

Section 87 of the Solicitors Act 1974 defines *client* as including:

'(a) in relation to contentious business, any person who as a principal or on behalf of another person retains or employs, or is about to retain or employ, a solicitor, and any person who is or may be liable to pay a solicitor's costs; and

(b) in relation to non-contentious business, any person who, as a principal or on behalf of another, or as a trustee or executor, or in any other capacity, has power, express or implied, to retain or employ, and retains or employs or is about to retain or employ a solicitor, and any person for the time being liable to pay a solicitor for his services any costs.'

Despite the statutory definition, it is not always clear who the client is. This chapter briefly examines some of the problems that arise in practice, particularly in the context of:

- supervening incapacity. If a client becomes mentally incapable, can a solicitor still act on his or her behalf?
- the Court of Protection. Who is the client: the patient or the receiver?
- enduring powers of attorney. Who is the client: the donor or the attorney?
- a conflict or potential conflict of interests between two or more clients.

A solicitor has a duty to act in the best interests of his or her client.[1] When acting for incapacitated, vulnerable or elderly clients, a solicitor should take into account:

- so far as ascertainable, the past and present wishes and feelings of the client;
- the need to encourage and permit the client to participate in any decision-making to the fullest extent of which he or she is capable; and
- the general principle that the course least restrictive of the client's freedom of decision and action is likely to be in his or her best interests.[2]

---

1 Solicitors' Practice Rules 1990, r 1(c).
2 *Mental Incapacity* (1995) Law Com No 231 (HMSO, 1995), paras 3.26–3.36, and the draft Mental Incapacity Bill, cl 3.

Supervening incapacity of the client

A solicitor is an *agent* acting on behalf of a *principal* – the client. As with most other forms of agency, a solicitor's retainer may be terminated by operation of the law if the client becomes 'mentally incapable'[1] which, for these purposes, means 'incapable, by reason of mental disorder, of managing and administering his or her property and affairs'.

Occasionally the solicitor is completely unaware of the supervening incapacity of the client. The traditional view is that, in these circumstances, if the solicitor enters into a contract or transacts any business with a third party on the client's behalf, the solicitor will be personally liable to that third party for any loss or damage caused by reason of the termination of his or her authority.

> ### Yonge v Toynbee (1910)[1]
>
> Yonge threatened to sue Toynbee and another for defamation. In August 1908, Toynbee gave instructions to Wontner & Sons to act on his behalf. On 8 October 1908, he was certified as a 'lunatic'. On 20 October 1908, Yonge commenced the action. Wontners entered an appearance and drew up proceedings on Toynbee's behalf. On 29 February 1909, Toynbee's wife was appointed as his receiver. In April 1909, Wontners learnt of Toynbee's incapacity for the first time. The Master in Lunacy made an order that the appearance and subsequent proceedings on Toynbee's behalf should be struck out, but refused to make an order for the payment of Yonge's costs by Wontners personally. Yonge appealed, and a judge in chambers affirmed the Master's refusal. Yonge appealed to the Court of Appeal.
>
> **HELD** – that by acting on Toynbee's behalf, Wontners had impliedly warranted that they had the authority to act, and were therefore liable personally to pay the plaintiff's costs in the action.

In *The Guide to the Professional Conduct of Solicitors*,[2] The Law Society states in the commentary on Principle 12.17 that 'where the client suffers mental incapacity the solicitor should take reasonable steps to ensure that the client's interests are protected. This may involve contact with the relatives. The solicitor may also contact the Court of Protection or the Official Solicitor'.

Where a mentally incapacitated client is involved in contentious business, proceedings can only be conducted in the client's name, or on his or her behalf, by a *next friend* if the client is bringing the proceedings, or by a *guardian ad litem* if he or she is defending or responding to the proceedings.[3]

Where a mentally incapacitated client is involved in non-contentious business, it is recommended that the solicitor should first establish whether the client has made an enduring power of attorney (EPA). If the client has, and the power has been registered with the Public Trust Office, the solicitor should only act on the instructions of the attorney(s). If the incapacitated client has made an EPA, but it has not yet been registered, it should be registered immediately. If the business is urgent, a supplemental application could be made to the Court of Protection requesting emergency relief.[4]

If the client has not executed an EPA, or if for any reason the EPA is invalid, it is recommended that the solicitor should first consider applying to the Public Trustee for a direction. Depending on the nature of the business and the size of the client's estate, a direction from the Public Trustee might be more appropriate than the appointment of a receiver. Alternatively, an application could be made to the Court of Protection:

- for the appointment of a receiver;[5] or
- for interim provision (including, if necessary, the appointment of an interim receiver) if the business is urgent; or
- to exercise its powers for emergency provision where the business is exceptionally urgent.[6]

---

1 [1910] 1 KB 215, 99 LJKB 208, CA.
2 (6th edition, 1993), Principle 12.17, Commentary 3, p 265.
3 RSC Ord 80, r 2.
4 Enduring Powers of Attorney Act 1985, s 5.
5 See Forms A–D of the Court of Protection Rules 1994 (SI 1994/3046), reproduced in Chapter 10.
6 Mental Health Act 1983, s 98.

Who is the client where there are Court of Protection proceedings?[1]

The general rule is that a solicitor instructed by a receiver to act in connection with a patient's affairs is the patient's solicitor, not the receiver's. The receiver is merely the statutory agent of the patient.

Re EG (1914)[2]

Every & Phillips received instructions from FG, the receiver, to act in connection with the renewal of leases on properties owned by the patient, EG. The solicitors' costs were not paid because all of the patient's income was applied for her benefit and no surplus funds were available.

HELD, by the Court of Appeal – that the receiver was the statutory agent for the patient and was not personally liable to pay the costs of the solicitors appointed by him to act on the patient's behalf. The costs were payable out of the patient's estate. The relationship of solicitor and client did not exist between the solicitors and the receiver.

The general rule does not apply in all circumstances. For example:

- the receiver only becomes the patient's statutory agent when his or her appointment is entered by the Court of Protection.[3] However, the court takes the view that, once it has received an application for the appointment of a receiver, which is complete and regular on the face of it, the solicitor involved in making that application is deemed to be acting on behalf of the patient;
- in proceedings relating to a statutory will, or the gift or settlement of a patient's property, the Official Solicitor is usually appointed to represent the patient[4] in order to resolve the problem of a potential, if not actual, conflict of interests between the applicant and the patient. The solicitor who has prepared the application for a statutory will, gift or settlement is usually, for the purposes of the application, deemed to be acting for the applicant;
- in theory, a patient who has testamentary capacity could instruct any solicitor[5] to prepare a will for him or her, without the involvement of the receiver or even the solicitor who is acting in the receivership;[6]

- where a solicitor is employed by a local authority, the client is the local authority itself, not the patient, nor the officer of the local authority (usually the Director of Social Services) who is, or is applying to be appointed as, the receiver.[7]

Difficulties arise when there are counter-applications for the appointment of a receiver. The court has power, if it considers that the interests of the patient are not adequately represented, to direct that the Official Solicitor shall act as solicitor for the patient either generally in the proceedings or for any particular purpose connected with the proceedings.[8] However, the Official Solicitor's consent to act is required, and in the past it has been his policy not to act in contested receivership applications.

Problems also occur where there are conflicting applications for the appointment of a receiver and the registration of an EPA. The court's usual practice is to follow the EPA route as far as possible, only considering the appointment of a receiver when it proves impossible to register the EPA. The reasoning behind this is that, on the face of it, the donor decided to execute an EPA in preference to having his or her affairs handled by a receiver, and this decision should be respected wherever possible.[9] The Master may give a directions hearing, once a conflict has become apparent, in order to identify the issues and dispose of them.

Where someone objects to the registration of an EPA, the solicitor acting for the objector acts solely for the objector and not for the donor of the power unless, of course, the donor is the objector.

---

1 See the Practice Direction issued by the Master of the Court of Protection on 9 August 1995: *The Law Society's Gazette*, 11 October 1995, p 21.

2 [1914] 1 Ch 927, 83 LJCh 586.

3 An order takes effect from its date, but it can always be withdrawn, altered or modified by the court until it is drawn up, passed or entered: *Re Harrison's Settlement* [1955] Ch 260.

4 Court of Protection Rules 1994 (SI 1994/3046), r 15.

5 Rule 1 of the Solicitors' Practice Rules 1990 provides that 'A solicitor shall not do anything ... likely to compromise or impair ... (b) a person's freedom to instruct a solicitor of his or her choice'.

6 In *The Guide to the Professional Conduct of Solicitors* (6th edition, 1993), The Law Society states (as Principle 12.10) that 'A solicitor must not accept instructions to act in a matter where another solicitor is acting for the client in respect of the same matter until the first retainer has been determined'. The execution of a will by a patient with testamentary capacity is probably a separate matter from the management and administration of his or her property and affairs.

7 Employed Solicitors' Code 1990, para 6.

8 Court of Protection Rules 1994 (SI 1994/3046), r 15.

9 P.D. Lewis, Assistant Public Trustee, 'The Enduring Powers of Attorney Act 1985 – Twelve Months On', *The Law Society's Gazette*, 29 April 1987, p 1219.

Enduring powers of attorney

Where a solicitor is instructed to prepare an EPA, the client is the donor.[1] The attorney is the statutory agent of the donor, just as a receiver is the statutory agent of a patient.[2]

When asked to prepare an EPA on written instructions alone, a solicitor should always consider carefully whether these instructions are sufficient, or whether he or she should see the client to discuss them.[3]

Where instructions for the preparation of an EPA are received not from the client (the prospective donor), but from a third party purporting to represent that client, a solicitor should obtain written instructions from the client that he or she wishes the solicitor to act. In any case of doubt, the solicitor should see the client or take other appropriate steps to confirm the instructions.[4] The solicitor must also advise the prospective donor without regard to the interests of the source from which he or she was introduced.[5]

The donor remains the client after he or she has become mentally incapable.[6]

If an EPA is registered, and it is silent on the question of disclosure of the donor's will,[7] it may be necessary to obtain a direction from the Court of Protection as to whether the will can be disclosed to the attorney.[8]

---

1 The Law Society, *The Guide to the Professional Conduct of Solicitors* (6th edition, 1993), Principle 12.01, Commentary 4. In *Enduring Powers of Attorney: A Report to the Lord Chancellor* (Lord Chancellor's Department, June 1991), Stephen Cretney et al noted a widespread divergence in practice among solicitors as to whether they considered that they were acting for the donor, the attorney, or the family generally. Cretney and his colleagues stated (at para 2.6) that 'it does seem to us questionable whether a solicitor should accept instructions to prepare an EPA from a person other than the donor'.

2 *Re EG* [1914] 1 Ch 927, CA.

3 The Law Society, *The Guide to the Professional Conduct of Solicitors* (above), Principle 12.05, Commentary 2.

4 *Ibid*, Principle 12.05.

5 *Ibid*, Principle 12.05, Commentary 1.

6 *Ibid*, Principle 12.01, Commentary 4.

7 For a precedent of a clause authorising the donor's solicitor to disclose the contents of the donor's will to the attorney, see Chapter 9, Precedent 8 at p 255 below.

8 The Law Society, *The Guide to the Professional Conduct of Solicitors* (above), Principle 16.01, Commentary 4.

Conflict of interests

The rules of professional conduct draw a distinction between:

- initially *accepting instructions to act* for two or more clients where there is a conflict, or a significant risk of a conflict, between the interests of those clients;[1] and
- *continuing to act* when a conflict of interest arises.[2]

(1)   Accepting instructions to act

A solicitor or firm of solicitors should not accept instructions to act for two or more clients where there is a conflict or a significant risk of a conflict between the interests of those clients.[3] A solicitor may, however, act as a conciliator or mediator between parties in a domestic dispute, but cannot subsequently act for either party in respect of that dispute.[4]

Accepting instructions to act for two or more parties in a conveyancing transaction is generally prohibited by r 6(1) of the Solicitors' Practice Rules 1990. However, provided no conflict of interest appears, this rule does not apply if, inter alia, the parties are related by blood, adoption or marriage;[5] or if both parties are 'established clients',[6] which includes persons related by blood, adoption or marriage to established clients.[7]

(2)   Continuing to act

A solicitor or firm of solicitors must not continue to act for two or more clients where a conflict of interests arises between those clients.[8] If a solicitor has already accepted instructions in a matter and a conflict of interests subsequently arises, the solicitor:

- must cease to act for both clients; but
- may continue to act for one client, provided that he or she can do so without embarrassment and with the consent of the other client. The solicitor may continue to represent one client only if he or she is not in possession of relevant confidential knowledge concerning the other obtained whilst acting for the other. The consent should be sought of the other client (usually through his or her new solicitors), and the solicitor should proceed in the absence of such consent only if there is no good cause for its refusal.[9]

The same rule applies where a solicitor has already accepted instructions to act for two or more related parties or established clients in a conveyancing matter and a conflict of interests arises during the course of that transaction.[10]

(3)   Waiver by the clients

These strict rules of professional conduct may be waived by the very clients whose interests conflict or potentially conflict. In *Boulting v Association of Cinematographic Television and Allied Technicians*,[11] the Court of Appeal held that 'the person entitled to the benefit of the rule may release it, provided he is of full age and sui juris, and fully understands not only what he is doing but also what his legal rights are and that he is in part surrendering them.[12] . . . The reason why the law permits the rule to be relaxed is obvious. It is frequently very much better in the interests of the client that they should be advised by someone on the transaction, although he may be interested on the other side of the fence'.[13]

The circumstances in which clients may waive the rules on separate representation were considered recently by the Privy Council in *Clark Boyce v Mouat*, an appeal from the New Zealand Court of Appeal.[14]

Clark Boyce v Mouat (1993)

Dorothy Mouat was a widow aged 72. Her son Robert, 45, was a chartered accountant and management consultant. He wanted to raise $100,000, partly for improvements to his house, and partly for business purposes. His house was already mortgaged to the hilt, so he asked his mother whether she could mortgage hers. She agreed. Their usual solicitors, Meares Williams, declined to act for either of them. So they went to Martin Boyce of Clark Boyce. He recommended that Mrs Mouat should be independently advised. She refused to obtain independent advice, and went ahead and signed the mortgage deed. Robert defaulted with the repayments and was eventually adjudged bankrupt. Mrs Mouat was left with a debt of $110,000 plus arrears of interest. She sued Clark Boyce. In the High Court, Holland J gave judgment for the solicitors. The New Zealand Court of Appeal (by a majority) allowed Mrs Mouat's appeal. Clark Boyce then appealed to the Privy Council.

HELD – allowing Clark Boyce's appeal – that what Mrs Mouat required of the solicitors was that they should complete all the necessary conveyancing formalities. She was already aware of the consequences if her son defaulted, and was not concerned about being advised on the wisdom of the transaction. By offering to arrange independent legal advice for her, Clark Boyce had done all that was reasonably expected of them, and accordingly there was no breach of contract or fiduciary duty.

In the course of his judgment, Lord Jauncey said:

'There is no general rule of law to the effect that a solicitor should never act for both parties in a transaction where their interests may conflict. He may act provided that he has obtained the informed consent of both to his acting. Informed consent means consent given in the knowledge that there is a conflict between the parties and that as a result the solicitor may be disabled from disclosing to each party the full knowledge which he possesses as to the transaction, or may be disabled from giving advice to one party which conflicts with the interests of the other. If the parties are content to proceed on this basis, the solicitor may properly act.'[15]

His Lordship also considered whether a solicitor is under any obligation to advise an elderly client on the *wisdom* of his or her action.

'When a client in full command of his faculties and apparently aware of what he is doing seeks the assistance of a solicitor in the carrying out of a particular transaction, that solicitor is under no duty, whether before or after accepting instructions, to go beyond those instructions by proffering unsought advice on the wisdom of the transaction. To hold otherwise would impose intolerable burdens on solicitors.'[16]

It is doubtful, however, that the principle in *Clark Boyce v Mouat* would rebut the presumption of undue influence.[17]

---

1 The Law Society, *The Guide to the Professional Conduct of Solicitors* (6th edition, 1993), Principle 15.01 ('When instructions must be refused').
2 *Ibid*, Principle 15.03 ('Conflict arising between two or more current clients').
3 *Ibid*, Principle 15.01.
4 *Ibid*, Principle 15.01, Commentary 2.
5 Solicitors' Practice Rules 1990, r 6(2)(b).
6 The test of whether a person is an *established client* is an objective one, namely, whether a reasonable and fair-minded solicitor would regard the person as an established client. An existing client is not the same as an established one: The Law Society, *The Guide to the Professional Conduct of Solicitors* (above), Principle 24.01, Commentary 3.
7 Solicitors' Practice Rules 1990, r 6(2)(c).
8 The Law Society, *The Guide to the Professional Conduct of Solicitors* (above), Principle 15.03.
9 *Ibid*, Principle 15.03, Commentary 1.
10 *Ibid*, Principle 24.01, Commentary 2.
11 [1963] 1 All ER 716, CA.
12 *Ibid*, at p 729D–E, per Upjohn LJ.
13 *Ibid*, at p 729I, per Upjohn LJ.
14 [1993] 4 All ER 268, PC.
15 *Ibid*, at p 273g, per Lord Jauncey.

16 *Ibid*, at p 275b, per Lord Jauncey.
17 See *Inche Noriah v Shaik Allie Bin Omar* [1929] AC 127, PC, summarised at p 108 below.

Financial abuse of a client

Particular care needs to be taken where clients are elderly or otherwise vulnerable to pressure from others. A solicitor must not accept instructions where he or she suspects that they may have been given by a client under duress or undue influence.[1] In such circumstances, the solicitor should:

- see the client alone, in order to satisfy himself or herself that the instructions were, in fact, freely given; or
- refuse to act.[2]

As far as the solicitor's own relationship with the client is concerned:

- a solicitor must not take advantage of the age, inexperience, want of education, business inexperience or ill health of the client.[3]
- a solicitor who holds a power of attorney from a client must not use that power to gain a benefit which, if acting as a professional adviser to that client, he or she would not be prepared to allow to an independent third party.[4]

1 The Law Society, *The Guide to the Professional Conduct of Solicitors* (6th edition, 1993), Principle 12.04. See, generally, Chapter 5, 'Introduction', at p 107 below.
2 *Ibid*, Principle 12.04, Commentary.
3 *Ibid*, Principle 12.14.
4 *Ibid*, Principle 15.07.

PRECEDENTS

1 REQUEST FOR WRITTEN CONFIRMATION OF INSTRUCTIONS GIVEN BY AN INTERMEDIARY

(*date*)

Dear (*client*)

(*Your daughter*) has informed me that you would like to make an enduring power of attorney appointing (*her*) as your sole attorney.

I would be grateful if you could kindly confirm that you wish me to draw up such a power of attorney. I am enclosing a prepaid envelope for your reply.

I apologise for writing what may seem to be an unnecessary letter, but The Law Society's rules on professional conduct are extremely strict about receiving a client's instructions from somebody else, and in the circumstances I am required to obtain written instructions from you personally that you wish me to act on your behalf.[1] [I should also point out that I have a duty to advise you without regard to the interests of anyone else, including (*your daughter*).][2]

When you reply, please let me know whether you would like to place any restrictions on the power of attorney. Otherwise, (*your daughter*) will be able to assume complete control over your property and affairs straightaway, and will be able to do anything with your property and finances that you could do yourself. The idea of an enduring power of attorney is that it remains in force if a person becomes mentally incapacitated and, if that happens, they cannot change it without permission from the court.

If you would like (me to come and see you)/(to come and see me)[3] to discuss this matter further, let me know and we can arrange a mutually convenient time.

Yours sincerely

---

1 The Law Society, *The Guide to the Professional Conduct of Solicitors* (6th edition, 1993), Principle 12.05: 'Where instructions are received not from a client but from a third party purporting to represent that client, a solicitor should obtain written instructions from the client that he or she wishes the solicitor to act'.

2 *Ibid*, Principle 12, Commentary 1: 'In such circumstances a solicitor must advise the client without regard to the interests of the source from which he or she was introduced'.

3 *Ibid*, Principle 12.05: 'In any case of doubt the solicitor should see the client or take other appropriate steps to confirm instructions'.

2 CONSENT ENABLING A SOLICITOR TO CONTINUE TO ACT FOR ONE PARTY WHERE HE OR SHE HAD BEEN ACTING FOR BOTH PARTIES UNTIL A CONFLICT OF INTERESTS AROSE[1]

To: (*name and address of solicitors*)

I (*full name*) of (*address*) CONSENT to you continuing to act for (*full names*) in connection with (*describe the transaction*).

Signed ....
Dated ....

---

1 See, generally, 'Conflict of Interests', at p 27 above. 'A solicitor or firm of solicitors must not continue to act for two or more clients where a conflict of interests arises between those clients': The Law Society, *The Guide to the Professional Conduct of Solicitors* (6th edition, 1993), Principle 15.03. A solicitor may continue to represent one client with the other's consent, but only if he or she can do so without embarrassment and with propriety, and if he or she is not in possession of relevant confidential knowledge concerning the other obtained whilst acting for the other. Even in such a case, the consent should be sought of the other client (usually through his or her new solicitors) and the solicitor should proceed in the absence of such consent only if there is no good cause for its refusal: *Ibid*, Principle 15.03, Commentary 1.

---

3 CONFIRMATION OF INSTRUCTIONS TO ACT FOR ONE OF TWO OR MORE CLIENTS WHOSE INTERESTS MAY CONFLICT[1]

Dear (*solicitor*)

Despite your recommendation that I should receive separate advice and representation on the [wisdom,][2] implications and possible risks and consequences of (*transferring my house to my son*), I do not wish to be independently advised or represented, and I instruct you to act on my behalf in this matter even though you will also be acting for (*my son*).

I am aware that there could be a conflict between my interests and (*my son's*), and that by acting for both of us you may be unable to disclose to each of us your full knowledge of the matter, or may be unable to give advice to one of us which conflicts with the interests of the other. Nevertheless, you have my consent to act for both of us in this transaction.[3]

I relieve you of any civil liability or breach of professional conduct for acting in accordance with these instructions.[4]

Yours sincerely

1 See, generally, 'Conflict of Interests', at p 27 above.

2 At first instance in *Clark Boyce v Mouat*, Holland J differentiated between the duties owed by a solicitor in those cases of limited retainer where all that was required was assistance to carry a transaction into effect, and those cases where clients sought advice as to the wisdom of entering into a transaction and a discussion of any risk such a transaction entailed: [1991] 1 NZ Conv C 190, 794 (HC). In the Privy Council, Lord Jauncey stated that 'When a client in full command of his faculties and apparently aware of what he is doing seeks the assistance of a solicitor in the carrying out of a particular transaction, that solicitor is under no duty whether before or after accepting instructions to go beyond those instructions by proferring unsought advice on the wisdom of the transaction. To hold otherwise could impose intolerable burdens on solicitors': *Clark Boyce v Mouat* [1993] 4 All ER 268, at p 275b.

3 A solicitor may act for both parties in a transaction where their interests may conflict 'provided he has obtained the informed consent of both to his acting. Informed consent means consent given in the knowledge that there is a conflict between the parties and that as a result the solicitor may be disabled from disclosing to each party the full knowledge which he possesses as to the transaction, or may be disabled from giving advice to one party which conflicts with the interests of the other. If the parties are content to proceed on this basis, the solicitor may properly act': *Clark Boyce v Mouat* [1993] 4 All ER 268, at p 273g, per Lord Jauncey.

4 See The Law Society's Council statement on limitation of liability by contract (27 May 1987, as amended): The Law Society, *The Guide to the Professional Conduct of Solicitors* (6th edition, 1993), Annex 12A. Inter alia, liability for fraud or reckless disregard of professional obligations may not be limited.

CHAPTER 3: CAPACITY

INDEX

Text

Checklists

Precedents

CAPACITY

TEXT

Introduction

Capacity means someone's ability to do something and, in a legal context, it refers to a person's ability to perform a specific juristic act, such as making a will, a gift, a contract or an enduring power of attorney, or generally being able to manage his or her property and affairs.

Incapacity, or the inability to enter into a transaction, is either imposed by the law for policy reasons or arises by reason of mental disorder. In the past, married women, convicted felons and enemy aliens were incapable of performing most juristic acts by operation of the law. Nowadays, incapacity by operation of the law applies principally to children, the underlying policy being that they need to be protected from their own inexperience and imprudence and from the rapacity of others. Similar considerations apply in the case of mentally disabled adults.

Mental incapacity is never really constant except in the case of wholly insensate patients. It can fluctuate. Everyone has their 'good days' and 'bad days'. It also varies according to the nature of the task to be performed. It has been said that 'the mental capacity required by the law in respect of any instrument is relative to the transaction which is being effected by means of the instrument, and may be described as the capacity to understand the nature of that transaction when it is explained'.[1] This suggests that incapacity is function-specific, although this is difficult to reconcile with the notion of being mentally incapable of managing one's property and affairs generally. It also suggests that the essence of incapacity is *understanding* an explanation, but this may be inappropriate in some cases – particularly testamentary capacity where other qualities such as memory, judgement and the ability to reason play an important role.

---

1 *Gibbons v Wright* (1954) 91 CLR 423, at p 438, per Dixon CJ; approved by the English High Court in *Re Beaney (Deceased)* [1978] 2 All ER 595, at p 601 et seq.

Capacity and evidence

Whether or not a person is mentally capable of performing a juristic act is ultimately a legal, rather than a medical, decision. Neville J expressed this particularly robustly when he said: 'It is obvious that an idea obtained that this was a question for the doctors to decide ... in my opinion this is not so; it is for the court to decide, although the court must have the evidence of experts in the medical profession who can indicate the meaning of symptoms and give some idea of the mental deterioration which takes place in cases of this kind'.[1] Although the court attaches a great deal of weight to the evidence of a registered medical practitioner on questions of incapacity, it does not automatically prefer medical opinion to lay opinion.[2] The Court of Protection, however, is required only to consider medical evidence as to whether or not it has jurisdiction under the Mental Health Act 1983.[3]

Proof of incapacity depends on the operation of two rebuttable presumptions:[4]

- *the presumption of capacity*.[5] A person is presumed to be capable until the contrary is proved; and
- *the presumption of continuance*. Once it has been proved by acceptable evidence that a person is mentally incapable of doing something, that incapacity is presumed to continue until the contrary is proved.

The burden of proof operates on the usual principle that the person who alleges rather than denies something has to prove his or her case.[6] In cases involving incapacity the onus is on the person who alleges that:

- an individual lacks capacity;
- an individual who previously lacked capacity has recovered and is now capable;
- something was done by an otherwise incapacitated individual during a lucid interval.

The standard of proof is the usual standard in civil proceedings – *the balance of probabilities*. When seeking medical or lay evidence as to a person's capacity, it is important to remind the assessor that his or her opinion should be based on the balance of probabilities rather than the higher standard – beyond reasonable doubt – which applies in criminal proceedings.

In cases of borderline capacity, a medical practitioner or anyone else making an assessment should immediately record his or her examination and findings.[7] A laconic certificate or record which fails to explain the reasons why the assessor arrived at his or her decision is likely to be of little evidential value.[8]

It is recommended that, wherever possible, an assessment should take place at a time and location favourable to the person whose capacity is being assessed. Some people are at their best in the morning; others in the afternoon. And most are likely to be less confused or intimidated in their own home environment than in a solicitor's office or doctor's surgery. By seeing clients at their best, it is easier to gauge the maximum extent of their capabilities.[9]

It is essential to remember that it is the client's capacity that is being assessed; not his or her wisdom. Although the law insists that individuals should be capable of understanding the nature and effects of their actions, it does not require them to behave 'in such a manner as to deserve approbation from the prudent, the wise, or the good'.[10]

1 *Richmond v Richmond* (1914) 111 LT 273, at p 274, per Neville J.
2 See the discussion in *Birkin v Wing* (1890) 63 LT 80, at pp 83 and 84, in which Kekewich J preferred the evidence of a solicitor as to his client's contractual capacity to a doctor's evidence alleging incapacity. In a Canadian case, *Re Price* [1964] 2 DLR 592, at p 595, Laidlaw J stated that a judgment as to capacity 'is a practical question which may be answered by a layman of good sense with as much authority as by a doctor'.
3 Mental Health Act 1983, s 94(2) (but see s 98); Court of Protection Rules 1994 (SI 1994/3046), r 36(2).
4 On the presumptions of sanity and continuance, the effect of a lucid interval, and the burden of proof, see, generally, *Attorney-General v Parnther* (1792) 3 Bro CC 440, 2 Dick 748, 27 ER 962.
5 The Law Commission, in cl 2(6) of its draft Mental Incapacity Bill, proposes to place this presumption on a statutory footing.
6 This rule is sometimes expressed by the Latin maxim, affirmanti non neganti incumbit probatio.
7 *Kenward v Adams* (1975) *The Times*, 29 November, per Templeman J; repeated by him in *Re Simpson, Deceased: Schaniel v Simpson* (1977) 121 SJ 224.
8 See, for example, the decision of the Social Security Commissioner in *CS 773/81*.
9 See, generally, *Assessment of Mental Capacity: Guidance for Doctors and Lawyers*, published jointly by The Law Society and the British Medical Association in December 1995. Pages 95–98 consider the duty to enhance capacity.
10 *Bird v Luckie* (1850) 8 Hare 301, at p 306, per Sir L.J. Knight-Bruce V-C. The Vice-Chancellor went on to say that 'a testator is permitted to be capricious and improvident, and is, moreover, at liberty to conceal the circumstances and motives by which he has been actuated in his dispositions'.

The Law Commission, in cl 2(4) of its draft Mental Incapacity Bill, provides that 'a person shall not be regarded as unable to make a decision by reason of mental disability merely because he makes a decision which would not be made by a person of ordinary prudence'.

Capacity to make a will

A person making a will should have testamentary capacity at two stages:

- when he or she gives instructions to a solicitor for the preparation of the will; or, if it is written or typed by the testator or testatrix personally, at the time of writing or typing it;[1] and
- when the will is executed.

Occasionally, the maker becomes ill, or his or her condition deteriorates, between giving instructions and executing the will. In these circumstances, if it has been prepared strictly in accordance with the instructions given, the will may still be valid even though, when it is executed, the testator or testatrix merely recalls giving the instructions to the solicitor and believes that the will he or she is executing complies with those instructions.

Parker v Felgate and Tilly (1883)[2]

Georgina Compton was a 28-year-old widow. In 1882, she contracted glomerulon-ephritis or Bright's Disease. She gave her solicitor, Mr Parker, instructions to prepare a new will on her behalf, leaving legacies to her father and brother and her residuary estate to Great Ormond Street Hospital. She subsequently suffered acute renal failure and the will was signed by a friend on her behalf, in her presence and at her direction.

She died four days later, and her father and brother contested the will on the grounds that she had lacked testamentary capacity at the time of its execution.

HELD, by Sir James Hannen, President of the Probate Division – in a case of this nature three questions must be asked in the following order of priority: (1) When the will was executed, did she remember and understand the instructions she had given to her solicitor?; (2) If it had been thought advisable to rouse her, could she have understood each clause of the will when it was explained to her?; and (3) Was she capable of understanding, and did she understand, that she was executing a will for which she had previously given instructions to her solicitor? If the answer to any of these questions is affirmative, the will will be valid. In this particular case, the jury answered 'No' to the first two questions, but 'Yes' to the third, and accordingly Mrs Compton's will was valid.

In *Battan Singh v Amirchand*, in 1948, the Privy Council held that the principle in *Parker v Felgate* should be applied with the greatest caution and reserve when the testator does not personally give instructions to the solicitor who drafts the will but gives the instructions to a lay intermediary who repeats them to the solicitor.[3] Before making any presumption in favour of validity, the court ought to be strictly satisfied that there are no grounds for suspicion, and that the instructions given to the intermediary were unambiguous and clearly understood, faithfully reported by him and rightly apprehended by the solicitor.[4]

The classic definition of testamentary capacity was given by the Chief Justice, Sir Alexander Cockburn, in *Banks v Goodfellow* in 1870, and was essentially a restatement of the law prior to 1848 when the court espoused the doctrine of *monomania*,[5] according to which doctrine, any degree of mental disorder, however slight, and however unconnected with the testamentary disposition in question, is necessarily fatal to the testator's capacity.[6]

Banks v Goodfellow (1870)[7]

John Banks was a bachelor who lived with his teenaged niece, Margaret Goodfellow, in Arkleby, Cumberland. He owned 15 houses in Keswick. He had a history of psychiatric disorder and would probably nowadays be diagnosed as a paranoid schizophrenic. He was convinced that a Keswick grocer, Featherstonhaugh Alexander (who was, in fact, dead), was pursuing and persecuting him. In 1863, with legal assistance, he drew up a short, simple will, leaving his entire estate to his niece. He died in 1865, aged 53. Margaret inherited his estate, but died soon afterwards unmarried and under age. The Banks' properties then passed to her half-brother, who was not related to the testator. Various members of the Banks family contested the will on the grounds that John had lacked testamentary capacity because of his insane delusions.

HELD – partial unsoundness of mind, not affecting the general faculties, and not operating on the mind of a testator in regard to testamentary disposition, is not sufficient to render a person incapable of disposing of his property by will. 'The only legitimate or rational ground for denying testamentary capacity to persons of unsound mind is the inability to take into account and give due effect to the considerations which ought to be present to the mind of a testator in making his will, and to influence his decision as to the disposal of his property'.[8]

In the course of delivering the court's judgment, Sir Alexander Cockburn said:

> 'It is essential . . . that a testator shall understand the nature of the act and its effects; shall understand the extent of the property of which he is disposing; shall be able to comprehend and appreciate the claims to which he ought to give effect; and, with a view to the latter object, that no disorder of the mind shall poison his affections, pervert his sense of right, or prevent the exercise of his natural faculties – that no insane delusion shall influence his will in disposing of his property and bring about a disposal of it which, if the mind had been sound, would not have been made.'[9]

This definition sets out three, possibly four, separate tests. The testator or testatrix must be able to:

- understand the nature of the act *and* its effects; and
- understand the extent (as distinct from the value)[10] of the property of which he or she is disposing; and
- comprehend and appreciate the claims to which he or she ought to give effect.

These tests are based mainly on *understanding*, which involves receiving, believing, evaluating and making a decision on information which is already known to the testator or testatrix or which could perhaps to a limited extent be communicated or explained to him or her by someone else, for example, a solicitor.[11] The final test, 'comprehending and appreciating the claims to which he ought to give effect', extends beyond understanding and requires other qualities, such as: judgment; the ability to discern, distinguish and compare; the ability to reason; moral responsibility; memory; sentiment and affection.

The extent to which an individual's testamentary capacity can be enhanced is an open question. The Law Commission has recently suggested that 'a person should be considered unable to take the decision in question if he or she is unable to understand an explanation in broad terms and simple language of the basic information relevant to taking it'.[12] However, there is a substantial body of authority which insists that 'unquestionably, there must be a complete and absolute proof that the party who had so formed the will did it without any assistance',[13] and that 'a disposing mind and memory is one able to comprehend, of its own initiative and volition, the essential elements of will-making . . . merely to be able to make rational responses is not enough, nor to repeat a tutored formula of simple terms'.[14]

In *Banks v Goodfellow*, John Banks' persecutory delusions had no influence whatsoever on the way in which he drew up his will. By contrast, in *Re Belliss*, the testatrix's delusional beliefs that she had already given substantially more money to one daughter than the other did materially affect the substance of her will, thereby rendering it invalid.

Re Belliss: Polson v Parrott (1929)[15]
In 1922, Margaretta Belliss made a will leaving her estate equally between her two daughters. In 1927, when she was 93, she made a new will leaving a larger share to her younger daughter, Theodora. She actually stated in the will: 'I desire to place on record that I have for years given to my daughter Mary more financial assistance than to her sister, and this has been present in my mind when framing the provisions of this my will, and I have sought to put matters on a fair basis between the sisters'. She died in February 1928 leaving an estate of £19,000. Mary contested the will.

HELD, by Lord Merrivale P – Mrs Belliss had executed the will under the delusional belief that she had already benefited one daughter far more than the other, and her memory had failed in that she could no longer remember her past actions towards her daughters so as to displace the delusional notions. Accordingly, at the material times she did not have testamentary capacity as defined in *Banks v Goodfellow.*

An additional point emerging from the decision in *Re Belliss* is that, wherever possible in cases of borderline capacity, it is preferable that the testator or testatrix be seen by a solicitor or legal executive who knows him or her fairly well.[16] It is essential in such cases that the will be witnessed or approved by a doctor who satisfies himself or herself as to the testator's capacity and understanding and makes a record of his or her examination and findings.[17]

The Times report of *Kenward v Adams* (1975)[18] stated:

'When a solicitor is drawing up a will for an aged testator or one who has been seriously ill, it should be witnessed or approved by a medical practitioner, who ought to record his examination of the testator and his findings. That was the golden, if tactless rule, Mr Justice Templeman said when finding that the testatrix, Mrs Martha Price, retired hospital almoner of Mitcham, did not have testamentary capacity when she signed a second will in July 1972 or the capacity to revoke a will of 1951 by destroying it if, in fact, she did destroy it. Other precautions were that if there was an earlier will it should be examined and any proposed alterations should be discussed with the testator.'

Dysphasia – the loss of the ability to communicate, usually following a stroke – can present enormous practical difficulties in terms of assessing testamentary capacity.[19] It is usually necessary for a speech therapist to work with the testator or testatrix to ensure that a consistent, clear and unequivocal method of communication is established.[20] The Law Commission has recommended that a person should be considered unable to take the decision in question if he or she is unable to communicate it to others who have made reasonable attempts to understand it.[21]

Testamentary capacity and marriage

A will is revoked by the subsequent marriage of the testator or testatrix, unless it was expressed to be made in expectation of that marriage.[22] This can create problems if an elderly person is capable of entering into a valid marriage but lacks the capacity to make a valid will. In *Re Park*, considered below, the Court of Appeal held that in order to have capacity to marry:

- it is not enough that a party appreciates that he or she is taking part in a marriage ceremony, and is able to follow the words of the ceremony;[23]
- a party must be able to understand the nature of the contract he or she is entering into;[24]
- he or she must understand the rights and responsibilities that marriage involves; and
- he or she must be free from the influence of any morbid delusions.[25]

The Court of Appeal was not prepared to accept counsel's submission that one of the essential attributes of capacity to marry is that each party should be capable of taking care of his or her own property and person,[26] and it also held that no useful purpose would be served in suggesting that 'a lesser degree of capacity is required to consent to a marriage than in the making of a will'.[27]

In the Estate of Park, Deceased (1954)[28]

Robert Park was 77 when his wife died in January 1948. He made a will in March 1948, and had a stroke in May 1948. Twelve months later, when he was undoubtedly senile, he became romantically attached to Wyn Hughes who worked as a cashier at his London club. They were married at Kensington Register Office at 11.30 am on 30 May 1949. By 3 o'clock that afternoon, when he went to bed, he had executed a new will making modest provision for Wyn. Apparently, he behaved towards her like a foolish schoolboy, and wouldn't let her out of his sight, and was extremely disappointed that she wasn't willing to let him consummate the marriage. He died on 17 June 1949 leaving an estate of £120,000. In the action reported as *In re Park: Culross v Park* (1950) *The Times*, December 2, a jury found that he was not of sound mind, memory and understanding when he executed the will on his wedding day, and probate was refused. This rendered him intestate, and further litigation ensued as to the validity of the marriage which had revoked his earlier will.

HELD, by the Court of Appeal – Mr Park had the capacity to enter into, and did enter into, a valid and binding marriage, which had the effect of revoking the will he made in March 1948. Accordingly, he died intestate and his widow was entitled to a substantial portion of his estate.

If such a situation were to arise today, it would be advisable to inform the Court of Protection of the facts and, if necessary, an application could be made for an order authorising the execution of a statutory will.[29] The statutory will jurisdiction is considered in detail in Chapter 14.

---

1 *In the Estate of Wallace, Solicitor of the Duchy of Cornwall v Batten* [1952] 2 TLR 925.

2 (1883) 8 PD 171, (1883) 52 LJP 95. The principle in *Parker v Felgate and Tilly* was applied by the Privy Council in *Perera v Perera* [1901] AC 354.

3 On third party instructions, generally, see The Law Society, *The Guide to the Professional Conduct of Solicitors* (6th edition, 1993), Principle 12.05.

4 *Battan Singh v Amirchand* [1948] AC 161, Privy Council on appeal from the Supreme Court of Fiji. The principle in *Parker v Felgate* also applies if the will was prepared by the testator personally at a time when he was competent, because the draft constitutes 'instructions' within the meaning of this principle: *In the Estate of Wallace, Solicitor of the Duchy of Cornwall v Batten* (fn 1 above), per Devlin J.

5 For the origins of *monomania*, see Isaac Ray, *A Treatise on the Medical Jurisprudence of Insanity* (Boston, USA, 1838), pp 102–108.

6 *Waring v Waring* (1848) 6 Moo PC 341. Lord Brougham's view that, because the mind is one and indivisible, any degree of mental disorder renders it unsound, was followed in *Smith v Tebbitt* (1867) 1 P & D 398 and *Hancock v Peaty* (1867) 1 P & D 351.

7 (1870) LR 5 QB 549, (1870) 39 LJQB 237.

8 (1870) LR 5 QB 549, at p 566, per Cockburn CJ.

9 *Ibid*, at p 565, per Cockburn CJ.

10 Considerable practical difficulties can arise where a testator's portfolio is managed by someone else and there are no recent statements or valuations. In such cases, it may be necessary to apply a 'reasonableness' test.

11 See, for example, the definition of *incapacity* proposed by The Law Commission in *Mental Incapacity* (1995) Law Com No 231 (HMSO, 1995), and draft Mental Incapacity Bill, cl 2(3): 'unable to understand an explanation in broad terms and simple language of the basic information relevant to taking the decision in question . . .'.

12 *Ibid*, cl 2(3).
13 *Cartwright v Cartwright* (1793) 1 Phill Ecc 90, at p 101, per Sir William Wynne, Judge of the Prerogative Court of Canterbury.
14 *Leger v Poirier* [1944] 3 DLR 1 (Supreme Court of Canada), at pp 11 and 12, per Rand J.
15 (1929) 141 LT 245.
16 *Ibid*, at p 247. See also *Re Simpson, Deceased: Schaniel v Simpson* (1977) 121 SJ 224.
17 The warnings issued by Templeman J in *Kenward v Adams* (see below) were repeated by him in *Re Simpson, Deceased: Schaniel v Simpson* (above).
18 (1975) *The Times*, November 29.
19 *King and Thwaits v Farley* (1828) 1 Hagg Ecc 502.
20 See, generally, Pam Enderby, 'The Testamentary Capacity of Dysphasic Patients' (1994) 62 *Medico-Legal Journal* 70–80.
21 Law Com No 231 (HMSO, 1995), and draft Mental Incapacity Bill, cl 2(5).
22 Wills Act 1837, s 18, as substituted by the Administration of Justice Act 1982.
23 Following the dicta of Sir James Hannen P in *Hunter v Edney* (1885) 10 PD 93, at p 95.
24 *Durham v Durham* (1885) 10 PD 80: 'the contract of marriage is a very simple one, which does not require a high degree of intelligence to comprehend. It is an engagement between a man and woman to live together and love one another as husband and wife to the exclusion of all others', per Sir James Hannen P.
25 Following *Hunter v Edney* (fn 23 above), and *Jackson v Jackson* [1908] P 308, at p 310.
26 Counsel was relying on dicta of Sir John Nicholl in *Browning v Reade* (1812) 2 Phill Ecc 69, at p 70.
27 Disapproving the dictum of Karminski J in *Re Park* at first instance: [1954] P 89, at p 97.
28 [1954] P 89, CA.
29 *Re Davey (Deceased)* [1981] 1 WLR 164, [1980] 3 All ER 342.

Capacity to revoke a will

The leading authority on the mental capacity required to revoke a will is the following case, which was reported very briefly in *The Solicitors' Journal* on 9 January 1970 and establishes that a testator or testatrix must have the same degree of understanding, when revoking a will, as he or she had when making it. It is understood that the Court of Protection applies the same principle to the revocation of an enduring power of attorney.[1]

Re Sabatini, Deceased (1970)[2]

In June 1940, Ruth Sabatini made a will leaving her residuary estate to her nephew Anthony Dixon-Green. On 16 September 1965, when she was suffering from mental illness due to old age, she tore up the will. She died on 14 May 1966, aged 92. Seven nephews and nieces were entitled to share on her intestacy. Her gross estate came to £51,000. Mr Dixon-Green alleged that when his aunt tore up the will, she was not of sound mind, memory or understanding. Counsel for the other nephews and nieces submitted that a lower standard of capacity – a lesser degree of concentration – was acceptable when a will was destroyed, and that a testator incapable of making a new will might understand that a beneficiary had become unworthy of his bounty and wish to deprive him of benefit by tearing up the will and dying intestate.

HELD, by Baker J – as a general rule, a testator must have the same degree of understanding, when destroying his will, as when he made it. It would be illogical if different methods of revocation were to be judged by different standards. In view of the evidence, the only possible conclusion was that the destruction of Mrs Sabatini's will was not a rational act, and that she was not of sound disposing mind, memory and understanding when she destroyed it.

The unfortunately named *doctrine of dependent relative revocation* might also have applied in this case. Where a testator's intention to revoke a will is conditional in some way and the condition is not fulfilled, the revocation is ineffective. So, if Mrs Sabatini had been mentally capable of revoking her will, and had revoked it in the (incorrect) belief that she would completely disinherit her nephew, the doctrine would have operated so as to preserve the validity of the will.[3]

1 For the revocation of a registered EPA, see Enduring Powers of Attorney Act 1985, ss 7(1)(a) and 8(3). The Court of Protection will confirm the revocation if it is satisfied 'that the donor has done whatever is necessary in law to effect an express revocation of the power and was mentally capable of revoking a power of attorney when he did so (whether or not he is so when the court considers the application)'. It is understood that, in practice, where the donor of a registered EPA seeks to revoke it, the attorney usually disclaims, thus obviating the need to investigate the donor's capacity to revoke.
2 (1970) 114 SJ 35.
3 *Re Southerden* [1925] P 177; *Re Jones* [1976] 1 All ER 593, CA.

Capacity to make a gift

The leading case on capacity to make a gift is *Re Beaney (Deceased)* (below).

Re Beaney (Deceased) (1978)[1]

Maud Beaney was a 64-year-old widow with three grown-up children. She owned and lived in a three-bedroomed semi-detached house in Cranford, Middlesex. Her elder daughter, Valerie, lived with her. Mrs Beaney suffered from advanced dementia and, in May 1973, she was admitted as an in-patient to the National Hospital for Nervous Diseases. A few days later, she purported to sign a deed transferring the house to Valerie. She died intestate in June 1974. Her estate came to about £1150, whereas the house was worth £14,000. Her son and younger daughter applied to the court for a declaration that the transfer was void because their mother lacked capacity when she signed it.

HELD – in this case, the degree of understanding required was as high as that required for a will. In the circumstances, Mrs Beaney had not been capable of making a valid transfer of the house, and her son and younger daughter were entitled to a declaration that the transfer was void and of no effect.

Martin Nourse QC (as he then was), sitting as a deputy judge of the High Court, set out the following criteria for capacity to make a gift.

'The degree or extent of understanding required in respect of any instrument is relative to the particular transaction which it is to effect. In the case of a will, the degree required is always high. In the case of a contract, a deed made for consideration or a gift inter vivos, whether by deed or otherwise, the degree required varies with the circumstances of the transaction. Thus, at one extreme, if the subject-matter and value of a gift are trivial in relation to the donor's other assets a low degree of understanding will suffice. But, at the other, if its effect is to dispose of the donor's only asset of value and thus for practical purposes to pre-empt the devolution of his estate under his will or on his intestacy, then the degree of understanding required is as high as that required for a will, and the donor must understand the claims of all potential donees and the extent of the property to be disposed of.'[2]

He added that, even where the degree of understanding in respect of a gift is not as high as that required for a will, the donor must be capable of understanding that he or she is making an outright gift and is not, for example, transferring property to someone else simply to facilitate its sale.[3]

---

1 [1978] 2 All ER 595.
2 *Ibid*, at p 601f–h.
3 *Ibid*, at p 602g–h.

Capacity to create an enduring power of attorney

The Enduring Powers of Attorney Act 1985 gives no indication of the mental capacity required of the donor at the time of creating an EPA. The position was clarified in an appeal and a reference from the Court of Protection, which were heard together.

Re K, Re F (1988)[1]

The facts of both cases were basically the same. An elderly lady suffering from dementia signed an enduring power of attorney, and a day or two later the attorneys applied for the power to be registered. In both cases, there was evidence that, when she executed the power, the donor understood its nature and effect, but there was also evidence that both of the donors were incapable, by reason of mental disorder, of managing and administering their property and affairs. The question arose as to whether the EPAs were valid.

HELD, by Hoffmann J – the test of validity of the power was whether, at the time of its execution, the donor had the mental capacity, with the assistance of such explanation as she may have been given, to understand the nature and effect of the power, not whether the donor would hypothetically have been able to perform all the acts authorised by the power. On the facts, both donors had understood the nature and effect of the power, even though they were incapable of managing and administering their property and affairs. Accordingly, both EPAs were valid and should be registered under the 1985 Act.

At the end of his judgment, the judge considered the degree of understanding involved in understanding the nature and effect of an EPA.

'Plainly, one cannot expect that the donor should have been able to pass an examination on the provisions of the 1985 Act. At the other extreme, I do not think that it would be sufficient if he realised only that it gave [the attorney] power to look after his property . . . I accept the [following summary] as a statement of the matters which should ordinarily be explained to the donor . . .   and which the evidence should show he has understood:
- first, if such be the terms of the power, that the attorney will be able to assume complete authority over the donor's affairs;
- second, if such be the terms of the power, that the attorney will in general be able to do anything with the donor's property which the donor could have done;

- third, that the authority will continue if the donor should be or become mentally incapable;
- fourth, that if he should be or become mentally incapable, the power will be irrevocable without confirmation by the court.'[2]

If the donor is already mentally incapable of managing and administering his property and affairs when he executes an EPA, the obligation to register the EPA arises immediately.[3]

The above criteria are not a substitute for the explanatory information in Part A of the prescribed form,[4] which the donor must read, or have read to him or her, before signing an EPA.[5]

There is no statutory duty to obtain medical evidence of the donor's capacity to execute an EPA, but in cases of borderline capacity there may be an obligation at common law to ensure that the donor's capacity is assessed by a registered medical practitioner.[6]

The decision in *Re K, Re F* has been criticised for setting too simple a test of capacity,[7] but its simplicity or complexity depends largely on the questions asked and the manner in which they are asked. For example, if the four pieces of basic relevant information described in *Re K, Re F* were explained to the donor, and she was then asked 'Do you understand this?' in such a way as to prompt an affirmative reply, she would almost certainly pass the test, and it would be too simple. But if the assessor were specifically to ask her 'What will your attorney be able to do?', 'What will happen if you become mentally incapable?', and 'Can you revoke the power?' the test would be a more realistic assessment of the donor's capacity, but substantially harder to pass. It can be inferred from the decision in *Re Beaney (Deceased)* that questions susceptible to the answers 'Yes' or 'No' are inadequate for the purpose of assessing capacity.[8]

---

1 [1988] Ch 310, [1988] 1 All ER 358.

2 *Re K, Re F* [1988] 1 All ER 358, at p 363d–f, per Hoffmann J. Law Com No 231 (HMSO, 1995), draft Mental Incapacity Bill, cl 2(2)(a) suggests that a person should also be capable of understanding the reasonably foreseeable consequences of taking or failing to take a decision – in this case, creating an enduring power of attorney.

3 *Re K, Re F* [1988] 1 All ER 358, at p 362f.

4 In the case of the first prescribed form, which was valid from 10 March 1986 to 30 June 1988 (both dates inclusive), the explanatory information appeared at the end of the form.

5 Enduring Powers of Attorney Act 1985, s 2(2)(b)(ii).

6 See what Templeman J described as the 'golden if tactless rule' in *Kenward v Adams* (1975) *The Times*, November 29, that when a will is drawn up for an elderly person or one who has been seriously ill, it should be witnessed or approved by a medical practitioner who should record his examination and findings. For a suggested form of medical certificate of capacity to create an EPA, see Precedent 3 at p 68 below.

7 Law Com Consultation Paper No 128 (HMSO, 1993), paras 7.12 and 7.13.

8 *Re Beaney (Deceased)* [1978] 2 All ER 595, at p 602c–d, j, per Martin Nourse QC: '[The solicitor] said that she asked Mrs Beaney certain questions, but that they were all susceptible to the answer "Yes" or "No". She asked her whether she understood what would happen and whether that was what she wanted. The questions were put to her twice and on both occasions she nodded affirmatively. All three persons present said they thought she understood what she was doing . . . [Counsel] offered some criticisms of [the solicitor] for the way in which she handled the transfer. However, a criticism by the court, particularly of a solicitor, is of a different order and I wish to make it clear that I have not considered whether any such criticism would be justified or not'.

Capacity to manage and administer one's property and affairs

There is a remarkable shortage of information about the criteria for assessing whether someone is mentally capable of managing and administering his or her property and affairs. This is particularly surprising since it is the cornerstone of the Court of Protection's jurisdiction under both the Mental Health Act 1983 and the Enduring Powers of Attorney Act 1985.

The functions of the judge under Part VII of the Mental Health Act 1983 are exercisable where 'after considering medical evidence, he is satisfied that a person is incapable, by reason of mental disorder, of managing and administering his property and affairs'.[1] An attorney acting under an enduring power has a duty to register the power with the Court of Protection if he 'has reason to believe that the donor is or is becoming mentally incapable'.[2] In this context, 'mentally incapable' means 'in relation to any person, that he is incapable by reason of mental disorder of managing and administering his property and affairs.'[3]

The definition of *mental incapacity* in both Acts contains three prerequisites. A person must:

- be suffering from *mental disorder*; and
- have *property and affairs* that need to be managed and administered; and
- *be incapable* (or, in the case of the donor of an EPA, *be becoming incapable*) by reason of mental disorder, of managing and administering such property and affairs.

The three do not always coincide. A person suffering from mental disorder might have no property and affairs to manage other than social security benefits and, if he or she is incapable of claiming, receiving and dealing with these, an appointee could be appointed by the Secretary of State to act on his or her behalf.[4] A person suffering from mental disorder might be more than capable of looking after his or her affairs – even financially astute – and people who are not suffering from any form of mental disorder could be incapable of managing and administering their property and affairs, because they are tired, physically ill or lazy.

Mental disorder

Mental disorder is defined in the Mental Health Act 1983, s 1(2). It means:

- mental illness;
- arrested or incomplete development of mind (in other words, learning disability or mental handicap);
- psychopathic disorder;[5]
- any other disorder or disability of mind.[6]

People are not to be regarded as suffering from mental disorder if their only problem is:

- promiscuity;
- immoral conduct;
- sexual deviancy;
- dependence on alcohol; or
- dependence on drugs.[7]

Mental illness is not defined in the 1983 Act. In *W v L*,[8] Lawton LJ said that the words *mental illness* are 'ordinary words of the English language. They have no particular medical significance. They have no particular legal significance . . . [and] should be construed in the way that ordinary sensible people would construe them'.[9] In 1976, in an appendix to its review of the Mental Health Act 1959, the Department of Health and Social Security issued the following guidelines on the symptoms commonly associated with mental illness.[10]

> 'Mental illness means an illness having one or more of the following characteristics:
> - more than temporary impairment of intellectual functions shown by a failure of memory, orientation, comprehension, and learning capacity[11]
> - more than temporary alteration of mood of such a degree as to give rise to the patient having a delusional appraisal of his situation, his past or his future, or that of others, or to the lack of any appraisal
> - delusional beliefs: persecutory, jealous or grandiose
> - abnormal perceptions associated with delusional misinterpretation of events
> - thinking so disordered as to prevent the patient making a reasonable appraisal of his situation or having reasonable communication with others.'

Property and affairs

Property and affairs means 'business matters, legal transactions and other dealings of a similar kind'.[12] It does not include matters relating to personal welfare or medical treatment. Strictly speaking, neither the Court of Protection[13] nor an attorney acting under an enduring power has any jurisdiction or authority to make personal or medical decisions[14] on behalf of a patient or the donor of an EPA, although inevitably 'power over the purse' confers a certain degree of 'power over the person'.[15]

Incapacity to manage

Assessing someone's capacity to manage and administer his or her property and affairs is very subjective. The individual's ability to cope depends largely on the value and complexity of his or her property and affairs, and the extent to which he or she may need to be protected from himself, herself, or others.

The leading textbook on Court of Protection practice cites an unreported decision of Wilberforce J in 1962[16] as the authority for its conclusion that 'the degree of incapacity of managing and administering a patient's property and affairs must be related to all the circumstances, including the state in which the alleged patient lives and the complexity and importance of the property and affairs which he has to manage and administer, and the Court has a discretion of deciding whether in the circumstances and upon the facts it is right for a receiver to be appointed'.[17]

A checklist of points to consider when assessing whether a person is incapable by reason of mental disorder of managing and administering his or her property and affairs can be found at p 62 below.

---

1 Mental Health Act 1983, s 94(2).

2 Enduring Powers of Attorney Act 1985, s 4(1).

3 *Ibid*, s 13(1).

4 Social Security (Claims and Payments) Regulations 1987 (SI 1987/1968), reg 33. See Chapter 7, 'Social Security Agents and Appointees'.

5 *Psychopathic disorder* means a persistent disorder or disability of mind (whether or not including significant impairment of intelligence) which results in abnormally aggressive or seriously irresponsible conduct on the part of the person concerned: Mental Health Act 1983, s 1(2).

6 The conditions falling within this residual category depend to some extent on how broadly *mental illness* is defined, but are likely to include disabilities resulting from head injuries, brain tumours, and toxic confusional states.

7 Mental Health Act 1983, s 1(3).

8 [1974] QB 711, at p 719B, CA.

9 Applying the dictum of Lord Reid in *Cozens v Brutus* [1973] AC 854, at p 861.

10 Department of Health and Social Security, *A Review of the Mental Health Act 1959*, (HMSO, 1976), Appendix II.

11 Compare the standard definition of *dementia*: 'an acquired global impairment of intellect, memory and personality but without impairment of consciousness ... as such, it is almost always of long duration, usually progressive, and often irreversible, but these features are not included as part of the definition': William A. Lishman, *Organic Psychiatry: The Psychological Consequences of Cerebral Disorder* (2nd edition, Blackwell Scientific, 1987).

12 *F v West Berkshire Health Authority* [1989] 2 All ER 545, HL, at p 554d, per Lord Brandon.

13 The Court of Protection's parens patriae jurisdiction over mental patients appears to have been abolished in 1960 as a consequence of the enactment of the Mental Health Act 1959: see *T v T* [1988] Fam 52; [1988] 1 All ER 613.

14 For example: where to live; who to live with; who to see; who not to see; what social activities and pastimes to have; decisions about diet, dress, and appearance; whether to consent to medical treatment, or withdraw or withhold consent, or accept treatment on a trial basis, or refuse outright.

15 See *Re W (EEM)* [1971] 1 Ch 123. A limited 'power over the person' is given under the Mental Health Act 1983, s 8(1), to a guardian, usually the director of social services for a local authority. The guardian has power: (a) to require the patient to reside at a place specified by the authority or person named as guardian; (b) to require the patient to attend at places and times so specified for the purpose of medical treatment, occupation, education or training; and (c) to require access to the patient to be given, at any place where the patient is residing, to any registered medical practitioner, approved social worker or other person so specified.

16 *Re CAF* (No 2367 of 1961), unreported, 23 March 1962.

17 Heywood and Massey, *Court of Protection Practice* (12th edition, Sweet & Maxwell, 1991), p 17.

Capacity to issue a cheque

The case of *Manches v Trimborn*[1] suggests that the essence of mental capacity is real consent to any transaction, and that an individual must be capable of exercising (a) the reason, and (b) the deliberations, necessary for real consent.

Manches v Trimborn (1946)

Mrs Caroline Trimborn was a wealthy widow aged 86. She was friendly with her neighbours, the Balassas, and in 1941 and 1942 had given them more than £5000. On 31 January 1945, she issued a cheque for £1300 in favour of Jack Manches to settle a debt incurred by Mr Balassa in a complicated series of transactions. It was dishonoured on presentation. Mrs Trimborn pleaded that, when she signed the cheque, she was suffering from senile degeneration and was incapable of understanding what she was doing, and that Manches was aware of her incapacity.

HELD, by Hallett J – 'there cannot have been, on the part of this old woman, the real consent to the transaction of which her cheque formed part which our law fundamentally requires'.

According to the judge, the ability to understand the nature and effect of the transaction was not simply a question whether of Mrs Trimborn was capable of understanding that: (a) she was signing a cheque; (b) it would transfer £1300 to the payee; and (c) the transfer of funds was for the benefit of Mr Balassa. She probably was capable of understanding, and did understand, all of these things. At the heart of the matter lies the need for *real consent*, that is full and free consent. Consent is an act of reason accompanied by deliberation and, in order that it could be said that she understood the nature and effect of the cheque she signed, it would be necessary to establish that she understood the nature and effect of the transactions of which her cheque formed part.

---

1 (1946) 174 LT 344, WN 63. Applied in *Re Beaney (Deceased)* [1978] 1 WLR 770, which is summarised at p 45 above.

Capacity to litigate

Although capacity is generally function-specific, the rules of court regard the capacity to sue or be sued as an aspect of an individual's general capacity to manage and administer his or her property and affairs.

The relevant rules are:

- Rules of the Supreme Court[1] Ord 80
- County Court Rules[2] Ord 10
- Family Proceedings Rules 1991,[3] Part IX
- Insolvency Rules 1986,[4] Chapter 7.

Where a person is considered to be 'incapable, by reason of mental disorder, of managing and administering his property and affairs', legal proceedings can only be conducted in his name and on his behalf by a *next friend* if the incapacitated person is bringing the proceedings, or a *guardian ad litem* if he is defending or responding to the proceedings.

The incapacitated person is technically referred to as a *patient* and, although the basis for assessing whether someone is capable of bringing or defending proceedings is the same as for the appointment of a receiver in the Court of Protection,[5] an incapacitated individual who is involved in litigation does not automatically have to become a Court of Protection patient.

---

1 SI 1965/1776.
2 SI 1981/1687.
3 SI 1991/1247 (L.20).
4 SI 1986/1925.
5 See pp 48–50 above, and the checklist at pp 62–63 below.

Contractual capacity

The law relating to contractual capacity is a complex combination of common law and statutory rules, from which it is possible to extract a few principles of general application.

Contractual capacity relates to a specific contract, rather than to contracts in general. An individual must be capable of understanding the nature and effect of the specific contract that he or she is entering into.[1] The degree of understanding required obviously varies according to the transaction itself,[2] for example, buying a bus pass would require a relatively low degree of understanding, whereas a complicated consumer-credit transaction would demand a higher level of comprehension.

In considering contractual capacity, the courts have to counterbalance two important policy questions. The first is the need to protect individuals who are incapable of looking after themselves, and the second is the need to ensure that other people are not prejudiced by the actions of a person whose incapacity they have no reason to suspect. Accordingly, an incapacitated individual will be bound by the terms of a contract unless it can be proved that the other party was aware or ought to have been aware of the incapacity at the time when the contract was made.[3] The burden of proof is on the incapacitated person, and if he or she is able to discharge that burden the contract is voidable at his or her option.[4] However, the circumstances may be such that any reasonable person would have been aware of the patient's incapacity.[5]

There are two main exceptions to the general rule on voidability at the patient's option. The first relates to contracts for *necessaries*, and the second applies to patients within the jurisdiction of the Court of Protection.

A mentally incapacitated person who agrees to pay for goods which are *necessaries* is legally obliged to pay a reasonable price for them. *Necessaries* are defined in the Sale of Goods Act 1979, s 3(3) as 'goods suitable to [the individual's] condition in life and his actual requirements at the time of sale and delivery'. Again the countervailing policy considerations apply. The rule is designed partly to protect shopkeepers, and partly to protect the patient who is obliged to pay a *reasonable price* for the goods supplied,[6] which is not necessarily the same as the asking price.[7] Although the Sale of Goods Act 1979 applies to goods, the principles regarding necessaries would govern the supply of essential services such as accommodation and care in a nursing home.[8]

A patient whose affairs are managed by a receiver under the supervision of the Court of Protection cannot make any contract which is inconsistent with the court's powers. Any such contracts are automatically voidable, regardless of whether the patient had contractual capacity at the time, and regardless of whether the other party was aware of the Court of Protection's involvement.[9] The court does, however, have power to make orders or give directions or authorities for the carrying out of any contract entered into by the patient.[10]

---

1 *Boughton v Knight* (1873) LR 3 PD 64, at p 72.
2 *Re Beaney (Deceased)* [1978] 1 WLR 770.
3 *Imperial Loan Co v Stone* [1892] 1 QB 599, CA.
4 'A defendant must plead and prove both his insanity and the knowledge of the plaintiff: the burden of proof of both of these facts lies on the defendant': *ibid*, at pp 602–603, per Lopes LJ.
5 *York Glass Co v Jubb* (1925) 134 LT 36, CA.
6 Sale of Goods Act 1979, s 8(3): 'What is a reasonable price is a question of fact dependent on the circumstances of each particular case'.
7 *Acebal v Levy* (1834) 10 Bing 376, at p 383, per Tindal CJCP.
8 *Re Rhodes: Rhodes v Rhodes* [1890] 44 ChD 94, CA.
9 *Re Walker* [1905] 1 Ch 160; *Re Marshall* [1920] 1 Ch 284.
10 Mental Health Act 1983, s 96(1)(h).

Proposed reforms

In its report on *Mental Incapacity*, the Law Commission has made the following recommendations.[1]

- Legislation should provide that a person is without capacity if at the material time he or she is: (1) unable by reason of mental disability to make a decision on the matter in question; or (2) unable to communicate a decision on that matter because he or she is unconscious or for any other reason.[2]
- A person should be regarded as unable to make a decision by reason of mental disability if the disability is such that, at the time when the decision needs to be made, he or she is unable to understand or retain the information relevant to the decision, including information about the reasonably foreseeable consequences of deciding one way or another or failing to make the decision.[3]
- A person should be regarded as unable to make a decision by reason of mental disability if the disability is such that, at the time when the decision needs to be made, he or she is unable to make a decision based on the information relevant to the decision, including information about the reasonably foreseeable consequences of deciding one way or another or failing to make the decision.[4]

- A person should not be regarded as unable to understand the information relevant to a decision if he or she is able to understand an explanation of that information in broad terms and simple language.[5]
- A person should not be regarded as unable to make a decision by reason of mental disability merely because he or she makes a decision which would not be made by a person of ordinary prudence.[6]
- A person should not be regarded as unable to communicate his or her decision unless all practicable steps to enable him or her to do so have been taken without success.[7]
- The Secretary of State should prepare, and from time to time revise, a code of practice for the guidance of persons assessing whether a person is or is not without capacity to make a decision or decisions on any matters.[8]

The Law Commission is not proposing to replace any of the existing definitions of capacity at common law with its new statutory definition, but is of the opinion that, after the implementation of the new statutory definition, it is likely that common law judges would consider it and then adopt it if they saw fit. The new definition expands upon, rather than contradicts, the terms of the existing common law tests. The only point of difference is the provision requiring an explanation of the relevant information to have been made if a finding of incapacity is to have prospective effect.[9]

---

1 *Mental Incapacity* (1995) Law Com No 231 (HMSO, 1995).
2 *Ibid*, para 3.14, and draft Mental Incapacity Bill, cl 2(1).
3 *Ibid*, para 3.16, and draft Mental Incapacity Bill, cl 2(2)(a).
4 *Ibid*, para 3.17, and draft Mental Incapacity Bill, cl 2(2)(b).
5 *Ibid*, para 3.18, and draft Mental Incapacity Bill, cl 2(3).
6 *Ibid*, para 3.19, and draft Mental Incapacity Bill, cl 2(4).
7 *Ibid*, para 3.21, and draft Mental Incapacity Bill, cl 2(5).
8 *Ibid*, para 3.22, and draft Mental Incapacity Bill, cl 31(1)(a).
9 *Ibid*, para 3.23.

CHECKLISTS

1 CAPACITY TO MAKE A WILL (TESTAMENTARY CAPACITY)[1]

'When a solicitor is drawing up a will for an aged testator or one who has been seriously ill, it should be witnessed or approved by a medical practitioner, who ought to record his examination of the testator and his findings. That is the golden, if tactless, rule.'[2]

Any person making a will must understand:

1. The nature of the act of making a will:

- that he or she will die;
- that the will will come into operation on his or her death, but not before;
- that he or she can change or revoke the will at any time.

2. The effects of the will:

- who the executor is, and possibly why he or she is being chosen as executor;
- who gets what under the will;
- whether a beneficiary's gift is absolute, or whether it is limited or conditional in some way (for example, a life interest, or a legacy contingent on attaining a particular age);
- whether he or she has already made a will and, if so, how and why the new one differs from the old one;[3]
- if he or she has not made a will, (roughly) the reasonably foreseeable consequences of not making one.[4]

3. The extent[5] of the property being disposed of:

- the extent of all the money and property owned solely by the testator or testatrix which is capable of being disposed of by will;
- the fact that any jointly owned property might automatically pass to the other joint owner, regardless of anything the will says;
- whether there are benefits payable on his or her death which would be unaffected by the terms of the will: for example, the proceeds of an insurance policy, pension rights, or rights under a trust in which the testator or testatrix has a life interest;
- the fact that assets could be sold, and new assets acquired during his or her lifetime;
- the fact that his or her assets might increase or decrease in value during his or her lifetime;
- whether he or she has any debts, and how they are to be paid;[6]
- (the incidence of inheritance tax may be relevant if it would have been of importance to the testator or testatrix in his or her pre-morbid state).

4. A person making a will should also be able to comprehend and appreciate the claims to which he or she ought to give effect.[7]

Why are some beneficiaries preferred and others possibly excluded? For example:

- some may be better provided for than others;
- some may be more deserving than others because they have been kind to the testator or testatrix;
- some may have upset, offended or disregarded him or her;
- some may be in greater need than others because of, say, their age or state of health.[8]

5. It is essential that no delusions should influence the testator or testatrix and bring about a disposal of his or her property which would not have been made if he or she were not mentally disordered.[9]

6. The testator or testatrix should not be regarded as lacking testamentary capacity merely because he or she makes a will which would not be made by a person of ordinary prudence.[10]

---

1 See, generally, 'Capacity to make a will' at p 44 above. This checklist is based on the criteria for testamentary capacity set out by Cockburn CJ in *Banks v Goodfellow* (1870) LR 5 QB 549, at p 565.

2 *Kenward v Adams* (1975) *The Times*, November 29, per Templeman J. The golden rule was reiterated by Templeman J in *Re Simpson, Deceased: Schaniel v Simpson* (1977) 121 SJ 224.

3 If there is an earlier will it should be examined and any proposed alterations should be discussed with the testator or testatrix: *Kenward v Adams* (fn 2 above).

4 The Law Commission, in *Mental Incapacity* (1995) Law Com No 231 (HMSO, 1995), recommends at paras 3.16 to 3.18 that a person should be considered unable to take the decision in question if he or she is unable to understand an explanation in broad terms and simple language of the basic information relevant to taking it, including information about the reasonably foreseeable consequences of taking or failing to take it.

5 Note that in *Banks v Goodfellow* (fn 1 above), Cockburn CJ referred to the *extent*, rather than the *value*, of the property being disposed of under the will.

6 *Birkin v Wing* (1890) 63 LT 80, at p 82, per Kekewich J.

7 The previous tests are based on the testator's *understanding*. Understanding involves receiving and evaluating information which might have been communicated by others. This final test requires the testator to be able to distinguish and compare the claims of the potential beneficiaries, and to exercise moral judgment.

8 'Among those, who, as a man's nearest relatives, would be entitled to share the fortune he leaves behind him, some may be better provided for than others; some may be more deserving than others; some from age, sex, or physical infirmity, may stand in greater need of assistance. Friendship and tried attachment, or faithful service, may have claims that ought not to be disregarded. In the power of rewarding dutiful and meritorious conduct, paternal authority finds a useful auxiliary; age secures the respect and attentions that are one of its chief consolations': *Banks v Goodfellow* (fn 1 above), at p 564, per Cockburn CJ.

9 *Banks v Goodfellow* (fn 1 above), at p 565, per Cockburn CJ. See *Re Belliss: Polson v Parrott* (1929) 141 LT 245.

10 See *Bird v Luckie* (1850) 8 Hare 301, at p 306. See also the Law Commission's draft Mental Incapacity Bill, cl 2(4).

2 CAPACITY TO MAKE A GIFT[1]

1. Are the subject matter and value of the gift insignificant in the context of the donor's assets?

- If they are, a low degree of understanding is probably sufficient.
- If they are not, the degree of understanding required could be as high as (or possibly even higher than)[2] that required for making a will,[3] and the following questions may need to be asked.

2. Does the donor understand the nature of the transaction?

- that he or she is making an outright gift rather than, say:
  - a loan[4]
  - a mortgage
  - acquiring a beneficial interest in property being purchased by the recipient of the gift
  - acquiring a stake in the recipient's business
  - transferring property into the recipient's name in order to facilitate a sale on the donor's behalf;[5]
- whether he or she expects to receive payment or anything else in return;
- whether he or she intends the gift to take effect immediately, or whether it is to take effect at a later date, maybe on the donor's death;
- who the recipient is;
- whether he or she has already made substantial gifts to the recipient;
- whether he or she has already made substantial gifts to anyone else;
- whether this gift is a 'one off' or part of a larger transaction or series of transactions;
- the underlying motive or purpose of the transaction.[6]

3. Does the donor understand the effects of making the gift?

- that, if the gift is outright, the donor will not be able to ask for the asset to be returned to him or her;
- the effect that disposing of this asset will have on the donor's future standard of living, having regard to his or her current and anticipated:
  - age
  - life expectancy
  - income
  - earning capacity (if any)
  - financial resources
  - financial obligations
  - financial needs;
- the effect that the gift could have on the recipient;
- whether there are alternative ways of rewarding the recipient which would involve less risk to the donor;[7]

- the possibility that the gift could be challenged if it is intended to defeat creditors, or defeat a claim for financial relief in family proceedings, or secure entitlement to or greater entitlement to means-tested benefits or community care funding;
- the possibility that the relationship between the donor and the recipient might not always be amicable;
- the possibility that the recipient could predecease the donor, or become involved in bankruptcy or divorce proceedings, in which case the subject matter of the gift could pass into the hands of someone else;
- any other foreseeable consequences of making the gift;
- the reasonably foreseeable consequences of not making the gift.[8]

4. Does the donor understand the extent of the property of which he or she is disposing?

- that the subject matter of the gift belongs to the donor and that he or she is able to dispose of it;
- the extent (and maybe the approximate value)[9] of the gift in relation to all the circumstances and, in particular, the donor's other assets.

5. Is the donor capable of comprehending and appreciating other claims to which he or she ought to give effect?

- Why is the recipient of the gift more deserving than any other potential beneficiaries under the donor's will or on his or her intestacy? Perhaps the recipient is:
  - more deserving;
  - less well provided for;
  - in need of greater assistance.
- What effect is the gift going to have on the other potential beneficiaries under the donor's will or intestacy?
- Is it necessary to compensate the others: perhaps by making a new will?

6. The donor should not be regarded as mentally incapable of making the gift merely because the gift would not be made by a person of ordinary prudence.[10]

---

1 See, generally, 'Capacity to make a gift' at p 45 above.
2 Because of the potential detriment the donor could suffer as a result of making such a gift.
3 *Re Beaney (Deceased)* [1978] 2 All ER 595, at p 601f–h.
4 Property case-law reveals that there is often confusion as to the actual nature of a transaction, even in cases where capacity is not an issue. For example, see *Hussey v Palmer* [1972] 3 All ER 744 and *Sekhon v Alissa* [1989] 2 FLR 94.
5 *Re Beaney (Deceased)* (fn 3 above), at p 602g–h.
6 In *Re Craig (Deceased)* [1971] Ch 95, various gifts were set aside by Ungoed-Thomas J partly because none of them could be accounted for on the ground of 'ordinary motives on which ordinary men act'.
7 *Inche Noriah v Shaik Allie Bin Omar* [1929] AC 192, PC.
8 *Mentally Incapacitated Adults and Decision-Making: A New Jurisdiction* (Law Com Consultation Paper No 128) (HMSO, 1993), para 3.24.

9 In *Banks v Goodfellow* (1870) LR 5 QB 549, at p 565, Cockburn CJ stated that one of the pre-requisites of testamentary capacity is that the testator 'shall understand the *extent* of the property of which he is disposing'. *Extent* was specified rather than *value*. Possibly in the context of an outright gift, the donor should be aware of its value as well: partly because of the potential detriment the transaction could cause to the donor, and partly because it is not unreasonable to expect the donor to be aware of the approximate value of one asset comprised in an outright gift, as distinct from all of the assets which would be included in a testamentary disposition.

10 See *Bird v Luckie* (1850) 8 Hare 301, at p 306. See also the Law Commission's draft Mental Incapacity Bill, cl 2(4).

3 CAPACITY TO EXECUTE AN ENDURING POWER OF ATTORNEY[1]

1. Has the explanatory information in Part A of the prescribed form of EPA been read by or to the donor?[2]

- The solicitor owes a general duty to the donor to explain the document to him or her.[3]
- The solicitor should explain any unusual provisions,[4] or any provisions of particular relevance to the donor's property and affairs.[5]
- The solicitor should ensure that the donor understands and agrees to the provisions of the EPA.[6]

2. Have the following matters been explained to the donor, and does he or she understand:[7]

- first, that the attorney will be able to assume complete authority over his or her affairs?
- secondly, that the attorney will, in general, be able to do anything with the donor's property which he or she could have done personally?
- thirdly, that the attorney's authority will continue if the donor is or is becoming mentally incapable?
- fourthly, that if he or she is or is becoming mentally incapable, the EPA cannot be revoked without confirmation by the Court of Protection?

3. Is the donor aware of the reasonably foreseeable consequences of not creating an EPA?[8]

4. In assessing the donor's capacity, try to avoid asking questions which are susceptible of the answers 'Yes' or 'No'.[9]

5. If the donor's capacity is borderline:

- the EPA should be witnessed or approved by a registered medical practitioner;[10] and
- the medical practitioner should, as soon as practicable, record his or her examination and findings.[11]

---

1 See, generally, 'Capacity to create an enduring power of attorney' at pp 46–48 above, and Chapter 9, 'Enduring powers of attorney', at p 216 ff.
2 Enduring Powers of Attorney Act 1985, s 2(2)(b)(ii).
3 'A solicitor, whatever may be his other duties towards his client, ought always to make his client distinctly acquainted with the legal effect of any step he may take ... Where their clients are unacquainted with the law, solicitors should always be extremely careful to explain to them fully what their duty is': *Re A Solicitor ex parte Incorporated Law Society* (1895) SJ 219.
4 *Stannard v Ullithorne* (1834) 10 Bing 491; *Phillips v Millings* (1871) 7 Ch App 244.
5 *Transportation Agency v Jenkins* (1972) 223 EG 1101.

6 'It seems most unusual not to do one of two things, viz, either to read over the whole of the document which the party is about to sign or go through it passage by passage, and say there is a clause to this effect and a clause to that effect and so on. In some states of a testator's health or in some states of a testator's mind disturbed by pain it might be expedient to shorten the process, but in some way or other, so far as my experience goes, I should say that it is the practice of solicitors either to read over the whole instrument or to read and explain clause by clause the effect that each clause would have': *Morrell v Morrell* (1888) PD 68, at p 73, per Sir John Hannen P.

7 *Re K, Re F* [1988] 1 All ER 358, at p 363d–f, per Hoffmann J.

8 'A person should be considered unable to take the decision in question (or decisions of the type in question) if he or she is unable to understand an explanation in broad terms and simple language of the basic information relevant to taking it, including information about the reasonably foreseeable consequences of taking it or failing to take it, or to retain the information for long enough to take an effective decision': *Mentally Incapacitated Adults and Decision-Making: A New Jurisdiction* (Law Com Consultation Paper No 128) (HMSO, 1993), para 3.24. This recommendation appears in cl 2 of the draft Incapacity Bill appended to *Mental Incapacity* (1995) Law Com No 231 (HMSO, 1995).

9 *Re Beaney (Deceased)* [1978] 2 All ER 595, at p 602c–d.

10 See the dicta of Templeman J, in the context of Wills, in *Kenward v Adams* (1975) *The Times*, November 29; repeated in *Re Simpson, Deceased: Schaniel v Simpson* (1977) 121 SJ 224.

11 For a precedent of a medical certificate of the donor's capacity to create an EPA, see Precedent 3 at p 68 below.

4 CAPACITY TO MANAGE ONE'S PROPERTY AND AFFAIRS[1]

An attorney acting under an enduring power has a duty to register the power, as soon as practicable, if he or she 'has reason to believe that the donor is or is becoming mentally incapable'.[2] 'Mentally incapable' means 'incapable by reason of mental disorder of managing and administering his [or her] property and affairs'.[3]

The attorney may care to consider the following points when deciding whether the donor is, or is becoming, mentally incapable.[4]

1. Is the donor suffering from mental disorder? *Mental disorder* means:[5]

- mental illness;
- arrested or incomplete development of mind;
- psychopathic disorder; or
- any other disorder or disability of mind.

2. If so – on the balance of probabilities – is the donor incapable or *becoming* incapable,[6] by reason of mental disorder, of managing and administering his or her property and affairs?

3. What property and affairs does the donor have to manage? For example:

- income;
- earning capacity;
- occupation;
- the value of his or her house;
- the nature and value of his or her other assets;
- debts;
- outgoings;
- financial needs;
- financial responsibilities;
- family responsibilities;
- social responsibilities;
- the time, skill, and specialised knowledge needed to manage such property and affairs;
- whether the management of these affairs has already got into a mess because of the donor's mental state;
- whether the management of these affairs is likely to get into a (further) mess because of his or her mental state if no action is taken;
- whether there are likely to be any changes in the donor's property and affairs in the foreseeable future;
- whether the donor could manage better if his or her affairs were rationalised or simplified in some way.

4. Consider the donor's personal circumstances, for example:

- his or her age;
- life expectancy;
- psychiatric history;
- prospects of recovery;
- prospects of progressive deterioration;
- the possibility that capacity could fluctuate;
- the condition in which he or she lives;
- the family background;
- the degree of support and back-up he or she receives from others;
- the ascertainable past and present wishes and feelings of the donor.

5. Consider the donor's vulnerability.

- Do the donor's property and affairs need to be protected from his or her own recklessness, carelessness or irresponsibility?
- Does the donor need to be protected from exploitation by others – including close relatives?
- Do other people need to be protected from the donor's inability to manage his or her affairs properly?

6. Is the registration of the EPA in the donor's best interests, and is there any alternative course of action which is less restrictive of the donor's freedom of decision and action?[7]

---

1 See, generally, 'Capacity to manage and administer one's property and affairs' at p 48 above.
2 Enduring Powers of Attorney Act 1985, s 4(1), (2).
3 *Ibid*, s 13(1).
4 The Court of Protection applies similar criteria when deciding whether a person is a patient for the purposes of Part VII of the Mental Health Act 1983.
5 Mental Health Act 1983, s 1(2).
6 The expression *is becoming mentally incapable* refers to incipient incapacity to manage and administer one's property and affairs, rather than incipient mental disorder. The attorney has a duty to register an EPA when the donor: (1) is suffering from mental disorder; and, as a result, (2) is or is becoming incapable of managing his or her property and affairs.
7 The Law Commission has suggested that the attorney must act in the donor's best interests, taking into account the general principle that the course least restrictive of the donor's freedom of decision and action is likely to be in his or her best interests: *Mental Incapacity* (1995) Law Com No 231 (HMSO, 1995), and draft Mental Incapacity Bill, cl 3(2)(d).

PRECEDENTS

1 CLIENT'S CONSENT TO THE DISCLOSURE OF CONFIDENTIAL INFORMATION FOR THE PURPOSE OF ASSESSING HIS OR HER CAPACITY

I ....
of ....
born on ....
CONSENT to the following:

1. My solicitor (*name*) of (*address*) may disclose to my doctor (*name*) of (*address*) such confidential information about my property and affairs as (he)/(she) considers is necessary to enable my doctor to form an opinion on whether I am capable of (making a will)/(making a gift of my (*house*) to my (*children*))/(managing my property and affairs generally).[1]

2. My doctor may disclose (his)/(her) opinion to my solicitor together with such other confidential information about my health as (he)/(she) considers relevant in the circumstances.[2]

Signed ....
Dated   ....

---

1 The Law Society, *The Guide to the Professional Conduct of Solicitors* (6th edition, 1993), Principle 16.03: 'The duty to keep confidential a client's business continues until the client permits disclosure or waives the confidentiality'.
2 General Medical Council, *Professional Conduct and Discipline: Fitness to Practise* (May 1992), para 77: 'Where a patient, or a person properly authorised to act on a patient's behalf, consents to disclosure, information to which the consent refers may be disclosed in accordance with that consent'.

2 LETTER TO GP REQUESTING EVIDENCE OF A CLIENT'S MANAGERIAL AND TESTAMENTARY CAPACITY[1]

(*GP's name and address*)   (*reference*)

                                                                                     (*date*)

Dear (*GP*)

(Full name, address and date of birth of client)

I have received a letter from (*client*) dated (*date*) in which she states that on her death her four children (*names*) are to receive legacies of £ . . . . each, and the rest of her estate is to go to her daughter (*name*). A photocopy of the letter is enclosed.

I am aware that (*client*) is suffering from dementia, and I am conscious of the possibility that she might have been persuaded to write the letter. However, it appears to have been written in her own handwriting, and the wishes are coherent. They may be entirely reasonable in the circumstances.

The letter is, of course, inadequate as a will or codicil, but I have interpreted it as instructions to take whatever steps are necessary to prepare a will or codicil which would give effect to these wishes. After receiving the letter, I went to see (*client*) personally and she has confirmed these instructions.)[2]

There is a procedure whereby the Court of Protection can authorise the execution of what is known as a 'statutory will' on behalf of a patient who is mentally incapacitated,[3] but it will only make such an order if, after considering medical evidence, it is satisfied that the patient is both:

- incapable, by reason of mental disorder, of managing and administering her property and affairs; and
- incapable of making a valid will.[4]

I would be grateful, therefore, if you could visit (*client*) as soon as possible to assess her capacity, and then let me have a certificate or report stating whether in your opinion she is: (a) incapable, by reason of mental disorder, of managing and administering her property and affairs; and (b) incapable of making a valid will.

I enclose a consent form signed by (*client*) in which she has agreed that I can disclose to you confidential information about her income, capital and will. You will note that she has also consented to your disclosing to me your opinion on her capacity.[5]

Capacity to manage her property and affairs

I enclose the standard form of medical certificate (Form CP3) issued by the Court of Protection, together with the 'Notes to accompany Certificate of Incapacity' which were prepared by the court in consultation with the Royal College of Psychiatrists and the British Medical Association.[6]

In essence, the court needs to know whether (*client*) is:

- suffering from 'mental disorder' as defined in the Mental Health Act 1983;[7] and
- by reason of that mental disorder, incapable of managing and administering her property and affairs.[8]

The statutory definition of 'mental disorder' in the margin of Form CP3 is not particularly helpful but, as far as the Department of Health is concerned, 'mental illness' includes an illness which is characterised by 'more than temporary impairment of intellectual functions shown by a failure of memory, orientation, comprehension and learning capacity',[9] which, I understand, is almost a classic definition of dementia.

I am enclosing a brief statement of the approximate current values of her property and other assets, together with a note of her annual income and outgoings, because her ability to manage her property and affairs may very well be linked to their value and complexity.

Capacity to make a will

It is possible that, although (*client*) may be incapable of managing her property and affairs, she is capable of making a valid will for herself. The tests for the two types of capacity are different.

In order to be capable of making a will, (*client*) must be able to:[10]

- understand the nature of the act of will-making;
- understand the effects of making a will in the form she proposes;
- understand the extent (although not necessarily the value) of the property which she is disposing of under her will; and
- comprehend and appreciate the claims of all the people to which she ought to have regard. Unlike the other tests, which are based on 'understanding', this final test involves the ability to distinguish between individuals and to reach some kind of moral judgment. For example, she might prefer her daughter (*name*) to her other children because:
  - she may be less well provided for; or
  - she may be more deserving; or
  - she may be in need of greater financial assistance because of her family responsibilities, or her state of health.[11]

I am enclosing a photocopy of her existing will dated (*date*) in which you will note, in Clause (*number*), that she has given her residuary estate to her five children in equal shares.

Generally

In either case, your assessment of (*client's*) capacity should be based 'on the balance of probabilities'. In other words, is it more likely that she is capable or she is incapable? You do not need to be satisfied 'beyond reasonable doubt'.

If an application is made to the Court of Protection, I suspect that it may be contested by the children who stand to lose part of their present inheritance, although I doubt whether it will be necessary for you to provide any further medical evidence. Obviously, the fact that the children might contest any application for a statutory will should have no bearing on your opinion as to (*client's*) capacity.

If you consider you have insufficient experience of assessing mental states and different types of functional capacity, please feel free to decline these instructions or to refer the matter to a specialist.

There is no standard fee for producing this sort of evidence. It largely depends on the amount of time you spend reading the patient's notes, visiting her, assessing her capacity, and writing your report. I would think that anything within the region of (£ . . .) would be considered reasonable in the circumstances.

If you are of the opinion that (*client*) is capable of making a valid will for herself, I would be grateful if you could kindly act as one of the witnesses when the time comes for her to sign it.[12]

Please let me know whether you require any further information. I look forward to hearing from you as soon as possible.

Yours sincerely

Enclosures

- [• Copy of client's letter]
- Client's consent to disclosure[13]
- Form CP3
- Notes to accompany Form CP3
- Statement of client's property and affairs
- Copy of client's existing will
- Stamped addressed envelope

---

1 See, generally, 'Capacity to manage one's property and affairs' at p 48 and Checklist 4 at p 62 above; 'Capacity to make a will' at p 39 and Checklist 1 at p 55 above.

2 The Law Society, *The Guide to the Professional Conduct of Solicitors* (6th edition, 1993), Principle 12.05, Commentary 2: 'When asked to prepare a will on the basis of written instructions alone, a solicitor should always consider carefully whether these are sufficient or whether the solicitor should see the client to discuss the instructions'.

3 Statutory wills are discussed in detail in Chapter 14.

4 Mental Health Act 1983, s 96(4)(b).

5 The Law Society, in *The Guide to the Professional Conduct of Solicitors* (6th edition, 1993), states as Principle 16.03 that 'the duty to keep confidential a client's business continues until the client permits disclosure or waives the confidentiality'. Similarly, the General Medical Council has directed that 'where a patient, or a person properly authorised to act on a patient's behalf, consents to disclosure, information to which the consent refers may be disclosed in accordance with that consent': *Professional Conduct and Discipline: Fitness to Practise* (May 1992), para 77. For a precedent consent form, see Precedent 1 at p 64 above.

6 Form CP3 is reproduced in Chapter 10, at p 291 below.

7 Mental Health Act 1983, s 1(2).

8 *Ibid*, s 94(2).

9 Department of Health and Social Security, *A Review of the Mental Health Act 1959* (HMSO, 1976), Appendix II.

10 *Banks v Goodfellow* (1870) LR 5 QB 549, at p 565.

11 *Ibid*, at p 564.

12 For the need for the will to be witnessed by a medical practitioner, see *Kenward v Adams* (1975) *The Times*, November 29; *Re Simpson, Deceased: Schaniel v Simpson* (1977) 121 SJ 224; and Court of Protection Procedure Note PN5.

13 For a precedent consent to the disclosure of confidential information for the purpose of assessing a client's capacity, see Precedent 1 at p 64 above.

---

3 MEDICAL CERTIFICATE OF DONOR'S CAPACITY TO EXECUTE AN ENDURING POWER OF ATTORNEY

Enduring Powers of Attorney Act 1985

In the matter of a power given by .... (the donor)
to .... (the attorney)

I (*full name and medical qualifications*) of (*address including postcode*)
CERTIFY as follows.

1. I have been the donor's GP since (*date*), and see (him)/(her) approximately (*number*) times a year.

2. The donor is suffering from a mental disorder, namely (*description of disorder*).

3. On (*date*), I attended on the donor when (he)/(she) executed an enduring power appointing the attorney(s) to be (his)/(her) attorney(s) with general authority to act on (his)/(her) behalf in relation to all (his)/(her) property and affairs.

4. In my opinion, notwithstanding (his)/(her) mental disorder, when the donor executed the enduring power (he)/(she) was capable of understanding the nature and effect of the power and, in particular, understood that:

- the attorney(s) would be able to assume complete authority over (his)/(her) affairs;
- the attorney(s) would in general be able to do anything with (his)/(her) property that (he)/(she) could do personally;
- the authority given to the attorney(s) will continue if (he)/(she) should be or become mentally incapable;
- (he)/(she) can revoke the power at any time, provided that (he)/(she) is mentally capable of doing so;
- if (he)/(she) should be or become mentally incapable, (he)/(she) could not revoke the power without confirmation by the court.

5. This certificate is limited to my opinion on the donor's capacity to execute an enduring power of attorney, and I express no opinion on (his)/(her) capacity to do anything else.

Signed ....
Dated ....

4 MEDICAL CERTIFICATE ON DONOR'S RECOVERY[1]

Court of Protection
Enduring Powers of Attorney Act 1985

In the matter of a power given by

.... (a donor)

to .... (attorney)

and .... (attorney)

MEDICAL CERTIFICATE

I .... *(full name and medical qualifications)* ....
of .... *(address including postcode)* ....
CERTIFY as follows.

1. I have been the donor's GP since *(date)*.

2. On *(date)*, I examined the donor for the purpose of ascertaining the state of (his)/(her) mind.

3. As a result of such examination, I am of the opinion that the donor:

- (is)/(is not) suffering from mental disorder as defined in the Mental Health Act 1983 [namely, *(diagnosis)*];
- is capable of managing and administering (his)/(her) property and affairs; and
- is likely to remain capable of managing and administering (his)/(her) property and affairs.[2]

4. I base my conclusions on the following grounds: ....
....
....
....

Signed ....
Dated ....

---

1 'The court shall cancel the registration of an [EPA] . . . on being satisfied that the donor is and is likely to remain mentally capable': Enduring Powers of Attorney Act 1985, s 8(4)(c).

2 'This would involve a complete recovery rather than a return to, say, the becoming incapable level': Law Commission Report No 122, *The Incapacitated Principal*, Cmnd 8977 (July 1983), p 47.

5 CERTIFICATE OF TESTAMENTARY CAPACITY GIVEN BY A SOLICITOR ACTING AS AN EXPERT WITNESS

I ....

of ....

CERTIFY as follows.

1. I was admitted as a solicitor in (*year*) and specialise in private client work. I am familiar with the law and practice relating to testamentary capacity.

2. Between (*state times*) on (*date*) I attended on (*name of testatrix*) at her home (*address*) for the purposes of ascertaining whether she had testamentary capacity and, if so, to act as one of the witnesses to her will. Also present were her solicitor (*name*) and GP (*name*).

3. I understand that (*testatrix*) was born in (*year*) and has been suffering from a mild form of dementia for the last (*period*).

4. In my opinion she was capable of executing the will, and I base my opinion on the following grounds.

5. She clearly understood the nature of the will and its effects. She was aware that it would come into operation on her death, but not before. She knew that she had an existing will, although she could not recall when she had made it. She knew that in her existing will she had divided her residuary estate equally between her three children.

6. She clearly recalled that she had written to her solicitor giving instructions for the preparation of a new will in which she proposed to leave half of her residuary estate to her son (*name*), and a quarter to each of her daughters (*name*) and (*name*).

7. She intended, and understood her will to provide, that if any of her children died before her, his or her share of the estate would go to his or her children.

8. She believed that the variation from her existing will was fair and reasonable in the circumstances. She expressly stated that her daughters were better off financially than her son.

9. It was clear to me that (*testatrix*) is particularly fond of her son, and she mentioned in conversation that he is in closer contact with her than his sisters, by telephone, correspondence and personal visits. Since (*year*), she and her late husband have spent Christmas with (*son's forename*) and his family, and at least a week with them during the summer holidays.

10. (*Testatrix's*) husband died three months ago, and she could still vividly recount the circumstances of his final illness and death. Her husband (*name*) had always managed their financial affairs, and she admitted that she was not well-versed in business matters. Her solicitor explained to her that, before deducting inheritance tax, her estate was worth roughly £450,000, and she considered that this estimate was probably correct. She knew that her estate consisted of

the house, which she thought could be worth somewhere in the region of £150,000, though she acknowledged that the property prices in the area had fallen during the last few years. She knew that she had a current account at the (*branch name*) branch of the National Westminster Bank, although she was unaware of the current balance. In her own words, 'It could be anything between £500 and £5000 for all I know'. She knew that much of her capital was tied up in investments managed by (*stockbrokers*). She was aware that her state retirement pension and the widow's pension she receives from her late husband's company (*name of company*) would cease to be payable on her death, and seemed rather surprised that I should have asked her a question to which the answer was so obvious.

11. She was fully aware of the extent of her family. She knew the full names and, in most cases, the actual date of birth of her children and grandchildren. She knew all about the current whereabouts and activities of everyone in the family. I sensed that she was slightly more devoted to (*son's children*) because she sees more of them. I have no reason to doubt that she was fully able to comprehend and appreciate the claims to which she ought to give effect in her will.

12. One of the symptoms of (*testatrix's*) illness is a mild loss of short-term memory. On two or three occasions, she repeated comments that she had already made. These were generally social niceties about the weather, whether we had travelled very far, and an invitation to join her for a glass of sherry. The repetition was not unreasonably excessive, and is probably of greater consequence in the context of her ability to manage her property and affairs generally. I am satisfied that her short-term memory deficit did not in any way affect her testamentary wishes.

13. There was no evidence of any delusion which might have affected her attitude towards any member of her family, and there was no evidence to suggest that any pressure or undue influence had been applied in connection with the making of her will.

14. I was satisfied that on the balance of probabilities (*testatrix*) had testamentary capacity. Her GP was also satisfied as to her capacity and will be making a separate record of his own findings. Her GP and I acted as subscribing witnesses to the will.

Signed ....

Dated ....

CHAPTER 4: SHARING RESIDENTIAL ACCOMMODATION

INDEX

Text

Precedents

SHARING RESIDENTIAL ACCOMMODATION

TEXT

Introduction[1]

There are four fairly common scenarios where an elderly person shares owner-occupied accommodation with other people – usually a son or daughter, although occasionally an unrelated friend.[2] They are:

- simply moving in with the children, ie no capital changes hands;
- contributing towards the purchase price of a larger house to accommodate the extended family;
- paying all or part of the cost of constructing a granny flat, annexe or extension; and
- making a promise along the lines that 'if you come and look after me, I'll leave you the house when I die'.

Solicitors are rarely involved in the early stages of any of these transactions – except, perhaps, the second – but, when they do receive instructions to advise or act, they should try to establish the common intention of the parties concerned and draw up the appropriate documentation to record and give effect to that common intention.[3] In some cases, a declaration of trust will be necessary to establish the existence and extent of a beneficial interest. In other cases, a contractual licence or documentary evidence of a loan or gift may be required. In the context of declarations of trust, in particular, the courts have stated on several occasions that it is deplorable that solicitors and licensed conveyancers generally fail to find out and declare the beneficial interests when a property is being acquired.[4] Indeed, failure to do so can give rise to an action for professional negligence.[5]

The following notes briefly consider what might happen in each of these four situations in the absence of any proper documentation. The remedies may appear confusing and their application extremely inconsistent, but equity is currently in a state of flux.[6] Resulting trusts have been more or less completely subsumed by remedial constructive trusts, and the doctrines of proprietary estoppel and constructive trusts are now referred to interchangeably – at least by the judiciary,[7] if not by academic lawyers. It has been predicted that within the next decade both concepts will be reduced to a single principle of unconscionability.[8]

---

1 For a detailed examination of the legal implications of informal arrangements for the co-occupation of residential property, see Jean Warburton, *Sharing Residential Property* (Sweet & Maxwell, 1990).

2 The advantages and disadvantages of: (a) staying at home; (b) moving in with a son or daughter; and (c) moving into residential care, are neatly summarised in tabular form on p 142 of Alison Norman's chapter, 'Assessing Risk', in Julia Johnson and Robert Slater (eds), *Ageing and Later Life* (Sage Publications, 1993).

3 See, generally, Godfrey Gypps, 'Living-in Relatives: Some Legal Consequences', *The Law Society's Gazette*, 14 September 1983, pp 2198–2204.

4 For example, *Cowcher v Cowcher* [1972] 1 All ER 943, at p 959, per Bagnall J; *Bernard v Josephs* (1983) FLR 178, at p 187F, per Griffiths LJ; *Walker v Hall* [1984] FLR 126, at p 129E, per Dillon LJ; and *Springette v Defoe* [1992] 2 FLR 388, per Dillon LJ.

5 *Taylor and Harman v Warners* (unreported) 21 July 1987. See the article on this case by Ross Crail in *The Law Society's Gazette*, 29 June 1988, at pp 26 and 27.

6 JD Davies, 'A State of Flux', in Peter Birks (ed), *The Frontiers of Liability, vol 2* (Oxford University Press, 1994), pp 224–226. Part IV of the volume contains five essays by distinguished academics on the subject of remedial constructive trusts. The Law Commission has just begun a research project to examine the property rights of people who live together in a shared household.

7 For example, 'Once a finding to this effect is made it will only be necessary for the partner asserting a claim to a beneficial interest against the partner entitled to the legal estate to show that he or she has acted to his or her detriment or significantly altered his or her position in reliance on the agreement in order to give rise to a constructive trust or proprietary estoppel': *Lloyds Bank plc v Rosset* [1990] 1 All ER 1111, HL, at p 1119a, per Lord Bridge.

8 DJ Hayton, 'Equitable Rights between Cohabitees' (1990) *Conveyancer and Property Lawyer* 370. But see Patricia Ferguson, 'Constructive Trusts: A Note of Caution' (1993) 109 *Law Quarterly Review* 114.

Where no capital is contributed

What happens when an elderly person simply moves in with a younger couple and makes no capital contribution towards the purchase of a new home or the extension of their existing home? The main legal issue is the nature and extent of their occupation rights. Someone who shares residential accommodation with the owner's consent is a licensee. A licence is a personal right to occupy. There are three types of licences: bare licences, contractual licences, and equitable licences.[1]

(1)   Bare licences

In the vast majority of cases where the people sharing residential accommodation are related, nothing will have been said about the terms and conditions of occupation, and they will be sharing informally. In the absence of any formal legal basis for his or her occupation, the non–owner will be merely a bare licensee.

A bare licence confers the minimum protection on the licensee. It confers no interest in the property, but it does provide a defence to any action for trespass. It arises, usually orally, where the owner gives the licensee permission to occupy the property or part of it without payment and on an informal basis.

A bare licence is automatically terminated on the death of the licensor or on the sale of the property.[2] The licensor can revoke a bare licence at any time without the need for a notice to quit[3] and, if the property is jointly owned, one joint owner can revoke a bare licence without reference to the other.[4] A bare licence can be terminated by the licensee without notice.

If a bare licence is revoked by the licensor, the licensee must be given a *reasonable time to leave*.[5] What is reasonable will depend on the facts of each case. The court will take into account the time required by the licensee to find alternative accommodation, given his or her particular circumstances and the housing conditions in the area.[6] Where the accommodation was originally intended to be long term, six months may be considered a reasonable time for an older married couple to make alternative arrangements. Where the accommodation was intended to be short term, three weeks' packing-up time may be reasonable. If the parties have argued to such an extent that their continued joint occupation is likely to be injurious to the health of either of them, an even shorter period for vacating the property may be considered reasonable.[7]

(2)   Contractual licences[8]

A contractual licence is a personal right to occupy based on an express or implied contractual agreement.[9] Such licences are fairly unusual where relatives share residential accommodation, because of the need to show an intention to create legal relations, but they may occur in cases where the parties, although intending to enter into a formal agreement, fail to establish a lease because, for example, exclusive possession cannot be given.

In order to establish the existence of a contract, whether it be express or implied by law, it has to be shown that there was:

- an intention to create legal relations;
- consideration;[10] and
- a reasonably clear definition of the contractual terms and conditions.[11]

As long as these criteria are satisfied, the licence does not have to be in any particular form, and may be written or oral.[12]

The licensor cannot revoke the licence in breach of the contract. If the licensor does not reside in the property, four weeks' written notice to quit must be given under the Protection from Eviction Act 1977, s 5(1A). If no contractual notice period is specified in the licence, the court will usually infer that reasonable notice must be given and, as with bare licences, what is reasonable will depend on the facts of each case.

(3)   Equitable licences

An equitable licence is a licence awarded by the court in order to satisfy the equity raised by proprietary estoppel,[13] and can vary from a right to remain in the property until money previously paid to the licensor is repaid to a right for the licensee to occupy the premises rent-free for the rest of his or her life. The following cases provide examples.

Greasley v Cooke (1980)[14]
In 1938, when she was 16, Doris Cooke went to work as a maidservant for the Greasley family in their home at Riddings, Derbyshire. She was not paid any wages, and was treated as a member of the family. She was assured that she could live in the family home for the whole of her life. In 1975, the family asked her to leave.

HELD – the family would be estopped from denying her occupation, and she would be granted an equitable licence to remain in the house until she died.

Matharu v Matharu (1994)[15]

Mr Matharu bought a house in Ilford in 1968. It was subsequently occupied by his son, Raghbir, daughter-in-law, Kamaljit, and their children. In 1983, Raghbir carried out and paid for extensive improvements with his father's approval. Raghbir died in 1991. Kamaljit had a modern kitchen installed at her own expense, and a few months later Mr Matharu demanded possession.

HELD – the elements of proprietary estoppel had been established, and Kamaljit had an equitable licence to occupy the house for the rest of her life or such shorter period as she might decide, conditional on her paying the outgoings and keeping the property in good decorative repair.

In order to prevent an irrevocable licence for life amounting to a tenancy for life under the Settled Land Act 1925,[16] the court may require the landowner to grant the claimant a long lease, determinable on his or her death, at a nominal rent, and with an absolute covenant against assignment.[17]

---

1 See, generally, Jean Warburton, *Sharing Residential Property* (Sweet & Maxwell, 1990), chapter 2, and Godfrey Gypps, 'Living-in Relatives: Some Legal Consequences', *The Law Society's Gazette*, 14 September 1983, pp 2198–2204.

2 *Terunnanse v Terunnanse* [1968] AC 1086, at pp 1095–1096, per Lord Devlin.

3 *Crane v Morris* [1965] 1 WLR 1104, at p 1108, per Lord Denning MR.

4 *Annen v Rattee* (1984) 273 EG 503, CA.

5 *Minister of Health v Bellotti* [1944] 1 KB 298, at p 309, per Goddard LJ.

6 *Hannaford v Selby* (1976) 239 EG 811.

7 *Ibid.*

8 For a precedent of a contractual licence, see Precedent 1 at p 89 below. Gypps, *op cit*, at p 2200, suggests that if no capital is changing hands between an elderly person and the relatives with whom he or she is living, 'a fairly straightforward licence agreement is all that is required, the main essentials being to record the limited nature of the transaction and the period of notice which is required to end the licence'.

9 See, generally, *Street v Mountford* [1985] AC 809.

10 Even where no payment is made, a contractual licence may exist because some other form of consideration has been given. For example, in *Tanner v Tanner* [1975] 3 All ER 776, giving up a secure tenancy to move into another property was held to be sufficient consideration for the purposes of a contractual licence.

11 *Horrocks v Forray* [1976] 1 WLR 230, at p 236, per Megaw LJ.

12 Law of Property (Miscellaneous Provisions) Act 1989, s 2 does not apply because a contractual licence is not an 'interest in land'.

13 See p 87 below.

14 [1980] 3 All ER 710, CA.

15 [1994] 2 FLR 597, CA.

16 See Martin, *Contractual Licensee or Tenant for Life* [1972] Conv 266.

17 *Griffiths v Williams* (1977) 248 EG 947.

Where capital is contributed

The situation envisaged here is where, say, an elderly widow contributes towards the purchase of a new, larger home by her son and daughter-in-law, in whose names the legal title is to be vested, or where she pays towards the cost of building an extension to their existing home. She moves in and, after a while, they fall out.

The first issue is to identify the common understanding of the nature of the contribution.

- Was it a gift?
- Was it a loan?
- Was it intended that she would acquire a beneficial interest? or
- Was it intended that she would have the right to reside in the property (perhaps rent-free) for the rest of her life?

The second issue is to identify the extent of her occupation rights.

Documentary evidence

The precedents that appear at the end of this chapter consider various circumstances in which capital changes hands between an elderly person and his or her relatives. They include:

- a declaration of trust where an elderly person and a younger couple buy a property jointly (Precedent 2, p 91);
- a declaration of trust where an elderly person pays for the construction of a granny annexe and acquires a beneficial interest in the property (Precedent 3, p 94);
- an agreement recording the terms of a loan made by an elderly person towards the cost of constructing a granny annexe (Precedent 4, p 97);
- a declaration of trust of 'right to buy' property (Precedent 6, p 102).

In the absence of any documentary evidence of this kind, the court will seek to establish the common understanding about the nature of the parent's contribution by reference first to any express discussions between the parties, and secondly (in default of any express discussions) by examining their conduct.

Express discussions

In *Lloyds Bank plc v Rosset* [1990] 1 All ER 1111, at p 1118, Lord Bridge said:

'The first and fundamental question which must always be resolved is whether, independently of any inference to be drawn from the conduct of the parties in the course of sharing the house as their home and managing their joint affairs, there has at any time prior to acquisition, or exceptionally at some later date, been any agreement, arrangement or understanding between them that the property is to be shared beneficially. The finding of an agreement to share in this sense can only, I think, be based on evidence of express discussions between the parties, however imperfectly remembered and however imprecise their terms may have been.

Once a finding to this effect is made it will only be necessary for the party asserting a claim to a beneficial interest against the party entitled to the legal estate to show that he or she has acted to his or her detriment or significantly altered his or her position in reliance on the agreement in order to give rise to a constructive trust or proprietary estoppel.'

Conduct

Lord Bridge continued:

> 'In sharp contrast with this situation is the very different one where there is no evidence to support a finding of an agreement or arrangement to share, however reasonable it might have been for the parties to reach such an agreement if they had applied their minds to the question, and where the court must rely entirely on the conduct of the parties, both as the basis from which to infer a common intention to share the property beneficially and as the conduct relied on to give rise to a constructive trust. In this situation direct contributions to the purchase price by the party who is not the legal owner, whether initially or by payment of mortgage instalments, will readily justify the inference necessary to the creation of a constructive trust. But, as I read the authorities, it is at least extremely doubtful whether anything less will do.'

Although Lord Bridge was referring specifically to the acquisition of a beneficial interest (which is more likely to be claimed when property values have risen substantially), this threefold test – namely, looking at (1) the documentary evidence, failing which (2) any express discussions between the parties, failing which (3) their conduct – would probably also apply where it was claimed that the contribution was a loan or a gift or that it was intended to acquire a right to occupy the property for life.

Occupation rights

Apart from the tensions of living within an extended family, inter-generational sharing arrangements usually present few problems until a third party, such as a mortgagee of a trustee in bankruptcy, becomes involved. The non-owner's legal rights against the third party will depend on (a) the legal relationship between the owner and non-owner, and (b) the general law in relation to third party rights in respect of registered or unregistered land. Readers are recommended to refer to the standard textbooks on conveyancing and property law, or the useful chapter on the enforcement of property rights against third parties in Jean Warburton's book, *Sharing Residential Property*.[1]

Capital contribution cases

It is impossible to extract any universal principles – other than maybe the desire to achieve some sort of restitution or a return to the status quo ante – from the variety of ways in which the courts have disposed of capital contribution cases in recent years. In some cases, they have awarded the elderly person a beneficial interest; in others, they have ordered the repayment of his or her contribution; in some, they have awarded damages; and, in a few, they have created an equitable licence conferring occupation rights for life. The right to remain in shared accommodation where the relationship has broken down irretrievably is almost certainly unworkable. The courts acknowledge this and have imported the 'clean break' doctrine from mainstream family law.

Hussey v Palmer (1972)[2]

Emily Hussey, a widow in her 70s, was invited to live with her daughter and son-in-law, the Palmers, in Wokingham. A bedroom extension was built, and Mrs Hussey contributed £607 towards the cost. After 15 months, differences arose and she left. She sued for recovery of her money. The judge held that there was no resulting trust.

HELD, by the Court of Appeal (Cairns LJ dissenting) – the money paid by Mrs Hussey was not intended as a gift and, although there were no arrangements for its repayment, it would be unconscionable for the Palmers to retain the benefit without repayment. Accordingly, the Palmers held the property on a resulting trust (or, per Lord Denning, a constructive trust) for Mrs Hussey in proportion to her payment. Cairns LJ, incidentally, was of the opinion that Mrs Hussey's contribution was a loan and that this was quite inconsistent with a resulting trust.

Broughall v Hunt (1983)[3]

After her husband died in 1969, it was suggested that Mrs Broughall should go and live with her daughter and son-in-law, Mr and Mrs Hunt. She did, and in 1972 paid £1000 towards the cost of constructing a granny annexe. The Hunts paid the rest. Nothing was said about the legal nature of her contribution. In 1981, after increasing friction, the Hunts' solicitor wrote to Mrs Broughall purporting to terminate her licence to occupy and requiring her to remove her goods from the house.

HELD, by Michael Wheeler QC, sitting as a deputy judge of the Chancery Division:

(1) the cash contribution was neither a gift, nor a loan (as had been argued);
(2) the intention had been that she should live at the property for as long as she wished, and that on her death or when she decided to leave, the extension would belong to the Hunts unencumbered;
(3) the purported termination of her licence to occupy had been wrongful;
(4) she had no beneficial interest in the property, there being no grounds for imputing to the parties a common intention that she should have one.

Mrs Broughall was awarded £1500 damages. The Hunts had to sell the house in order to pay the award and the costs which were estimated at £10,000. Mr Hunt was quoted in the *Daily Express* as saying, 'our only crime was giving the mother-in-law a home'.

Burrows v Sharp (1989)[4]

Mrs Sharp bought her council house in 1986 with a mortgage funded by her granddaughter, Mrs Burrows. The idea was that Mrs Burrows and her husband would eventually inherit the property. In 1987, the Burrows realised that they couldn't afford to pay the mortgage as well as the rent on their own flat, so they moved in with Mrs Sharp. The relationship broke down. The judge held that Mrs Sharp held the house on trust for sale so long as the Burrows continued to pay the mortgage instalments, and that all of them had the right to reside there.

HELD, by the Court of Appeal – the judge's order was unworkable, and, in the circumstances, a 'clean break' was more appropriate even though it meant that the Burrows would lose their expectation. Mr and Mrs Burrows were to give up possession within 42 days; the endowment policy would be released to them; and Mrs Sharp would reimburse them to the extent that the mortgage instalments they had paid exceeded the rent of their old flat.

Bonner v King (1991)[5]

In 1965, Mrs Bonner contributed £650 towards the purchase of a house for £4500 by her sister and brother-in-law, Mr and Mrs King. She lived with them and paid a weekly sum towards their common living expenses. The Kings moved out in 1970 and made no further payments towards the mortgage. In 1972, Mrs Bonner paid off the mortgage arrears and remained in occupation. She claimed to be a beneficial owner of the house or, alternatively, that the Kings held the property in trust for themselves and her in such shares as the court should determine.

HELD – Mrs Bonner did not have a beneficial interest for three reasons:

(1) The mere fact that she had paid part of the purchase price did not automatically give her a beneficial interest. At the time when she made the contribution there had to be some form of agreement, arrangement, understanding or common intention, however informal and however imperfectly thought through, that she should share in the beneficial ownership: *Lloyds Bank v Rosset* [1991] AC 107 applied.

(2) Except in very rare cases, beneficial interests crystallise at the time of acquisition and do not depend on subsequent events. Exceptions could be: (a) a subsequent contract; or (b) a common intention at the time of acquisition that the shares should be quantified at some future date: *Gissing v Gissing* [1971] AC 886 applied. The court will, however, look at the conduct after an acquisition to draw inferences as to the common intention at the time of purchase.

(3) It is not the law that, in a case of this kind, the court can decide by looking backwards and deciding what it now thinks would be fair in all the circumstances. The evidence was that Mrs Bonner's £650 was a loan. Money provided by way of loan, and not as part of the purchase price, is outside the resulting trust doctrines. Possession would not be ordered while the £650 loan was still outstanding. The Kings could not turn her out and keep the money: *Re Sharpe* [1980] 1 WLR 219 applied.

Baker v Baker (1993)[6]

In 1987, Edward Baker went to live with his son and daughter-in-law, Peter and Julie. He contributed £33,950 towards the purchase of a house in Torquay. The intention was that he would live with them for the rest of his life. They fell out and, in June 1988, he left. He claimed a beneficial interest in the property on alternative grounds: resulting trust, in which he was unsuccessful; and equitable estoppel, in which he succeeded. The judge ordered that Edward's contribution plus interest should be repaid and that, until it was repaid, the sum should be charged on the house. Peter and Julie appealed.

HELD, by the Court of Appeal – Edward's contribution was designed to achieve two objectives: (1) the provision of a family home; and (2) to provide him with rent-free accommodation for the rest of his life. What he had lost was not his £33,950 but merely the right to rent-free accommodation for life. The appeal was allowed and remitted to the lower court for assessing the compensation payable on the loss of his rent-free accommodation for life.

Cheese v Thomas (1994)[7]

In 1990, Charlie Cheese, 86, sold his flat in Peacehaven and moved back to Hayes, Middlesex. He paid £43,000 to his great nephew, Aubrey Thomas, 36, towards the purchase of a house costing £83,000. The house was acquired in Mr Thomas's sole name and it was agreed that Mr Cheese could live there for the rest of his life. Thereafter it would belong to Mr Thomas, who had raised the balance of £40,000 by means of a mortgage. He failed to keep up the mortgage payments, and Mr Cheese, fearing that his security was jeopardised, sought repayment of the £43,000. The judge ordered that the house be sold and that the proceeds be divided 43:40. It was sold for £55,000 and Mr Cheese appealed against the judge's order.

HELD, by the Court of Appeal – the judge had correctly decided on the division of the net proceeds of sale. Although the transaction was clearly disadvantageous to Mr Cheese as he had used all his money to buy the right to live in a house for the rest of his life, and that right was insecure and tied him to a particular house, the basic objective of the court is to restore the parties to their original positions as nearly as may be.

---

1 (Sweet & Maxwell, 1990), Chapter 8, p 129 ff.
2 [1972] 1 WLR 1286, CA.
3 (1983) *The Law Society's Gazette*, 14 September.
4 [1989] EGCS 51, CA.
5 [1991] NPC 131.
6 [1993] 2 FLR 247, CA.
7 [1994] 1 All ER 35, CA.

'If you come and look after me, I'll leave you the house when I die'

The law reports contain a number of cases which have involved a promise of this kind. However, it is impossible to say whether such an arrangement occurs fairly often and is generally successful, or whether it is comparatively rare and, when it does occur, is an unmitigated disaster.

(1)　Contracts relating to wills

An agreement that 'if you come and look after me, I'll leave you the house when I die' is both (a) a contract relating to a will, and (b) a contract relating to land. As far as contracts relating to wills are concerned, individuals can contractually bind themselves as to the contents of their will in such a way that, whether they die testate or intestate, their personal representatives must give effect to the terms of the contract.

Schaefer v Schuhmann (1972)[1]

Edward Seery was a retired market gardener. His wife died in 1962. Shortly after her death, he made a new will leaving $2000 to each of his four daughters and the residue of his estate to his three sons. In May 1966, he took on a housekeeper, Mrs Schaefer, at a weekly wage of $12. In June 1966, he instructed his solicitor to draw up a codicil. The solicitor prepared the codicil and sent it to him for approval. It said: 'If my housekeeper Elizabeth Schaefer is still my housekeeper at the time of my death, then I give her my house at 124 Nuwarra Road, Chipping Norton, New South Wales and all my furniture and household effects therein free of tax'. Mr Seery showed the codicil to Mrs Schaefer, and then went off to his bank to execute it. On the following day, he told her that he would no longer pay her wages because he had left the house to her when he died, but that if she was short of cash she was to let him know. She was still his housekeeper when he died on 16 November 1966, aged 76. His net estate came to $68,700. The house and contents were worth $14,500. His four daughters applied to the court for an order under the Testator's Family Maintenance Act 1916 (the precursor of our Inheritance (Provision for Family and Dependants) Act 1975). The

Supreme Court of New South Wales imposed a charge on the house for the whole of its value except for $2300, the rationale being to compensate Mrs Schaefer for her unpaid wages from June to November 1966, which came to roughly $300, and to make her a gift of $2000. Mrs Schaefer appealed.

HELD, by the Privy Council, allowing the appeal – at the end of June 1966 there had been a change in the contractual relationship between Mr Seery and his housekeeper whereby her contract of employment at a weekly wage was changed to a contract to serve him for no wages on the understanding that she would inherit the house and its contents when he died. Her rights arose independently from the will or codicil. The result in law would have been exactly the same if she had subsequently worked for him without wages for five years (instead of five months); if he had no family to provide for; and if he had revoked the codicil before his death and left the house to some new friend: per Lord Cross at p 626j.

---

1 [1972] 1 All ER 621.

---

(2)   Contracts relating to land

Contracts relating to land must now comply with the provisions of s 2 of the Law of Property (Miscellaneous Provisions) Act 1989, which came into force on 27 September 1989. This section states, inter alia, that:

- a contract for the sale or other disposition of an interest in land can only be in writing;
- the document incorporating the terms of the agreement must be signed by or on behalf of each party;
- it does not apply to contracts made before 27 September 1989;
- it supersedes s 40 of the Law of Property Act 1925, which then ceased to have effect.

In practice, a contract of this kind is rarely committed to writing. The well-known case of *Parker v Clark* was an exception.

Parker v Clark (1960)[1]

Bert Clark, 77, and his wife Connie, 78, lived in a large house in Torquay. In September 1955, Connie's niece Madeline Parker and her husband Dudley spent a few days with them. Just as they were leaving, Bert said to Dudley, 'Why don't you come and live with us?', and on 25 September 1955, he followed up this suggestion in a letter which in broad terms said that 'if you come and look after us, we'll leave you the house when we die'. The Parkers accepted the offer, sold their cottage in Sussex, and moved in with the Clarks in March 1956. It was a disaster. Both couples got on each other's nerves and after 18 months the Parkers, who had been threatened with eviction anyway, found the atmosphere so unbearable that they decided to leave. They then sued the Clarks for damages. The Clarks argued – unsuccessfully – that this had been a purely social or domestic arrangement, and that there had not been any intention to create a legal relationship.

HELD – Bert's letter of 25 September 1955 was a sufficient 'memorandum or note' of a contract relating to land to satisfy the requirements of s 40 of the Law of Property Act 1925, and that the Parkers had accepted the offer by selling up and moving in. The judge awarded £1300 damages to the Parkers jointly, and £3400 to Madeline to compensate for the loss of her potential inheritance.

Parker v Clark would be decided differently today. Under s 40 of the Law of Property Act 1925 – which was superseded in 1989 – the signature of Bert Clark, as 'the party to be charged', was sufficient. The signatures of all parties to the agreement would be required now.

---

1 [1960] 1 All ER 93.

---

(3)   The effects of a written contract

The effects of a written contract that 'if you come and look after me, I'll leave you the house when I die' are as follows.

- The carer's rights exist under the contract – independently of the elderly person's will or the distribution of his or her estate on intestacy.
- The carer has the usual remedies for breach of contract: damages; specific performance; and injunction.
- The carer could obtain an injunction to stop the elderly person selling, giving away, or otherwise disposing of the property in breach of the agreement.
- If the elderly person sells the property during his or her lifetime, the carer can recover damages. These will be assessed subject to a reduction for (a) accelerated benefit, and (b) the contingency that the carer might fail to survive the elderly person.
- If the elderly person becomes insolvent, the carer can claim as a creditor in the insolvency, although the trustee in bankruptcy might seek to disclaim the contract.
- If the elderly person dies, having failed to leave the property to the carer, the carer can apply to the court for specific performance of the contract.

(4)   Part performance

Most arrangements along the lines of 'if you come and look after me, I'll leave you the house when I die' are unwritten, and there are usually evidentiary difficulties in establishing the existence of an oral agreement, especially after the death of the alleged promisor.

If an unwritten agreement of this kind was entered into before 27 September 1989, the carer has two choices of remedy – *part performance* or *proprietary estoppel*. Part performance was, in effect, abolished when s 2 of the Law of Property (Miscellaneous Provisions) Act 1989 came into force.

To succeed in a claim of part performance, the applicant has to prove that:

- there was an oral agreement whereby the owner of the property had promised that 'if you come and look after me, I'll leave you the house when I die';
- the agreement was made before 27 September 1989;

- the applicant has done things which could only be explained on the basis that the alleged oral agreement must have existed, and the applicant's actions are entirely consistent with the terms of the alleged agreement;
- it would be unconscionable to allow the owner of the property, or his or her estate, to take advantage of the fact that the agreement was not in writing;
- the agreement is one that the court could enforce anyway;
- there is no bar on the equity. He or she who comes to equity must come with clean hands.

The evidentiary problems presented by the doctrine of part performance accounted for a low success rate in applications for this remedy, as the following examples reveal. In only one of these cases, *Wakeham v Mackenzie*, was the applicant able to establish the existence of an oral contract.

Maddison v Alderson (1883)[1]

Thomas Alderson owned a 92-acre farm at Moulton, North Yorkshire. Mrs Elizabeth Maddison was his housekeeper. In 1860, she told him that she was thinking about getting a job elsewhere, and he induced her to remain with him by saying words to the effect that 'if you stay and look after me for the rest of my life, I'll see to it that you can remain at the farm for the rest of your life'. In April 1874, he signed a will which would have left her a life interest in the farm, but it was not properly witnessed. Alderson died in 1877, and his nephew inherited the farm. He brought possession proceedings, and Mrs Maddison counterclaimed by applying to the court for a declaration that she was entitled to a life interest in the farm.

   HELD, by the House of Lords – there was no contract between Mr Alderson and Mrs Maddison. Although he may have made representations to her of the benefits she might expect to receive if she remained in his service, there was never any binding agreement to confer those benefits on her and, even if there had been, her service was not unequivocal and referable to any contract.

Wakeham v Mackenzie (1968)[2]

Margaret Wakeham was a widow aged 67. George Ball was a widower aged 72. They lived in Southampton within half a mile of each other. She used to visit him practically every day. In October 1964, he suggested to her she should give up her council flat and move in with him. He told her that she could have her own room, and that he would leave her the house and its contents when he died. In December 1964, she gave up her flat and moved in with him. She looked after him, and shared their communal food and fuel bills. He died on 12 February 1966 having made no provision for her in his will. His executor, Mr Mackenzie, sought possession of the house. Mrs Wakeham pleaded part performance.

   HELD, by Stamp J – there clearly were acts of part performance. Mrs Wakeham had given up her flat. She had moved into the house. She had looked after Mr Ball, and had paid into the common kitty. The performance of these acts referred to the alleged oral contract, and raised an equity in her favour.

Re Gonin (Deceased) (1979)[3]

Dr Bertram Gonin was a Harley Street consultant. He and his wife Ellen lived in a large house in Bromley. In 1944, they asked their daughter Lucy to return home to look after them. According to Lucy, they promised that if she came and looked after them, they would leave her the house and its contents when they died. Dr Gonin died in 1957, and his wife died intestate in 1968. Her estate fell to be distributed equally amongst her three daughters.

HELD, by Walton J – Lucy's acts were not necessarily referable to any alleged contract relating to her parents' house, and could not constitute part performance. Indeed, she had failed to establish the existence of any such contract.

---

1 (1883) 8 App Cas 467, HL.
2 [1968] 1 WLR 1175.
3 [1979] 1 Ch 16.

---

(5) Proprietary estoppel

Proprietary estoppel is the only remedy available to the carer where there is an oral agreement made after 27 September 1989 to the effect that 'if you come and look after me, I'll leave you the house when I die'. It is an alternative remedy to part performance for an agreement made before that date.

To succeed in a defence of proprietary estoppel, carers must prove that:

- they have acted to their *detriment*, for example by:
  - incurring expenditure; or
  - altering their position; or
  - prejudicing themselves in some other way;
- they acted to their detriment *in reliance on a belief* that:
  - they had already acquired an interest in the property; or
    they would acquire an interest in the property at some future date – usually on the death of the owner;
- they acted to their detriment in reliance on a belief *induced or encouraged by the owner* or by someone acting on his or her behalf:
  - orally; or
  - in writing; or
  - by conduct; or
  - by acquiescence;
- there is no bar on the equity.

The following cases illustrate how these principles have been applied in practice. See also the discussion on equitable licences at pp 77–78 above.

Jones v Jones (1977)[1]

In 1967, old Mr Jones retired from his business in Kingston upon Thames and went to live in the Suffolk village of Blundeston. A year later, he bought a house in the same village for his son Fred. Fred liked the house and believed that his father had given it to him, so he gave up his job in Kingston and moved to Blundeston. Old Mr Jones died in 1972. The house was still in his name and it was inherited by his widow (Fred's stepmother). The stepmother brought possession proceedings.

HELD, by the Court of Appeal – she was estopped from turning Fred out of the house because of his father's conduct. Fred had acted to his detriment by giving up his job in Kingston and by paying money to his father in reliance on a belief that the house was his, and this belief had been induced or encouraged by his father.

Watts and Ready v Storey (1984)[2]

Storey was persuaded by his grandmother to give up the tenancy of his house in Leeds, and the prospects of finding employment there, in order to live in her house in Woodborough, Nottinghamshire. She promised that she would leave him the house in her will. Storey moved in, and a few weeks later his grandmother died. It transpired that she had not left him the house in her will after all, and her executors brought possession proceedings. Storey raised the defence of proprietary estoppel.

HELD, by the Court of Appeal – as far as any detriment was concerned, it had to be balanced by the countervailing benefits received. Storey had been entitled to rent-free accommodation in a house that he liked, and had received various other benefits under his late grandmother's will. In the circumstances, proprietary estoppel was inappropriate.

Re Basham (Deceased) (1987)[3]

Henry Basham married Joan Bird's mother in 1936, when Joan was 15. From then until his retirement, she worked for him without payment, first in his pub and later in his service station. They were a very close-knit family. After her mother's death in 1976, Joan looked after her stepfather. He assured her that she would inherit his estate when he died, and was still making such assurances on his deathbed. He died intestate on 13 April 1982, and his estate (worth just over £40,000) was inherited by his two nieces. Joan applied to the court for a declaration that she was entitled to the estate because Mr Basham had induced and encouraged her to believe that she would inherit his estate, and she had acted to her detriment in reliance upon that belief.

HELD – Joan had established a proprietary estoppel and was therefore entitled to her stepfather's estate.

---

1 [1977] 1 WLR 438, CA.
2 (1984) 134 NLJ 631, CA.
3 [1987] 1 All ER 405.

PRECEDENTS

1 CONTRACTUAL LICENCE[1]

THIS CONTRACTUAL LICENCE is made on..(*date*)
BETWEEN 'the parties' (1)..
of.. ('*couple*')
and (2) ....
of.. ('*parent*')

IT IS AGREED that:

1.   Recitals

1.1   (*Parent*) is (*one of the couple's*) (mother)/(father).
1.2   (*Couple*) own (*address*) ('the property') and have invited (*parent*) to live
        with them.
1.3   The parties wish to define the terms and conditions on which (*parent*)
        resides in the property and they intend that this agreement shall be legally
        binding on them.

2.   Licence

Subject to the terms and conditions of this agreement, (*couple*) permit
(*parent*) to:

2.1   live with them in the property; and
2.2   occupy (his)/(her) own bedroom; and
2.3   have unrestricted use of the lounge, kitchen, dining room, bathroom, toilets,
        hall, and garden(s) in common with the rest of the family.

3.   Payment

3.1   On (*day*) each week (*parent*) will pay to (*couple*) the sum of £ . . . as a
        contribution towards (his)/(her) accommodation and living expenses.
3.2   The sum payable by (*parent*) will be reviewed annually by the parties in
        (*month*) and any increase will not normally exceed the prevailing rate of
        inflation.

4.   (*Parent's*) obligations

(*Parent*) covenants with (*couple*) that (he)/(she) will:

4.1   contribute towards (his)/(her) accommodation and living expenses;
4.2   keep (his)/(her) bedroom clean and in good condition and keep the other
        parts of the property which (he)/(she) shares with the rest of the family
        reasonably clean and tidy;
4.3   not intentionally damage the property or any of the furniture and fittings;

4.4   not invite anyone else to stay overnight without first obtaining the consent of (*couple*);

4.5   not do anything that may annoy or cause a nuisance to (*couple*) or the owners or occupiers of the neighbouring premises;

4.6   consent to the sale of the property by (*couple*) or either of them, or the survivor of them, or their personal representatives, trustee in bankruptcy or mortgagee, and vacate the property before completion of the sale.

5.   (*Couple's*) obligations

So far as the circumstances of living in shared accommodation permit (*couple*) will use their best endeavours to ensure that (*parent*):

5.1   has as much privacy as possible, including the right to meet people, have conversations, make or receive telephone calls, engage in correspondence or receive visitors without being overlooked or overheard and without having to account for (his)/(her) actions;

5.2   is able to retain as much independence as possible, including the right to take personal risks provided that this does not endanger others or other people's property;

5.3   is not required to undertake any domestic or other tasks against (his)/(her) will.

6.   Notice

6.1   (*Parent*) can terminate this licence at any time without giving notice to (*couple*).

6.2   (*Couple*) or either of them can terminate this licence at any time by giving (*parent*) (four weeks') notice.

7.   Termination by couple

(*Couple*) are only likely to ask (*parent*) to leave the property if:

7.1   (his)/(her) health deteriorates to such an extent that they are no longer able to provide or arrange the level of care (he)/(she) needs; or

7.2   (he)/(she) persistently breaches or fails to perform (his)/(her) obligations under this agreement; or

7.3   the property is being sold; or

7.4   the relationship between the parties has broken down irretrievably.

8.   The nature of this licence

(*Parent*) acknowledges that:

8.1   this agreement is a licence which is personal to (him)/(her) and is not a lease or tenancy agreement;

8.2   this agreement does not automatically give (him)/(her) the right to live in the property or with (*couple*) in any other property for the rest of (his)/(her) life;

8.3   regardless of the contributions (he)/(she) makes towards the accommodation and living expenses, (he)/(she) will not acquire any legal estate or beneficial interest in the property.

SIGNED as a deed by (*couple*) and delivered in the presence of:

SIGNED as a deed by (*parent*) and delivered in the presence of:

---

1 Godfrey Gypps, 'Living-in Relatives: Some Legal Consequences', *The Law Society's Gazette*, 14 September 1983, pp 2198–2204, at p 2200, states that 'if no capital is changing hands a fairly straightforward licence agreement is all that is required, the main essentials being to record the limited nature of the transaction and the period of notice which is required to end the licence, this primarily to ensure the couple's ability to sell the house and move should they wish to do so. If the parent has exclusive occupation of a separate part of the premises (or effective possession of bedroom, kitchen and bathroom) this would be a particularly sensible document where payment is made in respect of overheads, so as to negative any question of a tenancy arising. It could also contain provisions to deal with *Williams and Glyn's Bank v Boland* [1981] AC 487 – a declaration of the nature of the occupation, and covenants to enter into any sale contract as required and to vacate'. See, generally, Jean Warburton, *Sharing Residential Property* (Sweet & Maxwell, 1990), Chapter 2.

---

2 DECLARATION OF TRUST WHERE AN ELDERLY PERSON AND A YOUNGER COUPLE BUY A PROPERTY JOINTLY[1]

THIS DECLARATION OF TRUST is made on ....
BETWEEN 'the trustees' (1) ....
and .... ('*couple*')
and (2) .... ('*parent*')
all of .... ('the property')

IT IS AGREED AND DECLARED as follows:

1.   Recitals

(1)   The trustees are the joint proprietors of the property, title to which is registered at the Land Registry under title number (*title number*).
(2)   The trustees purchased the property on (*completion date*).
(3)   The purchase price was £ ......
(4)   The incidental costs of the purchase came to £ ......
(5)   (*Parent*) contributed £ ...... towards the purchase price and purchase costs.
(6)   (*Couple*) contributed £ ...... towards the purchase price and purchase costs.
(7)   The property is mortgaged to (*mortgagee*) to secure an advance of £ ...... ('the mortgage').
(8)   (*Couple*) will be responsible for paying the mortgage.
(9)   The trustees wish to record their respective beneficial interests in the property and to define their respective rights and obligations.

2.   Trusts

The trustees declare that they:

(1)   hold the property on trust for sale;
(2)   have powers to postpone the sale;
(3)   have powers to deal with the property which are equal to those of a sole beneficial owner;
(4)   hold the property and its net proceeds of sale and its net income until sale in trust for themselves as beneficial tenants in common in the following shares.

3.   Shares

When the property is sold:

(1)   (*couple*) will receive (*percentage*)%[2] of the sale price less the amount required to redeem the mortgage[3] less (*percentage*)% of the costs of selling the property;
(2)   (*parent*) will receive (*percentage*)% of the sale price less (*percentage*)% of the costs of selling the property.

4.   Contingencies[4]

(1)   If the relationship between (*couple*) and (*parent*) breaks down irretrievably, the needs of (*couple*) will have priority.[5]
(2)   If (*parent*) wishes to realise (his)/(her) share of the property, (he)/(she) will give notice in writing to (*couple*) requiring them to pay the current market value of (his)/(her) share (subject to such discount, if any, as (*parent*) may think fit to reflect the fact that the property is held under a beneficial tenancy in common),[6] and if (*couple*) have not completed the purchase of (*parent's*) share within (six) months from the date on which the notice was given, (*parent*) may apply to the court for an order that the property be sold.[7]
(3)   If (*couple*) or (*parent*) contribute in money or money's worth to the improvement of the property, the person making such contribution will, if it is of a substantial nature, be treated as having acquired by virtue of his, her or their contribution an enlarged share of the net proceeds of sale of such an extent as the trustees may agree or, in default of agreement, as may seem in all the circumstances just to any court before which the question arises.[8]

5.   Legal advice[9]

(1)   (*Couple*) have been advised on the nature, effect and implications of this deed by Messrs (*name and address of firm*) Solicitors.
(2)   (*Parent*) has been advised on the nature, effect and implications of this deed by Messrs (*name and address of firm*) Solicitors.

SIGNED as a deed by (*couple*) and delivered in the presence of:

SIGNED as a deed by (*parent*) and delivered in the presence of:

1 See, generally, Godfrey Gypps, 'Living-in Relatives: Some Legal Consequences', *The Law Society's Gazette,* 14 September 1983, pp 2198–2204.

2 Presumably the percentage will be the proportion of the purchase price and purchase costs represented by the couple's original capital contribution and the mortgage advance.

3 Gypps, *op cit*, at p 2203, states that 'if there is a building society mortgage which is being repaid by the couple it would not seem right for the parent to derive a benefit from the reduction in the capital outstanding on that loan and the consequent increase in the value of the "equity" in the property. The proportions should therefore be defined by reference to a net value of the property itself defined so as to give credit to the couple for capital repayments made by them, and even perhaps for part of the interest paid'.

4 If the contingencies are likely to be lengthy, it may be preferable to introduce them briefly in the main body of the deed, and set out the substantive provisions in separate schedules, as in Precedent 3 at p 94 below.

5 Gypps, *op cit*, at p 2203, says that 'if one is concerned with the freedom or otherwise of the couple to sell one can require them to obtain the consent of the parent to a sale if the parent is to be given priority (Law of Property Act 1925, s 28), but otherwise it would be sensible to declare in the trust instrument the purposes of the trust, making it clear that the needs of the couple are to be given priority'.

6 For capital taxes purposes, the customary deduction for the inconvenience of holding as beneficial tenant in common was 10%: *Cust v Commissioners of Inland Revenue* (1917) reported in the *Digest of Law and Arbitration Cases 1918*, p 1, and in *Estates Gazette* 18 December 1917, p 538; 22 December 1917, p 587; and 5 January 1918, p 11. This was later raised to 15% in respect of jointly owned residential accommodation: *Wight v Commissioners of Inland Revenue* (1982) 264 EG 935. But see *Chief Adjudication Officer and Another v Palfrey; Same v Dowell; Same v McDonnell; Same v Pelter; Same v McNamara,* 8 February 1995, CA, reported briefly in *The Law Society's Gazette,* 15 March 1995, p 39.

7 Gypps, *op cit*, at p 2203, says that 'one must make provision for the sensible protection of both sides. Since one has a trust for sale an application to the court can be made, if necessary, under s 30 [of the Law of Property Act 1925]. The parent is unlikely to be interested in forcing a sale as such, but rather in having access to capital should the need arise. A separate agreement might usefully provide for the parent to serve notice on the couple calling for payment of the cash value of his or her interest (with provisions for its ascertainment and for sale in default of payment) to be made within a set period of time, again balancing the needs of both parties'.

8 This sub-clause is based loosely on the wording of the Matrimonial Proceedings and Property Act 1970, s 37.

9 Gypps, *op cit*, at p 2200, says that 'if capital changes hands far more care and thought must be taken to protect the different interests of the two sides. Because of the importance of the transaction to the couple and the parent, one might think it wise to suggest separate representation and if not, certainly to give written advice'. See, generally, 'Conflict of interests' in Chapter 2, at p 27 above, and footnote 1 to Precedent 6 at p 102 below (Declaration of Trust of 'Right to Buy' Property).

3 DECLARATION OF TRUST WHERE AN ELDERLY PERSON PAYS FOR THE CONSTRUCTION OF A GRANNY ANNEXE AND ACQUIRES A BENEFICIAL INTEREST IN THE PROPERTY[1]

THIS DECLARATION OF TRUST is made on ....
BETWEEN 'the parties' (1) .... and
.... ('*couple*')
and (2) .... ('*parent*')
all of .... ('the property')

IT IS AGREED AND DECLARED as follows:

1.   Recitals

(1)   (*Couple*) are the proprietors of the property, title to which is registered at the Land Registry under title number (*title number*).

(2)   The property is mortgaged to (*name of mortgagee*) ('the mortgage').

(3)   (*Parent*) is (*one of the couple's*) (mother)/(father) and has lived with them in the property since (*date*).

(4)   (*Parent*) has paid (£40,000) for the construction of an extension to the property.

(5)   The parties agree that before the extension was built the market value of the property with vacant possession was (£150,000); that the current market value of the property with vacant possession is (£210,000); and that (90) per cent of the increase in the value of the property is attributable to the extension.

(6)   The parties wish to record their respective beneficial interests in the property.

(7)   (*Couple*) have been advised on the nature and effect of this deed by Messrs (*name and address of firm*) and (*parent*) has been separately advised by Messrs (*name and address of firm*).[2]

2.   Trusts[3]

(*Couple*) declare that they:

(1)   hold the property on trust for sale;

(2)   have powers to postpone the sale;

(3)   have powers to deal with the property which are equal to those of a sole beneficial owner; and

(4)   hold the property and its net proceeds of sale and its net income until sale in trust for themselves and (*parent*) as beneficial tenants in common in the following shares.

3.   Shares[4]

(1)   (*Couple*) are entitled to (75) per cent of the sale price, less the amount required to redeem the mortgage, less (two thirds) of the costs of selling the property.

(2)   (*Parent*) is entitled to (25) per cent of the sale price, less (one third) of the costs of selling the property.

4.   Further assurances

(1)   (*Couple*) consent to the entry of a restriction on the Proprietorship Register at the Land Registry to the effect that 'Except under an order of the registrar no disposition or dealing other than a transfer to (*parent*) is to be registered without (his)/(her) consent'.

(2)   If (*parent*) requires them to do so, (*couple*) will appoint (him)/(her) to be a new trustee of the property and will complete the documentation needed to register (him)/(her) as a joint proprietor of the property.[5] The costs of the appointment and registration will be paid by (*parent*).

5.   Contingencies

(1)   If (*parent*) dies and (*couple*) or either of them do not become beneficially entitled to (his)/(her) share of the property, the provisions of Schedule 1 will apply.[6]

(2)   If (*parent*) wishes to realise (his)/(her) share of the property, the provisions of Schedule 2 will apply.[7]

(3)   If (*couple*) wish to sell the property or are compelled to do so, the provisions of Schedule 3 will apply.[8]

(4)   If the parties contribute in money or money's worth to the improvement of the property, the provisions of Schedule 4 will apply.[9]

(5)   If the relationship between (*couple*) and (*parent*) breaks down irretrievably, the provisions of Schedule 5 will apply.[10]

6.   The nature of this Declaration

This Declaration of Trust:

(1)   may be varied by a subsequent Declaration of Trust executed by all the persons who are competent to vary it;[11]

(2)   will be binding on the parties unless and until it is set aside by an order of the court or varied by all the persons who are competent to vary it;

(3)   contains the whole agreement between the parties and supersedes any previous agreements, representations and promises made by them in respect of the property.

SCHEDULES

(Set out in schedular form the parties' common intentions as to what will happen in the event of any of the contingencies referred to in clause 5 above.)

SIGNED by (*couple*) as a deed and delivered in the presence of:

SIGNED by (*parent*) as a deed and delivered in the presence of:

1 Godfrey Gypps, in 'Living-in Relatives: Some Legal Consequences', *The Law Society's Gazette*, 14 September 1983, pp 2198–2204, states at p 2203 that when documenting inter-generational sharing arrangements in which capital changes hands 'for most purposes the most sensible device to adopt seems to be that of co-ownership behind a trust for sale . . . one would envisage a separate trust instrument off the title *inter alia* declaring the beneficial interests'.

2 Gypps, *op cit*, at p 2200, suggests that 'because of the importance of the transaction to the couple and the parent, one might think it wise to suggest separate representation and, if not, certainly to give written advice'.

3 For a detailed discussion of each of these sub-clauses, see Denzil Lush, *Cohabitation and Co-ownership Precedents* (Family Law, 1993), at pp 23, 24.

4 Gypps, *op cit*, at p 2203, states that 'in defining the sizes of the beneficial interests, and in particular that of the parent, one should have regard to the existence or otherwise of the mortgage on the property. If there is a building society mortgage which is being repaid by the couple it would not seem right for the parent to derive a benefit from the reduction in the capital outstanding on that loan and the consequent increase in the value of the "equity" in the property. The proportions should therefore be defined by reference to a net value of the property itself defined so as to give credit to the couple for capital repayments made by them, and even perhaps for part of the interest paid'.

5 Gypps, *op cit*, at p 2203, states that 'although the couple and the parent could all three hold the legal estate, one might consider it sensible to appoint only the couple, especially where the parent is elderly, lest he or she become incapable of signing documents, in which case a replacement would have to be appointed under s 36(1) [of the] Trustee Act 1925, or an application for removal made to the court'.

6 Gypps, *op cit*, at p 2203, states that 'careful thought should be given to the position on the parent's death. Unless a joint tenancy is created the parent's interest will pass into his or her estate whence, if there are other children, it may not pass solely to one of the couple unless the parent's will so provides. This has caused practical problems where a couple have found themselves obliged to sell the home at an inconvenient time in order to put money into the estate for the benefit of other beneficiaries. The parent should be advised accordingly, and such arrangements as are appropriate made in the will, or perhaps in the trust instrument, for the greater safety of the couple. It may be fair for the parent's share to pass to the couple and not to the other children, who will have been freed from anxiety over the parent by reason of the couple having had the inconvenience (as it would usually be) of having the parent living with them. The net effect should be that they take the parent's beneficial interest in the property as their share of the estate, or if not are given a sensible period of time to buy it out if they wish'.

7 Gypps, *op cit*, at p 2203, suggests 'one must make provision for the sensible protection of both sides. Since one has a trust for sale an application to the court can be made, if necessary, under s 30 of the Law of Property Act 1925. The parent is unlikely to be interested in forcing a sale as such, but rather in having access to capital should the need arise. [The agreement] might usefully provide for the parent to serve notice on the couple calling for payment of the cash value of his or her interest (with provisions for its ascertainment and for sale in default of payment) to be made within a set period of time, again balancing the needs of both parties'.

8 Gypps, *op cit*, at p 2203, suggests that 'the agreement should provide for the parent to vacate the property on sale and to join in any sale contract if still in occupation (for the purposes of *Williams & Glyn's Bank Ltd v Boland* [1981] AC 487)'.

9 Consider the inclusion of a schedule based loosely on the wording of the Matrimonial Proceedings and Property Act 1970, s 37, for example: 'If any of the parties subsequently contributes in money or money's worth to the improvement of the property, he, she or they will, if the contribution is of a substantial nature, be treated as having acquired by that contribution an enlarged share of the net proceeds of sale of the property of such an extent as may have been declared or agreed by the parties. In default of such a declaration or agreement, the party who has made such a contribution will be treated as having acquired an enlarged share of such an extent as may in all the circumstances seem just to any court before which the question of the extent of the parties' beneficial interests arises'. For a more complicated formula whereby the parties' existing 'fixed shares' are converted into 'floating shares', see Denzil Lush, *Cohabitation and Co-ownership Precedents* (Family Law, 1993), at pp 33 *et seq*.

10 Gypps, *op cit*, at p 2203, states that 'it would seem sensible to declare in the trust instrument the purposes of the trust, making it clear that the needs of the couple are to be given priority'.

11 'If all the beneficiaries are sui iuris they can join together with the trustees and declare different trusts which supersede those contained in the original declaration. These new trusts operate proprio vigore by virtue of a self-contained instrument, namely the deed of arrangement or variation. The original declaration will have lost any force or relevance': *Re Holmden's Settlement Trusts* [1968] AC 685, at p 713C.

4 AGREEMENT RECORDING THE TERMS OF A LOAN MADE BY AN ELDERLY PERSON TOWARDS THE COST OF CONSTRUCTING A GRANNY ANNEXE[1]

THIS AGREEMENT is made on ....

BETWEEN (1) .... ('*husband*')

(2) his wife .... ('*wife*')

and (3) (his)/(her) (mother)/(father) .... ('*parent*')

all of .... ('the property')

1. Recitals

(1) (*Husband and wife*) own the property and have invited (*parent*) to live with them.

(2) To accommodate everyone comfortably it is necessary to build an extension.

(3) (*Parent*) has agreed to pay (*amount*) towards the cost of the extension.

2. The loan

(1) The sum of £ ...... paid by (*parent*) towards the cost of the extension will be a loan from (him)/(her) to (*husband and wife*) ('the loan') [and the balance of £ ...... will be a gift from (him)/(her) to them].

(2) (*Husband and wife*) will charge the property to secure the repayment of the loan.[2]

(3) [Except to the extent that the proceeds of sale of the property are charged with the repayment of the loan] (*parent*) will not acquire a beneficial interest in the property but will be entitled to occupy it as a licensee.

(4) No waiver of the repayment of all or any part of the loan will be valid unless it is evidenced in writing signed by (*parent*).[3]

3. Interest

(1) The loan will be interest-free until it becomes repayable.

(2) When the loan becomes repayable interest will be charged at (The Law Society's Interest Rate) on the principal sum outstanding.

4.   Repayment of the loan

The loan will become repayable when the first of the following events occurs, although nothing in this agreement prevents (*husband and wife*) from repaying it earlier:[4]

(1)   (*parent's*) death;[5] or

(2)   completion of the sale of the property; or

(3)   the expiration of (three months')[6] notice in writing given by (*parent*) requesting repayment; or

(4)   the date on which (*parent*) permanently ceases to reside in the property.[7]

5.   Covenant to vacate the property on sale

(*Parent*) covenants with (*husband and wife*) to vacate the property on sale and, if required to do so, to enter into the contract with the purchaser.[8]

[Additional clauses, if required][9]

SIGNED as a deed by (*husband*) and delivered in the presence of:

SIGNED as a deed by (*wife*) and delivered in the presence of:

SIGNED as a deed by (*parent*) and delivered in the presence of:

---

1 Although this precedent relates to a loan for the purpose of constructing a granny annexe, it could easily be adapted to record the making of a loan in connection with the purchase of a property. Such a loan does not normally create a beneficial interest in the property under either a constructive trust or a resulting trust: *Re Sharpe* [1980] 1 WLR 219. The relationship between the elderly person who makes the loan and the couple to whose home the extension is built is the personal one of creditor and debtor respectively. However, by obtaining a charging order against the property, the elderly person as creditor can convert his or her personal contract into what amounts to a proprietary interest and thereby gain protection against third parties. The charging order can relate to any land held by the debtor including an interest under a trust for sale: Charging Orders Act 1979, s 1. So if, for example, a mother makes a loan to her son alone for the purpose of building a granny annexe on a house he owns jointly with his wife, the mother can secure the loan by a charging order on his beneficial interest if there is disharmony within the family and she is forced to leave. See, generally, Jean Warburton, *Sharing Residential Property* (Sweet & Maxwell, 1990), pp 142–146.

2 See, generally, Godfrey Gypps, 'Living-in Relatives: Some Legal Consequences', *The Law Society's Gazette*, 14 September 1983, pp 2198–2204. At p 2203, he states: 'if one were advising the parent alone one would doubtless say that [the loan] should be secured by a charge on the legal estate of the property so as to give the parent the rights and remedies of a legal mortgagee under the Law of Property Act 1925; if advising the couple one might be less happy about a secured loan in the case of an elderly person lest he or she should become incapable of managing his or her own affairs and thus unable to execute a vacating receipt quickly in the event of a sale, a Mental Health Act receiver being needed. A prior building society mortgage anyway might contain a covenant forbidding a further charge'.

3 If appropriate, part of the debt could be released year by year to take advantage of the annual inheritance tax exemption.

4 Gypps, *op cit*, at p 2203, suggests that 'a provision preventing the couple from repaying the loan earlier could be a "clog" if oppressive in the circumstances'.

5 Gypps, *op cit*, at p 2203 states: 'On the parent's death the balance outstanding of the loan will fall into his or her estate and pass to the beneficiaries thereunder. Consideration should be given to this when drafting the parent's will if there are other beneficiaries. A failure to do so might leave the couple in difficulties in raising money quickly to repay all or part of the loan. Depending on the circumstances, a sensible course might be for the will to "forgive" the loan or to direct the executors to accept repayment by affordable instalments over a period of time, or for the charge document to cater for the position to the same effect'.

6 In selecting the period of notice, it is necessary to balance the parent's need to have reasonably prompt recourse to capital and the couple's need for time to raise the money or find somewhere else to live.

7 For a discussion of the meaning of expressions such as 'permanently ceases to reside', see *Re Coxen* [1948] 2 All ER 492, at p 500.

8 Gypps, *op cit*, at p 2203, recommends that 'there should be a covenant by the parent to vacate the original home on sale and to enter into the contract with the purchaser if so required for the purposes of *Williams & Glyn's Bank v Boland*' ([1981] AC 487).

9 Gypps, *op cit*, at p 2203, suggests that this kind of loan agreement 'might well include covenants by [the couple] to provide accommodation for the parent in their new property, and one by the parent to re-advance capital on the same terms on that new property'. It would preferable for the parties to enter into a new agreement when a new property is acquired, rather than commit either party to transfer this agreement to any alternative accommodation.

---

5 DECLARATION OF TRUST WHERE A CARER MOVES INTO AN ELDERLY PERSON'S HOME AND ACQUIRES A BENEFICIAL INTEREST[1]

THIS DECLARATION OF TRUST is made on ....

BETWEEN (1) ....

of .... ('*elderly person*')

and (2) ....

of .... ('*carer*')

IT IS AGREED AND DECLARED as follows:

1.   (*Elderly person*)

(*Elderly person*):

(1)   is the owner of (*address*) ('the property');

(2)   lives alone in the property and wishes to carry on living there for as long as possible;

(3)   realises that by reason of old age and infirmity [and (his)/(her) financial circumstances] it is becoming increasingly difficult for (him)/(her) to look after (himself)/(herself);

(4)   has invited (his)/(her) (son)/(daughter)/(*other*) (*carer*) to come and live in the property and look after (him)/(her);

(5)   has agreed that, in consideration of (*carer*) coming to live with and look after (him)/(her), (he)/(she) will give (*carer*) a beneficial interest in the property;

(6)   estimates that the current market value of the property with vacant possession is £ ......;

(7)   warrants that the property is free of any mortgage or charge of a financial nature;

(8)   estimates that the rest of (his)/(her) estate, excluding the property, is worth approximately £ ......;

(9)   has (*number*) [other] child(ren), namely (*name(s)*) and understands the effect that this declaration of trust will have on (his)/(her)/(their) inheritance prospects;[2]

(10)   has received legal advice in this matter from Messrs (*name and address of firm*) Solicitors.

2.   **(*Carer*)**

(*Carer*):

(1)   was born on (*date*);

(2)   is (unmarried)/(divorced)/(separated)/(a widow)/(a widower);

(3)   is (unemployed)/(retired)/(a self-employed (*occupation*))/(a (*occupation*));

(4)   lives in (rented)/(owner-occupied) accommodation;

(5)   has agreed to give up (his)/(her) home [and employment] in order to live with and look after (*elderly person*) [without payment];

(6)   has received legal advice in this matter from Messrs (*name and address of firm*) Solicitors.

3.   **Declaration of trust**

(*Elderly person*) declares that (he)/(she) holds the property and its net proceeds of sale and its net income until sale on trust for (himself)/(herself) and (*carer*) as beneficial tenants in common in the following shares.

4.   **Shares**

When the property is sold:

(1)   (*Carer*) will receive (20) per cent of the sale price in respect of the detriment initially suffered by (him)/(her) in giving up (his)/(her) home [and employment] in order to live with and look after (*elderly person*) ('(*carer's*) share');

(2)   (*Elderly person*) will receive the remainder of the sale price ('(*elderly person's*) share').

5.   **Gradual diminution of (*elderly person's*) share**[3]

(1)   In consideration of the continuing care given to (him)/(her) by (*carer*), (*elderly person*) declares that (his)/(her) share of the net proceeds of sale of the property will gradually decrease and that (*carer's*) share will gradually increase in the following manner.

(2)   (*Elderly person*) is now (80) years old and has an actuarial life expectancy of (7.315) years;

(3)   (*Elderly person's*) share will diminish on a daily basis so that at the expiration of (7.315) years from the date of this declaration it will be zero.

(4)   The amount by which (*elderly person's*) share diminishes will be added to (*carer's*) share so that at the expiration of (7.315) years from the date of this declaration (*carer*) will be entitled to the entire net proceeds of sale of the property.

(5)   (*Elderly person's*) share will cease to diminish and (*carer's*) share will cease to be augmented when the first of the following events occurs:

(a)   the death of (*elderly person*);

(b)   the death of (*carer*);

(c)   the date on which (*carer*) ceases, whether voluntarily or involuntarily, to be primarily responsible for the care of (*elderly person*).

5.   Sale costs

When the property is sold, the incidental costs of selling it will be borne by (*elderly person*) and (*carer*) in the proportions that their respective shares bear to each other.

6.   Occupation rights

Regardless of the extent to which (he)/(she) is entitled to a share of the net proceeds of sale of the property, (*elderly person*) shall have the right to live in the property for as long as (he)/(she) wishes or is able to.

[Additional clauses, if any][4]

SIGNED as a deed by (*elderly person*) and delivered in the presence of:

SIGNED as a deed by (*carer*) and delivered in the presence of:

---

1   This precedent is designed to offer a solution to some of the difficulties that can arise when an elderly person makes a promise along the lines of 'if you come and look after me, I'll leave you the house when I die'. For cases illustrating the problems associated with such an arrangement and for the law relating to such a promise, see p 83 ff above.

2   In most cases, this exercise will involve an element of gift, and it would be sensible to apply the guidelines set out in *Re Beaney* [1978] 2 All ER 595 on an individual's ability to understand the nature and effect of a gift and to record such understanding processes in the deed itself.

3   It is not clear how these provisions relating to the gradual diminution of the elderly person's share would be regarded by the Inland Revenue for tax purposes, or by the Department of Social Security or a local authority for the purposes of their respective deprivation of capital rules. As far as inheritance tax is concerned, it is arguable that there will only be a chargeable transfer to the extent that any transfer of value exceeds the commercial cost of employing a full-time carer. The Inheritance Tax Act 1984, s 10(1) provides that 'a disposition is not a transfer of value if it is shown that it was not intended and was not made in a transaction intended to confer any gratuitous benefit on any person and either: (a) it was made in a transaction at arm's length between persons not connected with each other; or (b) that it was such as might be expected to be made in a transaction at arm's length between persons not connected with each other'. As far as the notional capital rules are concerned, the significant operative purpose of the exercise is not to secure entitlement to or an increased amount of state benefits or local authority funding, but to enable the elderly person to remain in his or her home for the rest of his or her life, or for as long as is reasonably practicable, with assistance from a live-in carer who is entitled to a beneficial interest in the property, the extent of which reflects the detriment he or she has suffered.

4 For example, a clause stating who will be responsible for paying the outgoings on the property (including insurance), or a clause providing further assurance for the carer by agreeing to appoint him or her as a joint proprietor of the property: see Clause 4 of Precedent 3 at p 95 above. It would be preferable to deal with the carer's inheritance rights in the elderly person's will rather than in this declaration of trust just in case the relationship between the parties breaks down irretrievably.

---

6 DECLARATION OF TRUST OF 'RIGHT TO BUY' PROPERTY[1]

THIS DECLARATION OF TRUST is made on ....
BETWEEN (1) ....
of .... ('*parent*')
and (2) (his)/(her) (son)/(daughter) ....
of .... ('*child*').

IT IS AGREED AND DECLARED as follows:

1.   Recitals

(1)   This declaration of trust relates to (*address*) ('the property').
(2)   (*Parent*) bought the property from (*name of local authority*) Council ('the Council') on (*date*).
(3)   At the time of the purchase the property was valued at £ ......
(4)   Because (*parent*) had been a tenant of the Council for (*number*) years the value of the property was discounted by £ ...... ('*the discount*').[2]
(5)   The purchase price was £ ......
(6)   The additional costs of the purchase came to £ ......
(7)   (*Parent*) paid £ ...... towards the purchase price and purchase costs.
(8)   (*Child*) paid £ ...... towards the purchase price and purchase costs.

2.   Declaration of trust

(*Parent*) declares that (he)/(she) holds the net proceeds of sale of the property in trust for (himself)/(herself) and (*child*) as beneficial tenants in common in the following shares.

3.   Shares

When the property is sold:

(1)   (*Parent*) will receive (*percentage*)% of the sale price, representing the discount and (his)/(her) contribution towards the purchase price and purchase costs, less (50)% of the cost of selling the property ('(*parent's*) share');
(2)   (*Child*) will receive (*percentage*)% of the sale price, representing (his)/(her) contribution towards the purchase price and purchase costs, less (50)% of the cost of selling the property ('(*child's*) share');

(3)   if all or any part of the discount has to be repaid to the Council, it will be paid from ((*parent's*) share);[3]

(4)   If (*child's*) share is less than (his)/(her) contribution towards the purchase price and purchase costs, the shortfall will be paid from (*parent's*) share.

4.   Terms of continued occupation

(*Child*) agrees that (*parent*) can continue to live in the property rent-free for as long as (he)/(she) wishes on the terms that (*parent*):

(1)   pays all the outgoings; and

(2)   keeps the property insured to its full reinstatement value; and

(3)   keeps it in reasonable repair and condition; and

(4)   complies with all the covenants and conditions to which it is subject.

[Additional clauses, if any][4]

SIGNED as a deed by (*parent*) and delivered in the presence of:

SIGNED as a deed by (*child*) and delivered in the presence of:

---

1 Public sector tenants have the right to buy their home at a discount by virtue of Part V of the Housing Act 1985, as amended by the Housing and Planning Act 1986, and the Housing (Extension of Right to Buy) Orders 1987 and 1990 (SI 1987/1732 and SI 1990/197). Gordon Ashton in *Elderly People and the Law* (Butterworths, 1995), at p 103, suggests that 'it will not always be beneficial for an elderly secure tenant to purchase the property even if a substantial discount is available. For those on a limited income, interest on any mortgage arranged for the purpose may be covered by Income Support and MIRAS tax relief will also be available (though this is being phased out), but Housing Benefit can no longer be claimed because the rent ceases and the owner will be responsible for property insurance, all repairing obligations and any service charges (as before). Family members may offer to underwrite the mortgage and repair costs but serious problems arise if they later prove unable to do so. Some older people buy their council home with financial assistance from members of the family who do not reside therein. In each of these situations it is important to record the basis in a legal document (ie is it a gift or a loan, and if the latter, on what terms the loan is made) and to ensure that any inheritance expectations will be fulfilled, especially if there are other members of the family who are not involved in the arrangement'. In *The Law and Elderly People* (Sweet & Maxwell, 1995), Ann McDonald and Margaret Taylor state, at pp 166–167, that where a younger relative funds the purchase price 'the different parties should seek independent advice, almost certainly culminating in a trust deed, so that it is clear how the equitable interest is to be held, who is responsible for what outgoings, that the tenant/purchaser has the right to remain in residence for as long as they wish, and what happens to the proceeds of sale on death or earlier move into residential care'. The authors of *Precedents for the Conveyancer* (Sweet & Maxwell, looseleaf) state at p 9645 that 'separate advice is highly desirable'. For an illustration of how things can go wrong, see *Burrows v Sharp* [1989] EGCS 51, CA, summarised at p 81 above.

2 In the case of a dwelling-house, the discount is calculated by reference to a basic discount of 32 per cent if the purchaser has been a secure tenant for two years. Thereafter the value of the property is discounted by a further one per cent for each complete year up to a maximum of 60 per cent or £50,000 (whichever is less). In the case of a flat, there is a basic discount of 44 per cent for two years' secure tenancy plus an additional 2 per cent for each complete year to a maximum of 70 per cent or £50,000 (whichever is less): Housing Act 1985, s 129(2). The £50,000 limit was imposed by the Housing (Right to Buy) (Maximum Discount) Order 1989 (SI 1989/513).

3 If the purchaser makes a disposal within three years of the purchase, all or part of the discount will be repayable to the Council. The discount repayable is reduced by a third for each complete year after the purchase: Housing Act 1985, s 155. The execution of this declaration of trust is not a relevant disposal: Housing Act 1985, s 159.

4 For example, the parent could provide that when he or she dies, his or her beneficial interest in the property will pass to the child. It may, however, be preferable from the parent's point of view to deal with this separately in a will. For a clause providing for the gradual diminution of the parent's share, see Precedent 7 below.

7 CLAUSE PROVIDING FOR THE GRADUAL DIMINUTION OF THE PARENT'S BENEFICIAL INTEREST IN A 'RIGHT TO BUY' PROPERTY[1]

1. In recognition of the fact that (he)/(she) would not have been able to purchase the property without financial assistance from (*child*), and in consideration of the assurance from (*child*) that (he)/(she) can continue to live in the property rent-free for as long as (he)/(she) wishes, (*parent*) declares that the value of (his)/(her) share will gradually decrease and that the value of (*child's*) share will proportionately increase, and to that intent the following provisions will apply.

2. When the property is sold or when either party realises (his)/(her)/(his or her) share in it ('the disposal') (*parent's*) share will be reduced by (10) per cent for each complete year that has elapsed between the (first) anniversary of the completion of the purchase and the date of the disposal.

3. The amount by which (*parent's*) share is reduced will be added to (*child's*) share.

4. For the avoidance of doubt:

    (a) there will be no reduction of (*parent's*) share before the (first) anniversary of the completion of the purchase because of the provisions relating to the repayment of the discount to the Council;[2] and

    (b) there will be no reduction of (*parent's*) share in respect of any period of less than a complete year.

1 Although this clause relates to the gradual diminution of the parent's share of a right to buy property and is intended to be used as an additional clause in Precedent 6 above, it could fairly easily be adapted for incorporation in a declaration of trust of any property in which the parent has a beneficial interest. It is not clear how the Inland Revenue would regard this clause for capital taxes purposes; how the Department of Social Security would regard it for the purposes of the notional capital rule in reg 51 of the Income Support (General) Regulations 1987 (SI 1987/1967); or how a local authority would regard it for the purposes of the notional capital rule in reg 25 of the National Assistance (Assessment of Resources) Regulations 1992 (SI 1992/2977). For a brief discussion of these points, see Precedent 5, footnote 3 at p 101 above.

2 If the purchaser disposes of the property within three years of its purchase from the Council, there is an obligation to repay all or part of the discount. The amount of discount repayable is reduced by one-third for each complete year after the purchase: Housing Act 1985, s 155. Accordingly, the parent's share, if it only comprises the discount, will be valueless until the first anniversary of the purchase.

CHAPTER 5: GIFTS

INDEX

Text

Checklists

Precedents

GIFTS

TEXT

Introduction

This chapter is concerned mainly with lifetime or inter vivos gifts, rather than gifts intended to take effect on death, and in general the principles that apply to gifts also apply to financial transactions in which there is an element of gift.

A gift is a transaction whereby property is voluntarily transferred by the true owner in possession (the *donor*) to another person (the *recipient* or *donee*) without recompense and with the intention that the property shall not be returned to the donor. If, after making an alleged gift, dominion is restored to the donor, the gift is at an end.[1]

There cannot be a gift without the reciprocal acts of giving and receiving.[2] Accordingly, the donor should be competent to give,[3] and the recipient should be competent to receive.

Gifts are jealously scrutinised in equity, and may be set aside on proof of undue influence. Where no fiduciary relationship exists between the donor and the recipient, the onus is on the party alleging undue influence to prove it. But where there is a fiduciary relationship between the parties, the onus is on the recipient to prove that 'the gift was the spontaneous act of the donor acting under circumstances which enabled her to exercise an independent will, and which justify the court in holding that the gift was the result of the free exercise of her will'.[4] A presumption of undue influence arises where (a) the gift is so substantial that it cannot reasonably be accounted for by ordinary motives, and (b) there is a relationship between the donor and the recipient in which the donor has such confidence and trust in the recipient as to place the recipient in a position to exercise undue influence over the donor in making the gift. A fiduciary relationship exists, for example, between solicitor and client, doctor and patient, and priest and parishioner. It also applies to attorneys and others who manage the donor's property and affairs,[5] and to those in charge of mental hospitals[6] – and presumably, by extension, to people who run residential care homes or nursing homes. The courts have stressed that the list of such relationships is never closed.[7] The case below gives a further example.

Re Craig (Deceased) (1970)[8]

Alfred Craig, 83, was a kind, generous old man who depended on women's company and support and was extremely vulnerable to financial abuse. In January 1959, a couple of months after his wife's death, he took on Mrs Winifred Middleton as a secretary and companion. By the end of the year, he had made gifts in her favour of more than £13,500, and by the time he died in August 1964, the total value of the assets he had transferred to her was just short of £28,000. On two occasions, she had threatened to leave him if she did not get her own way. Mr Craig's estate came to £9500 for probate purposes, and his stepson, the residuary beneficiary under his will, applied to the court for an order that the gifts be set aside on the grounds of undue influence.

HELD, by Ungoed-Thomas J – the gifts could not be accounted for on the ground of the ordinary motives on which ordinary men act, and the relationship between Mr Craig and Mrs Middleton involved such a degree of confidence as to place her in a position to exercise undue influence over him. She had failed to discharge the burden of establishing that the gifts were only made after full, free and informed discussion so as to rebut the presumption of undue influence.

Unconscionable transactions other than those procured by undue influence may also be set aside by the court. Contracts of an improvident character made by poor and ignorant persons acting without independent advice will be set aside unless the other party can discharge the burden of proving that the transaction is fair and reasonable.[9] Bargains with expectants – people who hope to inherit under the donor's will or intestacy – will also be set aside unless the expectant can show that he or she paid a fair price,[10] namely the market price.[11]

---

1 *James v James* (1869) 19 LT 809.

2 *Cochrane v Moore* (1890) 25 QBD 57, CA, at p 76, per Lord Esher MR.

3 For capacity to make a gift, see *Re Beaney (Deceased)* [1978] 2 All ER 595, which is discussed in detail in Chapter 3, at p 45 above. For a checklist on capacity to make a gift, see p 57 above.

4 *Inche Noriah v Shaik Allie Bin Omar* [1928] All ER Rep 189, at p 192E, per Lord Hailsham, LC.

5 *Hunter v Atkins* (1834) 3 Myl & K 113; *Inche Noriah v Shaik Allie Bin Omar* [1928] All ER Rep 189, PC.

6 *Re CMG* [1970] Ch 574.

7 *Allcard v Skinner* (1887) 36 Ch D 145.

8 [1970] 2 All ER 390.

9 *Fry v Lane* (1888) 40 Ch D 312.

10 *Perfect v Lane* (1861) 3 De GF & J 369.

11 *Shelly v Nash* (1818) 3 Madd 232.

Capacity to make a gift

See Chapter 3, p 45 above.

Characteristics of legal advice

In *Inche Noriah v Shaik Allie Bin Omar,* an appeal to the Privy Council from the Court of Appeal of the Straits Settlements, the Lord Chancellor gave a few hints to solicitors advising elderly clients on making a gift.

Inche Noriah v Shaik Allie Bin Omar (1928)[1]

Inche Noriah was an illiterate Malay woman who was so old and infirm that she was never able to leave her house. She owned some valuable property in Singapore. In April 1922, she executed a deed of gift in which she gave practically all of this property to her nephew, Shaik Allie Bin Omar, 40. The deed was drawn up by a firm called Drew & Napier, but before she signed it she received independent legal advice from

James Aitken, a solicitor. He took the deed to her home, read it to her, explained it, and asked whether she was signing it voluntarily. However, Mr Aitken was not aware that she was parting with practically all of her property. He asked no questions about the value of her estate. He thought that she was about 80 and that she probably would not live long, but did not advise her that, if she wanted the properties to go to her nephew when she died, she would be better arranging so by will. In 1925, she issued a writ against her nephew claiming, inter alia, a declaration that the deed of gift was void. The judge decided in her favour, but his decision was reversed by the Court of Appeal. Inche Noriah appealed to the Privy Council.

HELD – the judgment of the trial judge should be restored, and the nephew must pay the costs of the action in all courts.

The Lord Chancellor, Lord Hailsham, said (at pp 135–136) that in order to rebut the presumption of undue influence:

'it is necessary for the donee to prove that the gift was the result of the free exercise of independent will. The most obvious way to prove this is by establishing that the gift was made after the nature and effect of the transaction had been fully explained to the donor by some independent and qualified person so completely as to satisfy the court that the donor was acting independently of any influence from the donee and with the full appreciation of what he was doing . . . their Lordships [are not] prepared to lay down what advice must be received in order to satisfy the rule where independent advice is relied upon, further than to say that it must be given with a knowledge of all the relevant circumstances and must be such as a competent and honest adviser would give if acting solely in the interests of the donor. In the present case their Lordships do not doubt that Mr Aitken acted in good faith; but he seems to have received a good deal of his information from the respondent; he was not made aware of the material fact that the property which was being given away constituted practically the whole estate of the donor, and he certainly does not seem to have brought home to her mind the consequences to herself of what she was doing, or the fact that she could more prudently, and equally effectively, have benefited the donee without undue risk to herself by retaining the property in her own possession during her life and bestowing it upon him by her will.'

---

1 [1929] AC 127, PC.

Ordinary powers of attorney

An attorney acting under an enduring power has rather limited authority to make gifts,[1] and it has been suggested that if, say for tax-planning reasons, the donor wants the attorney to have authority to make gifts beyond the scope permitted by the Enduring Powers of Attorney Act 1985, an ordinary power of attorney should be used instead of an enduring power.[2] In such a case, it would be a sensible precaution for the donor either to execute a specific power of attorney authorising the making of gifts, or at the very least to add a specific clause to that effect to an ordinary general power.[3]

In the absence of specific authorisation, the attorney probably could not make gifts, other than very trivial ones:[4]

- without obtaining the prior consent of the donor;[5]
- to himself or herself. The fiduciary nature of the relationship between principal and agent prohibits the attorney from using his position to acquire any benefit for himself,[6] and also raises the presumption of undue influence;[7] or
- to his or her close relatives[8] – on the same principles of secret profit and undue influence.

It is not entirely clear whether an attorney, acting under either an ordinary or an enduring power, has a duty to mitigate tax on the donor's behalf. Probably not, although there is a difference between the duty of a paid, professional attorney and that of a lay agent. On balance, it is unlikely that there is a duty for the attorney to minimise the ultimate tax burden on the donor's estate. The functions of an attorney are a facsimile of the functions of the donor,[9] and whereas the donor has a discretion to arrange his affairs, if he can, so that the tax attaching under the appropriate acts is less than it otherwise would be,[10] he has no duty as such to save tax for himself or for the ultimate benefit of his estate. As the attorney's authority is a facsimile of the donor's, the attorney likewise has a discretion – but not a duty – to minimise the amount of tax payable during the donor's lifetime and on his or her death.

An attorney, acting on express instructions from the donor, can make a donatio mortis causa by parting with dominion over money or property on the donor's behalf.[11]

---

1 Enduring Powers of Attorney Act 1985, s 3(5). See p 111 below.

2 Law Commission Report No 122, *The Incapacitated Principal*, Cmnd 8977 (July 1983), p 29, footnote 135, states that 'whilst the donor is still capable he can of course use an ordinary power to authorise the attorney to benefit others without limitation'.

3 See Precedent 3 at p 130 below.

4 *Rhodes v Bate* (1866) LR 1 Ch App 252; *Wright v Carter* [1903] 1 Ch 27.

5 *Parker v McKenna* (1874) LR 10 Ch App 96.

6 *Keech v Sandford* (1726) Sel Cas Ch 61, 2 Eq Cas Abr 741.

7 *Hunter v Atkins* (1834) 3 Myl & K 113. See, generally, *Bowstead on Agency* (15th edition, Sweet & Maxwell, 1985), p 171.

8 *Willis v Barron* [1902] AC 271.

9 F. E. Dowrick, *'The Relationship of Principal and Agent'* (1954) 1 MLR 24, at p 37.

10 *Inland Revenue Commissioners v Duke of Westminster* [1936] AC 1, at p 19, per Lord Tomlin.

11 'If the question in this case rested solely on the power of attorney, I should come to the conclusion that, even according to English law, there was no valid donatio. But the question does not rest on that, because there is clear evidence that, during the Channel crossing on the steamer, the testatrix had instructed her agent, her son, to get the particular shares and money transferred into his own name in the bank abroad, and there is evidence that he acted on that. By doing so, and getting the shares transferred into her son's name, the testatrix did what was necessary to part with dominion over the property [and] . . . the necessary conditions for a valid donatio mortis causa have been fulfilled': *Re Craven's Estate* [1937] 3 All ER 33, at p 39B–D, per Farwell J.

Enduring powers of attorney[1]

The extent to which an attorney acting under an enduring power can make a gift of the donor's property depends partly on whether the instrument is unregistered, in the process of being registered,[2] or registered with the Public Trustee.[3]

Section 3(5) of the Enduring Powers of Attorney Act 1985, which applies to both registered and unregistered powers but not those which are in the course of being registered, provides that:[4]

> 'Without prejudice to subsection (4) above, but subject to any conditions or restrictions contained in the instrument, an attorney under an enduring power, whether general or limited, may (without obtaining any consent) dispose of the property of the donor by way of gift to the following extent but no further, that is to say:
>
> (a) he may make gifts of a seasonal nature or at a time, or on an anniversary, of a birth or marriage, to persons (including himself) who are related to or connected with the donor, and
>
> (b) he may make gifts to any charity to whom the donor made or might be expected to make gifts,
>
> provided that the value of each such gift is not unreasonable having regard to all the circumstances and in particular the size of the donor's estate.'

The attorney's authority to make gifts is 'subject to any conditions or restrictions contained in the instrument', so the donor can, if he or she wishes, completely prohibit the attorney from making gifts, or impose conditions (for example, as to the maximum amount of any gift; or the persons to whom they are to be made, or the occasions on which they are made; or the frequency of such gifts; or the donor could require that gifts can be made only if the attorney obtains someone else's consent, perhaps that of the court, beforehand).

The attorney is authorised to make gifts within the prescribed parameters 'without obtaining any consent'. The subsection does not specifically state that the consent which does not need to be obtained is that of the donor, and it has been suggested that 'on the face of it the Act could be self-contradictory. First, it allows the power of attorney to impose conditions, which might certainly include the need to obtain someone's consent. Then it says that authorised gifts may be made without obtaining any consent'.[5]

Essentially, four conditions must be satisfied in order that any gift made by an attorney on behalf of the donor of an unregistered or registered EPA can be said to be valid.

1. There must be no restrictions in the EPA itself which prohibit the attorney from disposing of the donor's property by way of gift.[6]
2. The occasion of the gift must fall within the prescribed parameters. Presents on a christening, confirmation, barmitzvah, graduation, engagement or retirement are, in principle, excluded – as are potentially exempt transfers made at any time other than, say, Christmas, Easter or on a birthday or wedding anniversary. Incidentally, the Act does not specify on whose birthday or anniversary the gift may be made.

3. The recipient of the gift must either be *related to* or *connected with* the donor – neither term is defined in the Act[7] – or be a charity to which the donor actually made gifts or might be expected to make gifts if he or she had full mental capacity. A donor suffering from dementia, for instance, might be expected to make a donation to the Alzheimer's Disease Society.[8] The wording of the section prima facie excludes any purposes which are not charitable, for example political parties, animal rights groups or voluntary euthanasia societies.[9]

4. The value of the gift must be *not unreasonable* in the circumstances, particularly bearing in mind the size of the donor's estate. The attorney is the arbiter of 'reasonableness' in this context. The Court of Protection and the Public Trust Office do not – and would be unwilling to – set out any guidelines, or impose a quantum similar to that which applies to the 'small gifts' procedure in receivership cases.[10] So, if an attorney were to dispose of the donor's house by way of gift, and the donor had virtually no other assets in his or her estate, that would be unreasonable. But if the attorney were to make on the donor's behalf a gift of one of several or many houses, the gift might be reasonable in the circumstances.

Any provision in an EPA purporting to give the attorney a greater authority to benefit persons other than the donor is ineffective.[11] It has been suggested, however, that it may be possible for the donor to execute an ordinary power of attorney – whilst he or she is still mentally capable – authorising the attorney to benefit others without limitation,[12] and this is discussed in greater detail at p 109 above.

The Act does not specify what will happen if the attorney makes a gift which fails to comply with all of these conditions. The Law Commissioners who were responsible for drafting the Act decided not to create any specific new sanctions for EPA attorneys because they wished 'to encourage people to accept EPA attorney-ships: this purpose would be frustrated if honest prospective EPA attorneys were deterred by talk of penalties'.[13] Accordingly, the general law applies and, if an attorney has acted ultra vires in making a gift of the donor's property, he or she will be liable to the donor, or the donor's personal representatives, for any loss to the donor's estate.

---

1 For the results of research carried out, inter alia, on gifts made under an EPA, see Stephen Cretney, Gwynn Davis, Roger Kerridge and Andrew Borkowski, *Enduring Powers of Attorney: A Report to the Lord Chancellor* (Lord Chancellor's Department, June 1991), para 2.33.

2 For the position regarding EPAs in the course of registration, see p 113.

3 For the position regarding registered EPAs, see pp 114–115.

4 For the rationale behind s 3(5), see Law Commission Report No 122, *The Incapacitated Principal*, Cmnd 8977 (HMSO, 1983), paras 4.23–4.29.

5 Trevor Aldridge, *Powers of Attorney* (8th edition, Longman Practitioner Series, 1991), p 14.

6 Where an EPA is specifically subject to a restriction that the attorney is not to make gifts to the donor's friends or relatives, the powers of the Court of Protection under s 8 of the Enduring Powers of Attorney Act 1985 do not extend to directing the attorney to make provision for a third party by way of gift or in recognition of a moral obligation owed by the donor: *Re R (Enduring Power of Attorney)* [1990] 2 All ER 893.

7 Although Sch 1, para 2(1) to the Enduring Powers of Attorney Act 1985 defines the persons who are 'referred to in this Act as *relatives*', the list excludes, for example, a parent-in-law, son-in-law (unless widowed), daughter-in-law (unless widowed), step-parent, step-son, step-daughter, the spouse or partner of any of these persons, and the spouse or partner of any of the people defined as relatives in Sch 1 itself.

8 See, generally, the judgment of Hoffmann J in *Re C (Spinster and Mental Patient)* [1991] 3 All ER 866.

9 Compare Mental Health Act 1983, s 95(1)(c), which empowers the judge to do or secure the doing of all such things as appear necessary or expedient 'for making provision for other persons or purposes for whom or which the patient might be expected to provide if he were not mentally disordered'.

10 See 'Receivership' at p 115 below.

11 Law Commission Report No 122, *The Incapacitated Principal*, Cmnd 8977 (HMSO, 1983), p 29, note 134.

12 *Ibid*, note 135; but see 'Ordinary powers of attorney' (at pp 109–110 above) for a discussion of the limitations on attorneys making gifts under an ordinary power.

13 *Ibid*, p 52, para 4.100.

Enduring powers of attorney in the course of registration

Where an attorney acting under an enduring power has applied for registration of the power, then, until the application has been initially determined, the only action he can take is: (a) to maintain the donor or prevent loss to his estate; or (b) to maintain himself or other persons in so far as s 3(4) of the Enduring Powers of Attorney Act 1985 permits him to do so.[1]

So, prima facie, the attorney cannot make gifts in accordance with s 3(5) of the 1985 Act once he or she has applied for registration until the application has been initially determined. It is by no means uncommon for the donor of an EPA to die whilst an application for registration is pending,[2] and if the circumstances are urgent and it is necessary to make use of the attorney's power to dispose of the donor's property by way of gift (perhaps to take advantage of any unused inheritance tax exemptions), it is suggested that, when submitting the application to register the instrument, the attorney should also lodge an application for an order under s 5 of the 1985 Act,[3] which enables the Court of Protection[4] to confer wider powers on the attorney before the instrument has been registered.

---

1 Enduring Powers of Attorney Act 1985, s 1(2).

2 Mrs A.B. Macfarlane, 'The Court of Protection', (1992) 60 *Medico-Legal Journal*, Pt 1, p 33.

3 The precedent of the application for an order or directions authorising gifts to be made from the estate of the donor of a registered EPA (Precedent 12 at p 134 below) could be adapted to include a reference to the court's powers under the Enduring Powers of Attorney Act 1985, s 5.

4 Dealing with an application under s 5 is not a function exercisable by the Public Trustee: Court of Protection (Enduring Powers of Attorney) Rules 1994 (SI 1994/3047), r 6.

Registered enduring powers of attorney

The limited power to make gifts conferred on attorneys under s 3(5) of the Enduring Powers of Attorney Act 1985 applies regardless of whether the instrument is registered or unregistered. However, if the instrument is registered and the attorney proposes to make a more extensive gift of the donor's property – possibly as part of a tax-mitigation exercise – or a gift on an occasion or for a purpose that is not authorised by s 3(5), an application should be made to the Court of Protection for an order under s 8(2)(e) of the Act, which provides as follows:

> 'Where an instrument has been registered . . . the court may . . . authorise the attorney to act so as to benefit himself or other person than the donor otherwise than in accordance with section 3(4) and (5) (but subject to any conditions or restrictions contained in the instrument).'

If the EPA contains a specific restriction that the attorney is not to make gifts to the donor's friends or relatives, the court's powers under s 8(2) do not extend to authorising the attorney to make provision for a third party by way of gift or in recognition of a moral obligation owed by the donor.[1]

The procedure for applying for an order under s 8(2)(e) is similar to that under s 96(1)(d) of the Mental Health Act 1983 in receivership cases. The application will generally consist of:

- a General Form of Application (Form EP3);[2]
- medical evidence of the donor's mental incapacity, preferably in Form CP3;[3]
- evidence by way of affidavit or affirmation, with relevant exhibits.[4] The facts relating to the application should be set out in full, and the following information should be included:[5]
  - details of the donor's family, by way of a family tree showing the relationship between the donor and the other members of his or her family, naming the members of the family and giving their dates of birth or current ages;
  - particulars of the donor's current assets, with up-to-date valuations;
  - a statement of the donor's needs (both current and anticipated) and general circumstances;
  - where the donor is living in National Health Service accommodation, information as to the likelihood of discharge to Part III accommodation, or other fee-paying accommodation, or to his or her own home;
  - full particulars of the resources of any proposed beneficiary, with details of the likely changes if the application succeeds;
  - a clear explanation of the incidence of capital and income tax liabilities as a result of the proposals;
  - an illustration of the effect of the proposals on the donor's resources, preferably in the form of a 'before and after' schedule of assets and income.

Whereas in receivership cases an application for a gift of a patient's property can only be made by one or more of the persons specified in r 20 of the Court of Protection Rules 1994,[6] an application for a gift of any property of the donor of a registered EPA can be made by anyone with a sufficient interest in the matter. However, if the proposed applicant is neither the attorney nor any person who was served with a notice of intention to register the EPA, he or she should first apply to the Public Trustee for leave to make the application.[7]

Although the wording of s 8(2)(e) of the Enduring Powers of Attorney Act 1985 refers to benefiting persons other than the donor 'otherwise than in accordance with section 3(4) and (5)', it is understood that the Court of Protection will only consider gifts in favour of persons or purposes for whom or which the donor might be expected to provide if he or she were not mentally disordered.[8]

---

1 *Re R (Enduring Power of Attorney)* [1990] 2 All ER 893, at p 896, per Vinelott J.
2 For an application for an order or direction authorising gifts to be made from the estate of the donor of a registered EPA, see Precedent 11 at p 133 below.
3 Form CP3 is reproduced in Chapter 10, at p 291 below.
4 For an affidavit in support of an application to the Court of Protection authorising gifts to be made out of the estate of the donor of a registered EPA, see Precedent 12 at p 134 below.
5 See, generally, the Court of Protection's Procedure Note PN9, 'Applications for the execution of statutory wills and codicils, and for gifts, settlements and other similar dealings'.
6 SI 1994/3046.
7 Court of Protection (Enduring Powers of Attorney) Rules 1994 (SI 1994/3047), r 22.
8 See Mental Health Act 1983, s 95(1)(b) and (c); and *Re CMG* [1970] 1 Ch 574.

Receivership

Special rules apply where it is proposed to make gifts from the estate of a patient whose affairs are managed on a day-to-day basis by a receiver acting under the supervision of the Public Trust Office.

A gift of the patient's money or property, and any loan or other financial transaction in which there is an element of gift, must be authorised by either the Public Trustee or the Court of Protection under s 96(1)(d) of the Mental Health Act 1983.

The persons who are entitled to apply for an order authorising a gift of a patient's property are:[1]

(a) the receiver for the patient;
(b) any person who has made an application for the appointment of a receiver which has not yet been determined;
(c) any person who, under any known will of the patient or under his intestacy, may become entitled to any property of the patient or any interest therein;
(d) any person for whom the patient might be expected to provide if he were not mentally disordered;
(e) an attorney acting under a registered enduring power of attorney; or
(f) any other person whom the court or, where it relates to a function to be exercised by him, the Public Trustee, may authorise to make an application.

An application for a direction authorising the gift should be made to the Public Trustee in the first instance[2] if the proposed gift is:

- payable out of surplus income or capital; and
- insignificant in the context of the patient's assets; and
- for a sum not greater than £15,000.[3]

If the proposed gift does not fall within all of these parameters (for example, where the sum involved is less than £15,000, but is not insignificant in the context of the patient's assets as a whole), a formal application should be made to the Court of Protection for an order under s 96(1)(d) of the Mental Health Act 1983.[4] The procedure is virtually identical to that described above in respect of applications to the court for an order authorising larger gifts to be made out of the estate of the donor of a registered EPA, except that the application itself should be made in the general form of application (Form CP9), which appears as Form B in the Schedule to the Court of Protection Rules 1994. When making such an application, it is important to adhere to the court's requirements set out in its procedure note PN9, 'Applications for the execution of statutory wills and codicils and for gifts, settlements and other similar dealings', which is supplied free of charge.

A proposed gift cannot be considered unless it is 'for the maintenance or other benefit[5] of members of the patient's family'[6] or 'for making provision for other persons or purposes for whom or which the patient might be expected to provide if he were not mentally disordered'.[7] Although tax avoidance is a perfectly acceptable reason for applying for such a direction or order,[8] neither the Public Trustee nor the Court of Protection will countenance any gift which is primarily intended to avoid the payment of means-tested maintenance charges.[9]

---

1 Court of Protection Rules 1994 (SI 1994/3046), r 20.

2 For a precedent of a letter to the Public Trustee requesting a direction to make a gift of the patient's money or property, see Precedent 13 at p 137 below.

3 Court of Protection Rules 1994 (SI 1994/3046), r 6(1)(g).

4 For a precedent of an application to the Court of Protection for an order to make gifts from a patient's estate, see Precedent 14 at p 138 below. For the affidavit in support of such an application, see Precedent 12 at p 134 below, which, although it relates to an application for an order under s 8(2)(e) of the Enduring Powers of Attorney Act 1985, can easily be adapted to become an application for an order under s 96(1)(d) of the Mental Health Act 1983.

5 Mental Health Act 1983, s 95(1)(b). In *Re W (EEM)* [1971] Ch 123, which involved a divorce rather than a gift, Ungoed-Thomas J held that the word 'benefit' is 'of wide significance comprehending whatever would be beneficial in any respect, material or otherwise'. Similarly, in *Re E (Mental Health Patient)* [1985] 1 WLR 245, the Court of Appeal held that the benefit of the patient and his or her family is not confined to material benefit but extends to whatever may be meant by their true interests.

6 The words 'members of the patient's family' in s 95(1)(b) mean persons for whom the patient might prima facie be expected to provide, and do not include collateral such as nieces and nephews. Collateral, if to be benefited at all, would have to brought within the ambit of s 95(1)(c), 'persons for whom the patient might be expected to provide if he were not mentally disordered'.

7 Mental Health Act 1983, s 95(1)(c). In *Re CMG* [1970] 1 Ch 574, it was held that the court has to answer the following question: 'is the proposed gift such a gift as the patient might be expected to provide if she had ceased to be mentally disordered and was removed from any influence?' (at p 575H, per Stamp J).

8 *Re CWM* [1951] 2 KB 714, [1951] 2 All ER 707. Although the saving of tax may be an aspect
  or method of making provision, it does not convert persons for whom the patient would not
  otherwise be expected to provide into persons the patient might be expected to provide for:
  Re L (Case no 2121 of 1960) (unreported), per Ungoed-Thomas J.
9 Heywood and Massey, *Court of Protection Practice* (12th edition, Sweet & Maxwell, 1991), p 197.

Anti-avoidance provisions

Several statutory provisions are specifically designed to set aside a gift, or otherwise
penalise the recipient or donor, where Parliament considers the effect of the gift to
be socially undesirable. These provisions are far from uniform. In some cases, the
timing of the gift is relevant; in others, it is irrelevant and the donor's knowledge,
purpose or intention is the paramount consideration.

(1) Insolvency

The Insolvency Act 1986 contains two separate provisions relating to *transactions at
an undervalue*.[1] These transactions occur where an individual:

- makes a gift to another person, or otherwise enters into a transaction with that
  person on terms that provide for him or her to receive no consideration; or
- enters into a transaction with another person in consideration of marriage; or
- enters into a transaction with that person for a consideration the value of which,
  in money or money's worth, is significantly less than the value, in money's
  worth, of the consideration provided by himself or herself.[2]

Section 339 provides that where (a) an individual is adjudged bankrupt, and (b) he
or she has *at a relevant time* entered into a transaction at an undervalue, the trustee
in bankruptcy may apply to the court for an order restoring the position to what
it would have been if the transaction had never taken place.[3]

The timing of the transaction is *relevant* if it occurs less than:

- two years from the date of presentation of the petition on which the individual
  is adjudged bankrupt (regardless of whether he or she was insolvent at the time
  or became insolvent as a result of the transaction); or
- five years before the presentation of the petition if he or she: (a) is insolvent at
  that time; or (b) becomes insolvent as a result of the transaction.[4]

An individual is *insolvent* if (a) he is unable to pay his debts as they fall due, or (b)
the value of his assets is less than the amount of his liabilities, taking into account
contingent and prospective liabilities.[5]

There is a rebuttable presumption that an individual is insolvent at the time of the
transaction or has become insolvent as a result of it if he entered into the transaction
with an *associate*.[6] An associate is the individual's husband or wife, or a relative – or
the husband or wife of a relative – of the individual or his or her spouse.[7]

The second provision is s 423 (transactions defrauding creditors). A transaction at
an undervalue may be set aside by the court if it is satisfied that the individual
entering into the transaction did so for the purpose of (a) putting assets beyond the

reach of a person who is making, or may at some time make, a claim against him, or (b) otherwise prejudicing the interests of such a person in relation to the claim he is making or may make.[8]

The court may make such order as it thinks fit for restoring the position to what it would have been if the transaction had not been entered into and protecting the interests of persons who are victims of the transaction. A *victim* is someone who is, or is capable of being, prejudiced by the transaction.[9]

The persons entitled to apply for an order under s 423 are:

- where the individual is now bankrupt, the official receiver or trustee in bankruptcy, or, with the leave of the court, the victim of the transaction; or
- where a voluntary arrangement has been approved, the supervisor of the voluntary arrangement or the victim of the transaction; or
- in any other case – for example, where there is no bankruptcy – the victim of the transaction.[10]

The differences between ss 339 and 423 are as follows.

- Section 423 applies regardless of whether there are insolvency proceedings, whereas s 339 only applies where the individual is adjudged bankrupt.
- The court has a discretion in making an order under s 423, but there is no such discretion under s 339.
- There are no time-limits in respect of the date on which the transaction was entered into for the purpose of s 423.
- The purpose of the transaction must be proved for a s 423 order.
- Section 339 restores the position to what it would have been but for the transaction, whereas s 423 allows the court also to make provision for protecting the interests of the victim.

(2)   Family law

The court has powers to prevent assets from being disposed of with the intention of defeating a claim for financial relief in matrimonial proceedings,[11] and to set aside completed transactions intended to prevent or reduce financial relief.[12] Where a disposition takes place less than three years before the date of an application for financial relief, there is a rebuttable presumption that the disposition was intended to defeat the application.[13]

Where, less than six years before his or her death, the deceased made a disposition with the intention of defeating an application for financial provision under the Inheritance (Provision for Family and Dependants) Act 1975, the court may order the donee (regardless of whether he or she still has the money or property at the date of the order) to provide, for the purpose of making financial provision, such sum of money or other property as may be specified in the order.[14]

(3)   Social security

Claimants are treated as possessing capital of which they have deprived themselves for the purpose of securing entitlement to means-tested benefits or increasing the amount of those benefits.[15] This is known as the *notional capital rule*. The adjudication officer has to prove that claimants actually knew of the capital limit rule;[16] that they have deprived themselves of actual capital;[17] and that their 'significant operative purpose' was to secure entitlement to benefit or increase the amount of benefit payable.[18]

A supplementary rule, known as the *diminishing notional capital rule*, provides that, where a claimant has been assessed as having notional capital, that capital has to be reduced each week by the difference between the amount of benefit he or she actually receives and the amount he or she would have received if he or she were not treated as possessing the notional capital.[19]

(4) Community care

Residents may be treated as possessing actual capital of which they have deprived themselves for the purpose of decreasing the amount that they may be liable to pay for their accommodation.[20] This is similar to the notional capital rule for social security benefits, and a comparable diminishing notional capital rule also applies.[21] There is no time-limit in respect of the deprivation of assets – the key factor is the resident's purpose – although the CRAG guidelines advise local authorities that 'the timing of the disposal should be taken into consideration when considering the purpose of the disposal'.[22] If the local authority decides that a resident has disposed of capital in order to avoid or reduce the accommodation charges payable, it can choose either to recover the assessed charge from the resident personally (subject to the diminishing notional capital rule, if applicable) or, if the resident is unable to pay, transfer the liability for accommodation charges to the donee.

Liability can only be transferred to the donee if the resident knowingly, and with the intention of avoiding the accommodation charges, transferred any asset to some other person or persons less than six months before the date on which they began to reside in Part III accommodation, or while they are actually residing in such accommodation.[23]

It is understood that some local authorities make use of the insolvency legislation in order to avoid the burden of proving intent, and to take advantage of the wider facilities for recovery from the recipient.

(5) Inheritance tax

From the elderly client's point of view, the two most important anti-avoidance provisions for inheritance tax purposes are *gifts with a reservation of benefit*[24] and *associated operations*.[25]

A gift with a reservation of benefit occurs where an individual disposes of property by way of gift and either (a) possession and enjoyment of the property are not bona fide assumed by the donee before the beginning of the relevant period, or (b) at any time during the relevant period, the property is not enjoyed to the entire exclusion, or virtually the entire exclusion, of the donor. The relevant period is one which ends on the date of the donor's death and begins seven years before that date or, if later, on the date of the gift. Where a gift has been made with a reservation of benefit, the property comprised in the gift will still form part of the donor's estate for inheritance tax purposes on his or her death. A typical example is where an elderly mother transfers her house to her son on the understanding that she will be able to remain there for the rest of her life.

Associated operations are two or more operations of any kind affecting the same property, or any two operations, one of which is effected with reference to the other or with a view to facilitating the other. A typical illustration is where an elderly couple wish to give £100,000 to their daughter. The husband is wealthier than the wife, and has already made a large number of potentially exempt transfers, so he transfers the £100,000 to his wife (which would under normal circumstances be an exempt transfer between spouses) with the intention that she will pass it on to their daughter.

---

1 Section 423 of the Insolvency Act 1986 replaced s 172 of the Law of Property Act 1925; and s 339 of the Insolvency Act 1986 replaced s 42 of the Bankruptcy Act 1914.

2 Insolvency Act 1986, ss 339(3) and 423(1).

3 *Ibid*, s 339(1) and (2).

4 *Ibid*, s 341(1) and (2).

5 *Ibid*, s 341(3).

6 *Ibid*, s 341(2).

7 *Ibid*, s 435(2).

8 *Ibid*, s 423(3).

9 *Ibid*, s 432(2).

10 *Ibid*, s 424(1).

11 Matrimonial Causes Act 1973, s 37(2)(a).

12 *Ibid*, s 37(2)(b), (c).

13 *Ibid*, s 37(5).

14 Inheritance (Provision for Family and Dependants) Act 1975, s 10.

15 Income Support (General) Regulations 1987 (SI 1987/1967), reg 51; Family Credit (General) Regulations 1987 (SI 1987/1973), reg 34. See, generally, the detailed commentary on these regulations in the current edition of John Mesher and Penny Wood, *Income Related Benefits: The Legislation* (Sweet & Maxwell).

16 *CIS 124/1990* and *R(SB) 12/91*. It is not enough that the claimant ought to have known about the capital limit rule.

17 Income Support (General) Regulations 1987 (SI 1987/1967), reg 51(7).

18 *R(SB) 40/85*. Note that in *CIS 621/1991*, the Commissioner decided that, where the claimant had been warned about the consequences of a transaction by the local DSS office, and still went ahead with the transaction, this showed that he could not have had as any part of his purpose the securing of entitlement to, or continued entitlement to income support. The test seems to be whether the claimant would have carried out the transaction anyway, even if there had been no effect on the eligibility for benefit.

19 Income Support (General) Regulations 1987 (SI 1987/1967), reg 51A; Family Credit (General) Regulations 1987 (SI 1987/1973), reg 34A. The diminishing notional capital rule was introduced in October 1990.

20 National Assistance (Assessment of Resources) Regulations 1992 (SI 1992/2977), reg 25(1).

21 *Ibid*, reg 26.

22 Charging for Residential Accommodation Guide, para 6.064 (Amendment 2: January 1994). The paragraph advises local authorities to 'bear in mind, however, that deprivation can be considered for resources disposed of at any time. The six-month restriction only applies to using the provisions of the Health and Social Services and Social Security Adjudications Act 1983, s 21'.

23 Health and Social Services and Social Security Adjudications Act 1983, s 21(1).

24 Finance Act 1986, s 102.

25 Inheritance Tax Act 1984, s 268.

Inheritance tax

This section is an extremely brief summary of the exempt transfers for inheritance tax purposes and, where appropriate, elderly clients should be advised to use these exemptions to full advantage. The section numbers refer to the Inheritance Tax Act 1984.

Inheritance tax is charged on the value transferred by a chargeable transfer (s 1). A chargeable transfer is a transfer of value made by an individual which is not exempt (s 2(1)). The charge may apply to both lifetime transfers and transfers on death.

The main inheritance tax exemptions are as follows.

- Potentially exempt transfers (PETs) (s 3A). There is no liability on a PET at the time of the transfer, and it will become wholly exempt if the transferor survives for seven years after the transfer. If the PET becomes chargeable, tapering relief is available if the transferor survives for more than three years after the transfer.
- The nil rate band of £200,000, although technically it is not an exemption because inheritance tax is chargeable at a nil rate (s 7 and Sch 1).[1]
- Transfers between spouses, unless the recipient spouse is not domiciled in the UK, in which case the exemption is restricted to £55,000 (s 18).
- Annual exemption. Transfers up to a total of £3000 in any year, with a carry forward on any unused balance for one year only are exempt (s 19). A transfer of value which exceeds the annual exemption is a PET in respect of the excess.
- Small gifts. Transfers of value made by a transferor in any one year by outright gift to any one person are exempt if they do not exceed £250 (s 20).
- Normal expenditure out of income. A transfer of value is an exempt transfer if, or to the extent that it is shown: (a) it was made as part of the normal expenditure of the transferor; (b) that (taking one year with another) it was made out of his income; and (c) that, after allowing for all transfers of value forming part of his normal expenditure, the transferor was left with sufficient income to maintain his usual standard of living (s 21).[2]
- Gifts in consideration of marriage up to £5000 by any parent of the parties; up to £2500 by any party to the marriage or any remoter ancestor of a party to the marriage; and up to £1000 in other cases (s 22).
- Gifts to charities (s 23).
- Gifts to political parties (s 24).
- Gifts to housing associations (s 24A).
- Gifts for national purposes (s 25). The gift has to be made to one of the institutions listed in Sch 3, for example The National Trust, or public museums, art galleries and libraries.
- Gifts for public benefit (s 26).
- Maintenance funds for historic buildings (s 27).
- Employee trusts (s 28).

1 The nil rate band has been increased from £154,000 to £200,000 in respect of transfers made on or after 6 April 1996 (Finance Bill 1996, cl 169).

2 See, generally, *Bennett v IRC* [1995] STC 54.

Proposed reforms

The Law Commission's report on *Mental Incapacity*, published on 1 March 1995,[1] recommends the repeal of the Enduring Powers of Attorney Act 1985 and Part VII of the Mental Health Act 1983, and proposes in their place to create a new continuing power of attorney, which will only be operative while the donor is without capacity, and a new Court of Protection.

In view of its recommendation that anything done for, and any decision made on behalf of, a person without capacity should be done or made in the best interests of that person,[2] the Commission sees no need for comparable provision to ss 3(4), 3(5) and 8(2)(e) of the Enduring Powers of Attorney Act 1985. The power to act in the donor's best interests is more flexible and slightly wider than these powers since it requires the attorney to consider the wishes and feelings of the donor and the other factors he or she would have taken into account. Accordingly, in appropriate cases, the attorney would be quite able to meet other people's needs (including his or her own) or to make seasonal or charitable gifts, while still acting within the parameters of the best interests duty.[3]

The Commission has recommended that the powers of the new Court of Protection over the property and affairs of a person without capacity should cover the gift or other disposition of his property and the settlement of any of his property, whether for his own benefit or the benefit of others.[4]

The Labour Party has indicated in very broad terms a number of tax changes which it will introduce if elected at the next General Election. It is improbable that the existing provisions on potentially exempt transfers would continue and, instead, lifetime gifts would be likely to be subject to an immediate charge to inheritance tax.

1 Law Com Report No 231 (HMSO, 1995).

2 *Ibid*, para 3.25, and draft Mental Incapacity Bill, cl 3(1).

3 *Ibid*, para 7.11.

4 *Ibid*, paras 8.33 and 8.34, and Draft Bill, cl 27(1)(b) and (h).

CHECKLISTS

A checklist to assess a client's capacity to make a gift is included in Chapter 3, at p 57 above.

1 ETHICAL POINTS TO CONSIDER WHEN ACTING FOR AN ELDERLY PERSON WHO PROPOSES TO MAKE A SUBSTANTIAL GIFT[1]

(1) Who is the client?

Are you acting for:

- the elderly person?
- the recipient?
- both the elderly person and the recipient?

The rules of professional conduct state that you should not accept instructions to act for both parties where there is a conflict or a significant risk of conflict between the interests of those parties.[2]

Similarly, if you have accepted instructions to act for both parties and a conflict of interests arises during the course of the transaction, you should cease to act for both parties, but may continue to act for one of them provided that you can do so with propriety and without embarrassment, and provided you obtain the consent of the party for whom you have ceased to act.[3]

However, both clients can waive these rules provided that you obtain their informed consent to your acting for both of them.[4] Informed consent means consent given in the knowledge that there is a conflict between the parties and that as a result you may be disabled from disclosing to each party the full knowledge you possess of the transaction, or may be disabled from giving advice to one party which conflicts with the interests of the other. If the parties are content to proceed on this basis, you may properly act for both of them.[5]

Although a waiver of the rules of professional conduct by the informed consent of both parties may enable a solicitor to act for them where there is a conflict of interests, such a waiver is probably not sufficient for the purpose of rebutting the presumption of undue influence. The only way to rebut the presumption is to ensure that the gift was made after its nature and effect had been fully explained to the donor by some independent qualified person who was aware of all the relevant facts, including the size of the donor's estate.[6]

(2) You must not accept instructions to act if you suspect that they may have been given by the client under duress or undue influence

Particular care needs to be taken where clients are elderly or otherwise vulnerable to pressure from others. In such circumstances, you should either:

- see the client alone in order to satisfy yourself that the instructions were freely given; or
- refuse to act.[7]

(3) Does the elderly client have the capacity to make such a gift?

If the subject matter and value of the gift are trivial in relation to the donor's other assets, a low degree of understanding will suffice. But if the effect of the gift is to dispose of the donor's only asset of value and thus for practical purposes to pre-empt the devolution of his or her estate by will or on intestacy, then the degree of understanding is as high as that required for a will, and the donor must understand the claims of all potential donees and the extent of the property to be disposed of.[8]

There is a separate checklist on capacity to make a gift at p 57 above.

(4) Are you aware of all the relevant circumstances?

Your advice must be given with a knowledge of all the relevant circumstances and must be such as a competent and honest adviser would give if acting solely in the interests of the donor.[9]

For example, at the very least you need to know:

- the donor's age, state of health and life expectancy;
- the value of the property being disposed of;
- the value of the donor's estate generally.

(5) The client should be advised of the comparative advantages of disposing of the property to the donee by will, rather than by a lifetime gift.

If such is the case, the donor must be advised that he or she could more prudently, and equally effectively, benefit the donee without undue risk to himself or herself by retaining the property in his or her possession during his or her lifetime and bestowing it upon the donee by will.[10]

(6) If the client is in full command of his or her faculties and apparently aware of what he or she is doing, you are under no obligation to go beyond your instructions by proffering unsought advice on the wisdom of the transaction.[11]

1 This checklist considers some of the complex ethical problems that may arise when advising an elderly client who is proposing to make a gift of a substantial asset. It should be read in conjunction with the checklist on capacity to make a gift, which appears at p 57 above and contains an analysis of what is meant by understanding the nature and effect of the transaction.

2 The Law Society, *The Guide to the Professional Conduct of Solicitors* (6th edition, 1993), Principle 15.01. See, generally, 'Conflict of interests' in Chapter 2, at p 27.

3 *Ibid*, Principle 15.03. For a form of consent, see Precedent 2, Chapter 2, at p 32 above.

4 For a suggested form of informed consent, see Precedent 3, Chapter 2, at p 32 above.

5 *Clark Boyce v Mouat* [1993] 4 All ER 268, at p 273g, per Lord Jauncey. For a brief summary of this case, see p 28 above.

6 *Inche Noriah v Shaik Allie Bin Omar* [1928] All ER Rep 189, at p 193F, per Lord Hailsham LC.

7 The Law Society, *The Guide to the Professional Conduct of Solicitors* (6th edition, 1993), Principle 12.04.

8 *Re Beaney (Deceased)* [1978] 2 All ER 595, at p 601f–h, per Martin Nourse QC (as he then was). For a brief summary of this case, see p 45 above.

9 *Inche Noriah v Shaik Allie Bin Omar* [1928] All ER Rep 189, at p 193H, per Lord Hailsham, LC. For a brief summary of this case, see p 108 above.

10 *Ibid*, at p 193, per Lord Hailsham, LC.

11 *Clark Boyce v Mouat* [1993] 4 All ER 268, at p 275b, per Lord Jauncey: 'To hold otherwise would impose intolerable burdens on solicitors'.

2 MAKING GIFTS UNDER AN ENDURING POWER OF ATTORNEY[1]

(1) Does the EPA contain any restrictions or conditions on the making of gifts?

For example:

- the EPA may completely prohibit the making of gifts;[2]
- someone's consent may be needed before a gift can be made;[3]
- there may be restrictions on the amount payable to any one person, or in any one year,[4] or altogether.

(2) If the gift is being made to a charity, is it one to which the donor has made gifts in the past, or one to which he or she might be expected to make gifts?

- Gifts to causes which are non-charitable are outside the scope of the attorney's authority.[5]
- Any question as to what the donor might at any time be expected to do must be determined by assuming that he or she had full mental capacity at the time, but otherwise by reference to the circumstances existing at that time.[6]
- Unlike gifts to persons who are related to or connected with the donor, a gift to a charity can be made at any time of the year.
- The value of the gift should be 'not unreasonable having regard to all the circumstances and in particular the size of the donor's estate'.

(3) If the gift is to a person, is he or she related to or connected with the donor?

- Neither of these terms is defined in the 1985 Act.[7]
- The expression 'related to' is not restricted to the list of relatives who are entitled to receive notice of the attorney's intention to apply for registration.[8]

(4) If the gift is to a person, is it being made on an authorised occasion?

Gifts to persons must be of a seasonal nature or made:

- at the time of a birth;
- at the time of a marriage;
- on the anniversary of a birth; or
- on the anniversary of a marriage.

(5) Is the value of the gift not unreasonable having regard to all the circumstances, and in particular the size of the donor's estate?

- The attorney is the arbiter of what is not unreasonable in the circumstances.
- There are no defined maxima for small gifts, as there are in receivership cases.
- Consider whether it is worth obtaining an indemnity from the recipient.

(6) If the gift falls outside these parameters, and the EPA is registered (or in the course of being registered), an application should be made to the Court of Protection for an order authorising the making of the gift.

- If the EPA is unregistered, and the donor is mentally capable, the donor should make the gift personally or, at least, through channels other than an enduring power of attorney where the attorney's authority to make gifts is curtailed by s 3(5) of the Enduring Powers of Attorney Act 1985.
- If the EPA is in the course of being registered with the Public Trust Office, and it is necessary to make the gift before the power is registered (maybe because the donor is dying), an application should be made to the Court of Protection for an order under s 5 of the Act.
- If the EPA is registered, an application should be made to the Court of Protection for an order under s 8(2)(e) of the Act.

---

1 The extent to which an attorney acting under an enduring power can make gifts of the donor's property is described in the Enduring Powers of Attorney Act 1985, s 3(5). For a detailed discussion of this subsection, see pp 111–113 above.

2 See, for example, Precedent 5 at p 131 below.

3 See, for example, Precedent 6 at p 132 below.

4 See, for example, Precedent 11 at p 133 below.

5 In this respect, the EPA legislation differs from Part VII of the Mental Health Act 1983, where the judge can authorise a gift 'for making provision for other persons or purposes for whom or which the patient might be expected to provide if he were not mentally disordered': Mental Health Act 1983, s 95(1)(c).

6 Enduring Powers of Attorney Act 1983, s 13(2). See also *Re C* [1991] 3 All ER 866.

7 Ordinary words of the English language should be construed in the way that ordinary sensible people would construe them: *Cozens v Brutus* [1973] AC 854, at p 861, per Lord Reid.

8 The term 'relatives' is defined for the purposes of the 1985 Act in Sch 1, para 2(1).

PRECEDENTS

1 LETTER TO CLIENT CONSIDERING THE POSSIBLE CONSEQUENCES OF A PROPOSED GIFT BY REFERENCE TO THE LAW SOCIETY'S GUIDELINES[1]

(*date*)

Dear (*client*)

Thank you for your letter of (*date*) instructing me to act on your behalf in connection with the proposed transfer of (*your house*) to (*your children*). I would be pleased to assist you in this matter.

I have a duty to ensure that, before we actually go ahead with the transaction, you fully understand the nature, effect, and possible consequences of the proposed gift.[2] For this purpose, I am enclosing a copy of The Law Society's guidelines, which we send as a matter of course to any of our clients who are considering the transfer of substantial assets. I realise that most of the contents are inapplicable in your circumstances, but I would nevertheless be pleased to discuss any queries that may arise. If, having read and considered these guidelines, you wish to proceed with the gift, please let me know as soon as possible. I am enclosing a prepaid envelope for your reply.

Yours sincerely

Enclosures:

- The Law Society's guidelines
- Prepaid envelope

---

1 It may be preferable to deal with the sensitive issues raised by a proposed gift by reference to a general handout or brochure which considers the nature, effect and possible consequences of a gift on a strictly impersonal basis, such as the guidelines recently issued by The Law Society: *Gifts of property: Implications for future liability to pay for long term care: Guidelines for solicitors* (September 1995). Such a course of action is also likely to be more time-efficient and cost-effective than writing a comprehensive reply de novo to every enquiry of this nature.

2 *Inche Noriah v Shaik Allie Bin Omar* [1929] AC 127, PC.

2 DECLARATION OF TRUST RECORDING THE OCCUPATION AND INCOME RIGHTS OF AN ELDERLY PARENT WHO HAS TRANSFERRED A HOUSE TO HIS OR HER CHILDREN

THIS DECLARATION OF TRUST is made on ....
BETWEEN (1) ....
of ....
and ....
of .... ('the trustees')
and (2) ....
of .... ('*the parent*')

Whereas

(a)   This deed is supplemental to a transfer (of today's date but executed before this deed)/(dated (*date*)) in which (*the parent*) transferred to the trustees the (freehold)/(leasehold) property known as (*address*) ('the property').

(b)   Title to the property is registered at the Land Registry under title number (*number*).

(c)   The expression 'the trustees' means the trustees for the time being of this deed, whether original, substituted or added.

IT IS HEREBY DECLARED AND AGREED that:

(1)   The trustees hold the property on trust to sell it, with power to postpone the sale for as long as they think fit, and will hold the net proceeds of sale and the net income until sale and the investments from time to time representing the same upon the following trusts.

(2)   During the lifetime of (*the parent*) the trustees will not enforce the trust for sale or seek to obtain any rent or income from the property without the written consent of (*the parent*).

(3)   Until the property is sold the trustees will permit (*the parent*) to reside in it rent-free on the terms that (he)/(she):

(a)   pays all the outgoings;
(b)   keeps it in reasonable repair and condition;
(c)   keeps it insured to its full reinstatement value;
(d)   complies with all the covenants and conditions to which it is subject; and
(e)   does not, without first obtaining the trustees' consent in writing, grant any lease, licence or tenancy or allow anyone else to occupy the property in circumstances which could give that person protection from eviction.

(4)   So that (*the parent*) can move elsewhere during (his)/(her) lifetime, the trustees will, if asked to do so by (*the parent*), sell the property and apply the net proceeds of sale in or towards the purchase of such other property as (*the*

parent) directs, which will be held on exactly the same trusts as the property itself.

(5)   If the property is sold during (*the parent's*) lifetime, the trustees will invest the net proceeds of sale, or such part as has not been not applied in or towards the purchase of any other property for (*the parent*), in (whatever investments)/(whatever high income-yielding investments) they think fit and will pay the income from those investments to (*the parent*) during (his)/(her) lifetime.

(6)   Subject to the above, the trustees will hold the property, its net income until sale, its net proceeds of sale and the investments representing the same on trust for (themselves as beneficial tenants in common in equal shares).

SIGNED by (*the trustees*) as a deed
and delivered in the presence of:

SIGNED by (*the parent*) as a deed
and delivered in the presence of:

3 ORDINARY POWER OF ATTORNEY AUTHORISING THE ATTORNEYS TO MAKE GIFTS[1]

THIS GENERAL POWER OF ATTORNEY is made on ....
by me ....
of ....

I APPOINT ....
of ....
and ....
of ....
(jointly)/(jointly and severally) to be my attorneys in accordance with section 10 of the Powers of Attorney Act 1971.

I AUTHORISE my attorneys to dispose of my property by way of gift to such persons (including themselves) or such purposes, at such times, and on such terms and conditions as they may in their absolute discretion think fit [subject to any restrictions and conditions I may from time to time impose, but any person dealing with my attorneys shall assume that no such restrictions or conditions have been imposed].

SIGNED by me as a deed
and delivered in the presence of:

1 The limited power of making gifts of the donor's property under the Enduring Powers of Attorney Act 1985, s 3(5) has been criticised by many practitioners on the grounds that EPAs are thereby rendered inappropriate in cases where there is the prospect of significant lifetime giving for tax-planning purposes: Stephen Cretney et al, *Enduring Powers of Attorney: A Report to the Lord Chancellor* (Lord Chancellor's Department, June 1991), at para 2.33. The Law Commission has suggested that 'whilst the donor is still capable, he can of course use an ordinary power to authorise the attorney to benefit others without limitation': Law Commission Report No 122, *The Incapacitated Principal*, Cmnd 8977 (HMSO, July 1983), p 29, footnotes 134 and 135. See, generally, 'Ordinary powers of attorney' at p 109 above.

4 EPA CLAUSE PROHIBITING THE MAKING OF GIFTS

My attorney may not under any circumstances dispose of my property by way of gift to any person or charity.[1]

1 Section 3(5) of the Enduring Powers of Attorney Act 1985 authorises the attorney to dispose of the donor's property by way of gift in certain circumstances, subject to any conditions or restrictions contained in the instrument. Under s 8(2)(e), the Court of Protection can authorise the attorney to make gifts otherwise than in accordance with s 3(5), but its power to give such authorisation is also subject to any conditions or restrictions contained in the instrument. See *Re R (Enduring Power of Attorney)* [1990] 2 All ER 893.

5 EPA CLAUSE PROHIBITING THE MAKING OF GIFTS WITHOUT THE CONSENT OF THE DONOR'S SOLICITOR

My attorney may not dispose of my property by way of gift to any person without having first obtained the consent in writing of my solicitor (*name*) of (*address*) [who is one of the executors of my will].[1]

1 This clause is somewhat problematic, insofar as s 3(5) of the Enduring Powers of Attorney Act 1985 is self-contradictory. The subsection states that 'subject to any conditions or restrictions contained in the instrument, an attorney under an enduring power, whether general or limited, may (without obtaining any consent) dispose of the property of the donor by way of gift to the following extent but no further . . . '. It is submitted that this clause is a condition or restriction to which the making of such gifts is subject.

6 EPA CLAUSE DEFINING TRUSTEES AS PERSONS WHO ARE CONNECTED WITH THE DONOR

The trustees of any trust (including a protective or discretionary trust) which my attorney[s] consider[s] to be wholly or partly for the benefit of any person who is related to me are persons 'connected with' me for the purpose of making gifts of my property in accordance with s 3(5) of the Enduring Powers of Attorney Act 1985.[1]

1 Section 3(5) of the Enduring Powers of Attorney Act 1985 authorises an attorney to make gifts of the donor's property to 'persons (including himself) who are related to or connected with the donor'. The Act does not define the expressions 'related to' or 'connected with'.

7 EPA CLAUSE DEFINING 'SEASONAL'

The word 'seasonal' in s 3(5) of the Enduring Powers of Attorney Act 1985 includes the end of one tax year and the beginning of another [regardless of whether they occur during Easter in any year].[1]

1 Section 3(5) of the Enduring Powers of Attorney Act 1985 authorises an attorney to make gifts 'of a seasonal nature or at a time, or on an anniversary, of a birth or marriage'. The word 'seasonal' is not defined in the Act. The gift must still, of course, be 'not unreasonable'.

8 EPA CLAUSE DEFINING 'ANNIVERSARY OF A BIRTH'

For the purposes of s 3(5) of the Enduring Powers of Attorney Act 1985, my attorneys may make gifts on the anniversary of my birth to persons (including themselves) who are related to or connected with me, in addition to [or instead of] making gifts on the anniversary of the recipient's birth.[1]

1 Section 3(5) of the Enduring Powers of Attorney Act 1985 authorises an attorney to 'make gifts of a seasonal nature or at a time, or on an anniversary, of a birth or marriage, to persons (including himself) who are related to or connected with the donor'. The Act does not specifically state that the anniversary of the birth or marriage should be that of the recipient. The value of any such gift must, of course, be 'not unreasonable having regard to all the circumstances and in particular the size of the donor's estate'.

9 EPA CLAUSE IN WHICH THE DONOR AUTHORISES THE MAKING OF GIFTS FOR TAX-PLANNING PURPOSES

If this instrument is registered or is in the process of being registered, my attorneys may apply to the Court of Protection for an order authorising them to act so as to benefit themselves or other persons otherwise than in accordance with s 3(4) and (5) of the Enduring Powers of Attorney Act 1985, and I approve of taking whatever steps are necessary or expedient to reduce the amount of tax payable during my lifetime or on my death.[1]

1 Where an EPA is registered, the Court of Protection may authorise the attorney to act so as to benefit himself or other persons than the donor otherwise than in accordance with s 3(4) and (5) of the Act, but subject to any conditions or restrictions contained in the instrument: Enduring Powers of Attorney Act 1985, s 8(2)(e). See, generally, 'Registered enduring powers of attorney' at p 114 above. If the instrument is in the process of being registered, the attorneys could apply to the court for an order under s 5 of the Act, whereby it can exercise its powers under s 8(2). The confirmation by the donor at the end of this clause to the effect that he or she would take whatever steps are necessary or expedient to reduce the amount of tax payable is a convenient way of avoiding any questions 'as to what the donor of the power might at any time be expected to do': see Enduring Powers of Attorney Act 1985, s 13(2).

10 EPA CLAUSE RESTRICTING THE VALUE OF THE GIFTS MADE BY AN ATTORNEY IN ANY ONE YEAR

My attorney may make gifts of my property in accordance with s 3(5) of the Enduring Powers of Attorney Act 1985, provided that the value of all such gifts made in any one year does not exceed [£15,000].[1]

1 Section 3(5) of the Enduring Powers of Attorney Act 1985 authorises the attorney to make gifts of the donor's property in certain circumstances, 'subject to any conditions or restrictions contained in the instrument'. This clause imposes a restriction as to quantum.

11 APPLICATION FOR AN ORDER OR DIRECTION AUTHORISING GIFTS TO BE MADE FROM THE ESTATE OF THE DONOR OF A REGISTERED EPA[1]

Court of Protection/Public Trust Office
Enduring Powers of Attorney Act 1985
In the matter of a power given by
.... (a donor)
to .... (attorney)
and .... (attorney)

General form of application

(I)/(We) .... *(full name(s) of attorney(s))* ....
of .... *(address(es) including postcode(s))* ....
apply for an order or directions:

(1)   that, pursuant to s 8(2)(e) of the Enduring Powers of Attorney Act 1985, (I)/(we) may be authorised to dispose of the property of the donor by way of gifts otherwise than in accordance with s 3(4) and (5) of the Act; and that

(2)   the costs of and incidental to this application may be provided for out of the donor's estate;

and for any directions which are necessary as a result of (my)/(our) application.

The grounds on which (I)/(we) make this application are set out in the affidavit sworn by (me)/(us) on *(date)* which accompanies this application.[2]

Signed .... Dated ....
Address where notices should be sent ....
....

---

1 This precedent is based on Form EP3, 'General form of application', in Sch 1 to the Court of Protection (Enduring Powers of Attorney) Rules 1994 (SI 1994/3047). See, generally, p 114 above.

2 For an example of an affidavit in support of such an application, see Precedent 13 below.

---

12 AFFIDAVIT IN SUPPORT OF AN APPLICATION TO THE COURT OF PROTECTION FOR AN ORDER AUTHORISING GIFTS TO BE MADE OUT OF THE ESTATE OF THE DONOR OF A REGISTERED ENDURING POWER OF ATTORNEY[1]

Filed on behalf of:
Deponent:
Affidavit No.
Date sworn:

COURT OF PROTECTION   No.

ENDURING POWERS OF ATTORNEY ACT 1985
IN THE MATTER OF A POWER GIVEN BY

.... (A DONOR)
TO .... (ATTORNEY)

I *(attorney's full name)* of *(attorney's address and occupation or description)* MAKE OATH and say as follows:

(1) I am the attorney for my mother (*donor's full name*) under an enduring power which was registered with the court on (*date*). 'Exhibit 1' is a copy of the registered power.

(2) I make this affidavit in support of my application for an order under s 8(2)(e) of the Enduring Powers of Attorney Act 1985 authorising me to make gifts of my mother's property otherwise than in accordance with s 3(5) of that Act.

(3) The purpose of the proposed gifts is to reduce the amount of inheritance tax payable when my mother dies by making some potentially exempt transfers during her lifetime.

(4) My mother was born on (*date of birth*), and I understand that the actuarial life expectancy of a woman of her age is (*number*) years.

(5) 'Exhibit 2' is a medical certificate in Form CP3 completed by my mother's GP who is of the opinion that she is incapable, by reason of mental disorder, of managing and administering her property and affairs.[2] The GP also expresses the opinion that, although my mother is suffering from dementia, her general health is good, and that she could live for another five to ten years.

(6) 'Exhibit 3' is a 'family tree' which contains details of the full names and dates of birth of all the members of our immediate family.

(7) 'Exhibit 4' is a copy of my mother's last will executed on (*date*),[3] in which she has given her residuary estate to her children, including myself, in equal shares. It is proposed that these gifts of residue should be partially accelerated.

(8) For the last (*number*) years my mother has been living at (*name and address of residential care home*), a residential care home which accommodates (*number*) residents and specialises in caring for people suffering from dementia.

(9) The fees at the home are currently £ ...... a week, or £ ...... a year, and they are generally reviewed in (*month*). The fees are my mother's only outgoings.

(10) 'Exhibit 5' is a statement of my mother's present capital assets which amount in total to £ ......

(11) 'Exhibit 6' is a statement of my mother's current annual income and an assessment of her liability to income tax.

(12) I am advised by the solicitors acting in this matter that if my mother were to die today the inheritance tax payable on her death would amount to approximately £ ......

(13) I believe that if my mother were not suffering from mental disorder she would wish to reduce the amount of inheritance tax payable on her death and that, if she were properly and independently advised by a solicitor or accountant, she would not only make full use of all the available exemptions but would also make potentially exempt transfers of capital.

(14) I apply to the court for an order authorising me on my mother's behalf to make the following gifts from her estate or such other gifts as the court may direct:

Donee   Relationship to Donor   Amount

(15) 'Exhibit 7' contains particulars of the current resources of each of the proposed donees.

(16) The effect of the proposed gifts is that, if my mother were to live for another seven years, the amount of inheritance tax payable on her death would have been reduced from £ ...... to £ ......, based on the current nil rate band and rate of tax.

(17) 'Exhibit 8' gives an illustration of the effect that the proposed gifts will have on my mother's income. I am satisfied that they will not adversely affect her standard of living or care, and that there will be sufficient capital in her estate to meet any shortfall between her income and outgoings for the rest of her life.

Sworn by *(full name of applicant)*
at
this   day of   19

Before me

---

1 The application itself should be made in Form EP3 (General Form of Application): see Chapter 9, p 245 below. For the Court of Protection's requirements with regard to the contents of the affidavit, see Procedure Note PN9. The affidavit must conform with the requirements of the Practice Direction issued by the Master of the Court of Protection on 15 August 1984 ([1984] 1 WLR 1171, [1984] 3 All ER 128) following the Practice Direction issued by the Lord Chief Justice on 21 July 1983. In particular, attention is drawn to the marking at the top right-hand corner of the first page of the affidavit, and also on the backsheet. Where space allows, the first page of each exhibit should be marked in the same way as the affidavit. The affidavit must not be bound with a thick plastic strip or anything else which would hamper filing. The exhibits must not be bound up with, or otherwise attached to, the affidavit.

2 The court will require the original Form Med 3, not a photocopy, it being the rule that primary evidence is preferred to secondary evidence.

3 Note Principle 16.01, Commentary 4, at p 330 of The Law Society, *The Guide to the Professional Conduct of Solicitors* (6th edition, 1993): 'Whether a solicitor should disclose the contents of a will during the testator's lifetime to the donee of a power of attorney granted by the testator, will depend upon the extent to which the power of attorney enables the donee to stand in the place of the testator. Where there is an ordinary power of attorney in force it should be possible to obtain the donor's consent as he or she will have mental capacity. An enduring power of attorney will not be effective following incapacity until it is registered. Once registered, if the power is silent on the subject of disclosure, it is necessary to obtain a decision from the Court of Protection as to whether the will can be disclosed'.

13 LETTER TO THE PUBLIC TRUST OFFICE FOR A DIRECTION TO MAKE SMALL GIFTS ON BEHALF OF A PATIENT[1]

Public Trust Office
Protection Division
Stewart House
24 Kingsway
London WC2B 6JX

(*Address*)
(*Reference*)
(*Date*)

Dear Sirs

(*Patient's full name and matter number*)

The Receiver proposes to make the following gifts on the Patient's behalf subject to obtaining a direction from the Public Trustee:

Proposed Donee	Relationship	Proposed Amount
......	.....	.....
......	.....	.....
......	.....	.....

The purpose of the gifts is to make use of the annual inheritance tax exemption(s) for the year(s) (*tax year(s)*).

As you will appreciate, the proposed gifts are insignificant in the context of the Patient's assets as a whole, and the Receiver intends to make them out of (income)/ (capital) surplus to the Patient's requirements. The Receiver is satisfied that, if the gifts are authorised, the Patient's standard of living and personal care will not be adversely affected in any way.

The Receiver believes that, if the Patient were mentally capable and properly advised, (he)/(she) would make the proposed gift(s) personally.

We look forward to receiving a direction to proceed.

Yours faithfully

---

1 Under r 6(1)(g) of the Court of Protection Rules 1994 (SI 1994/3046), the Public Trustee can give a direction authorising the making of a gift of a patient's property if the proposed gift is:
   • payable out of surplus income or capital; and
   • insignificant in the context of the patient's assets as a whole; and
   • for a sum not more than £15,000.
   If the proposed gift does not fall within all three of these parameters, a formal application should be made to the Court of Protection for an order under the Mental Health Act 1983, s 96(1)(d).
   See, generally, 'Receivership' at p 115 above.

14 APPLICATION TO THE COURT OF PROTECTION FOR AN ORDER TO MAKE GIFTS FROM A PATIENT'S ESTATE[1]

COURT OF PROTECTION

19   no.

IN THE MATTER OF   A PATIENT

I .... *(full name of applicant)* ....
of .... *(applicant's address, including postcode)* ....
the receiver in this matter[2]
apply to the Court of Protection for an order that:

(1)   pursuant to s 96(1)(d) of the Mental Health Act 1983 I may be authorised to make gifts of the patient's property on the terms set out in the affidavit[3] sworn by me on *(date)* or in such other terms as the court may think fit; and that

(2)   the costs of and incidental to this application may be provided for out of the patient's estate,

and for any directions which are necessary as a result of my application.

Applicant's signature ....
Date ....

[OR]

Solicitors for the applicant:
of ....

---

1 This form is based on Court of Protection Form CP9, 'General Form of Application' (Form B in the Schedule to the Court of Protection Rules 1994 (SI 1994/3046) which is reproduced in Chapter 10, at p 285. For gifts from the estate of a patient under Part VII of the Mental Health Act 1983, see, generally, pp 115–117 above.

2 An application for a gift of patient's property can only by made by the persons having locus standi under r 20 of the Court of Protection Rules 1994 (SI 1994/3046).

3 The precedent of the affidavit in support (Precedent 12 at p 134 above), which relates to an application to make gifts from the estate of the donor of a registered EPA, can be adapted accordingly.

CHAPTER 6: RESIDENTIAL AND NURSING HOME CONTRACTS

INDEX

Text

Precedents

Clauses

RESIDENTIAL AND NURSING HOME CONTRACTS

TEXT

Introduction

There almost seems to have been a conspiracy to keep the negotiation and drafting of residential and nursing home contracts as far away from lawyers as possible. Where such contracts do exist, most have been drawn up by the home owners themselves from precedents supplied either by their professional associations or by local authority social services departments. They are usually presented to prospective residents or patients as an immutable fait accompli, and tend to be weighted heavily in favour of the home owners.[1] However, looking through the journals, books, reports and precedents in any well-stocked law library, a distinct impression emerges that during the last ten or twenty years practising and academic lawyers alike have shown a singular lack of interest in care home contracts. The loser, of course, is the elderly client. People in residential care have few clearly defined legal rights, and the practices in some homes leave them with little control over their affairs and may even lead to the denial of basic liberties.[2]

This chapter only considers contracts between the proprietors and residents or patients. There is little difference between a residential care home contract and a nursing home contract. Both types of home provide residential accommodation with board and personal care. A nursing home simply provides nursing care too.[3]

It is beyond the scope of this book to examine the contracts between local authorities as the purchasers, and care homes as the providers, of services. The documentation, policies and methods of negotiation[4] differ considerably from one county or metropolitan borough council to another, and a selection of precedents can be found in *Purchase of Service: Practice Guidance and Practice Material for Social Services Departments and Other Agencies* (Department of Health Social Services Directorate, 1991), and *Guidance on Contracting for Residential and Nursing Home Care* (Association of Metropolitan Authorities, 1994).[5]

The community care regime introduced on 1 April 1993 may have inadvertently diminished the ability of a resident or patient to contract with the service providers,[6] and it is not entirely clear whether a resident could bring an action for breach of a contract for his or her care made between the local social services department and the proprietors of the home.[7] Tripartite contracts between local authority, home and resident run the risk of merely paying lip-service to residents' rights, and the Consumers' Association has suggested that the key relationship is really between the home and the resident, and that the local authority's role should be purely facilitatory and regulatory in order to service that relationship.[8]

1 See, generally, the Consumers' Association policy paper, *Contracting for Residential Care: Individual Contracts for Older People in Residential Care and Nursing Homes* (June 1992), pp 3 and 4.

2 See, generally, National Institute for Social Work, Wagner Development Group, *Security of Tenure in Residential Homes: Code for a Contract* (1993), p 1, 'Why is a code for a contract needed?'.

3 For a discussion of the respective meanings of 'personal care' and 'nursing care', see Richard Jones, *Registered Home Act Manual* (Sweet & Maxwell, 1989).

4 Compare *R v Newcastle upon Tyne City Council ex parte Dixon* [1994] COD 217, reported in *The Independent* on 21 October 1993 under the heading 'Care services contract lawful', and *R v Cleveland County Council ex parte Cleveland Care Homes Association* [1994] COD 221, reported in *The Independent* on 30 December 1993 under the heading 'Care home contracts unlawful'.

5 Copies may be obtained from the Association of Metropolitan Authorities, 35 Great Smith Street, London SW1P 3BJ (tel: 0171 222 8100), priced £10.

6 Alison Brammer, 'The Registered Homes Act 1984: Safeguards the Elderly?' (1994) *Journal of Social Welfare and Family Law* 424–437, at p 434.

7 *Tweddle v Atkinson* (1861) B&S 393. See also the National Health Service and Community Care Act 1990, s 42(4).

8 Consumers' Association, *Contracting for Residential Care: Individual Contracts for Older People in Residential Care and Nursing Homes* (June 1992), p 8.

Format and contents

There is no legal requirement that residential care homes and nursing homes should enter into written contracts with individual residents.[1] However, *Home Life: A Code of Practice for Residential Care*, which enjoys almost semi-statutory status,[2] recommends that, before applying for admission to a residential care home, prospective residents should be given a clear statement of the terms and conditions under which the accommodation is offered. The statement should include the following information:

- the level of fees, time and method of payment, whether in advance or in arrears;
- the services covered by the fees;
- extra services which are charged separately (these should not include any essential facilities);
- procedure for increasing fees when this is necessary (increases should not normally exceed the prevailing rate of inflation);
- the personal items which the resident will be expected to provide for himself or herself;
- information regarding the home's policy on pets;
- the terms under which the resident can vacate the accommodation temporarily;
- the circumstances in which the resident might be asked to leave;
- procedure on either side for terminating the agreement or giving notice of changes;
- statement of insurance of the home and responsibility for insuring personal valuables (amounts of cover for residents' property should be made clear and details of insurers given);

- a statement to the effect that the home is registered as a residential care home by the local authority which is responsible for seeing that standards are maintained;
- a statement to the effect that the home is not registered as a nursing home by the health authority, unless dual registration is in force, in which case the situation should be explained;
- procedure for making complaints to the proprietor and information on how to contact the registration authority in the case of unresolved complaints;
- procedure on the death of a resident (this should take into account the known wishes of the resident and his social and cultural traditions).

In its *Code for a Contract*, the National Institute for Social Work[3] suggests that the contract between the home and the resident should consist of three elements – or perhaps three separate documents:[4]

- **Accommodation and services**. This is the main part of the contract or 'occupancy agreement' and should set out the terms of occupancy and the rights of residents to accommodation and related services. It should contain the substantive terms and conditions recommended above by *Home Life*.
- **Operational policies**. The second part of the contract should include all the policies and procedures for running the home, and can either be appended to the main document or contained in a separate residents' handbook. There should be policy statements on, for example: user involvement; catering; visitors; house rules; complaints procedures; equal opportunities; harassment; arrears; repairs and maintenance procedures; health and safety; drugs and medicine; and restraint.
- **Care and support services**. The third part of the contract should include the resident's individual care plan and outline the principles on which the care and support services are based. *Code for a Contract* suggests that the home's 'philosophy of care' should include statements on privacy, dignity, independence, choice, rights, and fulfilment.[5]

The Consumer Association in its policy paper *Contracting for Residential Care*[6] has also recommended a three-tier contract broadly fulfilling the functions described above. It suggests that contracts on audio tape (for blind people), in large print (for partially sighted people) and in translation (for ethnic minorities) would improve their accessibility to these groups of people.[7]

---

1 There does not have to be a written contract in order for a contractual relationship to exist between the resident and the home. If there is valuable consideration – for example, money changing hands in exchange for accommodation, board and care – a contract exists.

2 Report of a working party chaired by Kina, Lady Avebury, Centre for Policy on Ageing, London (1984), pp 19–20, para 2.2. Although *Home Life* has no formal legal status, the then Secretaries of State for Social Services and for Wales asked local authorities, in carrying out their duties in relation to residential care homes, to regard *Home Life* in the same light as the general guidance issued from time to time under the Local Authority Social Services Act 1970, s 7: *Home Life*, p 7, Foreword by the Secretaries of State.

3 National Institute for Social Work, Wagner Development Group, *Security of Tenure in Residential Homes: Code for a Contract* (1993). Copies of the Code may be obtained from the National Institute for Social Work, 5 Tavistock Place, London WC1H 9SN (tel 0171 387 9681), priced £4.

4 See, for example, the three separate documents issued by the British Federation of Care Home Proprietors, reproduced as Precedent 3 at pp 151–156 below.

5 These six values were identified by the Department of Health Social Services Inspectorate in *Homes are for Living In* (HMSO, 1989).

6 Consumers' Association policy paper, Kevin Steele (ed.), *Contracting for Residential Care: Individual Contracts for Older People in Residential Care and Nursing Homes*, (June 1992). Copies may be obtained from the Consumers' Association, 2 Marylebone Road, London NW1 4DX, priced £10.

7 *Ibid*, p 1.

Unfair terms

The effect of s 2 of the Unfair Contracts Terms Act 1977 is that: (1) a home cannot exclude or restrict liability for death or personal injury resulting from negligence; (2) in the case of any other loss or damage, it cannot exclude or restrict liability unless the restriction is reasonable; and (3) a resident's agreement to or awareness of a contract term purporting to exclude or restrict liability should not be taken as indicating his or her voluntary acceptance of any risk. Section 3(2)(b) provides that home owners cannot by reference to any contract term claim to be entitled to provide something substantially different from that which was reasonably expected, or to render no performance of their contractual obligations at all.[1]

The Unfair Terms in Consumer Contracts Regulations 1994[2] require all contracts to be drafted in plain, intelligible language.[3] Schedule 3 to the Regulations provides an indicative and illustrative list of terms which may be regarded as unfair. These include terms which have the object or effect of enabling the home to alter the terms of the contract unilaterally without a valid reason which is specified in the contract (for example, it is a very common, if not universal, practice in residential care home contracts to allow the home to raise the fees unilaterally), or enabling the home to terminate a contract of indeterminate duration without reasonable notice, except where there are serious grounds for doing so.

1 For a more detailed discussion on the unfair terms legislation in the context of residential care and nursing home contracts, see the Consumers' Association policy paper, *Contracting for Residential Care: Individual Contracts for Older People in Residential Care and Nursing Homes* (June 1992), pp 9–11.

2 (SI 1994/3159). The Regulations came into force on 1 July 1995, but apply to contracts entered into on or after 1 January 1995.

3 *Ibid*, reg 6.

PRECEDENTS

1 CLIENT HANDOUT: CHOOSING A RESIDENTIAL HOME

1. Don't be pressurised or rushed into making a decision you may later regret.

2. Consider all the accommodation options:

- staying in your own home;
- living with relatives;
- sheltered housing;
- residential care;
- nursing home;
- a dual registered home (a residential care and nursing home combined).

3. Contact your GP, social worker, or solicitor for advice.

4. Ask a friend or relative to help you with the decision-making.

If residential care seems the best option:

5. Consider your financial position. Find out whether any (additional) benefits are available. Find out whether social services will let you remain in a particular home if your funds run out.

6. Get hold of a list of homes in the area from social services or consult a care homes directory at the library.

7. Draw up a shortlist of the homes that seem to be most suitable.

8. Contact the social services' registration and inspection unit. Ask to see the inspection reports for the homes on your shortlist. (In some areas, copies of the reports are kept at the library). They're worth consulting because they'll give you an unbiased, expert opinion.

9. Contact the homes you like the sound of. Find out whether they've got any vacancies or whether there's a waiting list. Ask them to send you a copy of their:

- brochure;
- contract, or terms and conditions of residence;
- policy statements, or aims and objectives;
- scale of fees.

10. Arrange a visit. Before visiting draw up a list of the questions you need to ask (see Precedent 2). Take someone with you so you can compare notes later on. Take your time. Don't be rushed. Have a good look round. Talk to:

- the owner/manager;
- staff;

- residents;
- visitors.

11. When you've decided which home appeals to you most, arrange a trial stay for three or four weeks.

12. Don't sell your house or surrender your tenancy until you're entirely satisfied that the home will suit your requirements, that you'll fit in, and that you'll be happy there.

13. Make sure you receive a formal contract which clearly sets out your rights and responsibilities, and make sure you understand it.

2 CLIENT HANDOUT: VISITING A RESIDENTIAL HOME

(1) Accessibility

- Are there any problems with the location of the home? For example:
  - busy roads;
  - public transport;
  - how convenient it is for the shops, post office, church etc.
- How easy is it to enter, leave and move about inside the home?
- What difficulties will people who want to visit you encounter? For example:
  - getting there;
  - parking;
  - seeing you in private;
  - any restrictions on visiting hours.

(2) Accommodation

- What's your overall impression of the **building**?
  - Is it noisy; clean; well-maintained?
  - What's the temperature like?
  - Is it comfortable and inviting?
- How will you be able to make use of the **garden**?
- What do you think of the **bedroom**?
  - Is it too big or too small?
  - Can you personalise it?
  - What facilities does it have?
  - Is there enough cupboard space for all your clothes and personal belongings?
  - Is the bed comfortable?
  - What's the view like?
  - Will you have a key?
  - Do the staff knock the door before entering?
- How easy will it be to get to the **bathroom/toilet**?
  - What aids are there?
  - How many other people use it?
  - How often is it cleaned?
- What's the **lounge** like?
  - Is it comfortable; warm; noisy?
  - Who decides what to watch on TV?
  - Are people allowed to smoke?
- What are the arrangements for the **dining room**?
  - Can you sit on your own?
  - Do people always sit at the same table?
- Is the **kitchen** spotlessly clean?
  - Is it used just for preparing meals, or are the residents' clothes and bed linen washed there too?
- How easy will it be to manoeuvre the **stairs and corridors**?
  - Is there a lift?
  - Are there handrails?

- If there isn't a **phone** in your room, what arrangements are there for you to make and receive calls?
  - Will you be overheard?
  - How will you pay for the calls you make?
- What **fire safety** precautions are there?
  - Fire doors; alarms; smoke detectors; extinguishers; a fire escape.
- What **security** arrangements are there?

(3)   Care

- Does each resident have an individual care plan?
- Will you be able to remain in the home if your health deteriorates?
- Can you retain your own GP?
- How often is the home visited by a physiotherapist; chiropodist; hairdresser, etc?
- Are there set routines for when residents get up and go to bed?
- What are the laundry arrangements?
- Who looks after your drugs and medicine?
- What social activities and entertainments are provided for residents?
- Does the home have its own transport?

(4)   Catering

- What are the meal times?
  - Are they rigid or flexible?
- Is there a menu?
  - Is there much choice?
  - How often is the same menu repeated?
  - Do residents have any say in planning or preparing meals?
- Is the diet appetising and well-balanced?
- Can you have a snack between meals?
- What happens if you fancy a cup of tea or coffee at any time?
- Can you have your meals in your own room if you wish?
- Can visitors join you for a meal?

(5)   Finances

- What are the current fees?
  - When are they payable?
  - Are they paid in advance or arrears or a mixture of both?
  - How are they paid?
- When and how are the fees reviewed?
  - To what extent have they increased over the last few years?
- What services do the fees cover?
  - What extras will you have to pay?
- What retainer will you have to pay if you leave the home temporarily while you're on holiday, visiting family or friends, or in hospital?
- What happens about fees when a resident dies?

- Are you allowed to retain control of your own pension book?
- What will happen if you become unable to pay the full cost of the fees?

(6)   Management

- Is the home registered as a residential care home or nursing home or both?
- Who owns the home?
  - What qualifications and experience do they have?
  - Do they plan to sell up or retire in the foreseeable future?
- Will they let you see a copy of the latest inspection report?
- Will you be able to get on with the owner or manager?

(7)   Policy

- What is the home's general attitude towards residents':
  - privacy?
  - dignity?
  - independence?
  - choice?
  - rights?
  - fulfilment?
- What are the procedures for dealing with:
  - complaints?
  - arrears?
  - reporting faults in equipment?
  - damage caused by residents?
  - drugs and medicine?
  - anti-social behaviour?
  - pets?
  - smoking?
  - alcohol?

(8)   Residents

- How many residents is the home permitted to take?
  - How many are there at present?
- What is the age range?
  - Who has been there the longest?
- What is the proportion of males to females?
- How many are physically frail, mentally infirm, convalescent?
- Is there a residents' committee?
- How much say do the residents have in the way the home is run?
- Do they seem to be happy and well cared for?
- Will you be able to get on with the other residents?

(9)   Staff

- How many staff does the home employ?
- How many are on duty at any time during the day or night?
- What hours and what shifts do they work?

- What is the proportion of male staff to female staff?
- Do the staff seem to treat the residents with respect and sensitivity?
- Are they constantly busy, or are they able to find time for a chat?
- Do they look smart or slovenly?
- What is the home's record on staff turnover?
- Will you be able to get on with the staff?

(10) Terms and conditions

- Are there any particular criteria for admission?
- Can you stay for a trial period?
  - If so, how long?
- Does the home give residents a written contract?

Make sure you are aware of:

- how much the fees are, and when and how they are paid;
- the services included in the fees;
- the procedure for reviewing fees;
- the items you are expected to provide and pay for yourself;
- the retainer payable if you are away from the home in hospital or on holiday;
- the period of notice you need to give the home;
- the period of notice the home has to give you;
- the circumstances in which you might be asked to leave;
- what items are covered by the home's insurance policy, and what items you will need to insure for yourself;
- the facilities for looking after any cash or valuables;
- how to complain;
- what happens if you die.

3 BRITISH FEDERATION OF CARE HOME PROPRIETORS MEMBERSHIP INTRODUCTION PACK

(a)   Terms and Conditions of Residence

TERMS AND CONDITIONS OF RESIDENCE
at

Name of Home	

This document is a statement of the rights and responsibilities of both the resident and the management as parties to a binding contract between them. Full acceptance of the conditions expressed in this document will be signalled by the signatures of both parties (or authorised representatives) in the appropriate place below. Any alterations to this document should be initialled and dated by both parties.

Management and resident agree that it is not the intention to create between them the relationship of landlord and tenant and that legal possession and control of any room or rooms occupied by the resident remain at all times vested in management.

---

1. **NAME OF RESIDENT:** ....

2. **STARTING DATE OF AGREEMENT:**
    (Any part of a day of arrival or departure counts as a full day.)

    [/ /]

3. **TRIAL PERIOD**
    The resident shall initially be accommodated on a trial basis of one month. If at, or before, the expiry of the trial period the resident or management should decide that permanent residence would not be satisfactory, for whatever reason, residence shall terminate on notice in writing to the other party and the resident shall vacate the home at a time to be mutually agreed. Fees will be payable (see 6 below) from the beginning of the trial period.

4. **PERMANENCE**
    Every endeavour will be made to keep the resident in the home even if sick, provided that the doctor is satisfied that the home can give adequate care – with the support of national and community health services, where appropriate. However, management reserves the right to require the resident to leave **a)** if the home is unable to give or to arrange for the resident to receive the level of care required, or **b)** if the resident causes disharmony in the home.

5. **NOTICE PERIODS**
    After the completion of the initial trial period, the resident thereafter agrees to give ....
    weeks'/months' notice of leaving in writing to the home or to pay an equivalent period's fees in lieu of notice (whichever is applicable). Should the resident be assessed as unsuitable to continue in residence, for whatever reason, or should the payment of fees due be more than six weeks in ar·ears, management reserves the right to give the resident or family not less than **four** weeks' notice in writing to terminate this agreement and to require the resident to leave the home by the end of that notice period.

    Management may agree to waive this period of notice, without penalty if, on medical advice, it is decided that the resident is in need of a level of mental or physical care that the home is not capable of providing and relocation to a nursing home, hospital or other source of specialist care on a permanent basis is necessary.

    If the resident is required to leave, for whatever reason, management undertakes to make every effort to find suitable alternative living arrangements before the expiry of the period of notice. However, management can accept no responsibility if these efforts are not successful.

6. **FEES**

    i)   Fees payable at the start of this agreement and in return for the agreed care plan (See 19 below):   £ .... per month/week

    ii) Fees are to be paid one calendar month in advance. Publicly funded residents may choose to pay weekly in advance on the due pension/benefit day.

iii)   Payment is to be made by Direct Debit, Banker's Standing Order, cheque, cash, other

(please specifiy):...

iv)   Fees are normally reviewed annually on 1st .... but are kept under
continuing review in the light of changes in the level of care required by the resident (see 19
below). The fee previously quoted at i) above will be subject to confirmation at the end of
the probationary period in accordance with the pattern of care which is established at that
time in the light of experience.

v)   In addition, management reserves the right to change the fees payable at any time:

a)   if the resident changes his/her bedroom to one of a different standard or category.
b)   if increases in running costs, in management's sole discretion, justify such a change.

One month's prior notice of any change in fees will normally be given in writing to the resident
and/or the family (or other approved) representative.

7.   **LIABILITY FOR FEES DURING TEMPORARY ABSENCE OR WHILE ROOM IS VACANT**
Normal fees at the full current rate will be charged to the resident for the first .... **weeks**
while on holiday, in hospital or otherwise temporarily absent from the home. For any period in
excess of .... weeks, the normal fees will be subject to a reduction of......................**%.**

8.   **RESERVATIONS**
A prospective resident may ask, in writing, for a place in the home to be reserved in which case a
deposit calculated at £...................... per week will be required, payable in advance for the whole
period agreed whether or not the accommodation is occupied by someone else during any part
of the period involved. In the event that the prospective resident does not take up the place, a pro
rata refund may be agreed.

9.   **RESPONSIBILITY FOR FEES**
The resident and/or the family (or other approved) representative who signs this document as
party to the agreement accepts personal joint and several responsibility and liability for all the
terms and conditions of residence as well as the payment on demand of all fees, charges, extras
etc as may be claimed under this agreement. If the resident's affairs are to be managed by the
court of protection, his/her representative undertakes to accept responsibility for any debts
accruing to the home before and whilst the resident's affairs are being so managed.

10.   **FINANCIAL ADVICE**
Residents who are unable or who prefer not to control their own financial affairs are advised
to arrange to receive independent financial advice from a specialist source (solicitor, bank,
accountant, FIMBRA member, next-of-kin etc). Sources of appropriate and independent advice
can be identified by management but neither they nor staff can accept any responsibility for or
interest in a resident's financial resources or estate.

Management **will/will not** handle a resident's money or pension books and may require a relative
or appointee to deal with such matters.

11.   **CARE SERVICES**
a)   The agreed fees will cover the provision of the agreed pattern of care (see 19 below), furnished
accommodation, light, heat, all meals, beverages, normal washing and ironing of machine
washable clothing and linen and aid with personal needs during minor illness.

b)   The agreed fees cover the purchase or provision of additional personal goods and services as
indicated below: (tick as appropriate)

☐ clothing	☐ toilet requisites	☐ stationery	☐ dry cleaning
☐ hairdressing	☐ chiropody	☐ physiotherapy	☐ newspapers
☐ alcohol	☐ spectacles	☐ hearing aids	☐ batteries
☐ private television		☐ incontinence materials	
☐ non-prescription medicines			

c)   The agreed fees will not cover items of a luxury or personal nature, other treatment or care
requested or necessitated by a resident's state of health not provided by the NHS. Items not
covered by the agreed fees should normally be paid for at the time of purchase by the resident.
Alternatively and by prior agreement, management will organise the purchase and/or supply
raising a separate invoice for settlement under normal terms.

d)   Additional charges will also be raised in cases where private transport is required in the
interests of the resident for such things as visits to hospital, dentist etc.

e) Additional and/or special short-term care outside of the agreed standard pattern (see 19 below) will also be charged separately. Any change in the level of a resident's care services will take place only after discussion between the home and the resident and/or the family (or other approved) representative and/or (in appropriate cases) the Local Authority care officer.

12. **USE OF AND ACCESS TO FACILITIES**
All facilities of the home including bathrooms, lounges, gardens, and other communal areas are available for unrestricted use by the resident. Management is bound by the terms of a national **Residents' Charter** (copy available on request) which lays down guidance on the freedoms to be encouraged in and enjoyed by each resident within the home.

In the interests of all parties, the following considerations are requested:

● Family and friends are encouraged to visit at any time. Meals can be provided – by prior arrangement.
● Electrical appliances should be introduced and used by residents only after inspection and approval by management. Use of personal appliances is at the resident's own risk.
● All clothing must be name taped on admission to the home.
● No domestic pets or animals of any kind may be brought into the home by the resident or visitors without the prior permission of the management.
● Residents are encouraged to become involved in the social and recreational facilities available in the local community and to sustain a full social life outside of the home through friends and family. However, advance warning of the intention to be away from the home particularly for meals or overnight would be greatly appreciated. (It may be necessary for any medications which might be required during the proposed period of absence to be prepared.)
● Residents are advised to carry some form of identity in their handbag or wallet at all times.
● Within the terms of the Residents' Charter, management will seek to reach agreement with each resident on the question of the storage and administration of drugs and/or medication for personal use.

13. **TENURE OF ROOMS**
Although every effort will be made to accommodate and retain the resident in the room of his/her choosing, management reserves the right to negotiate the transfer of the resident to other accommodation within the home if necessitated by medical, social, practical or other significant considerations including the repair, maintenance, redecoration or refurbishment of the room or the home. In such cases, every effort will be made to allocate a room of similar or higher standard than that temporarily vacated.

14. **INSURANCE OF PERSONAL POSSESSIONS**
Residents' personal possessions, valuables and money are not insured by the home. Residents are advised to arrange their own insurance for such items. Beyond minimum statutory obligations, management can accept no responsibility whatsoever for a resident's personal effects that are lost, stolen, damaged, destroyed or mislaid through the resident's own actions or lack of care. Residents are strongly advised not to keep large sums of money in the home.

15. **SMOKING**
Either: To comply with fire regulations and for the safety of everyone in the home, residents are required to observe all 'No Smoking' signs and smoke only in designated areas. Residents who smoke do so at their own risk. Smoking in bedrooms is prohibited

Or: The home operates a strict no smoking policy.

16. **ALCOHOL**
Residents are permitted alcohol provided that its use is not individually prohibited on medical grounds or that drinking does not give rise to disruptive, violent or other anti-social behaviour.

17. **VACATING OF ROOMS**
When the resident leaves the home or permanently vacates the room for whatever reason, all furniture and personal effects must be removed with the minimum of delay. If possessions and effects are not removed within the time limit notified in writing by management, they will be disposed of at the resident's expense. A room is deemed to be still occupied and the full fees may be charged until all furniture and personal possessions are removed from the home.

18. **OTHER IMPLIED CONDITIONS**
The official brochure produced by the home (containing statements about such matters as the broad care philosophy, the general aims and objectives, location, the range of care and other facilities available, activities, support services on site, staff, meals etc) should be regarded as an integral part of the agreement binding upon both parties – particularly management. A copy will be

provided on request. In case of any discrepancy between the two, the terms of this document supercede any statement made in the brochure.

19. **INDIVIDUAL CARE PLAN**
As soon as possible after admission to the home has been proposed (or completed in the case of an 'emergency' admission), management will enter into negotiation to produce a mutually acceptable care plan which will define in detail the nature and extent of the care which the home undertakes to provide. This individual care plan, based on an assessment of the resident's care needs, will be produced in consultation with the resident, family doctor and, in appropriate cases, the Local Authority care officer(s). Management will be contractually bound to provide the range of services identified within this care plan which will be kept under continuing review (Please see 6 i), 6 iv), 11 a) and 11 e) above).

20. **GRATUITIES AND GIFTS**
Staff are forbidden under threat of dismissal to accept gifts from residents or their relatives without the prior written consent of the management. Staff are not allowed to act as witnesses nor to become executors of residents' wills.

Gratuities are not to be paid to individual members of staff. Voluntary donations may be made by residents to staff through the management who operate a special fund for staff welfare.

21. **FORMAL NOTICES AND CORRESPONDENCE**
All notices or correspondence relating to this agreement will be delivered to the resident at the home **OR** to the following named representative at the address indicated:

22. **ALTERATIONS AND AMENDMENTS TO AGREEMENT**
One month's notice in writing will normally be given by the management of any intended change to the terms of this agreement.

23. **COMPLAINTS PROCEDURE**
In the unlikely event that a resident (or approved representative) experiences a problem which cannot be satisfactorily resolved through discussions with the management, the matter can be referred to:

Name and address of Authority representative responsible for dealing with complaints

I have read and accept the conditions set out in this document.

Signed on behalf of the home:

.... Date: ....

Signed by/on behalf of the resident:

.... Date: ....

Address: ....

....

.... POST CODE: ....

Witness to signatures:

Signed: .... Date: ....

Address: ....

....

.... POST CODE: ....

Reorder Ref TCR/92/14

(b)   Members' Code of Practice

British Federation of Care Home Proprietors

MEMBERS' CODE OF PRACTICE

This code has been formulated on the assumption that the home owner is complying fully with the requirements of the 1984 Registered Homes Act and all subsequent legislation. Members in Scotland will be complying with all current Scottish legislation.

PHYSICAL

1. The member shall hold a current registration certificate issued by the relevant authority. This must be clearly displayed within the home.

2. At no time shall accommodation be provided for more than the number of residents authorised by the registration authorities.

3. Premises shall be clean, safe and well maintained with a good standard of freshness, decoration and furnishing.

4. An effective inter-communication system shall be provided.

5. The facility of a telephone, with privacy if required, must be available to residents.

6. Residents and their visitors should be allowed the freedom to communicate with one another as and when they wish and must have reasonable access to the person in charge.

7. There must be adequate reception, social, bedroom, bath and toilet facilities.

8. There must be adequate laundry, kitchen, food storage and refuse disposal facilities.

9. Residents must have access to an adequate open air rest area with suitable seating.

10. Physical and mobility aids shall be provided in accordance with the needs of the residents.

11. The BFCHP Membership Certificate shall be clearly displayed within the home and its plaque displayed in a conspicuous place outside the premises.

12. Residents and their relatives must be made aware of the member's association with the BFCHP and its Code of Practice to which the member has agreed to adhere.

13. Lapsed members shall be required to return their certificates and plaques.

CARE

1. A fresh, relaxed, welcoming and comfortable atmosphere must prevail.

2. Privacy and confidentiality must be accorded to all residents.

3. Accommodation and care must be provided with proper regard for the dignity and self-respect of residents.

4. Freedom of choice and independence shall be encouraged with due consideration given to the smooth and safe running of the home.

5. There must be an understanding of individual needs and a respect for opinions and beliefs.

6. A nourishing and varied diet shall be provided with correct attention given to special dietary needs.

7. Drugs must be correctly stored and administered in accordance with current legislative requirements.

8. Residents (or their representatives) shall be provided with appropriate information and assistance to enable them to claim any statutory benefits to which they may be entitled.

9. Terms and conditions of residency of the home shall be set out in writing in an explicit manner. These must not conflict with any policy dictated by the BFCHP.

10. Every endeavour shall be made to assess the needs of a prospective resident in order to ensure suitable placement.

11. A minimum of one month's trial period, on both sides, shall be normal procedure pending a decision on a long-term residency.

12. In the event of a resident proving unsuitable for the home, the member shall make every endeavour to assist in the seeking of suitable alternative accommodation, at the same time exerting no undue pressure on the resident to vacate within an unreasonably short period of time.

PROFESSIONAL CONDUCT

1. The member shall always strive to promote and safeguard the well-being and interest of residents.

2. The member shall take every reasonable opportunity to maintain and improve his/her professional knowledge and competence.

3. The member shall openly acknowledge both the physical and care limitations of the home, particularly in relation to the number of staff employed, their competence and skills.

4. The member shall ensure that all information of a confidential nature, gained in the course of work, shall not be divulged to third parties.

5. The member shall take all reasonable steps to ensure that staff employed have no previous history of work inconsistent with a caring profession.

6. The member shall ensure that adequate, suitably trained staff are on duty in the home at all times.

7. The member shall ensure that staff have the opportunity to maintain and improve their professional skills.

8. The member shall ensure that the terms and conditions of employment of management and staff are fair; that staff have a reasonable workload and adequate off-duty time and holiday allowances.

9. The member shall ensure that anyone on Government sponsored Training Schemes shall not be used as substitute labour otherwise performed by regular staff.

10. The member shall practice maximum integrity in all financial transactions and thereby safeguard the reputation of our profession and the BFCHP.

11. The member shall avoid any abuse of the privileged relationship which exists between himself/herself, staff and residents, especially concerning the residents' property and finances.

(c) Residents' charter

Name of Home	

RESIDENTS' CHARTER

ALL EMPLOYEES OF THIS ESTABLISHMENT ARE EXPECTED TO UPHOLD THE FOLLOWING PRINCIPLES OF CARE IN RESPECT OF THE RIGHTS OF ALL RESIDENTS IN THIS HOME.

1. THE RIGHT OF FULFILMENT:
to assist residents to achieve their full potential capacity, however small, in respect of their physical, intellectual, emotional and social needs.

2. THE RIGHT OF DIGNITY:
to preserve the self respect of residents by
a) maintaining status;
b) affording privacy in space, belief and opinions;
c) recognition, and use, where appropriate, of talents;
d) the practice of courtesy and respect toward residents at all times.

3. THE RIGHT OF AUTONOMY:
to maintain a resident's right to self-determination and freedom of choice, subject to the limitations of group living: the provision of choice, with assistance where necessary, to express wishes and preferences, including external help, (ie, doctor, solicitor, etc.).

4. THE RIGHT OF INDIVIDUALITY:
to respond to the individual needs of each resident to enable him/her to maintain a particular identity in respect of beliefs, opinions and reasonable idiosyncracies.

5. THE RIGHT TO ESTEEM:
to recognise the qualities, experiences, talents and previous higher status of each resident: to get to know relatives and visitors, then to use this information to maintain the morale of individual residents.

6. THE RIGHT TO A HIGH QUALITY OF LIFE:
to expect a wide range of normal activities to be available, to enable a resident to exercise freedom of choice, and to provide opportunities for shopping, visiting, etc: to provide facilities for each resident to follow his/her own particular religious or political pursuits, and to recognise the necessity at times, for privacy to carry them out.

7. THE RIGHT TO FREEDOM OF EMOTIONAL EXPRESSION:
to maintain the resident's right to have normal opportunities to develop personal relationships within and outside of the home.

8. THE RIGHT TO TAKE RISKS:
to allow all residents to undertake activities which contain an element of risk, the criteria being the resident's competence to judge, and the risks to others.

Reorder Ref: RC/92/10

Reproduced by kind permission of British Federation of Care Home Proprietors, 852 Melton Road, Thurmaston, Leicester LE4 8BN.

4 AGREEMENT TO STAY AT A RESIDENTIAL CARE HOME OR NURSING HOME FOR A TRIAL PERIOD[1]

THIS AGREEMENT is made on ....

BETWEEN (1) ....

of .... ('the owner')

and (2) ....

of .... ('the resident')

IT IS AGREED that:

1.   Trial period

In consideration of the fees paid to the owner by the resident, the owner will provide the resident with accommodation, board and personal care [and nursing] at (*name of home*) on a trial basis from (*commencement date*) until (*termination date*) or until the earlier termination of this agreement by either party.

2.   Fees

The resident will pay fees of £...... per day payable weekly in advance on (*day*) each week.

3.   Notice[2]

(1)   The resident may terminate this agreement by giving the owner at least (three days') notice and will be entitled to recover any fees overpaid from the expiration of the notice.

(2)   The owner may terminate this agreement by giving the resident at least (three days') notice and will be entitled to recover any unpaid fees to the expiration of the notice.[3]

4.   Standard terms and conditions

The standard terms and conditions of residence at the home (a copy of which is attached) are incorporated into and form part of this agreement, but where there is any inconsistency between this agreement and the standard terms and conditions, this agreement will prevail.

SIGNED by (*the owner*)

SIGNED by (*the resident*)

---

1 This agreement could easily be adapted for short-stay care. The Consumers' Association, *Contracting for Residential Care: Individual Contracts for Older People in Residential Care and Nursing Homes* (June 1992) recommends a trial period of at least one month for the resident to decide if the home is right for him or her and for the home to decide if the resident fits into the existing community. *Home Life: A Code of Practice for Residential Care* (Centre for Policy on Ageing, 1984) suggests at para 2.1.4 that 'the first two months, or longer, after a resident enters a home on a long-term basis should be mutually recognised as a trial period'.

2 The National Institute for Social Work, Wagner Development Group, *Security of Tenure in Residential Homes: Code for a Contract* (1993), p 7, suggests that 'the law does not take account of trial periods and for excluded licensees the notice during this period can be as little as a week, but for private sector licensees the minimum is a month. During the trial period the contract with the resident could be entered into on a fixed term basis, eg renewable on a weekly basis for a maximum of a month. Residents should not relinquish their previous accommodation during this period'.

3 *Ibid*, p 9, says that 'where there is early termination by either party and the fee has been paid in advance, it is good practice for a refund to be paid as soon as possible after the resident leaves'.

Clauses

5 FEES[1]

The fees are £ ...... a week.

The fees are payable (in advance)/(in arrears)/(half in advance and half in arrears)[2] on the (*first*) day of each month by standing order or cheque.

[OR]

The weekly fees are £ ...... which will be met from the following sources:[3]

£

(*County*) Council Social Services
The resident (excluding the personal allowance)
(*Third party contributions*)

£

The resident [and (*third party*)] agree[s] to pay the proprietor direct.[4]

---

1 *Home Life: A Code of Practice for Residential Care* (Centre for Policy on Ageing, 1984) states at para 2.2 that prospective residents should be given a statement containing details of 'the level of fees, time and method of payment, whether in advance or in arrears'. The National Institute for Social Work states at p 9 of *Security of Tenure in Residential Homes: Code for a Contract* (1993) that 'the contract should show the amount the resident or their representative is expected to pay and the amounts expected from elsewhere'. The Consumers' Association, in its policy paper *Contracting for Residential Care: Individual Contracts for Older People in Residential Care and Nursing Homes* (June 1992), recommends that there should be a statement about the levels of care for which the home has facilities, and the fees which are charged for each level, for example: Level 1 – residents with a need for a moderate level of care; Level 2 – a high level of care; and Level 3 – a very high level of care. The different levels of care would need to be defined in detail.

2 The Consumers' Association, *op cit*, p 13, recommends that the contract should contain 'a statement that the method of payment should be every calendar month, half of the month's fee being paid in advance and half being paid in arrears'.

3 *Ibid*, p 13, also suggests that there should be 'a breakdown of the contributions to the fees coming from the resident (stating whether direct or via the local authority), from friends/relatives, and from the local authority'.

4 National Health Service and Community Care Act 1990, s 42(4) allows residents to pay their own means-tested contribution direct to the home, rather than to the local authority if all three parties agree. The Consumers' Association, *op cit*, p 7, advises that 'for the purpose of strengthening the contractual relationship between resident and home, it would be preferable for the friend or relative's payment to be paid into the resident's bank account, and then paid from there to the home'.

6 SERVICES COVERED BY THE FEES[1]

The services covered by the fees include, but are not limited to:

(1)　residential accommodation;[2]

(2)　adequate light, heating and ventilation in all parts of the home occupied or used by the resident;[3]

(3)　suitable, varied and properly prepared wholesome and nutritious food in adequate quantities;[4]

(4)　regular laundering of linen and clothing [and the provision of adequate facilities for the resident to do his or her own laundry];[5]

(5)　personal care, including assistance with bodily functions where such assistance is required[6] [, and nursing].[7]

1 *Home Life: A Code of Practice for Residential Care* (Centre for Policy on Ageing, 1984) states, at para 2.2, that a prospective resident should be given a clear statement of the terms and conditions under which the accommodation is offered including details of the services covered by the fees.

2 Residential Care Homes Regulations 1984 (SI 1984/1345), reg 10(1)(b).

3 *Ibid*, reg 10(1)(f).

4 *Ibid*, reg 10(1)(l).

5 *Ibid*, reg 10(1)(n).

6 Registered Homes Act 1984, s 1(1) refers to homes which provide 'residential accommodation with both board and personal care'. Section 20(1) states that 'personal care' means care which includes assistance with bodily functions where such assistance is required. The DHSS in Circular LAC (77) 13, para 3, stated that 'The care provided in (residential care homes) is limited to that appropriate to a residential setting and is broadly equivalent to what might be provided by a competent and caring relative able to respond to emotional as well as physical needs. It includes for instance help with washing, bathing, dressing; assistance with toilet needs; the administration of medicines and, when a resident falls sick, the kind of attention someone would receive in his own home from a caring relative under the guidance of the general practitioner or nurse member of the primary health care team'.

7 The words 'and nursing' should only be included if the home is registered as a nursing home.

7 EXTRA SERVICES NOT COVERED BY THE FEES[1]

An account will be submitted to the resident every (three months) in respect of the provision of the following goods and services which are not covered by the fees:[2]

- clothing and footwear;
- hairdressing;
- chiropody;
- non-prescription medicines;
- newspapers and magazines;
- physiotherapy;
- speech therapy;
- incontinence materials;
- dry cleaning;
- transport;
- outings and excursions.

---

1 *Home Life: A Code of Practice for Residential Care* (Centre for Policy on Ageing, 1984) states, at para 2.2, that a prospective resident should be given a clear statement of the terms and conditions under which the accommodation is offered and that such statement should include details of 'extra services which are charged separately (these should not include any essential facilities)'. The National Institute for Social Work, Wagner Development Group states, at p 9 of *Security of Tenure in Residential Homes: Code for a Contract* (1993), that 'where there are likely to be extras the agreement should state this clearly from the outset, and the mechanism for charging extras should be made clear'.

2 The National Health Service is responsible for providing community health services to people in residential care homes on the same basis as to people in their own homes. Such services include the provision of district nursing, incontinence materials, nursing aids, physiotherapy, speech therapy and chiropody.

---

8 PROCEDURE FOR INCREASING FEES[1]

The fees will be reviewed:

- annually to allow for inflation; and
- when required because of any change in the level of care needed by the resident; and
- if necessary in order to comply with any statutory provisions which come into force after the date of this agreement.

The annual review will take place in (*month*) and the fees will be index-linked by reference to the change in the Retail Prices Index (or such other index as may replace it) during the preceding twelve months.[2] The revised fees will be payable with effect from the (*first*) day of (*month*), and the resident will be given written notice of the revised fees at least (four) weeks before they come into effect.

Any other change in the level of fees will only take place after discussion between the home and the resident and/or the resident's family and/or the resident's GP and/or the local authority care officer or advocate.[3]

---

1 *Home Life: A Code of Practice for Residential Care* (Centre for Policy on Ageing, 1984) states, at para 2.2, that prospective residents should be given a clear statement of the terms and conditions under which the accommodation is offered and that such a statement should contain details of the 'procedure for increasing fees when this is necessary (these should not normally exceed the prevailing rate of inflation)'.

2 The Consumers' Association suggests, at p 14 of its policy paper *Contracting for Residential Care: Individual Contracts for Older People in Residential Care and Nursing Homes* (June 1992), that an individual contract should include 'a statement that fees will be reviewed annually, with a general review to allow for inflation (saying what economic indicator the rise will be based on)'.

3 This clause is recommended by the Consumers' Association, *op cit*, p 14. Unfair Terms in Consumer Contracts Regulations 1994 (SI 1994/3159), Sch 3, para 1 states that a contract term may be regarded as unfair if it allows a supplier of services to alter the terms of a contract unilaterally.

---

9 PROCEDURE FOR INCREASING FEES IF THE RESIDENT IS IN RECEIPT OF INCOME SUPPORT[1]

Where the resident is in receipt of income support, the fees will be increased to the new applicable amount with effect from the date on which the Social Security Benefits Up-rating Order comes into force.[2]

---

1 For the applicable amounts for persons in residential care and nursing homes, see Income Support (General) Regulations 1987 (SI 1987/1967), reg 19, as amended by the most recent Social Security Benefits Up-rating Order.

2 The Social Security Benefits Up-rating Order is usually made in March each year and comes into force during the first fortnight in April.

---

10 ENDORSEMENT OF REVIEWED FEES[1]

On the date in Column 1, the weekly fee payable under this contract was reviewed for the reason stated in Column 2, and the proprietor and the resident agreed that the revised fee in Column 3 would be payable from the date in Column 4.[2]

1 Date of review	2 Reason for review	3 Revised fee	4 Payable from	Proprietor's signature	Resident's signature

---

1 This clause and schedule should be endorsed on or appended to the contract itself.

2 The Consumers' Association, in its policy paper *Contracting for Residential Care: Individual Contracts for Older People in Residential Care and Nursing Homes* (June 1992), suggests that the contract should contain a statement that the fees will be reviewed annually, with a general review to allow for inflation (saying what economic indicator the rise will be based on), and individual reviews of the level of care needed for each resident. It also recommends that the contract should include a statement that any change in the level of a resident's fees will only take place after discussion between the home and the resident and/or the resident's family and/ or the local authority care officer or advocate.

---

11 PERSONAL ITEMS WHICH THE RESIDENT IS EXPECTED TO PROVIDE FOR HIMSELF OR HERSELF[1]

The resident shall provide for the following goods and services from (his)/(her) own resources [including the personal allowance]:

(1)   clothing and footwear;
(2)   items of a luxury or personal nature;
(3)   hairdressing;
(4)   chiropody;
(5)   medical requisites (other than by prescription);
(6)   newspapers and magazines;
(7)   spectacles;
(8)   hearing aids;
(9)   batteries.

---

1 *Home Life: A Code of Practice for Residential Care* (Centre for Policy on Ageing, 1984) suggests, at para 2.2, that a residential care home contract should contain details of 'the personal items which the resident will be expected to provide for himself or herself'. This clause virtually repeats the list of goods and services in Precedent 7, 'Extra services not covered by the fees', at p 160 above, and attention is drawn to the footnotes to that precedent.

---

12 PETS[1]

(1)   The keeping of any pet at the home is at the absolute discretion of the proprietor.

(2)   If the circumstances justify it, the proprietor may at any time withhold or withdraw consent to keeping a pet at the home.

(3)   Residents are responsible for feeding and caring for their pets and paying for any veterinary treatment.

(4)   The proprietor reserves the right to charge such sum in addition to the resident's fees as (he)/(she) considers reasonable for accommodating the resident's pet at the home.

(5)   No pets are allowed in the kitchen.

(6)   No pets are allowed in the dining room except guide dogs for the blind.

(7)   Pets must be kept under proper control at all times so as not to frighten or be a nuisance or health risk to other residents.

(8)   Residents are responsible for the cost of making good any damage caused by their pet.

---

1   *Home Life: A Code of Practice for Residential Care* (Centre for Policy on Ageing, 1984), para 2.2, recommends that residents should be given a clear statement of the terms and conditions under which accommodation is offered, and that the statement should include, inter alia, 'information regarding the home's policy on pets'. The National Institute for Social Work, Wagner Development Group states at p 8 of *Security of Tenure in Residential Homes: Code for a Contract* (1993) that 'there must be a clear statement about keeping animals in the home and obtaining permission from the provider before keeping an animal'.

---

13 TEMPORARY ABSENCE FROM THE HOME[1]

If the resident is absent from the home for a continuous period of more than (42) days in the case of hospitalisation or (21) days for any other reason (or in either case for such other period as may be agreed between the parties), this contract may be reviewed.

Unless otherwise agreed in writing between the parties, until the resident returns or this contract is terminated the fees shall remain payable at the full rate during the first (7) days of absence and shall thereafter be payable at (80)% of the full rate.[2]

The proprietor may not let or otherwise use the resident's accommodation during any period of temporary absence without the resident's consent in writing.[3]

1 *Home Life: A Code of Practice for Residential Care* (Centre for Policy on Ageing, 1984), para 2.2
states that prospective residents should be given a clear statement of the terms and conditions
under which the accommodation is offered and that the statement should include 'the terms
under which the resident can vacate the accommodation temporarily'. The Association of
Metropolitan Authorities, in its *Guidance on Contracting for Residential and Nursing Home Care*
(1994), states at p 36: 'Temporary absence from the home may result from hospitalisation,
holiday or other unspecified reasons. It is essential to distinguish "temporary absences" from
individual service contract termination and the grounds on which each might occur. Where a
resident is temporarily absent it may be desirable to retain the accommodation, possibly for an
extended period in the case of hospitalisation. It is essential, therefore, that the conditions are
sufficiently flexible to allow review to take place'.
2 The Association of Metropolitan Authorities, *op cit*, p 36, states that 'the time periods and price
adjustments agreed for temporary absence are a matter for local discretion, but the following are
recommended inclusions:
- absences – six weeks in the case of hospital stays and three weeks otherwise;
- price adjustments – reduction to 80% of the price after the first three weeks.
Providers would not be incurring the full cost of caring for the absent person, therefore
reduction to 80% of the contract price is recommended'. Income Support (General)
Regulations 1987 (SI 1987/1967), Sch 7, para 16, makes provision for the payment of a
retaining fee 'not exceeding 80 per cent of the applicable amount'.
3 The Association of Metropolitan Authorities, *op cit*, p 36, states that 'it is essential also to
include a condition which prohibits the service provider from letting or using the bed/room to
any other party during temporary absences without the written agreement of all parties'.

14 CIRCUMSTANCES IN WHICH THE RESIDENT MIGHT BE ASKED TO LEAVE[1]

The (*proprietor*) is only likely to require the resident to leave the home if:[2]

(1)　the fees are more than (*number*)[3] weeks in arrears;[4] or

(2)　the local social services authority [or (*third party*)] withdraws financial
support for the resident; or

(3)　the home is no longer capable of providing or arranging the level of support
and care the resident needs; or

(4)　the home is provided for a specific rehabilitative purpose and the resident is
no longer in need of such services; or

(5)　the resident's behaviour is persistently antisocial to such an extent that it is
detrimental to the other residents' well-being;[5] and

(6)　suitable alternative accommodation (is available)/(has been found)[6] for the
resident; and

(7)　the (*proprietor*) has discussed the proposed termination of this agreement with
the resident's next of kin, GP and, where the resident is under the
supervision of an officer of the local authority's social services department,
that officer.[7]

1 See also Precedent 15, 'Termination of the contract', below. *Home Life: A Code of Practice for Residential Care* (Centre for Policy on Ageing, 1984), at para 2.2, states that prospective residents should be given a clear statement of the terms and conditions under which the accommodation is offered and that the statement should contain details of 'the circumstances in which the resident might be asked to leave'.

2 Unfair Terms in Consumer Contracts Regulations 1994 (SI 1994/3159), Sch 3, para 1(g) states that terms in a contract may be regarded as unfair if they have the object or effect of 'enabling the seller or supplier to terminate a contract of indeterminate duration without reasonable notice, except where there are serious grounds for doing so'.

3 The Consumers' Association policy paper, *Contracting for Residential Care: Individual Contracts for Older People in Residential Care and Nursing Homes* (June 1992), suggests, at p 13, that the home should only give notice to the resident 'if the fees are more than six weeks in arrears'.

4 The National Institute for Social Work, Wagner Development Group, *Security of Tenure in Residential Homes: Code for a Contract* (1993), p 15, recommends that care 'providers should have a clear arrears policy which minimises the possibility of eviction'.

5 *Ibid*, p 7, suggests that grounds for termination of a contract could include 'serious and persistent nuisance caused to other residents or neighbours, or acts of harassment on the grounds of race, ethnic origin, religion, gender, sexuality, age or disability'.

6 The Consumers' Association, *op cit*, p 13, states that the contract should stipulate that 'no resident will be required to leave in any circumstances until suitable alternative living arrangements have been found'.

7 Residential Care Homes Regulations 1984 (SI 1984/1345), reg 16(2) states that 'where arrangements for the accommodation of a resident are to be terminated the person registered shall notify the person who appears to be the resident's next of kin and, where the resident is under the supervision of an officer of a local social services authority, the person registered shall also notify that officer'.

15 TERMINATION OF THE CONTRACT[1]

This contract shall terminate on the expiration of at least (four)[2] weeks' notice in writing[3] given by either party to the other.[4]

This contract shall also terminate on the death of the resident[5] [although the fees shall remain payable until all the personal belongings of the resident have been removed from the home].

1 *Home Life: A Code of Practice for Residential Care* (Centre for Policy on Ageing, 1984) states, at para 2.2, that prospective residents should be given a clear statement containing details of the 'procedure on either side for terminating the agreement or giving notice of changes'. See also Precedent 14, above, 'Circumstances in which a resident might be asked to leave'.

2 The Consumers' Association policy paper, *Contracting for Residential Care: Individual Contracts for Older People in Residential Care and Nursing Homes* (June 1992), suggests, at p 13, that 'the notice to leave the home will be six weeks from the home to the resident and four weeks from the resident to the home'.

3 *Ibid*, p 11, commends the Australian legislation which requires the written notice from the home to the resident to include information about the resident's rights and the names and addresses of third parties they can contact for independent advice.

4 National Institute for Social Work, Wagner Development Group, *Security of Tenure in Residential Homes: Code for a Contract* (1993) states at pp 6–7: 'We have been advised that residents living in residential care homes in the private sector are legally entitled to at least four weeks' notice. Residents living in residential care homes provided by the public sector, charitable or registered housing associations, are entitled to reasonable notice. Residents living in residential care homes managed by voluntary organisations would be defined as living in the private sector, unless the primary objectives of the organisation are to provide residential accommodation. Residents living in private homes are protected by the Protection from Eviction Act 1977, and residents living in other sectors are excluded from the provisions of this Act. The term "reasonable" is not defined in the law, however failure to give reasonable notice could leave a provider open to charges of harassment. It is good practice to ensure that all residents living in residential care homes have the same rights, and the period of notice should be not less than four weeks for all homes. This period should also apply to residents giving providers notice'. Unfair Terms in Consumer Contracts Regulations 1994 (SI 1994/3159), Sch 3, para 1(g) provides that a contractual term may be regarded as unfair if it enables the supplier to terminate a contract of indeterminate duration without reasonable notice, except where there are serious grounds for doing so.

5 See Precedent 23, fn 4, below.

16 VARIATION OF THE CONTRACT[1]

The proprietor and the resident agree to let each other know as far in advance as possible of any situation which could materially affect the terms of this contract.

[OR]

The proprietor and the resident will give each other (*one month's*) notice in writing of any intended variation of the terms of this contract.

Any variation of this contract must be in writing and signed by both the proprietor and the resident or any person acting on the resident's behalf.[2]

1 *Home Life: A Code of Practice for Residential Care* (Centre for Policy on Ageing, 1984), para 2.2, recommends that a residential care home contract should include details of the 'procedure on either side for . . . giving notice of changes'.

2 For an example of an endorsement of revised fees on a contract, see Precedent 10 at p 161 above.

17 DISCHARGE WITHOUT NOTICE

If the resident leaves the home permanently without giving notice in advance to the proprietor, the date of departure will be treated as the beginning of the contractual notice period, and the fees will be payable at the full rate until the termination of the contractual notice period or until all of the resident's personal belongings have been removed from the home (whichever is the later).

18 INSURANCE[1]

(1)   The proprietor undertakes to maintain in force the home contents insurance policy number (*policy number*) effected with (*insurer*) covering loss of or damage to residents' property by fire, explosion, lightning, storm, flood, burst pipes and tanks, theft, vandalism, subsidence, heave and landslip [and accidental damage].

(2)   The policy is index-linked and currently provides cover to a maximum sum of (£2000) in respect of each resident's personal belongings.

(3)   It is the responsibility of the resident personally to arrange insurance cover for any belongings of significant value such as jewellery, watches, fur, curios, pictures and other works of art.[2]

---

1 *Home Life: A Code of Practice for Residential Care* (Centre for Policy on Ageing, 1984) suggests, at para 2.2, that a residential care home contract should contain a 'statement of insurance of the home and responsibility for insuring personal valuables (amounts of cover for residents' property should be made clear and details of insurers given)'. It suggests, at para 2.6.3, that 'residents should be fully informed about any insurance cover applying to the home which affects their own possessions and, if necessary, should be able to take out their own insurance cover'.

2 Most insurers stipulate a minimum sum to be insured (usually £15,000), and require receipts or valuations to be submitted with the completed proposal form in respect of any individual item worth over a specified sum (usually £1500).

19 SAFE CUSTODY OF RESIDENTS' CASH AND VALUABLES

(1)   Residents are responsible for the safe keeping of their own money, documents such as pension books, and other valuable possessions, unless some severe mental incapacity makes this impossible.[1]

(2)   The proprietor has a statutory duty to provide secure facilities for the safe keeping of the resident's money and other valuables.[2]

(3)   The resident will be given a receipt for each deposit made.

(4)   The proprietor also has a statutory duty to maintain a record of all money and valuables deposited by the resident for safe keeping,[3] specifying the date on which any sum of money or other item was received, returned to the resident or used, at the resident's request, on (his)/(her) behalf, and the purpose for which it was used.

---

1 *Home Life: A Code of Practice for Residential Care* (Centre for Policy on Ageing, 1984), para 2.6.3, states that 'residents should be made aware that they are responsible for the safe-keeping of their own money, etc'.

2 Residential Care Homes Regulations 1984 (SI 1984/1345), reg 10(1)(s).
3 *Ibid*, Sch 2, para 17.

20 REGISTERED STATUS OF THE HOME[1]

The home is registered as a residential care home by (*County or Metropolitan District*) Council which is responsible for seeing that standards are maintained.[2]

It is not a nursing home and is not registered as a nursing home by the health authority.

[*OR*]

The home is dually registered. It is registered as a residential care home by (*County or Metropolitan District*) Council and as a nursing home by (*Area*) Health Authority. Both the Council and the Health Authority are responsible for seeing that standards are maintained.[3] The purpose of dual registration is to enable a resident to stay and be cared for in the same home if his or her medical condition improves or deteriorates.

[*OR*]

The home is registered as a nursing home by (*Area*) Health Authority which is responsible for seeing that standards are maintained.[4]

[*AND*]

The address and telephone number of the registration officer are:[5] ....
....

1 *Home Life: A Code of Practice for Residential Care* (Centre for Policy on Ageing, 1984) states, at para 2.2, that prospective residents should be given a clear statement of the terms and conditions under which the accommodation is offered, and that this should include: (a) 'a statement to the effect that the home is registered as a residential care home by the local authority which is responsible for seeing that standards are maintained'; and (b) 'a statement to the effect that the home is not registered as a nursing home by the health authority, unless dual registration is in force, in which case the situation should be explained'.
2 Registered Homes Act 1984, s 20(1).
3 A dually registered home is registered under ss 20(1) and 23(3) of the Registered Homes Act 1984. The Guidance Notes appended to DHSS Circular LAC (84) 15, at para B7, stress the need for close co-operation between the two registration authorities and the desirability of joint inspections.
4 Registered Homes Act 1984, s 23(3).
5 In *Decision No 79*, Registered Homes Tribunal, the tribunal urged registration authorities to ensure that relatives and friends of the resident are given information on how to contact the local social services. This could be done by providing interested parties with a simple information sheet or a copy of the resident's contract.

21 ACCESS TO REGISTRATION OFFICER'S REPORTS[1]

At the request of the resident or any person acting on (his)/(her) behalf, the proprietor will make available for inspection any report on the home made by the registration authority.[2]

---

1 Registered Homes Act 1984, s 7 states that 'the registers kept by a registration authority for the purposes of this Part of this Act shall be available for inspection at all reasonable times, and any person inspecting such register shall be entitled to make copies of entries in the register on payment of such reasonable fee as the registration authority may determine'. These rights of inspection apply only to Part I of the Act, which relates to residential care homes. There is no similar statutory right to inspect and make copies of entries on the registers relating to nursing homes and mental nursing homes.

2 It has been suggested that all homes should post the latest inspection report in a prominent place and supply copies of it to interested parties because this 'would make available to those most concerned the inspector's report on the home and would enable someone reading the posted report to contrast what the inspector said with the reality around him': Mary A. Mendleson, *Tender Loving Greed* (1974), p 224.

---

22 COMPLAINTS[1]

It is suggested that any complaint relating to the home should be made in the following manner.

(1)   The resident should complain first to the relevant member of staff, who will try to solve the problem as quickly and courteously as possible without recourse to the more formal complaints procedures.[2]

(2)   If the resident wishes to bypass or is dissatisfied with the outcome of the preliminary problem-solving stage, he or she may register a formal complaint with the proprietor. The proprietor has a legal duty to investigate any complaint and to record details of it and the action taken to resolve it in the records which are inspected by the registration officer.[3]

(3)   If the proprietor is unable to resolve the complaint satisfactorily, the resident may refer the complaint to the registration officer whose address and telephone number are[4] ....
....

(4)   If the registration officer is unable to resolve the complaint satisfactorily, the resident may refer the complaint to the Commissioner for Local Administration (the Local Ombudsman).[5] A booklet on how to complain can be obtained from The Commissioner for Local Administration, 21 Queen Anne's Gate, London SW1H 9BU (tel: 0171 222 5622). A local councillor or the Citizens' Advice Bureau may be able to assist in referring the complaint to the Local Ombudsman.

(5)   This suggested complaints procedure does not affect the resident's right to pursue any complaint through the court.

---

1 *Home Life: A Code of Practice for Residential Care* (Centre for Policy on Ageing, 1984) states, at para 2.2, that prospective residents should be given a clear statement of the terms and conditions under which the accommodation is offered and that such a statement should contain details of the 'procedures for making complaints to the proprietor and information as to how to contact the registration authority in the case of unresolved complaints'. At para 2.3.7, it states that 'all complaints should be treated seriously and recorded. They should not be dismissed automatically as without foundation because of the personal characteristics or mental capacity of the complainant. It follows that a resident should be able to bring complaints on any subject to the proprietor without fear of incurring disapproval, and if he is not satisfied with the outcome, he or someone on his behalf should be able to take the matter up with the registration authority'. At para 6.12, it states that 'the majority of complaints regarding the management of a home will normally be satisfactorily resolved by the proprietor or home manager and there will be no need for the registration authority to be involved. Each home should have its own established complaints procedure and this should be outlined in the home's brochure/prospectus. When complaints cannot be resolved internally, the registration authority should be informed of the complaint. All complaints regarding a specific home should initially be made in writing to the registration authority, giving details of any action already taken and with whom the matter has been discussed. The registration authority will then take the necessary steps to investigate the complaint and arrange to interview the proprietor/manager, resident and other people relevant to the specific complaint. Following the investigation/interview, a letter should be sent to the proprietor and manager, resident and the complainant stating the outcome and specifying any action'.

2 The National Institute for Social Work, Wagner Development Group, *Security of Tenure in Residential Homes: Code for a Contract*, (1993), p 14, suggests that 'the complaints procedure should involve a number of simple stages and be written clearly. The first stage should involve problem solving, conciliation and negotiation and it should be made clear to residents and their relatives, where appropriate, how to set this first stage in motion. If the problem or difficulty is not resolved as a result of this process, the resident can take the problem to Stage 2, which is the registering of a formal complaint'.

3 Residential Care Homes Regulations 1984 (SI 1984/1345), reg 17(1) provides that 'the person registered shall inform every resident in writing of the person to whom and the manner in which any request or complaint relating to the home may be made, and the person registered shall ensure that any complaint so made by a resident or person acting on his behalf is fully investigated'.

4 *Ibid*, reg 17(2) states that 'the person registered shall also inform every resident in writing of the name and address of the registration authority to which complaints in respect of a home may be made'. For the circumstances in which the registration authority may cancel the registration of a person in respect of a residential care home, see Registered Homes Act 1984, s 10. Section 11 of the Act describes the procedure in urgent cases where it appears to a Justice of the Peace that there will be a serious risk to the life, health or well-being of the residents. The ordinary and urgent procedures whereby the Secretary of State may cancel the registration of a person in respect of a nursing home or mental nursing home are described in ss 28 and 30 respectively.

5 DHSS Circular LAC (88) 15, para 13 requires local authorities to ask the person registered: (a) to include in the information supplied to residents an explanation about the role of the Commissioner for Local Administration and the method of access to him (the local authority should inform the person registered how a complaint has to be made to the Local Commissioner); and (b) to ensure that the information is readily available at all times to residents and persons acting on their behalf.

---

23 PROCEDURE ON THE DEATH OF A RESIDENT[1]

If the resident dies:

(1) the proprietor will notify the resident's next-of-kin, personal representative, GP and any other responsible person as soon as possible or practicable;[2]

(2) the proprietor will have regard to any known wishes and religious, social or cultural practices of the resident;[3]

(3) the final payment of fees will include payment for the (seven) days immediately following the date of death;

[OR]

(3) the fees will be payable [at (. . . %) of the normal current rate] from the date of death until all of the resident's personal effects are removed from the home;[4]

(4) any fees overpaid will be refunded to the resident's estate;

(5) any fees underpaid will be recoverable from the resident's estate;

(6) the resident's next-of-kin or personal representative will be responsible for registering the death and for removing the resident's personal effects from the home as soon as possible or practicable;

(7) if the resident has no next-of-kin or personal representative, or if the next-of-kin or personal representative refuses to act, the proprietor may contact the local social services department for the purposes of making the funeral arrangements and removing and disposing of the resident's personal effects;[5]

(8) the proprietor may destroy (his)/(her) financial records relating to the resident after a period of (seven) years, and any other records after a period of (three) years, from the date of death.

---

1 *Home Life: A Code of Practice for Residential Care* (Centre for Policy on Ageing, 1984) recommends, at para 2.2, that the written statement of the terms and conditions on which the accommodation is offered should include details of the 'procedure on the death of a resident (this should take into account the known wishes of the resident and his or her social and cultural traditions)'. *Home Life*, para 2.75, 'Dying and Death', contains useful guidelines on caring for a dying resident, but is weak on good practice in respect of the fees payable on a resident's death.

2 If a resident dies in a nursing home, the person registered must give notice in writing of the death to the health authority within 24 hours: Nursing Homes and Mental Nursing Homes Regulations 1984 (SI 1984/1578), reg 8(1). Notification to the registration authority in respect of a death in a residential care home is only necessary if the resident was under the age of 70: Residential Care Home Regulations 1984 (SI 1984/1345), reg 14(1)(a).

3 See fn 1 above.

4 The extent to which fees remain payable after a resident's death is probably the most contentious part of any residential or nursing home contract. The National Institute for Social Work, Wagner Development Group, suggests, at p 9 of *Security of Tenure in Residential Homes: Code for a Contract* (1993), that 'where a resident has died in a home and the resident has paid in advance, any refund should be calculated on a weekly basis and be dependent on when the resident's possessions are removed, therefore allowing the room to be allocated to a new resident'. In *The Law and Elderly People* (1st edition, Routledge, 1990), Aled Griffiths, Richard Grimes and Gwyneth Roberts state, at p 181, that 'in a recent county court case (reported in the *Guardian* on 18 May 1988) the judge dismissed as "nonsense" a claim by proprietors of a residential home of a month's rent from the family of a deceased resident in lieu of notice in advance. The contract required one month's minimum notice of departure to be given by either side'.

5 For the local authority's powers in this respect, see Public Health (Control of Disease) Act 1984, s 46.

---

24 THE PROPRIETOR'S OBLIGATIONS[1]

The proprietor agrees:

(1) to provide residential accommodation, board and personal [and nursing][2] care for the resident;[3]

(2) to allow the resident to occupy his or her room without interruption or interference, except where reasonable access is required for cleaning or refurbishing the room or providing personal [and nursing] care for the resident;

(3) to make available for unrestricted use by the resident all the shared facilities at the home (such as the lounge, dining room, bathrooms and gardens) except during necessary cleaning and refurbishment;

(4) where necessary, to assist the resident with dressing, washing, bathing, toileting and any other routine personal care needed for his or her comfort and well-being;[4]

(5) to order, take charge of and administer the resident's prescribed medication if, for any reason, the resident is unable to do so himself or herself;

(6) to enlist the support of the NHS as necessary to enable the resident to remain in the home if he or she is ill, unless the resident's GP recommends that alternative arrangements be made;

(7) to respect the resident's cultural or religious beliefs and to provide reasonable facilities for the resident to continue to follow such beliefs;

(8) to take into account the resident's needs and preferences in the provision of facilities such as the quantity and nature of meals;

(9) to consult the resident before any changes are made to the home's services, policies and procedures which may affect the resident;

(10) to allow the resident access to his or her personal records;

(11) not without the resident's consent to divulge to any person any confidential information about the resident;

(12) to ensure that all residents have access to an independent advocacy service.[5]

---

1 To some extent this clause duplicates the statement of services covered by the fees: see Precedent 6 at p 159 above.

2 The words 'and nursing' are only applicable in the case of registered nursing homes or dually registered residential care and nursing homes.

3 See, generally, Registered Homes Act 1984, s 1, and Residential Care Homes Regulations 1984 (SI 1984/1345), reg 10.

4 Residential Care Homes Act 1984, s 20 defines 'personal care' as 'care which includes assistance with bodily functions where such assistance is required'. In *Wooding v Secretary of State for Social Services* [1984] 1 All ER 593, the House of Lords considered that the term 'bodily functions' is directed mainly to those functions which a fit person normally performs for himself or herself.

5 The Consumers' Association policy paper, *Contracting for Residential Care: Individual Contracts for Older People in Residential Care and Nursing Homes* (June 1992), p 15 suggests that a contract should contain 'a statement about the role, if any, of an advocate appointed to represent the resident: including who they are to be, to whom they are professionally answerable, and what exactly their role is'.

---

25 THE RESIDENT'S OBLIGATIONS[1]

The resident agrees:

(1) to pay the fees as and when they fall due;

(2) to provide for medical requisites, hairdressing, clothing, footwear, toilet requisites and items of a luxury or personal nature from (his)/(her) own resources;

(3) to permit the staff to inspect and ensure the safety of any furniture or electrical equipment the resident brings into the home;

(4) to report any faults in or repairs needed to furniture or equipment which is the responsibility of the home;

(5) to pay the cost of putting right any damage done to the accommodation, furniture or equipment by the resident or (his)/(her) visitors;

(6) not to remove or change the fixtures and fittings in (his)/(her) room without the proprietor's permission;

(7) not to cause a nuisance or annoy neighbours, staff and other residents;

(8) not to harass or offend anyone in any way which stops them feeling comfortable in the home because of their race, ethnic origin, religion, gender, sexuality, age or disability;

(9)   not to do anything which disrupts another person's right to live in the home or which causes them physical harm;

(10)   not to play a radio, television, record, tape, compact disc or musical instrument so loudly that it annoys the neighbours or other people living in the home;

(11)   not to use any prescribed or unprescribed medication without the proprietor's knowledge or approval.

---

1   The National Institute for Social Work, Wagner Development Group, states, at p 8 of *Security of Tenure in Residential Homes: Code for a Contract* (1993), that 'the obligations of the resident should be clearly spelt out in an occupancy agreement. It needs to be acknowledged that some people living in residential care homes have behaviour problems, and these obligations need to be placed in the context of the care provided and be sensitive to the needs of the users'.

---

26 SAFETY AND RISK-TAKING[1]

Although (*the proprietor*) wishes to give residents every possible choice in how they lead their lives, including the choice to take individual personal risks,[2] (he)/(she) reserves the right to take whatever steps are reasonably needed when the safety of the home or other residents is at risk.

---

1   The health and safety policies of a home usually relate to fire procedures, food preparation and environmental safety. There is a balance to be struck between protecting residents from risks and enabling them to be independent and to live according to their own lifestyle. The Consumers' Association, at p 14 of its policy paper, *Contracting for Residential Care: Individual Contracts for Older People in Residential Care and Nursing Homes* (June 1992), suggests that a contract should include 'a statement that although the home wishes to give the resident every possible choice in how they lead their lives, including the choice to take individual personal risks, the home reserves the right to take whatever steps are reasonably needed when the safety of the home or other residents is at risk'. The National Institute for Social Work, *Better Services for Older People* (1989), p 30 contains a specimen contract with the following clause: 'Residents are free to journey out alone at the proprietor's discretion or with the relatives' approval. The proprietor will not be responsible for the safety of residents outside the home'.

2   The Consumers' Association, *op cit*, states that 'in talking about the choice to take individual personal risks, we mean conscious decisions taken by residents of sound mind, for example someone with arthritis using a kettle despite the risk of burns, or someone with a weak liver drinking alcohol against a doctor's advice. We're not including situations in which a confused resident unintentionally puts themselves at risk, and in which the home clearly needs to protect them, for example a person with dementia who wanders out onto a main road'.

27 GIFTS TO THE MANAGEMENT OR STAFF

The proprietor and staff and their relatives are forbidden to accept from any resident any gratuity or gift except small token presents of a seasonal nature or on an occasion such as a birthday, engagement, wedding, anniversary or retirement.[1]

1 *Home Life: A Code of Practice for Residential Care* (Centre for Policy on Ageing, 1984), para 2.6.2, states: 'Because of the close relationship and dependence between the resident and those who manage and run the home, there is a need for a clear statement about the home's attitude to all personal gifts from residents. Ideally, and in order to avoid all suspicion of undue influence, the proprietor should make known to all staff and residents that it is the home's practice to decline all personal gifts, except for small token presents. Tipping of staff should be barred and a note of this, together with the prohibition on receipt of all other gifts, save those referred to above, should be included in each staff member's contract of employment'.

28 NON-DISCRIMINATION[1]

The proprietor and staff will have due regard to and respect for the resident's age, disability, gender, sexuality, religion, ethnic origin and cultural and linguistic background and will not discriminate against (him)/(her) on any of these grounds.[2]

1 The National Institute for Social Work, Wagner Development Group, states, at p 11 of *Security of Tenure in Residential Homes: Code for a Contract* (1993), that 'residents should know that they will not be unreasonably discriminated against on the grounds of their race, ethnic origin, religion, gender, sexuality, age or disability. An equal opportunities statement should be summarised in the occupancy agreement and detailed policies and procedures should be contained in a residents' handbook'. It suggests, at p 6, that the written agreement should be translated for people living in the home whose first language is not English, and that it may also be necessary to provide the agreement in braille or on audio cassette. The Association of Metropolitan Authorities provides an equal opportunities clause at p 28 of its *Guidance on Contracting for Residential and Nursing Home Care for Adults* (1994).
2 It is unlawful for anyone providing accommodation to the public, or a section of the public, in a hotel, boarding house or similar establishment to discriminate directly or indirectly against a person on racial grounds: Race Relations Act 1976, ss 20 and 22(2)(b).

29 VISITORS[1]

(1) Residents' families and friends are encouraged to visit regularly and to maintain contact by letter or telephone when visiting is not possible.[2]

(2) Visitors are welcome at all reasonable times,[3] and may join residents for a meal provided that the home is given reasonable notice in advance.

(3) Visitors are requested to let the person in charge know when they come and go.

(4) The proprietor will ensure that there are facilities whereby the resident may, if (he)/(she) wishes, communicate in private with (his)/(her) visitors.[4]

(5) The proprietor respects the resident's right to refuse to see a visitor and will wherever necessary accept the responsibility of informing the visitor of the resident's wishes.

(6) The proprietor may exclude any person from visiting the home if (he)/(she) has reason to believe that it is contrary to the resident's wishes or that it is not in the resident's best interests to be visited by that person.

(7) If the proprietor excludes any visitor from the home (he)/(she) will record the fact in writing and will explain to the registration authority the reasons for taking such action.

(8) Residents are responsible for the behaviour of their visitors.

---

1 These clauses are based on the section on visitors at para 2.5.3 of *Home Life: A Code of Practice for Residential Care* (Centre for Policy on Ageing, 1984). See also Residential Care Homes Regulations 1984 (SI 1984/1345), reg 11 and Sch 2, para 14; Nursing Homes and Mental Nursing Homes Regulations 1984 (SI 1984/1578), reg 12(1)(r). The National Institute for Social Work, Wagner Development Group, *Security of Tenure in Residential Homes: Code for a Contract* (1993) states, at p 14, that 'there should be a clear policy on visitors to the home'.
2 Residential Care Homes Regulations 1984, reg 10(2) states that 'the person registered shall arrange for the home to be connected to a public telephone service and shall, so far as may be reasonable and practicable in the circumstances, make arrangements for residents to communicate with others in private by post or telephone'.
3 *Ibid*, reg 11(3): 'The person registered shall keep affixed in a conspicuous place in the home a notice stating the times during which visits may be made and he shall, at the request of any person wishing to visit a resident, make available to that person details of such times'.
4 *Ibid*, reg 11(2): 'The person registered shall ensure that there are facilities in the home whereby residents may, if they so desire, communicate in private with their visitors'.

---

30 RESTRAINT[1]

'Restraint' means containing or limiting a person's freedom of action. In very exceptional circumstances, it may be necessary to restrain a resident for his or her own health or safety, or for the protection of other people or property.

The home has adopted the restraint procedures recommended in the Code of Practice issued by the Department of Health and the Welsh Office under the Mental Health Act 1983,[2] a copy of which will be made available to any resident on request.

1 In *Inspecting for Quality: Standards for the residential care of elderly people with mental disorders* (HMSO, 1993), the Department of Health's Social Services Inspectorate states, at para 3.48, that 'a clear written procedure on the use of restraint is useful'. The National Institute for Social Work, Wagner Development Group, *Security of Tenure in Residential Homes: Code for a Contract*, states, at p 17, that 'there needs to be a clear written policy specifying what sort of restraint is permissible, to what degree and for what clients, and in what circumstances. Where staff need to restrain someone physically, because they are a danger to themselves or other people, firm gentle restraint should be used and not physical force'. *What if they hurt themselves?*, published in 1992 by Counsel and Care, Twynam House, 16 Bonny Street, London NW1 9PG, contains an analysis of the uses and abuses of restraint in residential care homes and nursing homes for the elderly.

2 Department of Health and Welsh Office Code of Practice (HMSO, 1990), Chapter 18. This Code of Practice was laid before Parliament in December 1989, pursuant to s 118(4) of the Mental Health Act 1983. The second edition of the Code of Practice came into force on 1 November 1993. See, generally, Gordon Ashton, *Elderly People and the Law* (Butterworths, 1995), p 83.

CHAPTER 7: SOCIAL SECURITY AGENTS AND APPOINTEES

INDEX

Text

Forms

SOCIAL SECURITY AGENTS AND APPOINTEES

TEXT

Introduction[1]

The most widely used form of agency in the United Kingdom is the simple, sometimes mundane task of going along to the Post Office to collect someone else's retirement pension or other State benefits for them.

If the person entitled to the benefits ('the claimant') is mentally capable of managing his or her affairs, he or she can appoint an *agent* to cash the benefits.

If the claimant is mentally incapable of managing his or her affairs, the Secretary of State for Social Security can appoint an *appointee* to act on the claimant's behalf.

Agency – as distinct from appointeeship – operates on an entirely non-statutory basis. There are three ways of appointing an agent, each of which is designed to suit a particular set of circumstances: short-term agency; long-term agency; and agency where the claimant resides in Part III accommodation.

---

1 In February 1994, the Benefits Agency published an introductory leaflet for prospective agents or appointees: Leaflet AP1, *A Helping Hand: How you can help somebody with a disability claim the Social Security benefits due to them*. Copies can be obtained from BA Publications, Heywood Stores, Manchester Road, Heywood, Lancashire OL10 2PZ. See also Penny Letts, *Managing Other People's Money* (Age Concern, 1990).

Short–term agency

If the claimant is unable to get to the Post Office on a short-term basis (perhaps because of the weather or a temporary illness), he or she can appoint an agent by simply:

- crossing out the words 'I acknowledge receipt of the above sum' on the front of the order; and
- completing the authorisation on the back of the order.

The authorisation on the back of the order consists of two parts.

Part 1, which must be signed and dated by the claimant, says: 'I am the person whose name is on the front of this order book. I am entitled to the amount printed on this order.[1] I authorise .... to be my agent and to cash this order for me'.

Part 2, which must be signed and dated by the agent, says: 'I am the agent of the person whose name is on the front of this book, and who is alive today. I have received the amount printed on this order. I will pay this amount to the person whose name is on the front of this order straightaway'.

---

1 If, for any reason, the claimant is not entitled to the amount printed on the order, the misrepresentation is made by the claimant – rather than the agent – and could give rise to a recoverable overpayment under the Social Security Administration Act 1992, s 71.

Long-term agency – the agency card

If the claimant generally has difficulty in getting to the Post Office and wants somebody else to cash his or her order book on a regular basis, he or she can appoint a long-term agent by completing Form BF73,[1] which says: 'Until further notice I authorise (*name*) of (*address*) to cash my order books at (*a particular*) Post Office'.

The completed Form BF73 must be:

- dated;
- signed by the claimant in the presence of a witness;
- signed by the witness, who should add his or her full name, address and postcode; and then
- returned to the Benefits Agency.

The Benefits Agency will issue the agent with an 'Agency Card', Form BF74.[2] Every time the agent goes to the Post Office he or she should take the Agency Card with him or her. It contains this authorisation from the Benefits Agency to the postmaster: 'We have authorised this person to act as this payee's agent. Please pay the payee's money to the agent'.

---

1 Form BF73 is reproduced as Precedent 1 at p 191 below.
2 Form BF74 is reproduced as Precedent 2 at p 192 below.

Part III accommodation – the signing agent

Part III accommodation is the name given to residential accommodation provided by a local authority under Part III of the National Assistance Act 1948 for people who, by reason of age, infirmity, or any other circumstances, are in need of care and attention which is not otherwise available to them. Claimants in Part III accommodation may authorise a council official, commonly known as a 'signing agent', to draw their pension and other benefits for them. The signing agent is described by his or her office, rather than by name, in order to avoid any administrative complications and delays when the office holder changes.

The appropriate form, Form BR441,[1] has three parts.

- Part A must be signed by the claimant in the presence of any officer of the local authority other than the signing agent.
- Part B must be completed by the signing agent, and returned with Part A to the Benefits Agency.
- Part C is a tear-off slip which should be retained by the claimant. It advises the claimant that he or she can cancel the agency at any time, change the agent, and even draw single payments personally.

Unlike the other agents (short-term and long-term), the signing agent obtains payment by signing the order book as if he or she were the claimant. This means that the claimants no longer have control over their pension books, but the signing agent must give them the full amount of benefit due to them.[2]

People in Part III accommodation can, if they wish, appoint someone other than a council official to collect their benefits.

---

1 Form BR441 is reproduced as Precedent 3 at p 193 below.
2 Penny Letts, *Managing Other People's Money* (Age Concern, 1990), at p 30.

Appointeeship legislation

Unlike agency, appointeeship is regulated by statutory instrument. The current regulation which applies to people who are not hospital in-patients[1] is reg 33 of the Social Security (Claims and Payments) Regulations 1987[2], which says:

'(1) Where –
    (a) a person is, or is alleged to be, entitled to benefit, whether or not a claim for benefit has been made by him or on his behalf; and
    (b) that person is unable for the time being to act; and either
    (c) no receiver has been appointed by the Court of Protection with power to claim or, as the case may be, receive benefit on his behalf; or
    (d) in Scotland, his estate is not being administered by any tutor, curator or other guardian acting or appointed in terms of law,
the Secretary of State may, upon written application made to him by a person who, if a natural person, is over the age of 18, appoint that person to exercise, on behalf of the person who is unable to act, any right to which that person may be entitled and to receive and deal on his behalf with any sums payable to him.
(2) Where the Secretary of State has made an appointment under paragraph (1) –
    (a) he may at any time revoke it;
    (b) the person appointed may resign his office after having given one month's notice in writing to the Secretary of State of his intention to do so;
    (c) any such appointment shall terminate when the Secretary of State is notified that a receiver or other person to whom paragraph (1)(c) or (d) applies has been appointed.
(3) Anything required by these regulations to be done by or to any person who is for the time being unable to act may be done by or to the receiver, tutor, curator or other guardian, if any, or by or to the person appointed under this regulation . . . and the receipt of any person so appointed shall be a good discharge to the Secretary of State for any sum paid.'

Regulation 33 does not refer to enduring powers of attorney, and it is understood that the general approach is to treat an attorney in the same way as any other appointee. So, for example, attorneys may be interviewed to ensure that they are aware of their responsibilities, and their appointment – purely for social security purposes – may be revoked by the Secretary of State.

Regulation 16(2) of the Social Security (Hospital In-Patients) Regulations 1975[3] applies where a hospital manager is the appointee for a person receiving free in-patient treatment in hospital. The in-patient's social security entitlement can be reduced, or completely renounced, by the appointee if a medical officer certifies that the in-patient needs either a specified sum or nothing at all for his or her personal comfort or enjoyment.

Appointees have no authority to deal with the incapacitated claimant's capital, unless that capital represents accumulated social security benefits. If the appointee needs to deal with other capital, an application should be made to the Public Trust Office for a direction, a short order, or possibly the appointment of a receiver.

---

1 See the Social Security (Hospital In-Patients) Regulations 1975 (SI 1975/555).
2 SI 1987/1968.
3 SI 1975/555.

Capacity to handle benefits

Regulation 33 of the Social Security (Claims and Payments) Regulations 1987 does not define the meaning of the expression 'unable for the time being to act', but the DSS's internal *Income Support Manual* suggests that a person is unable to act if 'they do not have the mental ability to understand and control their own affairs, for example, because of senility or mental illness'.[1]

Although there are no formal legal criteria for this type of capacity,[2] it has been suggested[3] that, in order to have the mental capacity to claim, receive and deal with social security benefits, an individual should be able to:

(1)   understand the basis of possible entitlement;
(2)   understand and complete the claim form;
(3)   respond to correspondence from the DSS;
(4)   collect or receive the benefit(s);
(5)   manage the benefit(s) in the sense of knowing what the money is for, and be able to choose whether to use it for that purpose and, if so, how.

---

1 *Income Support Manual*, para 2.1002.
2 Several Commissioners' decisions explore the claimant's capacity in the context of overpayments. In *R(SB) 28/83*, Commissioner Watson held that it is necessary to show that the claimant either knew or with reasonable diligence ought to have known that he possessed certain capital assets. In *CSB/1093/1989*, Commissioner Mitchell held that the key question is

whether, at the time of signing a claim form, the claimant realised that he or she was signing a document in connection with a claim to benefit which could result in the payment of benefit. See also the decision of Commissioner Johnson in *CIS/545/1992*, and the decision of the Court of Appeal in *Chief Adjudication Officer v Sheriff* (1995) *The Times*, May 10: 'If she had the capacity to claim, surely she had the capacity to make the misrepresentation', per Nourse LJ.

3 Ruth Lavery and Laura Lundy, 'The Social Security Appointee System' (1994) *Journal of Social Welfare Law* 313–327, at p 316.

Procedure for appointment

The procedure for the appointment of an appointee is as follows.

- The prospective appointee[1] obtains and completes Form BF56[2] and returns it to the Benefits Agency.
- The Benefits Agency makes enquiries to ensure that the claimant is unable to act for himself or herself. There is generally no requirement that medical evidence of the claimant's incapacity should be obtained.[3] Sometimes the claimant is visited personally by a Benefits Agency officer to check that the appointment is needed, and is not being sought merely for the sake of convenience, and to establish that nobody else is already acting on the claimant's behalf.[4]
- The Benefits Agency interviews the prospective appointee to ensure that he or she is aware of his or her responsibilities and is suitable to act for the claimant.[5] If the benefits supervisor has any reservations about the applicant's suitability, he or she may ask for the names and addresses of possible referees.
- If everything is in order, the benefits supervisor will authorise the appointment on behalf of the Secretary of State.
- The appointee is notified of the appointment in Form BF57,[6] which also informs the appointee of his or her powers and responsibilities.
- Because this is technically a decision of the Secretary of State, there is no right of appeal to a Social Security Appeal Tribunal against the appointment, or refusal to appoint, or revocation of the appointment.
- There are provisions for a 'limited case check' every three years, in which the appointee's performance is reviewed.

The appointment covers all social security benefits. Before 11 April 1988, when the 1987 Regulations came into force it was possible, in theory, to have as many as five different appointees acting on a claimant's behalf.[7]

As soon as an appointment is made by the Secretary of State, the appointee should be advised to carry out an audit of all the benefits to which the claimant may be entitled, and apply for any which have not been claimed. Claims can be backdated for only a specified period – rarely exceeding twelve months before the date of claim[8] – and any further delay could result in a loss of benefit.

An appointee who is temporarily unable to collect the claimant's benefits may authorise an agent to collect those benefits on his or her behalf.

1 Usually a friend or relative who keeps in regular contact with the claimant, or the manager of a residential care home or nursing home. The DSS *Income Support Manual*, at para 2.1011, states that the proprietor or warden of a residential care home or nursing home should only be appointed as a last resort. Note that the Residential Care Homes (Amendment) Regulations 1988 (SI 1988/1192) require that the person registered under the Registered Homes Act 1984 must keep a record showing for each individual resident any money either received on his behalf or directly from him, and how it has been spent. *Home Life: A Code of Practice for Residential Care* (Centre for Policy on Ageing, 1994), at para 2.6.5, states that 'it is most undesirable that a manager or proprietor should take on this role whatever the pressures'.

2 Form BF56 is reproduced as Precedent 5 at p 194 below.

3 Ruth Lavery and Laura Lundy, 'The Social Security Appointee System' (1994) *Journal of Social Welfare Law* 313–327, at p 320, comment that 'the Northern Ireland Social Security Agency has stated that medical evidence should be sought if the claimant is not in hospital (letter, 28 June 1993) or if the social security officer has doubts about incapacity (letter, 1 July 1993)'.

4 DSS, *Income Support Manual*, para 2.1009.

5 People who cannot read or write, who are frail or confused, or who are known to be dishonest or unable to manage money are unlikely to be appointed: Penny Letts, *Managing Other People's Money* (Age Concern, 1990), p 45.

6 Form BF57 is reproduced as Precedent 6 at p 197 below.

7 Gordon Ashton and Adrian Ward, *Mental Handicap and The Law* (Sweet & Maxwell, 1992), p 565.

8 Social Security Administration Act 1992, s 1(2)(b): 'if the benefit is any other benefit except disablement benefit or reduced earnings allowance, the person shall not be entitled to it in respect of any period more than 12 months before that date'.

Revocation of appointment

An appointment may be revoked by the Secretary of State if the appointee fails to comply with his or her duty to apply the money in the claimant's interests. Before revoking an appointment it is usual practice for the appointee to be interviewed, the position explained, and his or her attention drawn to the notes on the reverse side of the certificate of appointment, Form BF57.[1] If he or she is then prepared to administer the benefits in a satisfactory manner, the appointment will be continued for a trial period. The Benefits Agency does not have the resources to visit the claimant and the appointee on a regular basis and, once an appointment has been made, it relies heavily on third parties, for example, social workers, health authorities, and even solicitors, to act as 'whistleblower' if an appointee is allegedly acting contrary to the terms of his or her appointment. Anyone who has reason to suspect that an appointee may be behaving improperly should contact the relevant office of the Benefits Agency and ask to speak to the benefit supervisor responsible for the claim.

1 Precedent 6 at p 197 below.

Personal liability of the appointee

An overpayment of benefits is recoverable from any person who has misrepresented or failed to disclose a material fact.[1] In *CIS/774/1992*, the appellant was the appointee of his mother, who had since died.[2] A Social Security Appeal Tribunal had decided that an overpayment of income support amounting to slightly over £4400 was recoverable from her estate, as there had been a failure to disclose the material fact that she had savings in excess of the prescribed limit of £8000. On appeal, the Commissioner held that there could be no recovery from the estate in view of the mother's mental capacity, and that the actions of the appointee could not be imputed to her. If the overpayment was recoverable,[3] it was recoverable from the appointee personally.

---

1 Social Security Administration Act 1992, s 71(3).

2 Reported briefly in (1994) 1 *Journal of Social Security Law* 3, at p D127.

3 In establishing whether the appointee had failed to disclose a material fact, it must be shown that: (a) the appointee had sufficient knowledge of the material fact (in this respect the position of an appointee can be contrasted with that of a receiver, who should have precise information about a patient's assets (see *R(SB) 28/83)*); and (b) there must be something which 'amounts to a failure to disclose and that necessarily imports the concept of some breach of obligation, ie that non-disclosure must have occurred in circumstances in which at lowest disclosure by the person in question was reasonably to be expected': *CIS/734/1992* (Commissioner J.M. Henty: 4 March 1994: Starred Decision: para 9).

Death of the claimant

There is some confusion as to whether an appointee can continue to act after the claimant's death.[1] It is submitted that an appointment under reg 33 is terminated on the death of the claimant and that, if there are matters still outstanding in respect of the claim, a further appointment should be made by the Secretary of State under reg 30 of the Social Security (Claims and Payments) Regulations 1987.[2] Paragraph (1) of that regulation states: 'On the death of a person who has made a claim for benefit, the Secretary of State may appoint such person as he may think fit to proceed with the claim'.

---

1 The standard textbook, Bonner et al, *Non-Means Tested Benefits: The Legislation 1995* (Sweet & Maxwell, 1995) states, at p 25: 'It seems that a tribunal has no jurisdiction where a claimant dies after having filed an appeal unless there is a personal representative appointed under a grant of probate or of letters of administration, or an appointee duly authorised by the Secretary of State under reg 33 of the Claims and Payment Regulations, willing to continue the appeal: *R(SB) 8/88*. Commissioner Goodman in *R(SB) 5/90* clarifies the decision in *R(SB) 8/88* in holding that the appointment of a person to act by the Secretary of State operates retrospectively. Thus, so far as tribunals are concerned, an appointment after the date of the appeal but before the date of the hearing will be sufficient to ground jurisdiction'. It is respectfully submitted that Bonner

is incorrect in referring to an appointment under reg 33. The two Commissioners' decisions referred to in that note both involved reg 28(1) of the Supplementary Benefit (Claims and Payments) Regulations 1981 (SI 1981/1525), which has now been replaced by reg 30 of the Social Security (Claims and Payments) Regulations 1987 (SI 1987/1968), 'Payments on death'.
2 SI 1987/1968.

Statistics

There is a surprising shortage of information on appointeeship. In the period from 16 January 1984 to 13 February 1984, the DHSS, as it then was, recorded 3898 appointments, making what was then an average yearly total of 46,776 appointments.[1] By comparison, the Court of Protection currently makes approximately 5000 first general orders for the appointment of a receiver each year, and registers about the same number of enduring powers of attorney. In 1988 it was estimated that one per cent of all benefits were paid to appointees.[2] There is evidence to suggest that an overwhelming majority of appointees deal principally with the disability benefits – attendance allowance, disability living allowance, invalidity benefit and severe disablement allowance – rather than retirement pensions.[3]

1 Age Concern, *The Law and Vulnerable Elderly People* (1986), p 104.
2 *Mentally Incapacitated Adults and Decision-Making: An Overview,* Law Com Consultation Paper No 119 (HMSO, 1991), at p 70.
3 Ruth Lavery and Laura Lundy, 'The Social Security Appointee System' (1994) *Journal of Social Welfare Law* 313–327, at p 314, quote the following statistics supplied by the Northern Ireland Social Security Agency: 'In Northern Ireland at 17 December 1991 there were 10,600 appointees dealing with Attendance Allowance; 10,000 dealing with Disability Living Allowance; and 326 with the Retirement Pension. In June 1993, there were 593 appointees dealing with Invalidity Benefit; 5017 with Severe Disablement Allowance, and 17 with Child Benefit'.

Agency and appointeeship: the differences

Agents	Appointees
An agent is appointed by the claimant.	An appointee is appointed by the Secretary of State for Social Security. The claimant's consent to the appointment is not required.
An agent is appointed if the claimant finds it difficult or inconvenient to go to the Post Office to cash his or her order.	An appointee is appointed where the claimant does not have the mental capacity to understand and control his or her affairs.
No medical evidence is required.	Medical evidence may be required.
There is no minimum age for acting as an agent.	An appointee must be 18 or over.
An agent's authority is limited to cashing the claimant's order.	An appointee can exercise all the rights and duties which the claimant has under the social security legislation, for example, claiming benefits, receiving benefits, notifying the office dealing with the claim of any change in the claimant's circumstances, appealing against the decision of an adjudication officer, etc.
An agent must hand the cash to the claimant straightaway.	An appointee must use the cash in the best interests of the claimant or the claimant's dependants.
There are no formal requirements for the resignation of an agent.	An appointee must give the Department one month's notice of his or her intended resignation.
The claimant can revoke the agency at any time.	The Secretary of State can revoke the appointment at any time.
There is no 'policing'.	There is limited 'policing' by means of limited case checks every three years.
An agent cannot sub-delegate.	An appointee can sub-delegate by appointing an agent to act for him or her temporarily.

Proposed reforms

In its report, *Mental Incapacity*, published in March 1995,[1] the Law Commission suggested various changes to the current appointeeship system. Because the regulations governing appointeeship are the responsibility of the Secretary of State for Social Security, the Law Commission did not presume to draft any new regulations itself.[2] The suggested changes are as follows.

(1)   The proposed statutory definition of *incapacity* in cl 2 of the draft Mental Incapacity Bill should be adopted for the purpose of establishing whether a claimant has the capacity to exercise his or her rights under the Social Security Administration Act 1992 and to receive or deal with sums payable.[3]

(2)   Consideration should be given to the sending out of an annual enquiry form to be completed by all appointees, giving at least a broad indication of the items on which money has been spent.[4]

(3)   A maximum time-limit, of perhaps three to five years, should be imposed on appointments, with a requirement that appointees apply for reappointment after that time.[5]

(4)   There should, perhaps, be a specific prohibition on managers of residential care homes or nursing homes acting as appointees for their residents.[6]

---

1 (1995) Law Com No 231 (HMSO, 1995). See also *Mentally Incapacitated Adults and Decision-Making: A New Jurisdiction*, Law Com Consultation Paper No 128 (HMSO, 1993), paras 5.7–5.9.

2 Law Com No 231, para 4.23.

3 *Ibid*, para 4.24.

4 *Ibid*, para 4.25.

5 *Ibid*, para 4.25.

6 *Ibid*, para 4.27.

FORMS

1 BF73 APPOINTMENT OF (LONG-TERM) AGENT

SOCIAL SECURITY

Authority for an agent

I have difficulty in getting to the Post Office. Until I tell you
something different, I authorise the person I have named to collect
my Social Security benefit at the Post Office I have named.

About you

Your surname — Mr Mrs Miss Ms

Other names

Address

Postcode

Date of birth

National Insurance (NI) number

or other reference number
This is on the front of your order book

About the agent

Their surname — Mr Mrs Miss Ms

Their other names

Their Address

Their daytime phone no.   Postcode

About the Post Office
Please tell us the name and address of the Post Office you
want your benefit to be collected from.
If you are not sure of the address, you can ask the Post Office to
stamp the form here

Your signature

Date

Are you sending your order book back with this form?

No ☐

Yes ☐

benefits
ba
agency

*An Executive Agency of
the Department of Social Security*

Signature of witness
This must not be the person you are asking to get your money for you.

Date

Name of witness
Mr Mrs Miss Ms

Address of witness

Postcode

BF73 tear-off

2 BF74 THE AGENCY CARD

Department of Social Security   Issuing office

Payment to an agent - Standing Authority

Details of agent

Name..

Address..

....

To the postmaster

.... Post Office

We have authorised this person to act as this payee's agent. Please pay the payee's money to the agent. Details of the payee and the agent are on the right.

Details of payee

Name..

Pension No, Allowance No or NI No

....

Form   BF 74   7/90

Your benefit - someone else can go to the Post Office

This form is to prove that someone else can get your money for you. We call this person your agent.

What you have to do

1 Keep this form with your order book.

2 Sign the front of each order before your agent cashes it.

Temporary change of agent

Sometimes you may want somebody else to go to the Post Office instead of your usual agent.

Fill in Part 1 on the back of the order, and get the person who goes to the Post Office to sign Part 2.

Permanent change of agent

If you want to change your agent or if you stop needing an agent at all, please let us know. Our address is on the front of this form.

Directions to agent

1 Take this form with you each time you go to the Post Office to cash the order book.

2 Sign Part 2 on the back of the order.

3 Hand over this form with the order book.

3 BR441 AUTHORISATION OF AGENT FOR A PERSON IN PART III ACCOMMODATION

SOCIAL SECURITY

Authorisation of an agent

This form authorises an agent to cash Social Security benefit for a person in accommodation provided under Part III of the National Assistance Act, 1948.

Part A should be signed by the beneficiary in the presence of an officer of the local authority. The officer must not be the person authorised to act as agent.

Name of beneficiary	
Address of Part III accommodation	
	Postcode

Part A

Until I tell you something different, I authorise the following officer of the local authority shown to act as my agent

I authorise this agent to cash my order book for the benefit named below at the Post Office shown.

official position	
local authority	
name of benefit	
reference number	
Post Office of payment	

Signature of payee

Date / /

Part B

Certificate

I certify that Part A of this form has been read over to the beneficiary named above and explained to them.

The beneficiary signed the form in my presence.

Part C of this form has been given to the beneficiary.

Signature of witness

This must be an officer of the local authority other than the agent.

Date / /

Declaration

I declare that the person who has signed this form at Part A did so voluntarily and is alive today. To the best of my knowledge and belief they are not getting any earnings which affect their benefit.

I agree on behalf of _____ local authority to notify the local office of the Department of Social Security immediately if the person —

- dies, or
- leaves the accommodation provided by the above local authority, or
- if anything changes which, according to the notes in the order book, may affect payment of the benefit.

Signature of agent

Official position

Date / /

BR441(OS)

Printed in the UK for HMSO A1569 1366L Dd 8359107 7 91 95M TP (17311)

SPECIMEN

4 BR442 STANDING AUTHORITY FOR PAYMENT TO THE SIGNING AGENT

PAYMENT TO AN AGENT

Standing authority

To the postmaster_____**Post Office**

The person named below is authorised to act as this payee's agent. Please pay the payee's money to the agent.

Details of the payee

Name (in full)_____

Reference number_____

Details of the agent

Official position_____

Local authority_____

BR442(OS)

Printed in the UK for HMSO. 3/90 Dd 8195077 M230 5924

SPECIMEN

_____ **continued**

Notes for the agent

You are authorised to act as the agent for the person named on the front of this form.

■ **What to do**

1 Take this form with you each time you go to the Post Office to cash the order book.

2 Sign the front of the order you are going to cash.
   You can do this in manuscript or by using a facsimile stamp.

3 Hand over this form with the order book.

■ **Temporary change of agent**

Sometimes the person you get money for may want somebody else to go to the Post Office instead. They should then fill in Part 1 on the back of the order, and get the person who goes to the Post Office to sign Part 2.

■ **Permanent change of agent**

If the person you get money for wants to change their agent or stops needing an agent, please let us know.

Please keep this for your information

5 BF56 APPLICATION FOR APPOINTMENT TO ACT ON BEHALF OF A PERSON UNABLE TO ACT

DEPARTMENT OF SOCIAL SECURITY

Social Security Acts   Industrial Injuries and Diseases (Old Cases) Act   Child Benefit Act

APPLICATION FOR APPOINTMENT TO ACT ON BEHALF OF A PERSON UNABLE TO ACT BY REASON OF MENTAL OR OTHER INCAPACITY

Particulars of person unable to act

Full names *(surname first)* .... Mr/Mrs/Miss/Ms
BLOCK CAPITALS please   *(Other names)*

Address ....
(including postcode)

....

NI No. [ ][ ][ ][ ][ ]   Ref No ..../.................Pension/Allowance No. ....

Nature of incapacity ....

Particulars of person applying to be appointed (A person under age 18 cannot be appointed)

Full names *(surname first)* .... Mr/Mrs/Miss/Ms
BLOCK CAPITALS please   *(Other names)*

Address ....
(including postcode)

....Tel No. ....

NI No. [ ][ ][ ][ ][ ]   Age (if over 18 write "over 18") ....

Method of payment

Some benefits can be paid by credit transfer direct into a bank or building society account. This is a safe way of getting the money and may be more convenient. Credit transfer is available for Retirement Pension, Widows' Benefits, Child Benefit, War Pensions, Attendance Allowance, Mobility Allowance and Family Credit. If you would like further information about the credit transfer arrangements, please tick this box. [ ]

Otherwise payment will be made by girocheque or order book cashable at the Post Office.
Please give the official name and address of the Post Office where you wish payment to be made. BLOCK CAPITALS PLEASE.

....   *If you are in doubt about this*
....   *ask the Post Office clerk to*
                                                                              impress the date stamp in here.

Application

I apply for appointment by the Secretary of State for Social Security to exercise on behalf of the person named above any right which he/she may have under the above Acts. No person has been legally appointed to administer his/her estate. I undertake to the best of my ability to give the Department's officer all the information required by him about the circumstances of that person and if there is any change in those circumstances to let him know at once.

I make application on the following grounds ....
(give a full statement of grounds)

....

....
                                                                              (continued overleaf if necessary)
Signature .... Date .... 19......

FOR OFFICIAL USE ONLY

ACT application form completed/issued on .... (Date)   Initials................Date................
Appointment authorised/refused   If authorised, other sections informed [ ]

Signature ....

Local Office .... Date ....19......

[ ] tick when BF57A issued   [ ] tick when NI205 issued   [ ] Leaflet AP1 issued

Post Office Code Number   [ ][ ][ ]—[ ][ ][ ]—[ ]

(To be entered in cases to be notified to either Newcastle or North Fylde Central Offices)

Appointeeship cancelled [ ]   Date of cancellation ....19......   Other sections informed [ ]

Form BF 56

6 BF57 NOTIFICATION OF APPOINTMENT OF APPOINTEE

DEPARTMENT OF SOCIAL SECURITY

National Insurance or Pension

Number 19

Dear Sir or Madam

You have been appointed to exercise on behalf of

.... (name)

of .... (address)

any right which that person may have under the Social Security Act and to receive and deal with any sum which may be payable.

This appointment takes effect immediately. It will end when the person recovers sufficiently to manage his or her own affairs, or may be revoked at any time. If you wish to resign your appointment you may do so by giving one month's notice in writing.

The notes overleaf give some general information and guidance. Especially important are those about claiming benefit and how it is to be used, and about the reporting of any change in circumstances. If you are in any doubt please get in touch with this office.

Yours faithfully

Manager

Form BF 57

NOTES

You are now responsible for attending to the national insurance affairs of the person named overleaf. This includes claiming and receiving benefit on behalf of that person. It is important when claiming sickness, invalidity benefit or severe disablement allowance to send doctors' statements promptly when they are due, and to claim any other benefit, such as retirement pension, at the proper time. Benefit may be lost if a claim is not made within the time limits.

Any benefit you receive under this appointment must be used in the interests of the person named overleaf. If that person is in hospital you should ensure that from the amount of benefit you receive, a sufficient weekly sum is provided to meet the patient's personal needs. This can be sent to the patient or to the hospital authorities or given to the patient on visiting days. Any balance of personal benefit remaining belongs absolutely to the patient, but you should use it to the best advantage of the patient and any dependants, taking into account any existing home or outside commitments.

Any increase of benefit which is paid for a dependant of the patient should be sent to the dependant or spent on maintaining the dependant. If the dependant is a child who is not in your care, the increase should be sent to the person who has care of the child.

If an overpayment of benefit occurs you may be required to repay the over-payment yourself, depending on how the overpayment arose.

You should notify this office of any change of circumstances which may affect the benefit or pension which is being paid, including benefit or pension which is being paid, including benefit for any dependants. A list of changes which must be reported is given in the notes issued with the first payment of benefit or is included in the instruction pages of a pension or allowance book. If you do not have this list you should ask your local office for a copy of the Notes on Sickness Benefit or the Notes on Invalidity Benefit or the Notes on Severe Disablement Allowance.

Examples of other changes which must be reported are:

If the person named overleaf—

- is admitted to hospital, is absent on leave or is discharged from hospital

- recovers sufficiently to manage his or her own affairs

- dies

- has a receiver appointed (in Scotland a tutor, curator or other guardian) by legal authority to administer his or her estate.

You should also tell this office if you intend to be absent from this country for a prolonged period.

10.90

7 BF57A NOTIFICATION OF APPOINTMENT OF HOSPITAL MANAGER AS APPOINTEE

DEPARTMENT OF SOCIAL SECURITY

National Insurance or Pension

Number   19

⌐ .... ⌐

....

....

....

....

⌐_ .... _⌐

Dear Sir or Madam

The ....

....

of the ....Hospital

has been appointed to exercise on behalf of the patient,

.... (name)

.... (address)

....

any right which that person may have under the Social Security Acts and to
receive and deal with any sum which may be payable.

This appointment takes effect immediately. It will end when the patient
recovers sufficiently to manage his or her own affairs, and may be revoked

Form BF 57A

at any time.   The appointment may be resigned by giving one month's notice in writing.

Any other change in circumstances affecting the appointment should be reported, for example, if the patient

- goes on leave or is discharged

- recovers sufficiently to manage his or her own affairs

- dies

- has a receiver appointed (in Scotland a tutor, curator or other guardian) by legal authority to administer his or her estate.

* On the information at present available, benefit at the rate of

£ .... a week from ....

£ .... a week from ....

will be payable on your next schedule.   I will notify you of any future change of rate.

Yours faithfully

Manager

Delete as necessary

6/93

CHAPTER 8: ORDINARY POWERS OF ATTORNEY

INDEX

Text

Precedents

ORDINARY POWERS OF ATTORNEY

TEXT

Introduction[1]

A power of attorney is a deed in which one person (*the donor*) gives another person (*the attorney*) the authority to act in his name and on his behalf. The word *ordinary* is used simply to describe a power of attorney which is not enduring. With one exception, ordinary powers are automatically revoked by operation of law when the donor becomes mentally incapable.

The exception is an irrevocable power. Section 4 of the Powers of Attorney Act 1971 provides that:

'(1) Where a power of attorney is expressed to be irrevocable and is given to secure:
   (a) a proprietary interest of the donee of the power; or
   (b) the performance of an obligation owed to the donee,
then, so long as the donee has that interest or the obligation remains undischarged, the power shall not be revoked:
   (i) by the donor without the consent of the donee; or
   (ii) by the death, incapacity or bankruptcy of the donor . . . '

Ordinary powers are governed by the common law and the Powers of Attorney Act 1971, which implemented the following reforms:

- a simplified method of proof of the contents of the power;[2]
- a new regime for the delegation of trustee powers;[3]
- clearer provisions for protecting attorneys and third parties against the consequences of the power having ended; and
- the ability to execute a power of attorney conferring general authority.

Before 1971 there was no such thing as a *general power of attorney*. The powers conferred on an attorney had to be listed specifically, and usually ran into twenty or thirty clauses concluding with a sweeping *eiusdem generis* clause. Section 10 of the 1971 Act enables a donor to grant a general power conferring 'authority to do on behalf of the donor anything which he can lawfully do by an attorney', and Sch 1 sets out the form of general power required for that purpose.[4]

Since the Enduring Powers of Attorney Act 1985 came into force, ordinary powers have rarely been used in private client work,[5] although they are employed extensively in company, commercial and international practice. Nevertheless, an elderly client may still require an ordinary power, for example where he or she:

- does not want to create an enduring power;
- wants a power of attorney for use abroad;
- wants the attorney to be able to appoint a substitute or successor;

- wants the attorney to make tax-planning gifts beyond those permitted under the Enduring Powers of Attorney Act 1985;[6]
- needs to appoint an attorney for one specific purpose, such as buying a house or obtaining a grant of representation to a deceased's estate;[7] or
- wishes to delegate temporarily his or her functions as a trustee.[8]

---

1 See, generally, Trevor Aldridge, *Powers of Attorney* (8th edition, Longman, 1991); Andrew Long, *Powers of Attorney and Other Instruments Conferring Authority* (ICSA Publishing, 1987); *Bowstead on Agency* (15th edition, Sweet & Maxwell, 1985).

2 For a precedent certificate, see Precedent 10 at p 213 below.

3 See further, 'Trustee powers of attorney' below. For a precedent of a trustee power, see Precedent 3 at p 208 below.

4 For a precedent of a general power of attorney, see Precedent 1 at p 207 below.

5 Stephen Cretney et al, *Enduring Powers of Attorney: A Report to the Lord Chancellor* (Lord Chancellor's Department, June 1991), p 11: 'It was evident that solicitors did not only regard EPAs as a substitute for Receivership. They also regarded them as a substitute for ordinary powers of attorney. We were often told that solicitors hardly ever made these for private clients now'.

6 For an ordinary power authorising the attorney to make gifts, see Precedent 3, Chapter 5, at p 130 above.

7 For a power of attorney given by an executor, see Precedent 5 at p 210 below.

8 See 'Trustee powers of attorney' below.

Trustee powers of attorney

Under s 25 of the Trustee Act 1925 (as amended), a trustee can delegate his or her functions to an attorney[1] provided that:

- the delegation cannot last for more than twelve months;[2]
- the attorney is not the only other co-trustee, unless the attorney is a trust corporation;[3]
- before or within seven days after giving the power of attorney, the trustee gives notice of the power to each of the other trustees and anyone who has power to appoint a new trustee;[4]
- the trustee remains liable for the acts and defaults of the attorney.[5]

The same rules apply to a tenant for life or statutory owner under the Settled Land Act 1925, and to a personal representative, although the persons to whom notice of the power must be given vary in each case.[6]

Under s 3(3) of the Enduring Powers of Attorney Act 1985, an attorney under an enduring power may exercise all the trusts, powers or discretions vested in the donor as trustee. This section is likely to be repealed in the near future,[7] and it is recommended that for the time being any delegation by a trustee should comply with the formalities of s 25 of the Trustee Act 1925.

---

1 For a form of trustee power of attorney, see Precedent 3 at p 208 below.

2 Trustee Act 1925, s 25(1), as amended by the Powers of Attorney Act 1971, s 9.

3 *Ibid*, s 25(2).

4 *Ibid*, s 25(4). For a form of notice, see Precedent 4 at p 209 below.

5 *Ibid*, s 25(5).

6 *Ibid*, s 25(8).

7 The Law Commission, *The Law of Trusts: Delegation by Individual Trustees* (Law Com No 220, HMSO, 1994).

Revocation[1]

Unless it is expressed to be irrevocable, and is given to secure a proprietary interest of the attorney or the performance of an obligation owed to the attorney,[2] an ordinary power of attorney may be revoked expressly or impliedly[3] by the donor; by effluxion of time;[4] and by the death, bankruptcy or supervening mental incapacity[5] of the donor or attorney.

The best way of expressly revoking a power of attorney is for the donor to execute a deed of revocation[6] or a new power of attorney which expressly revokes the former power. However, revocation on its own is insufficient, because the attorney's authority does not cease until he or she is given notice of the revocation,[7] and an attorney who carries on acting unaware of the revocation will not incur any liability to the donor or anyone else.[8]

If the donor is worried that in spite of the revocation the attorney will continue to act, he or she should ask for the attorney to return the original power and all copies of it, and, if necessary, notify every third party with whom the attorney has had dealings. If a power has been revoked and someone who does not know of the revocation deals with the attorney, the transaction between them is, in favour of that person, as valid as if the power were still in existence.[9]

The Powers of Attorney Act 1971 contains several conclusive presumptions designed to protect third parties. Where the interest of a purchaser (*C*) depends on whether a transaction between the attorney (*A*) and another person (*B*) was valid, it is conclusively presumed in favour of *C* that *B* did not at the material time know of the revocation of the power if:

- *either* the transaction between *A* and *B* was completed within twelve months of the date on which the power of attorney came into operation; *or*
- *B* makes a statutory declaration, before or within three months after the completion of the purchase, that he or she did not at the material time know of the revocation of the power.[10]

Where the attorney executes a stock transfer form, it is conclusively presumed in favour of the transferee that the power had not been revoked at that date if the attorney makes a statutory declaration to that effect on or within three months after that date.[11]

1 See, generally, Trevor Aldridge, *Powers of Attorney* (8th edition, Longman Practitioner Series, 1991), chapter 7.

2 Powers of Attorney Act 1971, s 4.

3 Implied revocation occurs where the donor does anything which is inconsistent with the continued operation of the power: *Cousins v International Brick Co Ltd* [1930] 2 Ch 90, CA.

4 For example, a trustee power of attorney usually expires by effluxion of time after twelve months: Trustee Act 1925, s 25(1) (as amended).

5 *Drew v Nunn* (1879) 4 QBD 661, CA.

6 For a precedent of a deed of revocation, see Precedent 6 at p 211 below.

7 *Drew v Nunn* (1879) 4 QBD 661, CA. For a solicitor's letter giving the attorney notice of revocation, see Precedent 7 at p 211 below.

8 Powers of Attorney Act 1971, s 5(1).

9 *Ibid*, s 5(2).

10 *Ibid*, s 5(4). For a precedent of a statutory declaration for land registration purposes, see Precedent 9 at p 212 below.

11 *Ibid*, s 6. For a precedent of a statutory declaration of non-revocation for the purposes of a Stock Exchange transaction, see Precedent 8 at p 212 below.

Proposed reforms

In its report, *Delegation by Individual Trustees*, the Law Commission has proposed that there should be a new statutory form of power of attorney for use by an individual trustee who wishes to delegate to one attorney all his or her powers under a single trust.[1]

In its report, *Mental Incapacity*, the Law Commission has recommended that the Enduring Powers of Attorney Act 1985 should be repealed and replaced by a new system of continuing powers of attorney which will only be effective if they are registered with the registration authority.[2] It is possible that, if and when this new legislation is introduced, ordinary powers of attorney will enjoy something of a renaissance because many donors may still wish to make provision for someone else to manage their property and affairs prior to the onset of incapacity.

1 Law Commission Report No 220, *The Law of Trusts: Delegation by Individual Trustees* (HMSO, January 1994, £8.25). The proposed General Trustee Power of Attorney appears in cl 5(6) of the draft Trustee Delegation Bill and is reproduced as Precedent 3 at p 208 below.

2 Law Commission Report No 231, *Mental Incapacity* (HMSO, March 1995, £21.85).

PRECEDENTS

A precedent for an ordinary power of attorney authorising the attorneys to make gifts is included in Chapter 5, as Precedent 3.

1 GENERAL POWER OF ATTORNEY[1]

THIS GENERAL POWER OF ATTORNEY is made this .... day of .... by me (*donor's full name*) of (*address*)

I APPOINT (*attorney's full name*) of (*address*) [and (*second or subsequent attorney's full name*) of (*address*) (jointly)/(jointly and severally)] to be my attorney(s) in accordance with section 10 of the Powers of Attorney Act 1971.[2]

SIGNED by me as a deed and delivered in the presence of:

---

1 This is almost verbatim the form of general power of attorney set out in Sch 1 to the Powers of Attorney Act 1971.
2 Section 10 of the Powers of Attorney Act 1971 provides as follows:
'(1) Subject to subsection (2) of this section, a general power of attorney in the form set out in Schedule 1 to this Act, or in a form to the like effect but expressed to be made under this Act, shall operate to confer:
   (a) on the donee of the power; or
   (b) if there is more than one donee, on the donees acting jointly or acting jointly and severally, as the case may be,
authority to do on behalf of the donor anything which he can lawfully do by an attorney.
(2) This section does not apply to functions which the donor has as a trustee or personal representative or as a tenant for life or statutory owner within the meaning of the Settled Land Act 1925.'
   On the effect of s 10(2), see *Walia v Michael Naughton Ltd* [1985] 3 All ER 673.

---

2 GENERAL POWER OF ATTORNEY SUBJECT TO RESTRICTIONS

I ....
of ....
APPOINT ....
of ....
to be my attorney for the purposes of the Powers of Attorney Act 1971.

(1)   My attorney does NOT have authority to:
   (a) sell any of my personal possessions;
   (b) sell my home;
   (c) make gifts out of my income or capital;
   (d) appoint a successor or substitute as my attorney;
   (e) exercise my functions as a trustee or personal representative.

(2)   Subject to the above restrictions, my attorney has authority to do on my behalf anything which I can lawfully do by an attorney.

SIGNED by me as a deed and delivered ....
on ....

in the presence of ....
Full name of witness ....
Address of witness ....

3 TRUSTEE POWER OF ATTORNEY[1]

THIS GENERAL TRUSTEE POWER OF ATTORNEY is made on *(date)*
by me .... *(name of one donor)*
of .... *(address of donor)*
as trustee of .... *(name or details of one trust)*

I APPOINT .... *(name of one donee)*
of .... *(address of donee)*
to be my attorney (from *(date)*)/(until *(date)*)/(from *(date)* until *(date)*)[2] with authority to execute or exercise all or any of the trusts, powers and discretions vested in me as a trustee of the said trust in accordance with section 25 of the Trustee Act 1925.[3]

SIGNED by me as a deed
and delivered in the presence of:

---

1 This precedent is largely based on the form of General Trustee Power of Attorney contained in cl 5 of the draft Trustee Delegation Bill, which forms Appendix A to Law Commission Report No 220, *The Law of Trusts: Delegation by Individual Trustees* (HMSO, 1994).

2 A trustee can delegate his or her functions to an attorney for a period not exceeding twelve months: Trustee Act 1925, s 25(1) (as amended by the Powers of Attorney Act 1971, s 9).

3 Before or within seven days after giving a power of attorney under this section, the donor must give written notice to each of the other trustees and each person who has power to appoint a new trustee: Trustee Act 1925, s 25(4) (as amended). For a form of notice, see Precedent 4 at p 209 below.

4 NOTICE OF CREATION OF A TRUSTEE POWER OF ATTORNEY[1]

To: (*each co-trustee and each person, if any, entitled to appoint a new trustee*)[2]

I ....
of ....
GIVE YOU NOTICE that
on ....
I gave a power of attorney (a copy of which is attached)[3]
to ....
of ....
which will come into operation on ....
and expire on[4] ....

I have delegated to my attorney (all)/(the following) trusts, powers and discretions vested in me as a trustee.

The power of attorney has been given because[5] ....

Signed ....

Dated ....

---

1 For the contents of the notice, see, generally, the Trustee Act 1925, s 25(4) (as amended by Powers of Attorney Act 1971, s 9).

2 Similar notice should be given by a personal representative to each of the other personal representatives except any executor who has renounced probate: *ibid*, s 25(8)(a) (as substituted by Powers of Attorney Act 1971, s 9).

3 The notice must be given before or within seven days after giving the power. If it is given beforehand, the wording should be amended accordingly.

4 A trustee may delegate his or her functions by a power of attorney for a period not exceeding twelve months: *ibid*, s 25(1) (as amended).

5 The reason why the power is given must be stated: *ibid*, s 25(4).

5 POWER OF ATTORNEY GIVEN BY AN EXECUTOR[1]

IN THE HIGH COURT OF JUSTICE
FAMILY DIVISION
THE   PROBATE REGISTRY

IN THE ESTATE OF   DECEASED

POWER OF ATTORNEY

I ....

of ....

APPOINT ....

of ....

to be my attorney for the purpose of obtaining a grant of letters of administration
with the will annexed[2]

to the estate of ....

late of ....

who died on ....

having in (his)/(her) will dated ....

appointed me as executor.

The grant of representation shall be limited for my use and benefit and until further
representation is granted, or in such other way as the Registrar may direct.[3]

SIGNED by me as a deed and delivered ....

on ....

in the presence of ....

Full name of witness ....

Address of witness ....

---

1 Notice that this power of attorney has been granted must be given to each of the other personal
representatives, if any, except an executor who has renounced probate, unless such notice is
dispensed with by the Registrar: Trustee Act 1925, s 25(8)(a) (as substituted by Powers of
Attorney Act 1971, s 9), and Non-Contentious Probate Rules 1987 (SI 1987/2024 (L 10)),
r 31(2). The notice of creation of a trustee power of attorney (Precedent 4 at p 209 above) can
easily be adapted for this purpose.

2 The lawfully constituted attorney of a person entitled to a grant may apply for administration
for the use and benefit of the donor, and such grant shall be limited until further representation
be granted, or in such other way as the Registrar may direct: Non-Contentious Probate Rules
1987 (SI 1987/2024 (L 10)), r 31(1).

6 DEED OF REVOCATION OF POWER OF ATTORNEY[1]

I ....

of ....

REVOKE the power of attorney dated ....

in which I appointed ....

to be my attorney(s).

SIGNED by me as a deed and delivered ....

on ....

in the presence of ....

---

1 Although an express revocation by deed is the most satisfactory way of revoking a power of attorney, it is not sufficient in itself because the attorney's authority does not cease until he or she receives notice of the revocation: *Re Oriental Bank ex parte Guillemin* (1885) 28 ChD 634. For a notice of revocation, see Precedent 7 below.

7 SOLICITOR'S LETTER GIVING ATTORNEY NOTICE OF REVOCATION[1]

(date)

Dear (Sir)/(Madam)

NOTICE OF REVOCATION OF POWER OF ATTORNEY

We write to inform you that the power of attorney granted by *(name of donor)* to you [and *(co-attorney(s), if any)*] on *(date)* has been revoked by *(donor)* as from *(date of revocation)*.

We enclose a photocopy of the (deed of revocation)/(new power of attorney)[2] which expressly revokes the authority under which you have been acting. You should take no further action under the revoked power.

Please return to us [the original and] all copies of the power of attorney in your possession so that they can be marked as cancelled, and let us know whether there are any other copies currently lodged elsewhere.[3] We are enclosing a prepaid envelope.

Yours faithfully

---

1 The revocation of an ordinary or enduring power of attorney is ineffective until it is communicated to all parties concerned. The revocation of a registered EPA is also ineffective until it is confirmed by the Court of Protection: Enduring Powers of Attorney Act 1985, ss 7(1)(a) and 8(3).

2 Where the donor creates a new power of attorney expressly revoking the former power, notice of revocation should be given to the attorneys appointed under the former power.

3 Where a power of attorney has been revoked and a person without knowledge of the revocation deals with the attorney, the transaction between them is, in favour of that person, as valid as if the power had been in existence: Powers of Attorney Act 1971, s 5(2). For this reason, it is recommended that, wherever possible, the original instrument and all copies should be returned to the donor for cancellation or destruction.

8 STATUTORY DECLARATION OF NON-REVOCATION FOR THE PURPOSE OF A STOCK EXCHANGE TRANSACTION[1]

I *(attorney's name)* of *(attorney's address)* SOLEMNLY AND SINCERELY DECLARE as follows:

(1)   By a power of attorney dated *(date)*, *(donor)* of *(address)* appointed me to be (his)/(her) attorney.

(2)   On *(date)*, I executed stock transfer forms transferring the following registered securities: *(specify the details)*

(3)   When I executed the stock transfer forms, the power of attorney had not been revoked.

AND I MAKE THIS SOLEMN DECLARATION conscientiously believing the same to be true and by virtue of the Statutory Declarations Act 1835.

DECLARED at
this   day of

Before me

A Commissioner for Oaths/Solicitor

---

1 'Where: (a) the donee of a power of attorney executes, as transferor, an instrument transferring registered securities; and (b) the instrument is executed for the purposes of a stock exchange transaction, it shall be conclusively presumed in favour of the transferee that the power had not been revoked at the date of the instrument if a statutory declaration to that effect is made by the donee of the power on or *within three months* after that date': Powers of Attorney Act 1971, s 6(1) (author's emphasis).

9 STATUTORY DECLARATION OF NON-REVOCATION FOR LAND REGISTRATION PURPOSES[1]

I *(name of person who dealt with the attorney)* of *(address)* SOLEMNLY AND SINCERELY DECLARE as follows:

(1)   By a power of attorney dated *(date)*, *(donor)* ('the donor') of *(address)* appointed *(attorney)* ('the attorney') to be (his)/(her) attorney.

(2)   On (*date*), I completed a transaction with the attorney, namely the purchase of (*address*).

(3)   At the time of the transaction, I did not know of any revocation of the power or of the occurrence of any event (such as the death of the donor) which had the effect of revoking the power of attorney.[2]

AND I MAKE THIS SOLEMN DECLARATION conscientiously believing the same to be true and by virtue of the Statutory Declarations Act 1835.

DECLARED at

this   day of

Before me

A Commissioner for Oaths/Solicitor

---

1 Section 5(4) of the Powers of Attorney Act 1971 provides as follows:
  'Where the interest of a purchaser depends on whether a transaction between the donee of a power of attorney and another person was valid . . . , it shall be conclusively presumed in favour of the purchaser that that person did not at the material time know of the revocation of the power if:
  (a)   the transaction between that person and the donee was completed within twelve months of the date on which the power came into operation; or
  (b)   that person makes a statutory declaration, before or within three months after the completion of the purchase, that he did not at the material time know of the revocation of the power.'
2 'Knowledge of the revocation of a power of attorney includes knowledge of the occurrence of any event (such as the death of the donor) which has the effect of revoking the power': *ibid*, s 5(5).

---

10 CERTIFICATION OF A COPY OF A POWER OF ATTORNEY[1]

I CERTIFY that this is a true and complete copy of the original.[2]

[OR]

I CERTIFY that this is a true and complete copy of the corresponding page of the original.[3]

[OR]

I CERTIFY that this is a true and complete copy of a copy of the original.[4]

Signed ....
Qualification[5] ....
Date ....

1 The rules on proof of instruments creating powers of attorney are contained in Powers of Attorney Act 1971, s 3. This section also applies to enduring powers of attorney: Enduring Powers of Attorney Act 1985, s 7(4).

2 Where an instrument creating a power of attorney consists of only one page, its contents may be proved by 'a certificate *at the end* to the effect that the copy is a true and complete copy of the original': Powers of Attorney Act 1971, s 3(1)(b)(i) (author's emphasis).

3 *Ibid*, s 3(1)(b)(ii): 'if the original consists of two or more pages, [its contents may be proved by] a certificate *at the end of each page* of the copy to the effect that it is a true and complete copy of the corresponding page of the original' (author's emphasis).

4 *Ibid*, s 3(2).

5 The certificate(s) must be 'signed by *the donor* of the power or by a *solicitor*, duly certificated *notary public* or *stockbroker*': *ibid*, s 3(1)(b) (as amended by the Courts and Legal Services Act 1990, s 125(2) and Sch 17) (author's emphasis).

CHAPTER 9: ENDURING POWERS OF ATTORNEY

INDEX

Text

Checklists

Forms

Precedents

ENDURING POWERS OF ATTORNEY

TEXT

Introduction

A power of attorney is a deed[1] in which one person (*the donor*) gives another person (*the attorney*) authority to act on his or her behalf and in his or her name. An ordinary power of attorney[2] is revoked by operation of the law if the donor becomes mentally incapable.[3] An enduring power, however, *endures* or remains in force despite the donor's mental incapacity, provided that it is registered with the Public Trust Office.[4]

Enduring powers have been available in England and Wales[5] since 10 March 1986, when the Enduring Powers of Attorney Act 1985 came into force.[6] The purposes and origins of the Act are described in the Law Commission's report *The Incapacitated Principal*, published in July 1983.[7]

EPAs can be created by anyone – even a minor[8] – and are a sensible precaution against the accidents, illnesses and injuries that can incapacitate a person of any age, but their principal uptake is among the over 70s. Research conducted in 1990 and 1991 by Professor Stephen Cretney and his colleagues at the University of Bristol revealed the following statistics for registered EPAs.[9]

Age of the donor at the time of application to register an EPA

90+	25%
80–90	54%
70–80	16%
60–70	3%
Under 60	2%

Period from the execution of an EPA to the application to register it

Under 1 month	26%
1 to 3 months	23%
3 to 6 months	18%
6 to 12 months	20%
Over 12 months	10%
Not recorded	3%

Sex of donor

Female	75%
Male	25%

Relationship of attorney to donor

Relative	62%
Solicitor	12%
Other/not known	26%

---

1 Powers of Attorney Act 1971, s 1(1).
2 Any power of attorney which is not an enduring power is referred to in this book as an 'ordinary power of attorney'. For notes and precedents relating to ordinary powers, see Chapter 8.
3 *Drew v Nunn* (1878) 4 QBD 661.
4 Enduring Powers of Attorney Act 1985, s 1(1).
5 For the temporary position in Scotland, see the Law Reform (Miscellaneous Provisions) (Scotland) Act 1990, s 71, whereby any power of attorney executed after 1 January 1991 will not be revoked by the incapacity of the granter.
6 Enduring Powers of Attorney Act 1985 (Commencement) Order 1986 (SI 1986/125 (C 5)).
7 Law Com No 122 (Cmnd 8977, HMSO, 1983).
8 *G(A) v G(T)* [1970] 2 QB 643, [1970] 3 All ER 546, CA. The attorney, however, has to have attained the age of 18 years when he executes the instrument creating the EPA: Enduring Powers of Attorney Act 1985, s 2(7)(a).
9 Stephen Cretney et al, *Enduring Powers of Attorney: A Report to the Lord Chancellor* (Lord Chancellor's Department, June 1991), pp 25–27.

The market for EPAs

It would be impossible to assess the number of EPAs that have been executed since the legislation came into force, but the number of registrations has grown steadily. In 1986 there were 350 registrations; in 1987 there were 1118; and during the last five years, the following picture has emerged.[1]

	1990	1991	1992	1993	1994
Applications received during year	3549	5688	5189	5767	6785
Number registered during year	2540	2930	3374	3826	5494
Total remaining registered	5688	7428	9956	12,989	18,826

The disparity between the number of applications and the number of EPAs registered each year can be attributed partly to the rejection of some applications; partly to the fact that not all applications are for registration; and also to the fact that many donors die during the period between submitting the application and registration.

New receivership applications have remained fairly constant – at about the 6000 level – since 1986, whereas there had been an average growth rate of 6.6% per year between 1980 and 1985. This suggests that EPAs are tapping a new market, as well as attracting cases which would otherwise have resulted in a receivership. It is almost universally agreed that, given a choice between receivership and an EPA, the EPA is preferable.[2] Receivership work is usually uneconomic and subject to bureaucratic constraints, or, to put it another way, 'the Court of Protection does things properly, but paternalistically and at a price'.[3] EPA work is not necessarily lucrative, but it is certainly more financially rewarding than receivership work.

The EPA legislation allows a trust corporation to be appointed as an attorney.[4] It is understood that most of the main high street banks offer attorneyship under an enduring power as part of their asset management service.

It is evident that solicitors not only regard EPAs as a substitute for receivership, but also as a substitute for ordinary powers of attorney, which are rarely made for private clients nowadays.[5]

In 1990, when a major survey was conducted into the impact of the Enduring Powers of Attorney Act 1985, there was still a fairly mixed approach among solicitors towards marketing EPAs to their clients.[6] However, there is a consistently growing body of responsible professional opinion which believes that solicitors have, at the very least, a duty to inform their clients about EPAs, and it is predicted that, within the next ten years, negligence actions could be brought against lawyers who have failed to advise their clients of the wisdom of planning in advance for possible incapacitation. The measure of damages in such a case would, presumably, be the cost of making a receivership application, plus the ongoing costs of the receivership.

---

1 Source: Lord Chancellor's Department, *Judicial Statistics Annual Report*: 1991 (Cm 1990); 1992 (Cm 2268); 1993 (Cm 2623); 1994 (Cm 2891). The annual report is published by HMSO in the July following the year ending 31 December.

2 Stephen Cretney et al, *Enduring Powers of Attorney: A Report to the Lord Chancellor* (Lord Chancellor's Department, June 1991), Conclusion 6, p 77.

3 J.T. Farrand, 'Enduring Powers of Attorney', in John Eekelaar and David Pearl (eds), *An Aging World: Dilemmas and Challenges for Law and Social Policy* (Clarendon Press, Oxford, 1989), at p 641.

4 Enduring Powers of Attorney Act 1985, s 2(7).

5 Cretney et al, *op cit*, para 2.1.

6 *Ibid*, para 2.1.

Who is the client?

This question is discussed in Chapter 2.

Capacity to create an EPA

See Chapter 3, and Checklist 3 in that chapter at p 60.

The prescribed form

An instrument cannot be a valid enduring power of attorney unless, when it was executed by the donor, it was in the form prescribed at that time by the Lord Chancellor.[1] There have been three prescribed forms since the Enduring Powers of Attorney Act 1985 came into force:

- The *first prescribed form* was drafted by the Law Commission.[2] It is most readily identifiable by the fact that the explanatory information appears at the end. This was the prescribed form *from 10 March 1986*[3] *to 30 June 1988 inclusive.*[4]
- The *second prescribed form* was drafted by the Public Trust Office in response to criticisms that the first form was difficult for a layman to follow and gave insufficient information as to its purpose.[5] This form is most easily identified by the fact that it is in three parts: 'Part A: About using this form'; 'Part B: To be completed by the donor'; and 'Part C: To be completed by the attorney(s)'. The instrument was under seal, and para 8 of Part A referred to the 1987 Regulations. This form was the prescribed form for an EPA executed by the donor *between 1 November 1987*[6] *and 30 July 1991 inclusive.*[7]
- The *third prescribed form* was introduced primarily because of the implementation of the Law of Property (Miscellaneous Provisions) Act 1989, which abolished any rule of law which required a seal for the valid execution of a deed.[8] It also made provision for the execution of an EPA at the direction of the donor.[9] The third form is virtually identical to the second form, except that para 9 of Part A of the form refers to the Enduring Powers of Attorney (Prescribed Form) Regulations 1990, and the attestation clauses state that the EPA is 'Signed by me as a deed and delivered'. This form is prescribed for EPAs executed by the donor *from 31 July 1990.*[10]

It is common practice among solicitors to produce EPAs on a word processor, rather than fill in a law stationer's form.[11] The reasons are partly cosmetic, partly because of the demise of manual typewriters, partly to enhance the firm's logo or corporate image, and partly to justify charging a higher fee for preparing the document. On balance, the law stationer's forms are preferable because:

- they are easier for third parties – such as banks or building societies – to identify, particularly where an additional clause has been inserted in the prescribed form;
- they are easier to complete, and can even be handwritten;
- they are usually simpler to photocopy;
- they are less bulky and easier to store; and
- there is less likelihood of making a mistake, or inadvertently excluding any part of the prescribed form.

---

1 Enduring Powers of Attorney Act 1985, s 2(1)(a), (2) and (13).

2 Law Commission Report No 122, *The Incapacitated Principal*, Cmnd 8977 (HMSO, 1983), Appendix C, 'Specimen Form of Enduring Power of Attorney'.

3 The Enduring Powers of Attorney (Prescribed Form) Regulations 1986 (SI 1986/126), which came into force on 10 March 1986.

4 The Enduring Powers of Attorney (Prescribed Form) Regulations 1987 (SI 1987/1612), which came into force on 1 November 1987.
5 P.D. Lewis, Assistant Public Trustee, 'Enduring Powers of Attorney Act 1985 – New Form and Regulations', *The Law Society's Gazette*, 28 October 1987, pp 3083–3085.
6 The Enduring Powers of Attorney (Prescribed Form) Regulations 1987 (SI 1987/1612).
7 Enduring Powers of Attorney (Prescribed Form) Regulations 1990 (SI 1990/1376), reg 5.
8 Law of Property (Miscellaneous Provisions) Act 1989, s 1(1)(b).
9 Enduring Powers of Attorney (Prescribed Form) Regulations 1990 (SI 1990/1376), reg 3(3) and (4).
10 *Ibid*, reg 1.
11 P.D. Lewis, *op cit*, p 3083.

Scope of authority

The donor of an EPA can confer on his or her attorney:

- general authority to act in relation to all his or her property and affairs;
- general authority to act in relation to specified property and affairs; or
- authority to do specified things on the donor's behalf.[1]

In each case, the authority can be conferred subject to conditions and restrictions.

According to the Court of Protection, 98.4% of EPAs presented for registration confer on the attorney general authority to act in relation to all the donor's property and affairs,[2] and it has been suggested that there could be 'a more imaginative use' of EPAs by practitioners.[3]

Where general authority is conferred then, subject to any restrictions imposed by the donor or by the Enduring Powers of Attorney Act itself,[4] the attorney has 'authority to do on behalf of the donor anything which the donor can lawfully do by an attorney'.[5] There is no statutory definition as to what a donor can lawfully do by an attorney. However, the following points seem to be fairly clear. An attorney acting under an enduring power cannot:

- make decisions about the donor's personal care and welfare.[6] For example:
  - where to live, whom to live with, whom to see and not to see;
  - whether to consent to, or refuse, medical treatment;
  - whether to marry or consent to a divorce;
- make a will on behalf of the donor;[7]
- perform any act which only the donor is competent to perform by virtue of some duty of a personal nature requiring skill or discretion for its exercise;[8]
- swear an affidavit on the donor's behalf;[9]
- sign a tax claim or tax return unless there may be difficulties where, owing to the age or physical infirmity of the taxpayer, he or she is unable to cope adequately with the management of his or her affairs, or where for the same reasons the taxpayer's general health might suffer if he or she were troubled for a personal signature.[10]

Despite the general prohibition on attorneys undertaking the donor's personal duties which require skill or discretion for their exercise, an attorney acting under an EPA can at present[11] 'subject to any conditions or restrictions contained in the instrument . . . (without obtaining any consent) execute or exercise all or any of the trusts, powers or discretions vested in the donor as a trustee and may (without the concurrence of any other person) give a valid receipt for capital or other money paid'.[12]

---

1 Enduring Powers of Attorney Act 1985, s 3(1).

2 Stephen Cretney et al, *Enduring Powers of Attorney: A Report to the Lord Chancellor* (Lord Chancellor's Department, June 1991), para 2.14.

3 J.T. Farrand, 'Enduring Powers of Attorney', in John Eekelaar and David Pearl (eds), *An Aging World: Dilemmas and Challenges for Law and Social Policy* (Clarendon Press, Oxford, 1989), at p 641.

4 For example, the limitations on gifts in s 3(5) of the Act; and the limited powers of maintenance and prevention of loss to the donor's estate when an application for registration is pending: s 1(2).

5 Enduring Powers of Attorney Act 1985, s 3(2), repeating verbatim the formula appearing at the end of s 10(1) of the Powers of Attorney Act 1971.

6 Matters of personal care and welfare do not come within the ambit of 'property and affairs', a phrase which means 'business matters, legal transactions and other dealings of a similar kind': *F v West Berkshire Health Authority* [1989] 2 All ER 545, at p 554d, per Lord Brandon. The Court of Protection itself has no power over the person of its 'patients'.

7 The attorney could, however, apply to the Court of Protection for an order authorising the execution of a statutory will under the Mental Health Act 1983, s 96(1)(e). See Chapter 14.

8 *Clauss v Pir* [1987] 3 WLR 493, [1987] 2 All ER 752.

9 *Ibid.*

10 Inland Revenue Practice Statement 8/1976.

11 Law Commission Report No 220, *Delegation by Individual Trustees* (HMSO, January 1994) recommends that s 3(3) of the Enduring Powers of Attorney Act 1985 should be repealed.

12 Enduring Powers of Attorney Act 1985, s 3(3). For the origins of this section, see R.T. Oerton, 'Trustees and the Enduring Powers of Attorney Act 1985: A Legislative Blunder', *Solicitors' Journal*, 10 January 1986, pp 23–25.

More than one attorney

If the donor wishes to appoint more than one attorney, he or she must appoint them to act either:

- *jointly*, which means that none of them can act independently: they must act together; or
- *jointly and severally*, which means that they may act together, or any one of them could act independently.[1]

The problem with appointing attorneys to act *jointly* (rather than jointly and severally) is that the EPA cannot be used if one of the attorneys:

- dies;
- disclaims his or her attorneyship, or refuses to act, or is unable to act; or
- becomes bankrupt.[2]

At present, it is difficult to create an EPA involving more than two attorneys who are required to act in a specified combination: for example, where the donor wishes to appoint four attorneys, any two of whom can act on the donor's behalf.[3] Such an appointment is, strictly speaking, neither joint nor joint and several. It may be that an inventive use of the 'conditions' provisions in the prescribed form could overcome this difficulty.[4]

---

1 Enduring Powers of Attorney Act 1985, s 11(1).
2 *Ibid*, s 2(10).
3 See, for example, Precedent 10 at p 255 below, where the donor's solicitor and any one of two or more other attorneys are appointed to act jointly on any one occasion.
4 See Stephen Cretney et al, *Enduring Powers of Attorney: A Report to the Lord Chancellor* (Lord Chancellor's Department, June 1991), para 2.18.

Notification prior to registration

If the attorney has reason to believe that the donor is or is becoming mentally incapable,[1] he or she has a duty, as soon as practicable, to apply to the Public Trust Office for the registration of the EPA.[2] However, before applying, the attorney must give notice of his or her intention to apply for registration (Form EP1)[3] to the following people:[4]

- the donor.[5] The Notice of Intention to Apply for Registration (Form EP1) must be given to the donor personally;[6] service by post is not sufficient. Form EP1 need not be served on the donor by the attorney personally, but may be served by a solicitor or agent acting on the directions of the attorney.[7] It is suspected that 'the usual pattern is for the notification of the donor to be fudged in one way or another';[8]
- any co-attorney who is not joining in making the application.[9] Service by first-class post is sufficient;[10]
- the donor's relatives.[11] Service by first-class post is sufficient.[12]

All of these notices should be served within fourteen days of each other.[13]

At least three of the donor's relatives must receive the Notice of Intention to Apply for Registration (Form EP1).[14] The three relatives must be taken in the following order of priority, set out in Sch 1 to the Enduring Powers of Attorney Act 1985:[15]

- the donor's husband or wife;
- the donor's children;
- the donor's parents;
- the donor's brothers and sisters, whether of the whole or half blood;
- the widow or widower of a child of the donor. It is not entirely clear whether a person in this category ceases to be entitled to receive notice if he or she remarries. If there is any doubt about a person's entitlement to receive notice it is safer to notify;
- the donor's grandchildren;

- the children of the donor's brothers and sisters of the whole blood;
- the children of the donor's brothers and sisters of the half blood;
- the donor's uncles and aunts of the whole blood;
- the children of the donor's uncles and aunts of the whole blood.

If there is more than one person in a particular class of relatives entitled to receive notice, then everyone in that class must be given notice.[16] If the attorneys are also notifiable relatives, they can count themselves as having been notified.[17]

A relative or co-attorney is not entitled to receive Form EP1 if:

- his or her address is not known to, and cannot reasonably be ascertained by, the attorney;
- the attorney has reason to believe that the relative or co-attorney is under 18;
- the attorney has reason to believe that the relative or co-attorney is incapable, by reason of mental disorder, of managing and administering his or her property and affairs.[18]

An application can be made by the attorney (on Form EP3)[19] to be dispensed from the requirement to give a Notice of Intention to Apply for Registration to the donor, or any co-attorney or any relative. The Court of Protection or Public Trustee will only grant such an application if satisfied that:

- it would be undesirable or impracticable for the attorney to give notice to him or her; or
- no useful purpose is likely to be served by giving notice to him or her.[20]

Applications to dispense with service on the donor are usually dealt with by the Master of the Court of Protection at an attended hearing, and are unlikely to succeed unless there is clear medical evidence that service would be detrimental to the donor's health.[21] Applications to dispense with service on a relative or co-attorney are dealt with on their merits. Clear grounds should be set out in the General Form of Application (Form EP3).[22] If the attorney believes that the donor would not want one of the prescribed relatives to be notified, he or she can apply to the court on Form EP3 supporting the application with appropriate evidence.

Applications to dispense with service on the donor are made in about 2% of registrations; and applications to dispense with service on a relative in about 4% of registrations.[23]

---

1 Enduring Powers of Attorney Act 1985, s 4(1). 'Mentally incapable' means 'in relation to any person, that he is incapable by reason of mental disorder of managing and administering his property and affairs': s 13(1).

2 *Ibid*, s 4(2).

3 Court of Protection (Enduring Powers of Attorney) Rules 1994 (SI 1994/3047), r 7(1). Form EP1 is reproduced at p 240 below.

4 Enduring Powers of Attorney Act 1985, s 4(3) and Sch 1.

5 *Ibid*, Sch 1, para 4.

6 Court of Protection (Enduring Powers of Attorney) Rules 1994 (SI 1994/3047), r 16(1).

7 P.D. Lewis, Assistant Public Trustee, 'The Enduring Powers of Attorney Act 1985', *The Law Society's Gazette*, 26 November 1986, p 3567.

8 Stephen Cretney et al, *Enduring Powers of Attorney: A Report to the Lord Chancellor* (Lord Chancellor's Department, June 1991), para 2.23.

9 Enduring Powers of Attorney Act 1985, Sch 1, para 7.

10 Court of Protection (Enduring Powers of Attorney) Rules 1994 (SI 1994/3047), rr 7(1) and 16(2).

11 For an empirical study of solicitors' experience of notifying relatives, see Cretney et al, *op cit*, para 2.24. The present system of notifying relatives may inadvertently encourage objections to registration.

12 *Ibid*.

13 Court of Protection (Enduring Powers of Attorney) Rules 1994 (SI 1994/3047), r 7(1).

14 Enduring Powers of Attorney Act 1985, Sch 1, para 2(3) and (4).

15 *Ibid*, para 2(1).

16 *Ibid*, para 2(4).

17 *Ibid*, para 3(1).

18 *Ibid*, paras 2(2) and 7(2).

19 For a precedent of an application to dispense with notification, see Precedent 11 at p 256 below.

20 Enduring Powers of Attorney Act 1985, Sch 1, para 3(2).

21 P.D. Lewis, *op cit*, p 3568.

22 *Ibid*. See Form EP3 at p 244 below.

23 Cretney et al, *op cit*, para 2.14.

Application to register

The application to register an enduring power of attorney must be made in Form EP2.[1] This form must be lodged with the Public Trust Office not later than ten days after the date on which:

- Notice of Intention to Apply for Registration (Form EP1) has been given to:
  - the donor;
  - every relative entitled to receive notice; and
  - every co-attorney; or
- leave has been given to dispense with notice,

whichever may be the later.[2]

An attorney lodging an application out of time must apply (in Form EP3) for an extension under r 15(3) of the 1994 Rules. Any late application should show good cause for the delay. If the application for registration is submitted more than a month after notice of intention to apply was given, the court will almost certainly reject the application, and the notification procedure will need to be started afresh.

Any discrepancy between the spelling of the donor's name or the attorney's name in the EPA and Form EP2 should be explained in a covering letter to the court, as should any discrepancy between the address of the donor in Form EP2 and the address at which he or she was personally served with a copy of Form EP1.[3]

The application to register an EPA should be sent to the Enquiries and Applications Branch, Public Trust Office, Protection Division, Stewart House, 24 Kingsway, London WC2B 6JX, and should comprise the following documents:

- Form EP2;
- the original EPA (not a copy);
- a cheque for the registration fee of £50 made payable to 'Public Trust Office';[4]
- wherever necessary, an accompanying letter explaining any discrepancies between the names and addresses; or an application in Form EP3 for an extension of the time-limit for applying for registration; or an application for 'emergency action' under s 5 of the Act.

It is not necessary to send copies of Form EP1 with the application, nor is it necessary to obtain or submit medical evidence of the donor's mental incapacity.[5] If, for any reason, the Public Trust Office refuses to register the EPA, it will retain the fee. The fee is payable in respect of the application, not the registration.[6]

According to figures published in 1991, only 25% of EPA registration applications are completely straightforward; 65% require additional enquiries; and the remaining 10% involve either a hearing, or the need for the court staff or the Master to spend additional time resolving exceptional queries.[7]

If there are no difficulties and no objections, the registration process will take approximately five weeks. When the EPA is registered it is rubber-stamped by the Public Trustee with the date of registration, sealed by the Court of Protection, and returned to the attorney(s) or their solicitor.[8]

While an EPA is in the course of being registered, the attorney's powers are extremely limited. The only actions he or she can take under the power are:

- to maintain the donor;
- to maintain himself, herself or anyone else in accordance with the provisions of s 3(4) of the Act; and
- to prevent loss to the donor's estate.[9]

If, however, the court is of the opinion that it is necessary to exercise wider powers before the EPA is registered, it can authorise the appropriate action.[10]

---

1 Court of Protection (Enduring Powers of Attorney) Rules 1994 (SI 1994/3047), r 8(1).
2 *Ibid*. The time-limit under the 1986 Rules was three days. This was extended to ten days by the 1994 Rules, r 8(1).
3 P.D. Lewis, Assistant Public Trustee, 'The Enduring Powers of Attorney Act 1985', *The Law Society's Gazette*, 26 November 1986, p 3568.
4 Court of Protection (Enduring Powers of Attorney) Rules 1994 (SI 1994/3047), r 27 and Sch 2.
5 Unless the donor has specifically stated in the EPA that it will not be registered unless the court is satisfied, after considering medical evidence, that the donor is mentally incapable. See Precedent 2 at p 249 below.
6 Court of Protection (Enduring Powers of Attorney) Rules 1994, r 27 and Sch 2.
7 Stephen Cretney et al, *Enduring Powers of Attorney: A Report to the Lord Chancellor* (Lord Chancellor's Department, June 1991), para 2.15.
8 Court of Protection (Enduring Powers of Attorney) Rules 1994 (SI 1994/3047), r 13.
9 Enduring Powers of Attorney Act 1985, s 1(2).
10 *Ibid*, s 5.

Objections to registration

A person on whom a Form EP1 (Notice of Intention to Apply for Registration) has been served can object to the registration of the EPA on any one or more of the following grounds:[1]

- that the power purported to have been created by the instrument was not valid as an enduring power of attorney;
- that the power created by the instrument no longer subsists;
- that the application is premature because the donor is not yet becoming mentally incapable;
- that fraud or undue pressure was used to induce the donor to create the power;
- that, having regard to all the circumstances and in particular the attorney's relationship to or connection with the donor, the attorney is unsuitable to be the donor's attorney.

Any objection to the proposed registration must be lodged with the Public Trustee within four weeks from the date on which the objector received Form EP1.[2] The objection must be in writing and contain the following details:[3]

- the name and address of the objector;
- the name and address of the donor, if the objector is not the donor;
- any relationship of the objector to the donor;
- the name and address of the attorney; and
- the grounds for objecting to the registration of the enduring power.[4]

An objection is lodged in approximately 8% of applications to register; 5% of the applications result in a formal hearing. Disputes about EPAs tend to be more acrimonious than those involving receivership: a possible reason being that receivership is seen to be more clearly under the supervision of the court.[5] The dispute often has a long history, pre-dating the creation of the power, and often concerns the ultimate destination of the donor's money when he or she dies. In many cases the objection has only a tenuous link with the EPA itself.

It has been suggested that one of the best ways to avoid problems is to encourage donors while they are still capable to be open with their families about their wishes should they become incapable. Donors who let their families know that they have made an EPA, and whom they have named as attorneys, may help the family to accept the situation, however unwelcome.[6]

---

1 Enduring Powers of Attorney Act 1985, s 6(5).
2 See Form EP1 itself: Court of Protection (Enduring Powers of Attorney) Rules 1994 (SI 1994/3047), Sch 1, reproduced at p 240 below.
3 *Ibid*, r 10(1).
4 For a precedent for an objection to the registration of an enduring power, see Precedent 13 at p 258 below.
5 Stephen Cretney et al, *Enduring Powers of Attorney: A Report to the Lord Chancellor* (Lord Chancellor's Department, June 1991), para 2.28.

6 Mrs A.B. Macfarlane, Master of the Court of Protection, in the notes on the court for the IBC Legal Studies and Services conference, *Handling the Problems of the Elderly,* held on 25 January 1995.

Substitutes and successors

Problems may arise where an attorney attempts to transfer the donor's investments into a discretionary management scheme. It has been suggested that the purported transfer could fall foul of s 2(9) of the Enduring Powers of Attorney Act 1985, which states that 'a power of attorney which gives the attorney a right to appoint a substitute or successor cannot be an enduring power'.

A distinction needs to be drawn between substitution and delegation. A delegate merely deputises for the attorney, whereas a substitute completely replaces him or her.[1] There are a number of exceptions to the general principle that an agent cannot delegate his or her authority: *delegatus non potest delegare.* At common law, an implied power to delegate may arise:

- where the act delegated is of a purely ministerial nature and does not involve any confidence or discretion;[2]
- where delegation is usual practice in the trade, profession or business of either the principal or the agent;[3]
- from the conduct of the parties;[4] or
- through necessity or unforeseen circumstances.[5]

Any power of delegation which is wider than these implied powers must be provided for expressly in the instrument.[6] The transfer of the donor's investments into a discretionary management scheme is unlikely to come within the range of implied powers of delegation because it involves the exercise of a discretion. In most cases, such a transfer will be a wider delegation for which the donor must make express provision in the EPA,[7] or, if the instrument were registered, the Court of Protection could authorise under s 8(2)(d) of the Enduring Powers of Attorney Act 1985.[8] In a few cases, however, the transfer could be a substitution which, by virtue of s 2(9), prevents the instrument from being an enduring power. Where, for example, the donor had given the attorney a power limited to the management of his or her investments, the transfer of assets by the attorney into a discretionary management scheme operated by a bank or stockbroker, could, in effect, be a complete replacement of the attorney's functions.

1 *Huth v Clarke* (1890) 25 QBD 391, at p 394 per Lord Coleridge CJ.
2 *Rossiter v Trafalgar Life* (1859) 27 Beav 377; *Allam v Europa Poster Services* [1968] 1 All ER 826.
3 *De Bussche v Alt* (1878) 8 ChD 286, CA, at p 310.
4 *Ibid.*
5 *Gwilliam v Twist* [1895] 2 QB 84, CA.

6 The reasoning behind s 2(9) of the Enduring Powers of Attorney Act 1985 is explained by the Law Commission in its report *The Incapacitated Principal* (Law Com No 122), Cmnd 8977 (HMSO, 1983), at para 4.22: 'As in the case of ordinary powers, the EPA attorney would have implied power to delegate any of his functions which were not such that the donor would have expected the attorney to attend to personally. Any wider power to delegate would have to be provided for expressly in the instrument. We would not wish, however, the attorney to be enabled to appoint a substitute or successor to himself. This would be contrary to the special relationship of trust subsisting between the EPA donor and the attorney, and would undermine some of the safeguards we recommend in this Report'.

7 For a precedent clause authorising the attorneys to delegate the management of investments, see Precedent 3 at p 250 below.

8 Section 8(2)(d) of the Enduring Powers of Attorney Act 1985 gives the Court of Protection a discretion to 'give any consent or authorisation to act which the attorney would have to obtain from a mentally capable donor'.

Proposed reforms

The Law Commission has made two separate proposals for the reform of the enduring powers of attorney legislation.

Law Commission Report No 220, *The Law of Trusts: Delegation by Individual Trustees*,[1] recommends that s 3(3) of the Enduring Powers of Attorney Act 1985 be repealed. That subsection currently provides that 'subject to any conditions or restrictions contained in the instrument, an attorney under an enduring power, whether general or limited, may (without obtaining any consent) execute or exercise all or any of the trusts, powers or discretions vested in the donor as trustee and may (without the concurrence of any other person) give a valid receipt for capital or other money paid'.[2] As a transitional measure, the effect of the repeal will be delayed in the case of EPAs created before the repealing Act comes into force. If the EPA is registered, or an application to register is made before the end of the first year after the repealing legislation comes into force, the repeal will not apply until the registration is cancelled. In all other cases, the repeal will take effect a year after the new legislation comes into force, thereby allowing time for alternative arrangements to be made.[3]

Law Commission Report No 231, *Mental Incapacity*,[4] recommends the repeal of the Enduring Powers of Attorney Act 1985 in its entirety. Instead, it will be possible to create a Continuing Power of Attorney (CPA) which may extend to matters relating to the donor's personal welfare, health care and property and affairs, including the conduct of legal proceedings.[5] Like enduring powers, CPAs will have to be in the prescribed form; executed in the prescribed manner; and include, at the time of execution by the donor, the prescribed explanatory information.[6] But unlike enduring powers, CPAs will be ineffective until they have been registered in the prescribed manner with the registration authority (presumably the Public Trust Office).[7] Once a CPA has been registered, the registration authority will give notice of that fact in the prescribed form to (a) the donor, and (b) a maximum of two people, not including the attorney, as specified in the CPA itself.[8] Subject to any contrary intention expressed in the document, the Court of Protection will have power to appoint an attorney in substitution for or in addition to the attorney mentioned in the CPA.[9] No enduring powers can be created after the new law in relation to CPAs comes into force, and transitional provisions will apply to any enduring powers made prior to the repeal of the 1985 Act.[10] An unregistered enduring power may be converted into a CPA by the donor and attorney executing a prescribed form and by registration.[11]

---

1 Law Commission Report No 220, *The Law of Trusts: Delegation by Individual Trustees* (HMSO, January 1994, £8.25). This followed the Law Commission's Consultation Paper No 118, *The Law of Trusts: Delegation by Individual Trustees* (HMSO, 1991, £4.80).

2 Section 3(3) has been criticised for a number of reasons: (1) it abandons the safeguards for beneficiaries; (2) the delegation remains operative after the delegating trustee has become mentally incapacitated, which is generally inappropriate unless he or she also has a beneficial interest in the property; (3) the delegation of trustee functions is automatic, unless expressly excluded in the EPA itself, and can occur inadvertently; (4) because s 25 of the Trustee Act 1925 (as amended) still remains in force, there is statutory duplication.

3 Law Commission Report No 220, para 4.4, and draft Trustee Delegation Bill, cl 4.

4 Law Commission Report No 231, *Mental Incapacity* (HMSO, March 1995, £21.85). This followed no less than four Consultation Papers: No 119, *Mentally Incapacitated Adults and Decision-Making: An Overview* (HMSO, April 1991, £6.90); No 218, *Mentally Incapacitated Adults and Decision-Making: A New Jurisdiction* (HMSO, February 1993, £8.50); No 129, *Mentally Incapacitated Adults and Decision-Making: Medical Treatment and Research* (HMSO, April 1993, £8.95); and No 130, *Mentally Incapacitated and Other Vulnerable Adults: Public Law Protection* (HMSO, May 1993, £7.95).

5 Law Commission Report No 231, para 7.7, and draft Mental Incapacity Bill, cl 16(1).

6 *Ibid*, para 7.24, and draft Bill, cl 13.

7 *Ibid*, paras 7.28 to 7.31, and draft Bill, cl 15(1).

8 *Ibid*, paras 7.36 to 7.38, and draft Bill, cl 15(6).

9 *Ibid*, para 7.56, and draft Bill, cl 17(3).

10 *Ibid*, para 7.59 and draft Bill, cl 21 and Sch 3, Parts II–V.

11 *Ibid*, para 7.61, and draft Bill, cl 21(2) and Sch 3, Part I.

CHECKLISTS

A checklist to ascertain capacity to create an EPA is included in Chapter 3 (Checklist 3) at p 60.

1 REGISTERING AN EPA

(1)   Remember that the donor is your client.[1] **The attorney is the donor's agent.**

(2)   Check that the EPA was valid at the time of its creation, and that it still is valid.

For example:

- was the correct prescribed form used?[2]
- was it properly executed by the donor and attorney(s)?
- has a subsequent event occurred (such as the disclaimer, death or bankruptcy of the attorney, or the revocation of the power by the donor) which affects the validity of the power?

If you have any doubts about the validity of the EPA, refer the matter to the court for a determination under s 4(5) of the Enduring Powers of Attorney Act 1985.

(3)   Is the donor incapable, or becoming incapable, by reason of mental disorder, of managing and administering his or her property and affairs?

- Is the donor suffering from a *mental disorder* as defined in the Mental Health Act 1983, s 1(2)?[3]
- As a consequence of the mental disorder is the donor incapable, or becoming incapable, of managing his or her property and affairs?
- What property and affairs need to be managed?
- How vulnerable is the donor?
- Is there a less restrictive alternative?

(4)   Prepare the notice of intention to apply for registration (Form EP1).

- Look at the list of relatives in Sch 1 to the Enduring Powers of Attorney Act 1985, and work out who is entitled to receive notice. At least three of the donor's nearest relatives should be notified in the following order of priority, class by class:[4]
  - the donor's husband or wife;
  - the donor's children;
  - the donor's parents;

- the donor's brothers and sisters (whether of the whole or half blood);
- the widow or widower of a child of the donor;
- the donor's grandchildren;
- the children of the donor's brothers and sisters of the whole blood;
- the children of the donor's brothers and sisters of the half blood;
- the donor's uncles and aunts of the whole blood; and
- the children of the donor's uncles and aunts of the whole blood.

- If there is more than one person in a particular class of relatives who are entitled to receive notice, then everyone in that class must be given notice.[5]
- Notice need not be given to anyone whose name or address is not known to and cannot reasonably be ascertained by the attorney.[6]
- Notice need not be given to any relative whom the attorney has reason to believe is under 18 or is mentally incapable.[7]
- Consider whether it is necessary to apply for leave to dispense with notice on the grounds that it would be undesirable or impracticable for the attorney to give notice to a particular person or that no useful purpose would be served by giving them notice.[8] (If so, an application must be made in Form EP3 and it should be accompanied by the original EPA.)[9]

(5)   Serve the notice of intention to apply for registration.

- Serve the notice on the donor *personally* – service by post is not sufficient.[10]
- Send Form EP1 by first-class post[11] to the nearest relatives who are entitled to receive notice (preferably with a photocopy of the EPA itself).
- All these notices must be served within fourteen days of each other.[12]

(6)   Send the application to the Public Trust Office.

An application for the registration of an EPA must be made in Form EP2 and lodged with the Public Trust Office not later than ten days after the date on which: (a) notice has been given to the donor and every relative entitled to receive notice and every co-attorney; or (b) leave has been given to dispense with notice (whichever may be the later).[13]

You need to send to the Public Trust Office:[14]

- Form EP2, duly signed and dated;
- the original EPA; and
- a cheque for £50 made payable to the Public Trust Office.

(7)   Let the attorney know about his or her limited authority to deal with the donor's property and affairs pending registration.

- The attorney only has authority to:
  - maintain the donor;
  - prevent loss to the donor's estate;
  - maintain other people insofar as s 3(4) of the Enduring Powers of Attorney Act 1985 permits.

• If the attorney needs wider powers pending completion of the registration, consider making an application to the Court of Protection for such wider powers.[15]

---

1 The Law Society, *The Guide to the Professional Conduct of Solicitors* (6th edition, 1993), Principle 12.01, Commentary 4. See, generally, the discussion on enduring powers of attorney in Chapter 2 at p 26 ff above.

2 Enduring Powers of Attorney Act 1985, s 2(1)(a). For details of the different prescribed forms, see p 220 above.

3 'Mental disorder' means 'mental illness, arrested or incomplete development of mind, psychopathic disorder and any other disorder or disability of mind': Mental Health Act 1983, s 1(2). For a detailed discussion of this definition, see p 49 above.

4 Enduring Powers of Attorney Act 1985, Sch 1, para 2(1).

5 *Ibid*, para 2(3) and (4).

6 *Ibid*, para 2(2)(a).

7 *Ibid*, para 2(2)(b).

8 *Ibid*, para 3(2).

9 Court of Protection (Enduring Powers of Attorney) Rules 1994 (SI 1994/3047), r 7(2).

10 Court of Protection (Enduring Powers of Attorney) Rules 1994 (SI 1994/3047), r 16(1): 'Any document required by these rules to be given to the donor shall be given to him personally'.

11 *Ibid*, r 16(2): 'Except where these Rules otherwise provide, any document required by these Rules to be given to any other person shall be given by sending it to him by first class post'.

12 *Ibid*, r 7(1).

13 Court of Protection (Enduring Powers of Attorney) Rules 1994 (SI 1994/3047), r 8.

14 For a letter to the Public Trust Office enclosing an application to register an EPA, see Precedent 19 at p 263 below.

15 Enduring Powers of Attorney Act 1985, s 5. The functions of the court under this section are not exercisable by the Public Trustee: Court of Protection (Enduring Powers of Attorney) Rules 1994 (SI 1994/3047), r 6.

2 CANCELLATION OF REGISTRATION OF AN EPA ON THE DONOR'S RECOVERY

(1) Assess the donor's capacity

Is the donor still suffering from mental disorder as defined in the Mental Health Act 1983, s 1(2)?

Is the donor now capable of managing and administering his or her property and affairs?

Is the donor likely to remain mentally capable of managing his or her property and affairs for the foreseeable future?[1]

(2) Medical evidence

Write to the donor's GP or any other medical practitioner who has recent knowledge of the donor's mental state, and explain the purpose for writing.

Remind the doctor of the criteria for assessing whether a person is incapable, by reason of mental disorder, of managing and administering his or her property and affairs.[2]

Obtain evidence in writing from the doctor which specifically answers the three questions raised under (1) above, and gives reasons for the opinion.[3]

(3) Confirmation by the donor

Clarify whether the donor wishes the registration of the EPA to be cancelled, or whether he or she wishes the EPA to be revoked.

(4) Prepare the application

The application may be in letter form, unless the Court of Protection directs that it should be formal, in which case it should be made on Form EP3.[4]

If the applicant is the donor, rather than the attorney(s), obtain concurrence from the attorney(s) in writing.

(5) Submit the application

Send the following to the Court of Protection,[5] Stewart House, 24 Kingsway, London WC2B 6JX (or DX 37965 Kingsway):

- the application itself (either in letter form, or in Form EP3);
- the medical evidence;
- the original registered EPA;
- the written concurrence of the attorneys, if they are not the applicants;
- written confirmation from the donor as to whether the EPA is to be revoked on cancellation of the registration, or whether it will remain in force.

(6) Cancellation of registration

On receipt of the application, the court may decide either that no hearing shall be held, or it may fix an appointment for directions for the application to be heard.[6] If the court cancels the registration, the instrument is stamped with details of the cancellation, and – assuming that the donor is not seeking to revoke the power – it reverts to being an unregistered EPA.

---

1 Section 8(4) of the Enduring Powers of Attorney Act 1985 states that: 'The court shall cancel the registration of an instrument . . . (c) on being satisfied that the donor is *and is likely to remain* mentally capable'. In *The Incapacitated Principal* (Law Com No 122), Cmnd 8977 (HMSO, 1983), at p 47, the Law Commission stated that 'this would involve a complete recovery rather than a return to, say, the *becoming incapable* level'.

2 See, generally, the section on capacity to manage and administer one's property and affairs in Chapter 3 at p 48 ff above.

3 For a precedent medical certificate on an EPA donor's recovery, see Precedent 4, Chapter 3, at p 69 above.

4 Court of Protection (Enduring Powers of Attorney) Rules 1994 (SI 1994/3047), r 9(1).

5 The cancellation of the registration of an EPA on the donor's recovery is not one of the functions exercisable by the Public Trustee: *ibid*, r 6.

6 *Ibid*, r 11(2).

FORMS

SCHEDULE TO THE ENDURING POWERS OF ATTORNEY (PRESCRIBED FORM) REGULATIONS 1990[1]: PRESCRIBED FORM OF EPA

Enduring Power of Attorney

Part A: About using this form

1. **You may choose one attorney or more than one.** If you choose one attorney then you must delete everything between the square brackets on the first page of the form. If you choose more than one, you must decide whether they are able to act:
   - Jointly (that is, they must all act together and cannot act separately) or
   - Jointly and severally (that is, they can all act together but they can also act separately if they wish).
   On the first page of the form, show what you have decided by crossing out one of the alternatives.

2. **If you give your attorney(s) general power** in relation to all your property and affairs, it means that they will be able to deal with your money or property and may be able to sell your house.

3. **If you don't want your attorney(s) to have such wide powers**, you can include any restrictions you like. For example, you can include a restriction that your attorney(s) must not act on your behalf until they have reason to believe that you are becoming mentally incapable; or a restriction as to what your attorney(s) may do. Any restrictions you choose must be written or typed where indicated on the second page of the form.

4. **If you are a trustee** (and please remember that co-ownership of a home involves trusteeship), you should seek legal advice if you want your attorney(s) to act as a trustee on your behalf.

5. **Unless you put in a restriction preventing it** your attorney(s) will be able to use any of your money or property to make any provision which you yourself might be expected to make for their own needs or the needs of other people. Your attorney(s) will also be able to use your money to make gifts, but only for reasonable amounts in relation to the value of your money and property.

6. **Your attorney(s) can recover the out-of-pocket expenses** of acting as your attorney(s). If your attorney(s) are professional people, for example solicitors or accountants, they may be able to charge for their professional services as well. You may wish to provide expressly for remuneration of your attorney(s) (although if they are trustees they may not be allowed to accept it).

7. **If your attorney(s) have reason to believe that** you may have become or are becoming mentally incapable of managing your affairs, your attorney(s) will have to apply to the Court of Protection for registration of this power.

8. **Before applying to the Court of Protection for registration** of this power, your attorney(s) must give written notice that that is what they are going to do, to you and your nearest relatives as defined in the Enduring Powers of Attorney Act 1985. You or your relatives will be able to object if you or they disagree with registration.

9. **This is a simplified explanation** of what the Enduring Powers of Attorney Act 1985 and the Rules and Regulations say. If you need more guidance, you or your advisers will need to look at the Act itself and the Rules and Regulations. The Rules are the Court of Protection (Enduring Powers of Attorney) Rules 1986 (Statutory Instrument 1986 No. 127). The Regulations are the Enduring Powers of Attorney (Prescribed Form) Regulations 1990 (Statutory Instrument 1990 No. 1376).

10. **Note to Attorney(s)**
    After the power has been registered you should notify the Court of Protection if the donor dies or recovers.

11. **Note to Donor**
    Some of these explanatory notes may not apply to the form you are using if it has already been adapted to suit your particular requirements.

YOU CAN CANCEL THIS POWER AT ANY TIME BEFORE IT HAS TO BE REGISTERED

Part B: To be completed by the 'donor' (the person appointing the attorney(s))

Don't sign this form unless you understand what it means

Please read the notes in the margin which follow and which are part of the form itself. Donor's name and address.	I _____ of _____
Donor's date of birth.	born on _____ appoint _____
See note 1 on the front of this form. If you are appointing only one attorney you should cross out everything between the square brackets. If appointing more than two attorneys please give the additional name(s) on an attached sheet.	of _____ • [and _____ of _____
Cross out the one which does not apply (see note 1 on the front of this form).	• jointly • jointly and severally] to be my attorney(s) for the purpose of the Enduring Powers of Attorney Act 1985
Cross out the one which does not apply (see note 2 on the front of this form). Add any additional powers.	• with general authority to act on my behalf • with authority to do the following on my behalf:
If you don't want the attorney(s) to have general power, you must give details here of what authority you are giving the attorney(s).	
Cross out the one which does not apply.	in relation to • all my property and affairs: • the following property and affairs:

Part B: continued

Please read the notes in the margin which follow and which are part of the form itself.

If there are restrictions or conditions, insert them here; if not, cross out these words if you wish (see note 3 on the front of this form).

- subject to the following restrictions and conditions:

If this form is being signed at your direction:
- the person signing must not be an attorney or any witness (to Parts B or C).
- you must add a statement that this form has been signed at your direction.
- a second witness is necessary (please see below).

I intend that this power shall continue even if I become mentally incapable

I have read or have had read to me the notes in Part A which are part of, and explain, this form.

Your signature (or mark).

Signed by me as a deed _____
and delivered

Date.
Someone must witness your signature.

on _____

Signature of witness.

in the presence of _____

Your attorney(s) cannot be your witness. It is not advisable for your husband or wife to be your witness.

Full name of witness _____

Address of witness _____

_____

_____

A second witness is only necessary if this form is not being signed by you personally but at your direction (for example, if a physical disability prevents you from signing).
Signature of second witness.

in the presence of _____

Full name of witness _____

Address of witness _____

_____

_____

Part C: To be completed by the attorney(s)

Note: 1. This form may be adapted to provide for execution by a corporation
2. If there is more than one attorney additional sheets in the form as shown below must be added to this Part C

Please read the notes in the margin which follow and which are part of the form itself.

Don't sign this form before the donor has signed Part B or if, in your opinion, the donor was already mentally incapable at the time of signing Part B.

If this form is being signed at your direction:
• the person signing must not be an attorney or any witness (to Parts B or C).
• you must add a statement that this form has been signed at your direction.
• a second witness is necessary (please see below).

Signature (or mark) of attorney.

Date

Signature of witness.

The attorney must sign the form and his signature must be witnessed. The donor may not be the witness and one attorney may not witness the signature of the other.

I understand that I have a duty to apply to the Court for the registration of this form under the Enduring Powers of Attorney Act 1985 when the donor is becoming or has become mentally incapable.

I also understand my limited power to use the donor's property to benefit persons other than the donor.

I am not a minor

Signed by me as a deed _____
and delivered

on _____

in the presence of _____

Full name of witness _____

Address of witness _____

_____

_____

A second witness is only necessary if this form is not being signed by you personally but at your direction (for example, if a physical disability prevents you from signing).
Signature of second witness.

in the presence of _____

Full name of witness _____

Address of witness _____

_____

_____

1 SI 1990/1376.

COURT OF PROTECTION (ENDURING POWERS OF ATTORNEY) RULES 1994, SCHEDULE 1

FORM EP1: Notice of Intention to Apply for Registration

Court of Protection/Public Trust Office
Enduring Powers of Attorney Act 1985

Notice of intention to apply for registration

To ....

of ....

TAKE NOTICE THAT

This form may be adapted for use by three or more attorneys.

I ....

of ....

and I ....

of ....

Give the name and address of the donor.

the attorney(s) of ....

....

of ....

....

It will be necessary for you to produce evidence in support of your objection. If evidence is available please send it with your objection, the attorney(s) will be given an opportunity to respond to your objection.

intend to apply to the Public Trustee for registration of the enduring power of attorney appointing me (us) attorney(s) and made by the donor on the .... 19 ....

1. If you wish to object to the proposed registration you have 4 weeks from the day on which this notice is given to you to do so in writing. Any objections should be sent to the Public Trustee and should contain the following details:

   - your name and address;

   - any relationship to the donor;

   - if you are not the donor, the name and address of the donor;

   - the name and address of the attorney;

The grounds upon which you can object are limited and are shown at 2 overleaf.

   - the grounds for objecting to the registration of the enduring power.

EP1

Note. The instrument means the enduring power of attorney made by the donor which it is sought to register.

2. The grounds on which you may object are:

- that the power purported to have been created by the instrument is not valid as an enduring power of attorney;

- that the power created by the instrument no longer subsists;

- that the application is premature because the donor is not yet becoming mentally incapable;

- that fraud or undue pressure was used to induce the donor to make the power;

- that the attorney is unsuitable to be the donor's attorney (having regard to all the circumstances and in particular the attorney's relationship to or connection with the donor).

The attorney(s) does not have to be a relative. Relatives are not entitled to know of the existence of the enduring power of attorney prior to being given this notice.

Note. This is addressed only to the donor.

3. You are informed that while the enduring power of attorney remains registered, you will not be able to revoke it until the Court of Protection confirms the revocation.

Note. This notice should be signed by every one of the attorneys who are applying to register the enduring power of attorney.

Signed .... Dated ....

Signed .... Dated ....

Court of Protection/Public Trust Office, Protection Division, Stewart House, 24 Kingsway, London WC2B 6JX

EP1

FORM EP2: **Application for Registration**

Court of Protection/Public Trust Office
Enduring Powers of Attorney Act 1985

Application for registration

Note. Give the full name and present address of the donor. If the donor's address on the enduring power of attorney is different give that one too.

The donor

Name ....

Address...

....

Address on the Enduring Power of Attorney (if different).........................

....

Note. Give the full name(s) and details of the attorney(s).

The attorney(s)

Name ....

Address...

age .... occupation ....

relationship to donor (if any) ....

This form may be adapted for use by three or more attorneys.

Name ....

Address...

age .... occupation ....

relationship to donor (if any) ....

The date is the date upon which the donor signed the enduring power of attorney.

I (we) the attorney(s) apply to register the enduring power of attorney made by the donor under the above Act on

the .... 19 ....

the original of which accompanies this application.

I (we) have reason to believe that the donor is or is becoming mentally incapable.

Notice must be personally given. It should be made clear if someone other than the attorney(s) gives the notice.

I (we) have given notice in the prescribed form to the following:

• the donor personally at..

....

on the .... 19 ....

- The following relatives of the donor at the addresses below on the dates given:

Names	Relationship	Addresses	Date

If there are no relatives entitled to notice please say so.

Note. Cross out this section if it does not apply.

- The Co-Attorney(s) ....

  at ....

  on ....

A remittance for the registration fee accompanies this application.

Note. The application should be signed by all the attorneys who are making the application.

I (we) certify that the above information is correct and that to the best of my (our) knowledge and belief I (we) have complied with the provisions of the Enduring Power of Attorney Act 1985 and of all the Rules and Regulations under it.

Signed .... Dated ....

This must not pre-date the date(s) when the notices were given.

Signed .... Dated ....

....

Address to which correspondence relating to the application is to be sent if different to that of the first-named attorney making this

application ....

....

When completed this form should be sent to:–
Court of Protection/Public Trust Office, Protection Division, Stewart House, 24 Kingsway, London WC2B 6JX

EP2

FORM EP3: General Form of Application

Court of Protection/Public Trust Office

Enduring Powers of Attorney Act 1985
In the matter of a power given by

> If this application is being made prior to an application for registration the original enduring power of attorney should accompany this application.

.... **(a donor)**

to.. **(attorney)**

and .... **(attorney)**

General form of application

I ....

of ....

> Note. Give details of the order or directions that you are seeking.

and I ....

of ....

Apply for an order or directions that ....

> State under which sub-section of the Enduring Powers of Attorney Act 1985 or which rule of the Court of Protection (Enduring Powers of Attorney) Rules 1994 this application is made.

....

....

....

....

....

and for any other directions which are necessary as a result of my/our application.

> Note. Give details of the grounds on which you are seeking the order or directions.

The grounds on which I/we make this application are:

....

....

> Evidence in support should accompany this application.

....

....

Signed.. Dated.........................

> Note. The application should be signed by all the applicants or their solicitors.

Signed.. Dated.........................

Address where notices should be sent.......................................

....

....

When completed this form should be sent to:–
Court of Protection/Public Trust Office, Protection Division, Stewart House, 24 Kingsway, London WC2B 6JX

EP3

FORM EP4: **Application for Search/Office Copy**

Court of Protection

No._____

Enduring Powers of Attorney Act 1985

Application for search/office copy

I (we)_____

of_____

_____

apply to be informed by the Court whether an enduring power of

attorney has been registered (or whether registration of an enduring

power of attorney is pending) in the name of

Note. Give the full name (if known) of the person who is the subject of your enquiry.

_____

alternative name _____

address (if known)_____

_____

alternative address_____

I (we) enclose the prescribed fee of £ _____

Note. Please fill in if applicable

Please supply me (us) with an office copy of the power.

- My/Our reasons for requesting a copy from the Court are _____

_____

_____

_____

_____

- It is not reasonably practicable to obtain a copy from the attorney

because: _____

_____

_____

_____

Signed _____

Dated_____

The Court of Protection, Stewart House, 24 Kingsway, London WC2B 6JX

EP4

Bas 273093/3/A19689 2m 4/89 P

FORM EP5:   Certificate of Result of Search

Court of Protection/Public Trust Office   No. ....

Enduring Powers of Attorney Act 1985

Certificate of result of search

> Your reference ....
>
> In reply to your enquiry made on...
>
> ☐ The following enduring power of attorney is registered
>   against the donor's name you give:
>
>   Donor's name...
>
>   Attorney's name...
>
>   Power made by donor on ....registered on ....
>
> ☐ There is an application pending for registration of the
>   following enduring power of attorney:
>
>   Donor's name...
>
>   Attorney's name...
>
>   Power made by donor on ....
>
> ☐ There was an enduring power of attorney registered
>   against the donor's name you give but the registration has
>   been cancelled:
>
>   Donor's name...
>
>   Attorney's name...
>
>   Power made by donor on ....registered on ....
>
>   Date cancelled ....
>
> ☐ There is no enduring power of attorney registered against
>   the donor's name (...
>   ....) you give.

Signed ....

Dated ....

EP5

FORM EP6: **Witness Summons**

Court of Protection

No ....

Enduring Powers of Attorney Act 1985

In the matter of a power given by

.... a donor

| **Witness summons** |

To ....

of ....

....

You are ordered to attend before ....

....

at ....

....

on the .... day of ....19 ....

at ....o'clock, to:

• give evidence in this matter

• bring with you and produce at the hearing the documents listed below:

....

....

....

....

....

Dated ....

This summons was issued at the request of

....

Solicitors for the ....

of ....

....

When completed this form should be sent to:– Court of Protection\Protection Division, Public Trust Office, 24 Kingsway London WC2B 6JX

FORM EP7: Notice of Appeal

COURT OF PROTECTION   No. _____

Enduring Powers of Attorney Act 1985

in the matter of _____

_____ a donor

Notice of appeal

I (we) _____

of _____

_____

wish to appeal to a judge against the order/decision of the Court made in this

matter on the _____ 19 __

_____

_____

_____

I intend to ask that the order/decision may be

☐ discharged

☐ varied in the following way

_____

_____

_____

_____

Signed _____ appellant

Dated _____

Solicitors for the appellant _____

of _____

_____

Note. If you are appealing against only part of the order/decision write down which part.

Note. Tick the box that applies.

Note. Give details of the new order/decision you are asking to be made.

Note. The form should be sent to the Court of Protection.

EP7 | To the appellant: You will be sent notice of the time, date and place of this appeal.

PUBLIC TRUST OFFICE STEWART HOUSE 24 KINGSWAY LONDON WC2B 6JX

PRECEDENTS

1 CLAUSE DEFERRING THE USE OF AN EPA UNTIL THE ONSET OF THE DONOR'S MENTAL INCAPACITY

This power shall come into effect when my attorney has reason to believe that I am or am becoming mentally incapable [or when the duty to register it arises].[1]

---

1 An EPA is usually 'live' from the moment it is executed by the donor. If the donor intends the power to come into operation at the onset of incapacity, he or she must specifically say so in the instrument creating the EPA. Such a power is sometimes referred to as 'springing', because it springs into action when needed.

The form of wording in the above clause may be preferable to stating that the power will only have effect 'if it is registered' for the following reasons.

- There is a minimum delay of five weeks between applying for the registration of an EPA and its actual registration. If anyone objects to the registration the delay could be substantially longer.
- During the interval between making the application to register and registration itself, the attorney can take the following action under the power: '(a) to maintain the donor or prevent loss to his estate; or (b) to maintain himself or other persons so far as section 3(4) permits him to do so': Enduring Powers of Attorney Act 1985, s 1(2). It is more likely to be in the best interests of the donor for the attorney to have at least these limited powers during the registration period, rather than no powers at all.
- Quite often the donor of an EPA dies in the period between the making of the application and the completion of the registration: Mrs A.B. Macfarlane, 'The Court of Protection', (1992) *Medico-Legal Journal*, vol 60, Pt 1, p 33.
- If the court considers that wider powers are needed prior to registration, these may be conferred by the court under s 5 of the Act.

---

2 CLAUSE REQUIRING MEDICAL EVIDENCE OF INCAPACITY TO BE PRODUCED PRIOR TO REGISTRATION OF AN EPA

This power shall not be registered by the court unless, after considering medical evidence, it is satisfied that I am [or am becoming] incapable by reason of mental disorder of managing and administering my property and affairs.[1]

1 An EPA is registrable 'if the attorney . . . has reason to believe that the donor is or is becoming mentally incapable': Enduring Powers of Attorney Act 1985, s 4(1). There is generally no obligation on the attorney to obtain medical evidence of the donor's mental capacity. This clause imposes a requirement on the attorney to obtain medical evidence of the donor's incapacity and to submit it to the Court of Protection when applying for the registration of the EPA. It is recommended that the medical evidence assume the form of the Medical Certificate (Form CP3) required by the court when considering the appointment of a receiver under Part VII of the Mental Health Act 1983. (See Chapter 10, p 289.)

3 CLAUSE AUTHORISING ATTORNEYS TO DELEGATE THE MANAGEMENT OF INVESTMENTS[1]

My attorneys may, on such terms and conditions as they think fit, without being liable for loss, arrange for my assets consisting of or including investments to be transferred into any discretionary management scheme, even though this means that investment decisions will be made by the managers of the scheme and my investments will be held in the name of the managers or their nominees.

1 There is potentially a problem here. Enduring Powers of Attorney Act 1985, s 2(9) states that: 'A power of attorney which gives the attorney a right to appoint a substitute or successor cannot be an enduring power'. For a detailed discussion of this problem, see 'Substitutes and Successors', fn 6, at p 229 above.

4 SOLICITOR ACTING AS ATTORNEY: PROFESSIONAL CHARGING CLAUSE[1]

(*Name of attorney*) may be paid such sums for acting as my attorney as are fair and reasonable in accordance with the Solicitors' (Non-Contentious Business) Remuneration Order 1994.[2]

1 An attorney is generally entitled to the reimbursement of out-of-pocket expenses: *Thacker v Hardy* (1878) 4 QBD 685, CA. An attorney has a fiduciary duty not to take any unauthorised financial benefit: *Dale v IRC* [1954] AC 11, [1953] 2 All ER 671, HL. The Council of The Law Society has expressed the opinion that, where a client appoints a solicitor to be his or her attorney, the solicitor is entitled to be paid not only for the professional services in preparing the power of attorney, but also for the non-professional services in acting as an attorney: Opinion, 14 March 1958 (*Law Society's Digest*, 4th Cum Supp, p 96).

The Enduring Powers of Attorney Act 1985 does not authorise the remuneration of an attorney, other than indirectly in s 8(2)(b)(iii), which says that, when the power is registered, 'the court may . . . give directions with respect to . . . the remuneration or expenses of the attorney, whether or not in default of or in accordance with any provision made by the instrument, including directions for the repayment of excessive or the payment of additional remuneration'. The current prescribed form of EPA contains the somewhat ambivalent statements in Part A, Note 6: 'Your attorney(s) can recover the out-of-pocket expenses of acting as your attorney(s). If your attorney(s) are professional people, for example solicitors or accountants, they may be able to charge for their professional services as well. You may wish to provide expressly for remuneration of your attorney(s) (although if they are trustees they may not be allowed to accept it)': Schedule to the Enduring Powers of Attorney (Prescribed Form) Regulations 1990 (SI 1990/1376).

It is recommended that whenever a solicitor is appointed as attorney, a charging clause should be expressly included in the instrument. If, when the power is registered, an application is made to the Court of Protection, the court may construe the charging clause an advance authorisation of the solicitor's fees by the donor, thereby avoiding the need for taxation of costs.

2 For the criteria as to the 'fairness and reasonableness' of the sum charged, see the Solicitors' (Non-Contentious Business) Remuneration Order 1994 (SI 1994/2616), which came into force on 1 November 1994. Note that 'a solicitor who holds a power of attorney from a client must not use that power to gain a benefit which, if acting as a professional adviser to that client, he or she would not be prepared to allow to an independent third party': The Law Society, *The Guide to the Professional Conduct of Solicitors* (6th edition, 1993), Principle 15.07. Similarly, 'a solicitor must not take advantage of the age, inexperience, want of education or business experience or ill health of the client': *ibid*, Principle 12.14.

---

5 CLAUSE (IN A SEPARATE INSTRUMENT) APPOINTING AN ALTERNATIVE ATTORNEY WHEN THE ORIGINAL ATTORNEY CEASES TO ACT[1]

My attorney's authority under this power shall not commence until the authority of *(full name of original attorney)*, whom I have appointed to be my attorney in a separate instrument dated *(date)*, is terminated.

---

1 'A power of attorney which gives the attorney a right to appoint a substitute or successor cannot be an enduring power': Enduring Powers of Attorney Act 1985, s 2(9). However, the donor can appoint a substitute or successor to act in the event of the original attorney ceasing to act. The Law Commission Report No 122, *The Incapacitated Principal*, Cmnd 8977 (HMSO, July 1983), at p 50, note 214, stated that 'it would, however, be possible to create the effect of successiveness by a donor granting EPAs in separate instruments so that the authority of an attorney under one power could commence only upon the termination of the authority of an attorney under another power'.

6 CLAUSE (IN THE ONE INSTRUMENT) APPOINTING AN ALTERNATIVE ATTORNEY WHEN THE ORIGINAL ATTORNEY CEASES TO ACT[1]

Ensure that the marginal notes on the prescribed form are not omitted

I ....

of ....

born on ....

appoint ....

of ....

to be my attorney for the purpose of the Enduring Powers of Attorney Act 1985 with general authority to act on my behalf in relation to all my property and affairs.

If for any reason (his)/(her) authority under this power is terminated, I appoint ....

of ....

instead to be my attorney for the purpose of the Enduring Powers of Attorney Act 1985 with general authority to act on my behalf in relation to all my property and affairs.

Continue with the standard provisions of the prescribed form.

Ensure that 'Part C: To be completed by the attorney' is completed by each attorney.

---

1 'A power of attorney which gives the attorney a right to appoint a substitute or successor cannot be an enduring power': Enduring Powers of Attorney Act 1985, s 2(9). However, there is no reason why the donor cannot appoint a substitute or successor to act in the event of the original attorney ceasing to act. The effect of successiveness could also be achieved by the donor granting two separate EPAs – the authority under one of which would only commence on the termination of the attorney's authority under the other power – which is the course recommended by the Law Commission in *The Incapacitated Principal*, Cmnd 8977 (HMSO, July 1983), p 50, note 214. For a precedent, see Precedent 5 at p 251 above.

Although s 11(1) of the Enduring Powers of Attorney Act 1985 provides that an instrument which appoints more than one attorney cannot create an enduring power unless the attorneys are appointed to act jointly or jointly and severally, the Court of Protection takes the view that an instrument which appoints one attorney but provides that, if he cannot or does not act, a named alternative attorney is appointed, is an instrument appointing only one person: P.D. Lewis, 'The Enduring Powers of Attorney Act 1985', *The Law Society's Gazette*, 26 November 1986, p 3567.

If successive attorneys are appointed, they should not both apply to register the EPA. Affidavit evidence will be needed to show which of them should register and act as attorney: P.D. Lewis, 'The Enduring Powers of Attorney Act 1985 – Twelve Months On', *The Law Society's Gazette*, 29 April 1987, p 1219.

7 CLAUSE REQUIRING THE ATTORNEY TO NOTIFY ADDITIONAL PERSONS OF INTENTION TO APPLY FOR REGISTRATION OF THE EPA[1]

In addition to those who are entitled by statute to receive notice of my attorney's intention to apply to the court for the registration of this power,[2] my attorney will give notice in the prescribed form to the following person(s), who may, with the leave of the court, object to the registration of this power:[3]

Name(s)[4]   Relationship (if any)   Address(es)[5]
                    to the donor

---

1 It is not possible to derogate from the statutory list of those who are entitled to receive notification of the attorney's intention to apply for registration, but it is possible to add to that list so as to include for example, a partner or, close friend; a stepchild, stepbrother or stepsister; a brother-in-law or sister-in-law; a doctor; a solicitor; a priest or pastor; a social worker; a voluntary worker; a home-help; a next-door neighbour; a residential care home or nursing home proprietor, etc.

Cretney et al, in *Enduring Powers of Attorney: A Report to the Lord Chancellor* (Lord Chancellor's Department, June 1991), at para 2.24, noted that 'the list of relatives to be notified often appeared somewhat arbitrary and out of keeping with present-day patterns of family relationships – as is the fact that it was not necessary to notify someone with whom the donor had been living for twenty years, but it would be necessary to notify a brother or cousin who had been living in Australia for this period. There was a general impression (among solicitors) that notifications had to be given to distant relatives who had no conceivable interest in the donor or in his finances'.

2 Enduring Powers of Attorney Act 1985, Sch 1. The list of relatives who have to be notified is reproduced at p 223 above under the heading 'Notification prior to registration'.

3 For applications for leave to apply for relief specified in the 1985 Act, see Court of Protection (Enduring Powers of Attorney) Rules 1994 (SI 1994/3047), r 22.

4 Note that, at para 7.18 of its Consultation Paper No 128, *Mentally Incapacitated Adults and Decision-Making: A New Jurisdiction*, circulated in February 1993, the Law Commission provisionally recommended that 'a donor should name in an EPA the two (or more) persons who are to be notified of its execution . . . '.

5 The problem with including addresses in this clause is that they may be out-of-date when the question of notification arises.

8 CLAUSE AUTHORISING DISCLOSURE OF THE DONOR'S WILL TO THE ATTORNEY[1]

I authorise my solicitor to disclose to my attorney(s) the contents of my will and any other testamentary document executed by me, provided that this power is registered, and provided that my solicitor considers such disclosure to be necessary or expedient for the proper exercise of the functions of my attorney(s).

---

1 'A solicitor is under a duty to keep confidential to his or her firm the affairs of clients and to ensure that the staff do the same': The Law Society, *The Guide to the Professional Conduct of Solicitors* (6th edition, 1993), Principle 16.01. Commentary 4 on that Principle states that: 'Whether a solicitor should disclose the contents of a will during the testator's lifetime to the donee of a power of attorney granted by the testator will depend upon the extent to which the power of attorney enables the donee to stand in the place of the testator. Where there is an ordinary power of attorney in force it should be possible to obtain the donor's consent as he or she will have mental capacity. An enduring power of attorney will not be effective following incapacity unless it is registered. Once registered, if the power is silent on the subject of disclosure, it is necessary to obtain a decision from the Court of Protection as to whether the will can be disclosed'. Disclosure may be authorised by the court under s 8(2)(d) of the Enduring Powers of Attorney Act 1985.

---

9 CLAUSE IN A NEW EPA REVOKING A FORMER EPA[1]

I REVOKE the enduring power of attorney made by me on *(date)*.

[OR]

I REVOKE all enduring powers of attorney previously made by me.

---

1 Unlike the express revocation of a previous will in a newly executed will, the revocation of a former EPA in a new EPA is, on its own, ineffective until the attorney receives notice of the revocation: *Re Oriental Bank ex parte Guillemin* (1885) 28 ChD 634. For a solicitor's letter giving the attorney notice of revocation, see Chapter 8, Precedent 7, at p 211 above. For a deed of revocation, see Chapter 8, Precedent 6, at p 211 above. If the former EPA is registered with the Court of Protection, the revocation by the donor will not be valid unless and until the court confirms the revocation: Enduring Powers of Attorney Act 1985, s 7(1)(a). The court will only confirm the revocation if it is satisfied that the donor has done whatever is necessary in law to effect an express revocation of the power and was mentally capable of revoking a power of attorney when he or she did so (whether or not he or she is so when the court considers the application): *ibid*, s 8(3).

---

10 SOLICITOR AND ANY ONE OF TWO OR MORE OTHER ATTORNEYS TO ACT JOINTLY ON ANY ONE OCCASION[1]

Ensure that the marginal notes of the prescribed form are not omitted

I ....

of ....

born on ....

appoint (my solicitor) ....

of ....

and (my children) ....

of ....

and ....

of ....

- ~~jointly~~
- jointly and severally

to be my attorneys for the purpose of the Enduring Powers of Attorney Act 1985

- with general authority to act on my behalf
- ~~with authority to do the following on my behalf~~

in relation to

- all my property and affairs
- ~~the following property and affairs~~

- subject to the following restrictions and conditions

(1) My solicitor and any one or more of my children shall act jointly on any one occasion;

(2) My solicitor may be paid such sums for acting as my attorney as are fair and reasonable in accordance with the Solicitors' (Non-Contentious Business) Remuneration Order 1994.

Continue as in the prescribed form.

---

1 P.D. Lewis, the former Assistant Public Trustee, asked the following question, and suggested possible solutions to it, in *The Law Society's Gazette*, 26 November 1986, p 3568: 'In a situation where a prospective donor has two children, neither of whom she wishes to alienate but as to neither of whom she feels confident enough to let them act solely or jointly, is it possible for her to make an enduring power whereby either child is empowered to act, provided he or she acts jointly with the donor's solicitor? The answer might be for the donor to grant two

enduring powers, one to child A and the solicitor jointly and the other to child B and the solicitor jointly. If there were no objections, it would seem the court could register both applications and both powers could be operated. The necessary concurrence of the solicitor in any proposed exercise by either child would guard against inconsistent dealings under the two powers. A better answer might be an enduring power appointing child A, child B and the solicitor to act jointly [*sic*], with a restriction included to the effect that only the solicitor and one of the two children should act on any one occasion. This would avoid the possible confusion caused by two powers'.

---

11 APPLICATION TO THE COURT OF PROTECTION TO DISPENSE WITH THE REQUIREMENT TO GIVE NOTICE TO THE DONOR OF THE ATTORNEY'S INTENTION TO APPLY FOR REGISTRATION OF AN EPA[1]

Court of Protection/Public Trust Office
Enduring Powers of Attorney Act 1985
In the matter of a power given by

.... (a donor)
to .... (attorney)
and .... (attorney)

General form of application

I ....
of ....
and I ....
of ....
apply for an order or directions that, pursuant to paragraphs 3(2) and 4(2) of Schedule 1 to the Enduring Powers of Attorney Act 1985, (I)/(we) may be dispensed from the requirement to give notice to the donor of (my)/(our) intention to apply for the registration of the enduring power of attorney executed by the donor on (*date*),

and for any directions which are necessary as a result of (my)/(our) application.

The grounds on which (I)/(we) make this application are: that it would be undesirable to give notice to the donor because such notification would be injurious to the donor's health for the reasons stated in the affidavit in support of this application sworn by (me)/(us) on (*date*).

Signed .... Dated ....
Signed .... Dated ....
Address where notices should be sent ....
....

---

1 Enduring Powers of Attorney Act 1985, Sch 1, paras 3(2) and 4(2); Court of Protection
  (Enduring Powers of Attorney) Rules 1994 (SI 1994/3047), r 11(1)(b). The application is made
  on Form EP3.

---

12 APPLICATION TO THE COURT OF PROTECTION FOR LEAVE TO SUBMIT AN OUT-OF-TIME APPLICATION FOR REGISTRATION OF AN EPA[1]

Court of Protection/Public Trust Office
Enduring Powers of Attorney Act 1985
In the matter of a power given by
.... (a donor)
to .... (attorney)
and .... (attorney)

General form of application

I ....
of ....
and I ....
of ....
apply for an order or directions that, pursuant to r 15(3) of the Court of Protection
(Enduring Powers of Attorney) Rules 1994, (I)/(we) may be granted leave to make
an application to register the power notwithstanding that the time limited by r 8
has expired; and for any directions which are necessary as a result of my/our
application.

The grounds on which (I)/(we) make this application are: that the donor was
critically ill when (he)/(she) was served with the notice of intention to apply for
registration of the power, and (his)/(her) condition deteriorated after service of that
notice. (I)/(we) had reason to believe that the donor's death was imminent, and
that accordingly an application to register the power would be unnecessary. The
donor's condition began to show signs of improvement on (*date*), and (I)/(we) now
wish to proceed with the application to register the power.

Signed .... Dated ....
Signed .... Dated ....
Address where notices should be sent ....
....

---

1 For the time-limit for submitting an application to register an EPA, see Court of Protection
(Enduring Powers of Attorney) Rules 1994 (SI 1994/3047), rr 5, 7 and 8. For the court's
discretion to extend the time-limit, see r 15(3).

---

13 OBJECTION TO THE REGISTRATION OF AN EPA[1]

Court of Protection/Public Trust Office
Enduring Powers of Attorney Act 1985
In the matter of a power given by
.... (a donor)
to .... (attorney)
and .... (attorney)

Objection to registration

I.. *(full name of objector)*
of...*(address, including postcode, of objector)*[2]
OBJECT to the registration of the enduring power of attorney
made by my .... *(state the relationship of the donor to the objector)*[3]
.... *(name of donor)*[4]
of.. *(address of donor)*
on ....*(date on which the EPA was executed, if known)*
appointing...*(full name of attorney)*
of...*(address of attorney)*
and..*(full name of attorney)*
of...*(address of attorney)*
as attorney(s).[5]

The grounds on which I object[6] are that *the power purported to have been created by
the instrument is not valid as an enduring power of attorney because, when it was executed
by (him)/(her), the donor lacked the mental capacity to create an enduring power of
attorney.*[7]

Signed...
Dated[8]...

1 There is no prescribed form of objection to the registration of an EPA, but the required contents are set out in Court of Protection (Enduring Powers of Attorney) Rules 1994 (SI 1994/3047), r 10(1).
2 *Ibid*, r 10(1)(a).
3 *Ibid*, r 10(1)(c).
4 *Ibid*, r 10(1)(b).
5 *Ibid*, r 10(1)(d).
6 *Ibid*, r 10(1)(e). A notice of objection to the registration of an EPA is valid if the objection is made on one or more of the five grounds listed in Enduring Powers of Attorney Act 1985, s 6(5).
7 Because of the presumption of capacity, and the principle that *affirmanti non neganti incumbit probatio*, the onus is on the objector to prove that the donor lacked capacity when he or she executed the EPA. Medical evidence should be produced. Form EP1 contains a marginal note advising any potential objector that 'it will be necessary for you to produce evidence in support of your objection. If evidence is available please send it with your objection'.
8 Any objection to registration received by the court on or after the date of registration shall be treated by the court as an application to cancel the registration: Court of Protection (Enduring Powers of Attorney) Rules 1994 (SI 1994/3047), r 10(2).

14 DISCLAIMER BY AN ATTORNEY ACTING UNDER AN EPA[1]

TO: (*Name and address of donor*)

TAKE NOTICE THAT

I ....

of ....

DISCLAIM my appointment as attorney under the enduring power of attorney made by you on (*date*).

SIGNED ....

DATED ....

1 'No disclaimer of an enduring power, whether by deed or otherwise, shall be valid unless and until the attorney gives notice of it to the donor or, where section 4(6) or 7(1) applies, to the court': Enduring Powers of Attorney Act 1985, s 2(12). Section 4(6) requires the attorney to give notice of disclaimer to the court, if the attorney has reason to believe that the donor is, or is becoming, mentally incapable. Section 7(1) requires the attorney to give notice of disclaimer to the court if the EPA is registered.

Court of Protection (Enduring Powers of Attorney) Rules 1994 (SI 1994/3047), r 6(1) provides that 'The Public Trustee may exercise the following functions: . . . (g) the receiving of a notice of disclaimer under sections 4(6) and 7(1)(b) of the Act'. It is not necessary for the disclaimer to be made by deed. Nor is it necessary for the attorney to disclose his or her reasons for disclaiming. If the attorney is one of two or more attorneys who have been appointed jointly (rather than jointly and severally) the remaining attorneys will no longer have the authority to act under the EPA.

15 NOTICE TO PUBLIC TRUST OFFICE OF DISCLAIMER OF ATTORNEYSHIP UNDER REGISTERED EPA[1]

(Address of attorney)

The Public Trust Office   *(Date)*
Protection Division
Stewart House
24 Kingsway
London WC2B 6JX

Dear Sirs

Disclaimer of attorneyship[2]

I *(full name of attorney)* disclaim my appointment as attorney under the enduring power of attorney made by *(full name and address of donor)* on *(date)* and registered on *(date of registration)*.

I intend that this disclaimer shall take effect as soon as you receive this letter.[3]

Please acknowledge receipt.

Yours faithfully

---

1 No disclaimer of an EPA which is, or is in the process of being, registered is valid unless and until the attorney gives notice of it to the Court of Protection: Enduring Powers of Attorney Act 1985, ss 2(12), 4(6), and 7(1)(b). Court of Protection (Enduring Powers of Attorney) Rules 1994 (SI 1994/3047), r 6(1)(g) states that 'the receiving of a notice of disclaimer under sections 4(6) and 7(1)(b) of the Act' may be exercised by the Public Trustee.

2 Court of Protection (Enduring Powers of Attorney) Rules 1994 (SI 1994/3047), r 9(1) provides that an application may be made by letter unless the Public Trustee directs that the application should be formal. Rule 9(8) of the now superseded 1986 Rules, required a notice of disclaimer to be in Form EP3. There is no requirement in the legislation that an attorney should state his or her reasons for disclaiming. On disclaimer generally, see Law Commission Report No 122, *The Incapacitated Principal*, Cmnd 8977 (HMSO, 1983), paras 4.54–4.56.

3 Court of Protection (Enduring Powers of Attorney) Rules 1994 (SI 1994/3047), r 11(7) provides that the disclaimer shall not take effect earlier than the day on which the notice of disclaimer is received at the Public Trust Office.

16 APPLICATION FOR CANCELLATION OF REGISTRATION ON DONOR'S RECOVERY[1]

Court of Protection/Public Trust Office
Enduring Powers of Attorney Act 1985
In the matter of a power given by

.... (a donor)

to .... (attorney)

and .... (attorney)

General form of application

I ....

of ....

apply for an order or directions that under s 8(4)(c) of the Enduring Powers of Attorney Act 1985 the registration of this power may be cancelled (although the power may remain in force)

and for any directions which are necessary as a result of my/~~our~~ application.

The grounds on which I/~~we~~ make this application are:
that I am and am likely to remain mentally capable, and medical evidence in support accompanies this application.

Signed .... Dated ....

Address where notices should be sent ....

....

---

1 Enduring Powers of Attorney Act 1985, s 8(4)(c): 'The court shall cancel the registration of an instrument . . . on being satisfied that the donor is and is likely to remain mentally capable'. This would involve a complete recovery rather than a return to, say, the 'becoming incapable' level: Law Commission Report No 122, *The Incapacitated Principal*, Cmnd 8977 (HMSO, July 1983), p 47.

17 ATTESTATION CLAUSE WHERE EPA IS EXECUTED AT THE DIRECTION OF THE DONOR[1]

(Prescribed form of Enduring Power of Attorney: Part B)

Executed as a deed by *(full name of signatory)*[2] at my direction and in my presence.

~~Signed by me as a deed~~..

~~and delivered~~

on ....

*(Two witnesses are necessary. Each should sign the
form and give their full names and addresses.)*[3]

---

1 Enduring Powers of Attorney (Prescribed Form) Regulations 1990 (SI 1990/1376), reg 3(3) provides as follows:

'Where an enduring power of attorney is executed at the direction of the donor—

    (a)   it must be signed in the presence of two witnesses who shall each sign the form and give their full names and addresses; and

    (b)   a statement that the enduring power of attorney has been executed at the direction of the donor must be inserted in Part B;

    (c)   it must not be signed by either an attorney or any of the witnesses to the signature of either the donor or an attorney.'

Although the Regulations do not specifically state that the person signing at the donor's direction must do so in the donor's presence, this requirement is imposed by the Law of Property (Miscellaneous Provisions) Act 1989, s 1(3)(a)(ii).

2 See reg 3(3)(c) above.

3 See reg 3(3)(a) above.

---

18 STATUTORY DECLARATION OF NON-REVOCATION OF EPA[1]

(I)/(WE) ....

of..

DO SOLEMNLY AND SINCERELY DECLARE as follows

(1)   By a transfer dated *(date)* the property known as *(address)* and registered at the Land Registry under title number *(number)* was transferred to (me)/(us) by *(full name of transferor)* acting by (his)/(her) attorney(s) *(full name of attorney(s))* under an enduring power of attorney ('the power') dated *(date)*.

(2)   At the time of the transfer (I)/(we) did not know:

    (a)   of any revocation of the power, whether by the donor or by an order of the Court of Protection; or

(b) of the occurrence of any event (such as the death of the donor or the bankruptcy of the donor or of a donee or a direction by the Court of Protection on exercising its powers under Part VII of the Mental Health Act 1983) which would have had the effect of revoking the power; or

(c) that the power was not a valid enduring power of attorney and had been revoked by the donor's mental incapacity; or

(d) of any other reason to doubt that the attorney(s) had authority to dispose of the property.

AND (I)/(we) make this solemn declaration conscientiously believing the same to be true and by virtue of the provisions of the Statutory Declarations Act 1835.

DECLARED at ....
this   day of   19

Before me

---

1 See, generally, Enduring Powers of Attorney Act 1985, s 9.

---

19 LETTER TO THE PUBLIC TRUST OFFICE ENCLOSING APPLICATION TO REGISTER AN EPA

Enquiries and Applications Branch
Public Trust Office
Protection Division   (*our reference*)
DX 37965 Kingsway[1]   (*date*)

Dear Sirs

APPLICATION TO REGISTER AN EPA

We apply for the registration of the enduring power given by (*full name of donor*) (donor) to (*full name(s) of attorney(s)*) (attorney(s)) on (*date*).

We enclose:

• the EPA itself;
• Form EP2;[2] and
• a cheque for £50 payable to the 'Public Trust Office'.[3]

We look forward to the return of the EPA duly registered.[4]

Yours faithfully

(*signature of firm of solicitors*)

1 If the application is being sent by post, the address is Stewart House, 24 Kingsway, London WC2B 6JX.
2 Court of Protection (Enduring Powers of Attorney) Rules 1994 (SI 1994/3047), r 8 provides that: 'An application to register an enduring power of attorney shall be made in Form EP2 and shall be lodged with the Public Trust Office not later than 10 days after the date on which: (a) notice has been given to the donor and every relative entitled to receive notice and every co-attorney; or (b) leave has been given to dispense with notice, whichever may be the later'.
3 *Ibid*, Sch 2 provides that the fee on lodging an application for the registration of an EPA shall be £50. Note that the fee is payable in respect of the application, rather than the registration. If the application is unsuccessful, or if the donor dies while the EPA is in the process of being registered, the fee will not be returned.
4 *Ibid*, r 13(2) provides that 'The Public Trustee shall retain a copy of the registered enduring power of attorney and shall return the original instrument to the attorney'.

20 AMENDMENT TO EXPLANATORY INFORMATION IN THE PRESCRIBED FORM OF EPA[1]

9. This is a simplified explanation of what the Enduring Powers of Attorney Act 1985 and the Rules and Regulations say. If you need more guidance, you or your legal advisers will need to look at the Act itself and the Rules and Regulations. The Regulations are the Enduring Powers of Attorney (Prescribed Form) Regulations 1990 (SI 1990/1376).

★ The Rules are the Court of Protection (Enduring Powers of Attorney) Rules 1994 (SI 1994/3047).

1 On 22 December 1994, the Court of Protection (Enduring Powers of Attorney) Rules 1994 came into force. No change has been made to the prescribed form of EPA, which is still governed by the Enduring Powers of Attorney (Prescribed Form) Regulations 1990, and no change to the Prescribed Form Regulations is likely in the foreseeable future. It is understood that the Court of Protection and Public Trust Office have no objection to the note 9 of Part A of the prescribed form being amended in the manner set out in this precedent.

CHAPTER 10: RECEIVERSHIP

INDEX

Text

Forms

The first four – bulleted – forms appear in the Court of Protection Rules 1994 (SI 1994/3046), as Forms A D respectively. The CP reference after each form is non-statutory.

Precedents

RECEIVERSHIP[1]

TEXT

The Court of Protection and the Public Trust Office

The Court of Protection is an office of the Supreme Court which exercises judicial functions over the property and affairs of persons who are incapable, by reason of mental disorder, of managing and administering their property and affairs themselves. Such people are technically known as *patients*, and their financial affairs are managed on a day-to-day basis by a *receiver*.

The origins of the court date from the Middle Ages,[2] when the Crown assumed a *parens patriae* jurisdiction over the persons[3] and estates of the mentally ill and mentally handicapped. In 1842 two Commissioners in Lunacy, later known as Masters, were appointed.[4] These were reduced to one in 1922.[5] In 1934 the Office of the Master in Lunacy was renamed the Management and Administration Department[6] which, although it sounds innocuous, had a most unfortunate set of initials, and actually issued forms headed MAD1, MAD2, etc! The Department became the Court of Protection in 1947.[7] It draws its current powers from the Mental Health Act 1983 and the Court of Protection Rules 1994.[8]

Although the first Public Trustee was appointed in 1906,[9] the Public Trust Office as such came into being on 2 January 1987[10] when it took over the administrative (as distinct from judicial) functions of the Court of Protection. It consists of four divisions or activities:

- Receivership, where the Public Trustee is the receiver;
- Protection, which deals with external receivers;
- Trust, where the Public Trustee is appointed as an executor or trustee;[11] and
- Court Funds, which provides a banking and investment service for funds deposited in court.

On 1 July 1994 the Public Trust Office became an executive agency within the Lord Chancellor's Department, the purpose being to enhance its ability to deliver its services more efficiently and effectively. The Public Trust Office employs 585 staff, has a gross budget of £18.73 m, and is responsible for the management of approximately £2.4 billion of the private assets of individuals.[12] The largest of the four activities − Protection − employs a staff of 214 and deals with 29,000 receivership cases and a current annual total of approximately 6800 EPA applications.[13]

The creation of the executive agency necessitated a new set of rules to clarify the relationship between, and the respective functions of, the Court of Protection and the Public Trust Office. The Court of Protection Rules 1994 came into force on 22 December 1994.[14]

Rule 6 provides that the Public Trustee may exercise all of the functions conferred on the judge by Part VII of the Mental Health Act 1983 *except* for the following functions which shall only be exercised by the Court of Protection:

(a)   the resolution of any contested application, including interim matters;
(b)   the appointment and discharge of a receiver;
(c)   the appointment of a new receiver;
(d)   the appointment of an interim receiver;
(e)   subject to r 9 (procedure for a short order or direction), the determination of the jurisdiction of the court under s 94(2) of the Act;
(f)   the making of orders on applications under s 96(1)(e) (the execution of a statutory will), s 96(1)(i) (conduct of legal proceedings in the name of the patient), s 96(1)(k) (the exercise of any power vested in the patient), s 98 (emergency cases), s 100 (vesting of stock in a curator outside England and Wales), s 103 (ordering that a patient be visited by one of the Lord Chancellor's Visitors) and s 104 (general judicial powers);
(g)   the making of orders on applications under s 96(1)(d) (settlements or gifts of the patient's property) except where, in respect of a gift, it is payable out of surplus income or capital, is insignificant in the context of the patient's assets and is for a sum of not more than £15,000;
(h)   the making of orders relating to loans or other financial transactions where there is an element of gift, except where it is payable out of surplus income or capital, is insignificant in the context of the patient's assets and is for a sum of not more than £15,000;
(i)   the making of directions under s 101 (preservation of interests in a patient's property) and for the severance of joint tenancies;
(j)   the making of directions relating to any assets of a patient that are the subject of specific bequests or devises in his will;
(k)   the making of orders under s 36(9) (appointment of new trustee where a patient is not only a trustee but also has some beneficial interest in the trust property) or s 54 of the Trustee Act 1925;
(l)   the making of orders determining proceedings;
(m)   the making of orders relating to assets situated outside England and Wales and for the transfer of assets out of England and Wales; and
(n)   the giving of such directions as may be appropriate in relation to a will made or proposed to be made by a patient.

One of the effects of r 6 is that sales and purchases are now authorised by the Public Trust Office and need no longer be the subject of an order of the court. However, when the need for an order is apparent at the time of the first application for the appointment of a receiver, an appropriate clause relating to the sale or purchase will continue to be included in the First General Order made by the court. The court no longer needs to settle and approve all mortgages, leases and other dispositions of a patient's land,[15] and, accordingly, there is no longer a transaction fee in respect of sales and purchases of land.[16] For procedure on the sale and purchase of property, and precedents of the documents required, see procedure note PN4.[17]

1 See, generally, *Heywood & Massey: Court of Protection Practice* (12th edition, Sweet & Maxwell, 1991); and Norman Whitehorn, *Court of Protection Handbook* (9th edition, Longman Practitioner Series, 1991).

2 The Statute *de Praerogativa Regis* (c 1325).

3 The *parens patriae* jurisdiction over a patient's person was effectively abolished by the Mental Health Act 1959: see *Re Eve* (1986) 2 SCR 388 (Supreme Court of Canada); *T v T* [1988] 1 All ER 613; *F v West Berkshire Health Authority* [1989] 2 All ER 545, at p 552, HL.

4 Lord Lyndhurst's General Order of 27 October 1842 under Stat 5 and 6 Vict, c 84: 'An Act to alter and amend the practice and course of proceeding under commissions in the nature of writs *de lunatico inquirendo*'. See, generally, T.C.S. Keely, 'One Hundred Years of Lunacy Administration', (1944) 8 *Cambridge Law Journal* 195–200.

5 Lunacy Act 1922, s 1(1).

6 Management of Patients' Estates Rules 1934 (SR&O 1934 No 269/L2), r 8.

7 Patients' Estates (Naming of Master's Office) Order 1947 (SR&O 1947 No 1235/L16).

8 SI 1994/3046.

9 Public Trustee Act 1906. See, generally, Patrick Polden, 'The Public Trustee in England, 1906–1986: The Failure of an Experiment?' (1989) 10 *Journal of Legal History* 228.

10 Public Trustee and Administration of Funds Act 1986.

11 The Lord Chancellor's Department is currently conducting a review of the trustee function of the executive agency.

12 Source: Public Trust Office Framework Document (1994), p 3.

13 Source: Public Trust Office Corporate Plan (1994), Annex B and C.

14 SI 1994/3046. The Court of Protection (Enduring Powers of Attorney) Rules 1994 (SI 1994/3047) came into force on the same day.

15 Rule 74 of the Court of Protection Rules 1984 (SI 1984/2035), which required the court's approval and settlement of transfers, etc has been revoked by the 1994 Rules.

16 Court of Protection Rules 1994 (SI 1994/3046), r 81 and Appendix, item 3.

17 Court of Protection Procedure Note PN4 (latest edition December 1994).

Is receivership necessary?

The Court of Protection's jurisdiction under the Mental Health Act 1983 is exercisable where, after considering medical evidence, it is satisfied that a person is incapable, by reason of mental disorder, of managing and administering his or her property and affairs.[1]

The meaning of 'incapable, by reason of mental disorder, of managing and administering his or her property and affairs' is considered in greater detail in Chapter 3, but in summary there are three prerequisites:

- alleged patients must be suffering from *mental disorder;*[2]
- they must have *property and affairs* that need to be managed and administered; and
- they must be *incapable*, by reason of mental disorder, of managing and administering their property and affairs.

An application for the appointment of a receiver is usually unnecessary if the incapacitated person has created a valid enduring power of attorney, and may not be necessary if his or her only assets consist of:

- social security benefits. The Secretary of State for Social Security could appoint an appointee to claim, collect and deal with the benefits;[3]

- a pension or similar payment payable by a government department, which can be administered by that department for the benefit of the patient and his or her dependants;[4]
- a pension or similar payment from a local authority;[5]
- entitlement under a discretionary trust. The trustees may apply the capital or income for the benefit of the patient as and how they think fit;
- property which does not exceed £5000 in value. The Court of Protection or the Public Trustee could deal with such a case by a short order or direction if it appears that the appointment of a receiver is unnecessary.[6]

---

1 Mental Health Act 1983, s 94(2).
2 'Mental disorder' is defined in Mental Health Act 1983, s 1(2).
3 Social Security (Claims and Payments) Regulations 1987 (SI 1987/1968), reg 33. Appointeeship is considered in detail in Chapter 7.
4 Mental Health Act 1983, s 142.
5 Local Government Act 1972, s 118(3).
6 Court of Protection Rules 1994 (SI 1994/3046), r 9.

The receiver

Who should be appointed as receiver for the patient is ultimately a matter for the Court of Protection to decide when the application and all the relevant facts are before it. The patient's nearest relative (usually the spouse) is normally proposed as receiver, but if he or she is of advanced age it may be preferable to appoint a younger member of the family, such as one of the patient's adult children. If no relatives are willing or able to act, a friend or neighbour of the patient, a solicitor or other professional adviser, or an officer of the local social services authority may be proposed. The following pie chart contains a breakdown of the different types of external receiver appointed in 1991.

Table 1: Receiver type (Protection Division, 1991)[1]

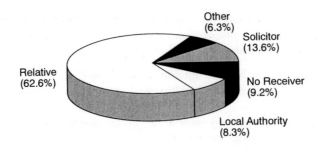

The court is generally reluctant to appoint as receiver anyone who:

- is resident outside England and Wales – although this is not automatically a bar to appointment;
- is an accounting party (eg the trustee of a trust in which the patient has an interest); or
- has interests which conflict with those of the patient, unless the court is satisfied that the patient's interests will not be prejudiced.[2]

Occasionally, applications are made for the appointment of joint receivers, especially where there are two or more opposing factions within the patient's family. Although such appointments are possible, they are discouraged by the court because they are rarely satisfactory. Each decision in the course of a receivership tends to become a bone of contention and can give rise to unnecessary delays and additional costs.[3] Where, in the opinion of the court, two or more persons ought to be appointed receivers for the same patient and one or more of them ought to continue to act after the death or discharge of any of the others, the court may direct that the receivership shall continue in favour of the surviving or continuing receiver.[4]

Where there is no other suitable person, or where there is family friction, the Public Trustee may be appointed. Such an appointment is disadvantageous from the solicitor's point of view in that the Public Trustee takes over conduct of the case once the First General Order has been issued. It is disadvantageous from the patient's point of view because the fees are higher in the Receivership Division than in the Protection Division,[5] and inevitably there is not the same degree of liaison between the receiver and the patient as when a close relative acts as receiver. In 1993–94, the Public Trust Office dealt with 29,137 external receiverships in the Protection Division and 2986 internal receiverships in the Receivership Division.[6]

The court or the Public Trustee may allow the receiver remuneration for his or her services at such rate or amount as the court or Public Trustee considers reasonable and proper. Any remuneration allowed constitutes a debt due to the receiver from the patient's estate.[7]

---

1 Source: Mrs A.B. Macfarlane, Master of the Court of Protection, 'The Court of Protection' (1992) *Medico-Legal Journal*, vol 60, Part 1, p 31. In most cases, 'no receiver' means that a short order or direction has been made under r 9 of the Court of Protection Rules 1994 (SI 1994/3046).
2 Norman Whitehorn, *Court of Protection Handbook* (9th edition, Longman, 1991), p 7.
3 *Ibid.*
4 Court of Protection Rules 1994, r 46.
5 See, generally, the Appendix to the Court of Protection Rules 1994.
6 Source: Public Trust Office Corporate Plan (1994), p 21, Annex C, Caseload assumption chart.
7 Court of Protection Rules 1994, r 45(1).

Applying for the appointment of a receiver

The forms for applying for the appointment of a receiver can be obtained free of charge from the Public Trust Office, Stewart House, 24 Kingsway, London WC2B 6JX.[1]

Before applying, the applicant must give notice of his or her intention to all the patient's relatives of a degree of relationship equal to or nearer than the applicant or the proposed receiver.[2] Where a solicitor is seeking to be appointed as receiver, it is probably sufficient to give notice of the proposed application to the patient's closest relatives rather than the entire family.

The following documents should be completed and sent to the Public Trust Office, Enquiries and Applications Branch:

- two copies of the First Application for the Appointment of a Receiver (Form CP1)[3]
- the Medical Certificate (Form CP3)[4]
- the Certificate of Family and Property (Form CP5)[5]
- a copy of the patient's will and any other testamentary document[6]
- a cheque for the Commencement Fee, currently £100, made payable to 'Public Trust Office'.[7]

If urgent action is necessary – for example, completion of the sale of a property or access to the patient's account in order to pay nursing home fees – an explanation why the matter is urgent should be given both in Form CP5 and in a covering letter. The court will then issue an interim order, certificate or directions as appropriate.[8]

On receiving these documents, the Public Trust Office will return one copy of Form CP1 marked with the date and time when the court will consider the application. Unless the solicitors are otherwise notified, no attendance on that date will be necessary.[9]

When it returns the application, the Public Trust Office will also send the applicant's solicitors a letter addressed to the patient telling him or her the date on which the application will be considered and explaining how representations and observations can be made.[10] Unless the court directs otherwise, this letter must be personally served on the patient,[11] and the person who serves it must complete a certificate to this effect.[12] The letter must be delivered to the patient at least ten clear days before the date when the application will be considered by the court.[13] Although the court has power to dispense with such notification, it is generally reluctant to do so because the patient may object to the appointment of a particular person or may have useful information to contribute. The court is only likely to dispense with notification if it is satisfied – after considering medical evidence – that the patient is incapable of understanding the letter, or that such notification would be injurious to his or her health.[14]

Where an order is to be made appointing anyone other than the Public Trustee as receiver, the receiver is required to give security for the due performance of his or her duties.[15] The order will not be entered until evidence of the security given has been produced. The court's requirements will be explained in a letter to the applicant's solicitors.[16]

The First General Order setting out the receiver's powers and duties is initially issued in draft form for approval or amendment, as the case may be, and should then be returned to the court. All dealings with the patient's capital must be authorised in the First General Order or subsequent orders or directions. After issue of the order, an office copy should be registered with all banks and building societies with which the patient has accounts and all companies in which he or she holds shares. The Public Trust Office has issued a charter statement which says that, assuming there are no complications or objections, the draft of the First General Order will be issued within eight weeks of lodgment of the application, and office copies of the order will be despatched within four weeks from the date on which the approved or amended draft is returned to the court.

---

1 Telephone 0171 269 7000; fax 0171 404 1725; DX 37965 Kingsway.
2 Court of Protection Rules 1994 (SI 1994/3046), r 27. This is a new rule, although for many years Form CP5 has contained a marginal note stating that 'Relatives of a degree equal to or nearer than the applicant (including those living abroad) are to be notified of this application. Confirmation that this has been done should be given'. For a precedent of a letter giving such notice, see Precedent 2 at p 302 below.
3 Court of Protection Rules 1994 (SI 1994/3046), r 8(1) and Form A. Form CP1 is reproduced at p 282 below. Paragraph 3 of that form, which requests the court to appoint 'some other suitable person as receiver' if for any reason the applicant is not acceptable, must not be deleted.
4 *Ibid*, r 36. Form CP3 is reproduced at p 289.
5 *Ibid*, r 36. Form CP5 is reproduced at p 293. It should be completed as fully, accurately and truthfully as possible. If it is not possible to supply all the information required, the reason should be explained and inquiries should be put in hand to find out the missing information. Any 'guesses' or estimates should be described as such.
6 Marginal note 6 to Form CP5. Rule 72 provides that the court may make inquiries as to testamentary documents executed by the patient.
7 Court of Protection Rules 1994 (SI 1994/3046), r 79 and Appendix.
8 *Ibid*, r 44.
9 *Ibid*, r 10.
10 The letter notifying the patient of the first application (Form CP6) is reproduced at p 300.
11 Court of Protection Rules 1994 (SI 1994/3046), r 26.
12 *Ibid*, r 28(1). The certificate of service of first application (Form CP7) is reproduced at p 301.
13 *Ibid*, r 48(1).
14 *Ibid*, r 26(2).
15 *Ibid*, r 58.
16 The manner of giving security is described in r 59.

Medical evidence[1]

The Medical Certificate (Form CP3) stating that the patient is incapable, by reason of mental disorder, of managing and administering his or her property and affairs must be completed by a registered medical practitioner.[2] The evidence of only one doctor is required, and ideally he or she should have examined the patient recently, say, within the last six months.

When requesting medical evidence, a solicitor should:

- send the doctor the blank Form CP3;
- send the doctor the notes to accompany Form CP3 issued by the Court of Protection and prepared in consultation with the Royal College of Physicians and the British Medical Association;
- (with consent wherever possible and practicable)[3] give the doctor sufficient background information about the patient's family and property to enable him or her to assess whether the patient is in fact incapable, by reason of mental disorder, of managing and administering his or her property and affairs;[4]
- remind the doctor that whether a person lacks capacity should be decided on *the balance of probabilities*;
- tell the doctor that in reply to question 12 on Form CP3 ('What is the Patient's life expectancy?'), the court is tactfully seeking some sort of prediction about how long the patient is likely to live because it needs to make investment decisions and needs to know whether it is aiming for a short-term or long-term target.[5]

If the patient has not seen his or her doctor recently and there are difficulties in obtaining the medical evidence, the Court of Protection has power to act in an emergency without prior medical evidence, provided it has reason to believe that the patient may be mentally incapable, and it is of the opinion that it is necessary to make immediate provision under Part VII of the Mental Health Act 1983.[6] However, such emergency powers are used extremely rarely.

If there are difficulties in obtaining evidence from the patient's doctor on the grounds that disclosure of Form CP3 would be in breach of the rules of professional conduct governing confidentiality, the doctor should be advised that he or she can send the medical certificate direct to the Court of Protection. Similarly, the court can write to the doctor direct requesting the medical evidence.[7]

If there is a dispute between two or more doctors about the patient's capacity, the court may direct one of the Lord Chancellor's Medical Visitors to visit the patient and report back on his or her capacity.[8]

---

1 See, generally, the contribution by Tony Whitehead on 'Medical Certification' in *Making the Most of the Court of Protection* (King's Fund Centre, 1987), pp 24–31.

2 Court of Protection Rules 1994 (SI 1994/3046), r 36(2). The court will not accept evidence from, say, a clinical psychologist who is not a registered medical practitioner, regardless of the quality of such evidence as to the patient's mental state.

3 For a precedent consent form to the disclosure of confidential information for the purpose of assessing capacity, see Chapter 3, Precedent 1, at p 64 above.

4 For a precedent of a letter requesting medical evidence as to both managerial capacity and testamentary capacity, see Chapter 3, Precedent 2, at p 65 above.

5 Mrs A.B. Macfarlane, Master of the Court of Protection, in 'The Court of Protection' (1992) *Medico-Legal Journal*, vol 60, Part 1, p 35.

6 Mental Health Act 1983, s 98.

7 Court of Protection Rules 1994 (SI 1994/3046), r 73. For a precedent letter alerting the Public
  Trust Office to such a problem, see Precedent 1 at p 302 below.
8 Mental Health Act 1983, s 103, and Court of Protection Rules 1994, r 69(1)(b).

Short procedure

The former Master of the Court of Protection, Mrs A.B. Macfarlane, described
proceedings in the court as 'a sledge-hammer to crack a nut where the estate is a
small one'.[1] The same applies if something needs to be authorised on a one-off
occasion where no continuing receivership is necessary. For these reasons, short
orders and directions are available.

Rule 9 of the Court of Protection Rules 1994 provides that:[2]

'(1) Without prejudice to the generality of rule 7, and where the conditions in
paragraph (2) below are satisfied—
  (a)   if an application for the appointment of a receiver for the patient has been made
        the court may instead make a short order under this rule; and
  (b)   if no such application has been made, the Public Trustee may—
        (i) give a direction under this rule; or
        (ii) require that such an application be made to the court.
(2) The conditions to be satisfied are that—
  (a)   the property of the patient does not exceed £5,000 in value; or
  (b)   it appears to the court or the Public Trustee that it is otherwise appropriate to
        proceed under this rule and that it is not necessary to appoint a receiver for the
        patient.
(3) A short order or direction under this rule is an order or direction directing an officer
of the Public Trust Office or some other suitable person named in the order or direction
to deal with the patient's property, or any part of it, or with his affairs, in any manner
authorised by the Act and specified in the order or direction.'

Short orders or directions may be particularly appropriate where, for example:

- the patient has received a legacy. The order will constitute a valid receipt as far
  as the personal representatives are concerned;
- the patient has won one of the smaller premium bond or national lottery
  prizes;
- an insurance policy has matured;
- the patient's consent in writing is needed by trustees;
- a tenancy agreement or a residential care home or nursing home contract needs
  to be signed; or
- a lease needs to be surrendered or terminated.

Sometimes, if the patient's property exceeds £5000 in value and an application has
been made for the appointment of a receiver, the court may make a short order if
it considers that an ongoing receivership is unnecessary.

To apply for a short order or direction:

- proceed initially as though you were applying for the appointment of a receiver;
  however, unlike an application for the appointment of a receiver or a new

receiver, there is no formal obligation to give notice of intention to apply for a short order or direction to the patient's next-of-kin;[3]

- obtain from the Public Trust Office a Medical Certificate (Form CP3) and a Certificate of Family and Property (Form CP5);[4]
- send the Medical Certificate to the patient's GP along with the 'Notes to Accompany Certificate of Capacity', and explain to the doctor why you are applying for a short order or direction;
- write to the Public Trust Office:[5]
  - enclosing the completed Medical Certificate (CP3);
  - enclosing the completed Certificate of Family and Property (CP5);
  - explaining the facts;
  - making proposals as to how the money or the matter should be dealt with to the best advantage for the patient;
  - stating whether the applicant has incurred any out-of-pocket expenses on the patient's behalf for which he or she should be reimbursed; and
  - enclosing a cheque for £100 made payable to 'Public Trust Office'.[6]

Where the court proposes to make a short order, or the Public Trustee proposes to give a direction under r 9, the patient must be notified of the application[7] unless the court or the Public Trustee directs that notification can be dispensed with on the grounds that the patient would be incapable of understanding it, or that it would be injurious to his or her health, or for any other compelling reason.[8]

Where an order or direction is made under r 9, it will not be entered until after the expiration of ten clear days from the date on which the patient was notified, unless notification has been dispensed with.[9]

Anyone who is directed to deal with the patient's property or affairs may be required to deliver accounts of his or her dealings to the court or the Public Trustee.[10]

Approximately 9% of the orders made by the Court of Protection under its Mental Health Act jurisdiction (ie about 500 per year) are short orders.[11]

---

1 Mrs A.B. Macfarlane, 'The Court of Protection' (1992) *Medico-Legal Journal*, vol 60, Part 1, p 41.
2 Court of Protection Rules 1994 (SI 1994/3046), r 9.
3 *Ibid*, r 27.
4 *Ibid*, r 36.
5 See Precedent 4, at p 305 below, for a fairly typical illustration of such a letter.
6 Court of Protection Rules 1994 (SI 1994/3046), r 79 provides that 'a commencement fee shall be payable on any first application for the appointment of a receiver or other originating process in respect of any patient'. The commencement fee of £100 is listed in the Appendix to the Rules.
7 *Ibid*, r 26(1)(b).
8 *Ibid*, r 26(2).
9 *Ibid*, r 48(1).
10 *Ibid*, r 68.
11 Mrs A.B. Macfarlane, *op cit*, p 41.

Court of Protection fees

The fees payable to the Court of Protection/Public Trust Office[1] are governed by Part XVIII of the Court of Protection Rules 1994, and are specified in the Appendix to the Rules.[2] The Appendix is reproduced at p 286 below.

In summary, the main fees are:

- **Commencement fee**. A commencement fee of £100 is payable on any first application for the appointment of a receiver or any other originating process (eg a short order or direction) in respect of a patient.[3]
- **Administration fee**. This is based on the clear annual income at the patient's disposal and is charged on an annual basis from the date of issue of the first application for the appointment of a receiver until the termination of the proceedings.[4]
- **Transaction fee**. A fee is payable in respect of a number of individual transactions, for example, £50 is payable in respect of a gift or settlement of a patient's property, and £100 for the execution of a statutory will on a patient's behalf.[5]
- **Fee on taxation**. A fee of £0.05 is payable for every £1, or fraction of £1, allowed on the taxation of a bill of costs.[6]
- **Receivership fee**. Receivership fees apply where the Public Trustee is appointed as receiver.[7] In the past, the Protection Division (which deals with external receivers) has subsidised the Receivership Division[8] and, to redress the balance, the 1994 Rules marginally reduced the annual administration fee payable in Protection activity cases and introduced higher fees in Receivership cases. For the same reasons, a *winding up fee* is payable on the death of a patient in cases where the Public Trustee has been appointed receiver.[9]

The Public Trustee may remit the payment of the whole or part of any fee where hardship might be caused to the patient or his or her dependants; where the circumstances are exceptional; or where the cost of calculation and collection would be disproportionate to the amount involved.[10]

---

1 The anticipated fee income for the year ended 31 March 1995 was £13,633,000, and represents approximately 72.5% of the Public Trust Office's total income of £18,730,000. (Source: Public Trust Office Business Plan (1994), Annex C.)

2 The Court of Protection Rules 1994 (SI 1994/3046).

3 *Ibid*, r 79 and Appendix.

4 *Ibid*, r 80.

5 *Ibid*, r 81 and Appendix.

6 *Ibid*, r 82 and Appendix.

7 *Ibid*, r 83.

8 Public Trust Office Business Plan (1994), para 4.2, and Annex C. For the year ended 31 March 1995, the total planned income of Receivership activity was £1,962,000 and its expenditure £3,923,000. By contrast, the total income and expenditure of the Protection Division during the same period were £8,213,000 and £6,252,000 respectively.

9 Court of Protection Rules 1994, r 84.

10 *Ibid*, r 86.

Solicitors' costs

All costs incurred in relation to proceedings under the Court of Protection Rules 1994 are in the discretion of the court or the Public Trustee.[1] Generally, they are awarded out of the patient's estate,[2] but in disputed cases there may be circumstances where some other order will be made, especially if the court is satisfied that an applicant or objector has acted unreasonably or has been motivated by self-interest rather than by the patient's best interests.[3]

Unless authorised by the court, receivers are not entitled at the expense of the patient's estate to employ a solicitor or any other professional person to do any work which does not usually require professional assistance.[4]

As far as solicitors' costs are concerned, there are three options: taxation; fixed costs; or agreed costs.

(1) Taxation

Taxation is the usual method of calculating the quantum of costs, which are normally awarded on an indemnity basis.

Order 62 of the Rules of the Supreme Court applies to taxation in Court of Protection proceedings:

- the bill should be prepared on A4 taxation paper following the format and with the item numbers used in App 2 of RSC Ord 62;
- items in the body of the bill should appear in type, but page and summary totals should appear in pencil until the bill has been checked and is ready for completion;
- the bill should be endorsed on the back with the title of the matter, and the name, address and telephone number of the firm;
- the bill should state the period covered (eg 1 November 1994 – 21 March 1995) and should be prefaced by a brief narrative indicating the issues involved, the status of the fee-earners concerned, and the expense rates claimed;
- each chargeable item of work done should be shown in chronological order with dates;
- the bill (one top copy only) should be lodged with the Supreme Court Taxing Office (Court of Protection Section), Royal Courts of Justice, Strand, London WC2A 2LL, together with all supporting documents, such as correspondence and attendance records, instructions to counsel, opinions, affidavits, orders, pleadings, all conveyancing documents where applicable, and accounts or receipts for disbursements included in the bill;
- if costs are to be taxed pursuant to an order of the Court of Protection, a copy of that order should be lodged with the bill;
- the bill will be provisionally taxed and returned by post;
- if desired, an appointment with the taxing officer will be made;
- the completed bill should be returned to the taxing office together with an office account cheque for the taxing fee made payable to 'HM Paymaster General';
- the certificate of taxation will then be issued and sent to the firm;

- costs must not be paid from any source until the certificate of taxation has been issued.

A survey carried out by the taxing office in June and July 1993 revealed that 91% of bills presented for taxation originated outside the London postal area; 38% of Court of Protection cases were handled entirely by a partner; 39% by an assistant solicitor; and 12% by a legal executive. The remaining 11% were dealt with by more than one grade of fee earner.

(2) Fixed costs

Fixed costs were introduced in 1983 at the suggestion of the then Chief Taxing Master who considered that his office was dealing with an excessive number of cases in which the amount of costs at issue was relatively small. Accordingly, fixed costs were originally intended to reduce this apparent waste of the taxing office's resources.

There are five categories:[5]

- Category I covers work up to and including the date on which the First General Order is entered. The current level of costs is £464.
- Category II applies to the preparation and lodgment of a receivership account. The level is currently £121, or, where the receivership account has been certified by a solicitor under the provisions of the Practice Notes dated 13 September 1984 and 5 March 1985, £137.
- Category III covers general management work in the second and subsequent years. The current level is £356 where there is a lay receiver, and £411 where a solicitor is the receiver. Categories II and III may be claimed together.
- Category IV relates to applications under the Trustee Act 1925, s 36(9) for the appointment of a new trustee in place of the patient and for the purpose of making title to land.[6] The current level is £255.
- Category V applies to conveyancing costs.[7] Two elements are allowable: (a) a fixed sum of £141 in respect of correspondence with the court or Public Trust Office; and (b) a value element of 0.5% of the consideration up to [£400,000] and 0.25% thereafter, with a minimum value element of £282.

In addition to the fixed costs in each category, VAT and disbursements are allowed.

Fixed costs are reviewed annually by the Supreme Court Taxing Office, the Court of Protection and The Law Society, and the revised levels usually come into effect in November or December each year.

Solicitors are under no obligation to accept fixed costs, and retain the option of having a bill of costs drawn up and taxed, if they prefer. The fixed costs take-up rates for the year ending 30 June 1994 were: Category I (55%); Category II (100%); Category III (70%); Category IV (100%); and Category V (77%).

(3) Agreed costs

If a solicitor's bill for costs incurred in the Court of Protection does not exceed £1000 excluding VAT and disbursements, the solicitor may submit the bill to the court and suggest a figure which he or she would be prepared to accept by way of costs. If the amount sought is reasonable, it will be agreed by the court.[8]

The bill submitted should contain a narrative of the work done, the time spent and the level of fee-earner involved, together with receipts for any disbursements.

If the costs are sought to be agreed are for categories of work for which there is already provision for fixed costs, it is unlikely that the court will agree a bill higher than the current level of fixed costs.

---

1 Court of Protection Rules 1994 (SI 1994/3046), r 87(1).
2 *Re Cathcart* [1893] 1 Ch 466.
3 Mrs A.B. Macfarlane, 'The Court of Protection's Role', notes for the IBC one-day conference on *Handling the Problems of the Elderly* held on 25 January 1995, at p 14.
4 Court of Protection Rules 1994 (SI 1994/3046), r 90(1).
5 The levels of fixed costs quoted have effect from 1 December 1995 in accordance with the Master's Practice Note dated 30 November 1995. The level of fixed costs is reviewed on an annual basis.
6 Category IV was introduced on 1 November 1986.
7 Category V was introduced on 1 November 1992.
8 For a precedent of a letter to the Public Trust Office requesting agreement of costs, see Precedent 5 at p 306 below.

Complaints procedures

(1) Public Trust Office

Any complaint about the service provided by the Public Trust Office should be directed:[1]

- first, to the caseworker involved, and if you wish to take the matter further;
- secondly, to the Principal of the Protection Division, who will acknowledge receipt of the complaint within three working days, investigate the complaint, and respond within fifteen working days. If you wish to take the matter further;
- thirdly, to the Head of the Mental Health Sector.

The Public Trust Office is subject to the jurisdiction of the Parliamentary Commissioner for Administration.

(2) Court of Protection: Review

Anyone who is aggrieved by a decision of the Court of Protection, which was not made on a hearing, or by a decision of the Public Trustee, may apply to the court within eight days to have the decision reviewed.[2] On hearing the application, the court may either confirm or revoke the previous decision or make any other order or decision it thinks fit.[3] Anyone who is aggrieved by the order or decision made on the hearing of the application for review may appeal to a nominated judge in the manner described below.[4]

(3) Court of Protection: Appeal

Anyone who is aggrieved by a decision of the Court of Protection which was made on a hearing may, within fourteen days from the date of entry of the order or, as the case may be, from the date of the decision, appeal to a nominated judge.[5] A notice of appeal must be served on everyone who appeared or was represented before the court when the order was made or the decision was given, and anyone else whom the court directs. A copy of the notice of appeal must be lodged at the court office. The time and place at which the appeal is to be heard will be fixed by the court and notice will be sent to all parties. Without the leave of the court, no further evidence to that given at the hearing may be filed in support of or in opposition to the appeal.[6]

---

1 Public Trust Office: Charter Statements on 'Protection' and 'Receivership'.
2 Court of Protection Rules 1994 (SI 1994/3046), r 56(1).
3 *Ibid*, r 56(3).
4 *Ibid*, r 56(4).
5 *Ibid*, r 57(1). The notice of appeal is reproduced at p 285.
6 *Ibid*, r 57(4).

Proposed reforms

The Law Commission's Report on *Mental Incapacity*,[1] published in March 1995, recommends that the existing Court of Protection should be abolished and replaced by a superior court of record, also to be known as the Court of Protection.[2] The jurisdiction of the new court would be exercisable by nominated district judges, circuit judges and judges of the Chancery and Family Divisions.[3] The new Court of Protection would have a central registry in London,[4] but may sit anywhere in England and Wales designated by the Lord Chancellor.[5]

The new court would have a general jurisdiction in respect of persons without capacity and would have power to make declarations, make decisions, appoint managers, and deal with personal welfare and health matters in addition to the traditional jurisdiction of the existing court over the property and affairs of persons without capacity.

---

1 Law Commission Report No 231 (HMSO, 1995).
2 *Ibid*, para 10.9, and Draft Mental Incapacity Bill, cl 46(1).
3 *Ibid*, para 10.13, and Draft Bill, cl 46(2).
4 *Ibid*, para 10.17, and Draft Bill, cl 46(7).
5 *Ibid*, para 10.16, and Draft Bill, cl 46(6).

FORMS

COURT OF PROTECTION RULES 1994, SCHEDULE

First Application for the Appointment of a Receiver (Form CP1)

SCHEDULE   Rule 2

FORMS

FORM A: FIRST APPLICATION FOR THE APPOINTMENT OF A RECEIVER

COURT OF PROTECTION

19   no

Rule 8

IN THE MATTER OF . . . .

. . . . A PATIENT

I . . . .

of . . . .

. . . .

Notes

apply to the Court of Protection for:

Complete EITHER
paragraph 1, OR paragraph 2.
Delete the one which does not
apply.

1. my own appointment as receiver for the patient

    a. I am not related to the patient*

    b. I am the . . . . of the patient
    (state relationship)*

2. the appointment of . . . .

* Delete whichever does not
apply.

of . . . .

. . . . as receiver for
the patient

    a. He/She is the. . . . . of the
    patient (state relationship)*

DO NOT DELETE
paragraph 3.

OR

3. the appointment of some other suitable person.

Where any other order in
addition to that at paragraphs 1.
2 and 3 is sought, a general
form of application should be
used.

Applicant's signature . . . .

Date . . . .

OR Solicitors for the applicant:

    of:

TO BE COMPLETED BY THE
COURT, +

THE COURT WILL CONSIDER THIS APPLICATION ON THE . . . . DAY

OF . . . . .19 . . . AT . . . . . . O'CLOCK

General Form of Application (Form CP9)

FORM B: GENERAL FORM OF APPLICATION

COURT OF PROTECTION

19   no

Rule 8

IN THE MATTER OF . . . .

. . . ., ... A PATIENT

I . . . .

NOTES

of . . . .

Where the application is one to
which rules 17, 19 or 20 applies
give details of your authority
to make the application
e.g. Receiver, Trustee, etc.

. . . .

. . . .

apply to the Court of Protection for an order that:

Give details of the order you
are asking the court to make

. . . .

. . . .

. . . .

. . . .

. . . .

. . . .

. . . .

. . . .

. . . .

and for any directions which are necessary as a result of my application.

Applicant's signature . . . .

Date . . . .

OR Solicitors for the applicant:

of

TO BE COMPLETED BY THE
COURT, +

THE COURT WILL CONSIDER THIS APPLICATION ON THE . . . . DAY

OF . . . . .19 . . . AT . . . . . . O'CLOCK

Witness Summons

FORM C: WITNESS SUMMONS

COURT OF PROTECTION

19   no

Rule 50

IN THE MATTER OF . . . .

. . . . A PATIENT

To . . . .

of . . . .

. . . .

You are ordered to attend before

. . . .

at . . . .

. . . .

on the . . . . day of . . . . 19 . . . .

at . . . . o'clock, to:

a. give evidence in this matter

b. bring with you and produce at the hearing the documents
   listed below:

. . . .

. . . .

. . . .

. . . .

. . . .

. . . .

Date . . . .

THIS SUMMONS WAS ISSUED AT THE REQUEST OF

. . . .

. . . . SOLICITORS FOR

THE . . . .

of . . . .

. . . .

Notice of Appeal

FORM D: NOTICE OF APPEAL

COURT OF PROTECTION

19   no

Rule 57

IN THE MATTER OF . . . .

. . . . A PATIENT

NOTES

I . . . .

of . . . .

. . . .

wish to appeal to a Judge against the order/decision* of the Court made in this matter on the . . . . day of . . . . 19 . . . . that:

. . . .

If you are appealing against only part of the order/decision write down which part.

. . . .

. . . .

. . . .

. . . .

. . . .

*Delete whichever does not apply.

I intend to ask that the order/decision* may be:

a. discharged*

b. varied in the following way:*

Give details of new order/decision you are asking to be made.

. . . .

. . . .

. . . .

. . . .

YOU WILL BE SENT NOTICE OF THE TIME, DATE AND PLACE OF THE HEARING OF THIS APPEAL.

Signed . . . . Appellant

Date . . . .

. . . . Solicitors for the

Appellant of: . . . .

. . . .

. . . .

APPENDIX TO THE COURT OF PROTECTION RULES 1994: COURT OF PROTECTION FEES

APPENDIX

COURT OF PROTECTION FEES   Rule 78

Column 1	Column 2
Item	Fee
Commencement fee (rule 79)	
1. On the first application for the appointment of a receiver or other originating process.	£100
Annual Administration fee (rule 80)	
2. On a certificate issued by the court.	In accordance with Table 1
Transaction fee (rule 81)	
3.—(1) On any order (or as the case may be, on any approval given by the court under an order) made by the court in the exercise of powers conferred by:—	
(i) section 96(1):—	
(d) (settlement or gift of property)	
(h) (carrying out of contract) or	
(k) (exercise of powers as guardian or trustee)	
of the Act:	
(ii) section 100 of the Act (vesting of stock in curator appointed outside England and Wales);	£50.00 or, in a "special case", 1/4% of the pecuniary consideration as defined in rule 81 if greater than £50.00.
(iii) section 36(9) of the Trustee Act 1925 (appointment of trustees)	
(iv) section 54 of the Trustee Act 1925 (concurrent jurisdiction with High Court over trusts);	
(v) section 1(3) of the Variation of Trusts Act 1958 (variation of trusts for the benefit of patient);	
provided that no fee under this item shall be taken if the property is worth less than £50.00 and no such fee shall exceed £500.00.	
(2) On the making by the court of any order or authority under section 96(1)(e) of the Act (execution of will).	£100.00
Taxation (rule 82)	
4. On the taxation of a bill of costs, for every £1 or fraction of £1 allowed.	£0.05
Receivership fees (rule 83)	
5. On the appointment of officer of the court as receiver, except where it appears that the patient's clear annual income is less than £1,000.	£250.00
6. On passing an account.	In accordance with Table 2
Winding up fee (rule 84)	
7. On the death of a patient where the Public Trustee had been appointed receiver.	£250 on the date of cessation of receivership and £100 on each anniversary of such date until the matter is completed.

TABLE 1 (Fee No. 2)

Income Band	Clear Annual Income		Fee
	Exceeding	Not Exceeding	
(i)		£1,000	£50
(ii)	£1,000	£2,000	£70
(iii)	£2,000	£3,000	£130
(iv)	£3,000	£5,000	£200
(v)	£5,000	£7,000	£350
(vi)	£7,000	£10,000	£550
(vii)	£10,000	£15,000	£800
(viii)	£15,000		£800 plus 5% of income exceeding £15,000

TABLE 2 (Fee No. 6)

Income Band	Clear Annual Income		Fee
	Exceeding	Not Exceeding	
(i)		£1,000	£100
(ii)	£1,000	£2,000	£250
(iii)	£2,000	£3,000	£525
(iv)	£3,000	£5,000	£800
(v)	£5,000	£7,000	£1,300
(vi)	£7,000	£10,000	£1,800
(vii)	£10,000	£15,000	£2,800
(viii)	£15,000		£2,800 plus 5% of income exceeding £15,000

NOTE

In relation to fees 2 and 6, and their corresponding Tables, where income exceeds the lower limit of a band by less than the difference between the fees for that band and the next lower band, the fee charged shall be the fee for the lower band plus the amount by which the income exceeds the upper limit of that band. For example, in calculating fee 2 on a clear annual income of £2,050 (which exceeds the lower limit (£2,000) on Band (iii) by less than the difference (£60) between the fee (£130) on Band (iii) and the fee (£70) on Band (ii)), the fee payable is—

£70 (the fee on Band (ii))

+£50 (the amount by which the income exceeds £2,000)

£120

MEDICAL CERTIFICATE ON THE RECOVERY OF THE PATIENT (FORM CP2)

C.P.2

MEDICAL CERTIFICATE

Court of Protection

19   No.

IN THE MATTER OF

(a) Insert full name, address and medical qualifications

I(*a*) ....

of ....

HEREBY CERTIFY as follows:—

    1.   I am the Medical Attendant of the above-named Patient and have so acted

since ....

    2.   I have to-day read a copy of

(b) Delete lines that do not apply.

(*b*) my $\frac{\text{Affidavit sworn}}{\text{Certificate given}}$ in this matter on the ....

(*b*) the $\frac{\text{Affidavit of}}{\text{Certificate of}}$ .... $\frac{\text{sworn}}{\text{given}}$ in this matter

on the ....

    3.   I have attended the Patient on the following dates ....

....

....

and I specially examined the Patient on the ....

with the object of ascertaining the state of h .... mind.

    4.   As a result of such special examination I am of the opinion that the Patient is

now capable of managing and administering h .... property and affairs and I base my

conclusions on the following grounds:—(*c*)

Set out fully the grounds on which you base your conclusions.

Signature ....

Date ....

MEDICAL CERTIFICATE (FORM CP3)

NO.

COURT OF PROTECTION

MEDICAL CERTIFICATE

In the matter of

(Full name of Patient) ....

(Please use **BLOCK CAPITALS**)

- Please read the attached notes before completing this form.
- Please answer all questions (except where indicated) as fully as you can.
- Correct boxes should be marked with a '✓'

INSTRUCTIONS **Insert your full name and address**	I .... of .... hereby certify as follows: **1.** I have the following medical qualifications ....
Insert the Patient's present address	**2.** I am medical attendant of the above-named Patient who resides at .... and have so acted since ....
For a definition of "mental disorder" see note 2 attached	**3.** I last examined the Patient on the .... 19 ...... and in my opinion the Patient is incapable by reason of mental disorder of managing and administering his/her property and affairs.
State the nature of the mental disorder and the reasons for the opinion expressed. Your attention is drawn to notes 5, 6 and 7 attached	**4.** My opinion is based on the following diagnosis and the following evidence of incapacity.

PD CP3 MM/8–95

5. The present mental disorder has lasted since ....

6. Is the Patient a danger to himself/herself or others in any way?   ☐ Yes   ☐ No

If yes, give details

7. Is the Patient capable of appreciating his/her surroundings?   ☐ Yes   ☐ No

Please comment

8. Does the Patient need anything to provide additional comfort?   ☐ Yes   ☐ No

If yes, what recommendations do you make?

9. Is there a reasonable prospect of the Patient:

(a) being moved to a nursing home or residential home   ☐ Yes   ☐ No

(b) returning to his/her own home if not living there at present   ☐ Yes   ☐ No

If yes, when?

10. Is the Patient visited by relatives or friends?   ☐ Yes   ☐ No

If yes:
    a)   How frequently?

    b)   By whom?

11. What is the Patient's age?

12. What is the Patient's life expectancy? ☐ Under 5 years ☐ Over 5 years

13. Please give a brief summary of the Patient's physical condition.

14. What are the Patient's prospects of mental recovery?

15. Have you or your family any financial interest in the accommodation in which the Patient is living? Yes ☐ No ☐

16. Additional comments (if any) *(Please see note 8)*

Signed ....

Dated ....

NOTES

- **Please read these notes before completing the Medical Certificate.**

- **Please note that when the medical certificate has been completed its contents will be confidential to the Court and the Public Trustee and those authorised by the Court or the Public Trustee to see it.**

- **These notes have been prepared in consultation with the Royal College of Psychiatrists and the British Medical Association.**

1. Doctors should be aware that if a person owning real or personal property becomes incapable, by reason of mental disorder, of safeguarding and managing his affairs, an application should be made to the Court of Protection for the appointment of a Receiver or to the Public Trustee for such directions as may be necessary.

2. An application to the Court of Protection for the appointment of a Receiver or to the Public Trustee for directions must be supported by a medical certificate stating that, in the doctor's opinion, the patient is incapable of managing and administering his property and affairs by virtue of mental disorder as defined in Section 1 of the Mental Health Act 1983. "Mental Disorder" is defined in Section 1(2) of the act as meaning "mental illness, arrested or incomplete development of mind, psychopathic disorder and any other disorder or disability of mind", and "psychopathic disorder" is defined as "disorder or disability of mind (whether or not including significant impairment of intelligence) which results in abnormally aggressive or seriously irresponsible conduct on the part of the person concerned".

3. Criteria for assessing incapacity are not identical with those for assessing the need for compulsory admission to hospital. The fact that a person is suffering from mental disorder within the meaning of the Mental Health Act 1983, whether living in the community of resident in hospital, detained or informal, is not of itself evidence of incapacity to manage his affairs. On the other hand, a person may be so incapable and yet not be liable to compulsory admission to hospital.

4. The certifying doctor may be either the person's general practitioner or any other registered medical practitioner who has examined the patient.

5. The medical certificate requires the doctor to state in paragraph 4 the nature of the mental disorder and the grounds on which he bases his opinion of incapacity. It is this part of the certificate which appears to give the doctor the most difficulty. What is required is a diagnosis and a simple statement giving clear evidence of incapacity which an intelligent lay person could understand, eg reference to defect of short-term memory, of spatial and temporal orientation or of reasoning ability, or to reckless spending (sometimes periodic as in mania) without regard for the future, or evidence of vulnerability to exploitation.

6. In many cases of senile dementia, severe brain damage, acute or chronic psychiatric disorder and severe mental impairment the assessment of incapacity should present little difficulty. Cases of functional and personality disorders may give more problems and assessment may depend on the individual doctor's interpretation of mental disorder. The Court and the Public Trustee tend towards the view that these conditions render a person liable to their jurisdiction where there appears to be a real danger that they will lead to dissipation of considerable capital assets.

7. **A person may not be dealt with under the Mental Health Act 1983, and may not be the subject of an application to the Court of Protection or the Public Trustee, by reason only of promiscuity or other immoral conduct, sexual deviancy or dependence on alcohol or drugs.**

8. The Court and the Public Trustee attach considerable importance to receipt by the patient of notice of the proposed proceedings, since the patient may have an objection, though irrational, to the appointment of a particular person or may, even unwittingly, contribute information of assistance to the Court or the Public Trustee. The Court and the Public Trustee are reluctant to exercise their power to dispense with notification, unless it could be injurious to the patient's health, because it is considered that a person has a right to know – or at least be given an opportunity to understand – if the management of his affairs is to be taken out of his hands and thereafter dealt with by someone on his behalf; if he has no understanding at all, then notification cannot affect him adversely, and a patient who has sufficient insight to appreciate the significance of the proceedings may need reassurance that they are for his benefit. If the certifying doctor believes that, in a particular case, notification of the proceedings by or under the supervision of the doctor is advisable, he should say so when completing the form CP3.

9. The grounds for dispensing with the need for notice being served are:–

   (a)   the patient is incapable of understanding it, or

   (b)   such notification would be injurious to the patient's health, or

   (c)   for any reason notification ought to be dispensed with.

10. The completed medical certificate should be returned to either the solicitors in the matter or to **The Public Trust Office, Protection Division, Stewart House, 24 Kingsway, London WC2B 6JX.**

CERTIFICATE OF FAMILY AND PROPERTY (FORM CP5)

IMPORTANT

C.P.5

NOTICE OF THIS APPLICATION WHEN ISSUED MUST BE DELIVERED TO THE PATIENT PERSONALLY WITHIN THE PRESCRIBED TIME UNLESS THE COURT OTHERWISE DIRECTS. ATTENTION IS DRAWN TO THE PROCEDURE NOTE ATTACHED.

Court of Protection

IN THE MATTER OF

(Full Name of Patient) ....

THE APPLICANT.

(a) Full name and address including postal code.

I *(a)* ....

of ....

(b) Occupation or description and in the case of a woman whether married, widowed or single.

(b) ....   *(c)* ....

(c) Relationship to Patient.

of the above named Patient hereby certify and say as follows:—

1. The following information and replies given to the undermentioned questions are true and accurate to the best of my knowledge and belief.

2. The details of the property given in this my certificate include the whole of the property belonging to the Patient, or in which the Patient has any interest whatsoever.

1. THE PATIENT	
Present address	and has resided there since 19
Home address prior to illness.	
Whether married, single or widowed.	
Date of birth (or year if exact date not known).	
Previous occupation and (for a widow) that of her late husband.	
Religion, if known.	
2. NEXT OF KIN	
Names, addresses, and relationship of all the Patient's nearest relatives (stating ages in the case of children under 18).	
Relatives of a degree equal to or nearer than the Applicant (including those living abroad) must be notified by letter of the identities of the Patient, the Applicant and the proposed Receiver and what the application is for.	
Please confirm that this has been done.	
3. GUARDIANSHIP	
Have powers of Guardianship under the Mental Health Act, 1983, been conferred on any person or Local Health Authority?; if so, give full name and address of Guardian and name of Local Health Authority.	

4. INCOME	The approximate net annual income from all sources that the Patient should receive if all available cash was invested and after deducting tax (if any) is £ a year.
5. MAINTENANCE	
Is the Patient:-	
(a) maintained free of charge under the National Health Service Act?	(a) YES/NO. If YES state weekly or annual amount required for clothing and extra comforts.
(b) in residential accommodation provided by the local authority under Part III of the National Assistance Act 1948 or Part III of the National Health Service Act 1946?	(b) YES/NO. If YES state - (i) which Act. (ii) weekly charge. (iii) date to which charges paid. (iv) weekly or annual amount required for clothing and extra comforts.
(c) in private care	(c) YES/NO. If YES state as appropriate:- (i) weekly, monthly or annual cost. (ii) date to which charges paid. (iii) annual amount required for clothing and extra comforts.
(d) in his own home?	(d) YES/NO. If YES state weekly or annual cost including clothing and comforts.
If provision is required for the maintenance of a wife and children etc., give details including annual amounts suggested.	
If income shown at 4 above is not sufficient to meet total expenditure state:- (a) if it is proposed the deficiency be met by resort to capital OR (b) who is prepared to make up the deficiency.	(a) YES/NO. (b)
6. WILL	
Has the Patient made a Will? If so, in whose possession is it? A copy of any testamentary document should, if possible, accompany the application.	N.B. Solicitors, if instructed, are expected to make all reasonable enquiries to ascertain if any Will has been executed.
7. POWER OF ATTORNEY	
Has the Patient at any time granted a Power of Attorney in favour of any person? If so, enter date thereof and full names of the person to whom it was granted. The Power of Attorney should accompany the application	
8. THE RECEIVER Name of proposed Receiver in full.	If the proposed Receiver is the same person as the Applicant it is sufficient to insert "Applicant" and to state age.
Address	
Age and Occupation	
Relationship to Patient	

9.	**REFEREE**	
	Name, address and occupation of someone who has known the proposed Receiver for at least 2 years to whom reference can be made as to his/her fitness to act. The following are not acceptable as referees:- A relative or partner of the proposed Receiver; A bank or an official of a bank; A solicitor acting in the matter; or The doctor who supplied the medical evidence.	

10.	**DRIVING LICENCE**	
	Does the Patient hold a driving licence?	YES/NO

11.		
	(a) A short history of the Patient stating what he was doing prior to his illness and giving any information concerning him or his relatives that may assist the Court.	
	(b) Further paragraphs should be added dealing with such matters as:-	
	(i) charitable contributions.	
	(ii) any proposed sale of portions of the estate.	
	(iii) the circumstances giving rise to these proceedings together with any further facts which should be brought to the notice of the Court.	
	(iv) where the Patient lives in his own home, details of the arrangements made or proposed to be made for the management of his establishment.	
	(v) names and relationships of any close relatives of the Patient whose affairs have been the subject of any order of the Court, including the Court's reference (if known) to be given.	
	(vi) if the proposed Receiver has been appointed in any other matter(s) give the names of the Patients(s) concerned and (if known) the Court's reference.	

SCHEDULE

PART I.
ABSOLUTE PROPERTY.
CASH

If none, say so.

(Either at Bank or elsewhere, giving name and address of Bank and stating whether on deposit or current account. If any of the money is not standing in the Patient's sole name the fact must be stated and the full names of the person under whose control the money is must be shewn and an explanation of the circumstances given in the body of this certificate.)

N.B. Where possible cash sums of over £500 not earning interest should be placed on deposit pending the directions of the Court.

PART II.
ABSOLUTE PROPERTY.
PENSIONS ANNUITIES ALLOWANCES LIFE POLICIES
& NATIONAL INSURANCE BENEFITS

If none, say so.

(Shewing full details of the Policies and premiums payable and, where surrender may be advisable, the surrender value. In the case of War Service Pensions, the Patient's rank, unit and regimental number must be stated and if possible the reference number of any correspondence with the Pensions Authorities).

Any additional sheets to be affixed here

PART III.
ABSOLUTE PROPERTY.
LAND AND HOUSE PROPERTY (INCLUDING TENANCIES)

If none, say so.

(Stating whether freehold or leasehold, or whether a mere tenancy, &c., and shewing Terms, Ground Rent, Tenants' Names and Rents together with particulars of any Mortgages thereon, stating the Mortgagees' names and the rate of interest; details of insurances should also be given.)

PART IV.
ABSOLUTE PROPERTY.
INVESTMENTS

If none, say so.

(Being a complete list of the Patient's investments and in the case of Bearer Bonds shewing the numbers and the coupon dates, and in the case of Mortgages shewing the names of the Mortgagors, the rate of interest, and particulars of the property on which the Mortgage is secured. If any of the investments are in joint names full particulars must be given and details should be furnished in the body of this certificate shewing the Patient's beneficial interest.)

PART V.
ABSOLUTE PROPERTY.
MISCELLANEOUS

If none, say so.

(Items such as rights under covenants, furniture and effects, jewellery, motor cars, stock-in-trade, fixtures and goodwill, or other property not otherwise appearing in this Schedule. A copy of the latest accounts of any business carried on by the Patient should accompany this application).

PART VI.
REVERSIONARY AND CONTINGENT INTERESTS, &c.

(Shewing the name and age of the person upon whose death the Patient will become entitled together with details of the property and particulars of the will or settlement and names of the Trustees.)

If none, say so.

Any additional sheets to be affixed here

PART VII.
LIFE INTERESTS

If none, say so.

(Shewing the date and nature of the Instruments creating the Trust, the Trustees' names and the property subject to the Trusts, and in the case of a voluntary settlement stating whether the same is revocable.)

PART VIII.
DEBTS

The debts of the Patient (other than Mortgages) are as follows:–

Name of Creditor and nature of debt.	£	Brought forward	£
Carried forward		Total	

Signed ....

Date ....

NOTIFICATION TO THE PATIENT OF FIRST APPLICATION (FORM CP6)[1]

Court of Protection
Stewart House
24 Kingsway
London WC2B 6JX

(date)
(reference)

(Full name of patient)

Dear *(patient)*

The court understands that, because of your present incapacity, it might be in your interests to take steps to protect and manage your property and affairs (while you are unable to do so yourself) by the appointment of *(proposed receiver)* of *(address)* as Receiver, which means that (he)/(she) will deal with your property and affairs on your behalf.

On *(date)* a Master will consider medical advice and will decide whether to appoint *(proposed receiver)* as Receiver or what other action should be taken in your interests to protect and manage your property and affairs.

If you wish to make any observations, or if you want to object either to the making of an order or as to the person whom it is suggested should act for you, you should write to the court at the following address:

The Court of Protection
Stewart House
24 Kingsway
London WC2B 6JX

or telephone 0171 (if out of London) 269 7076.

I will ensure that any letter or message received is placed before the Master, and if you wish to attend, an appointment will be arranged before a final decision is made.

Although if there are urgent matters requiring attention, the Master is able to give directions dealing with them before the above date, no final decision will be made until at least ten days after you receive this notification.[2]

Yours sincerely

(signature)

for Court of Protection

1 For notification to the patient of an application for the appointment of a receiver, see the Court of Protection Rules 1994 (SI 1994/3046), r 26. For the Certificate of Service (Form CP7) where the notice is not sent by the court to the patient direct, see below.
2 Court of Protection Rules 1994, r 48(1).

CERTIFICATE OF SERVICE OF NOTIFICATION OF FIRST APPLICATION[1] (FORM CP7)

COURT OF PROTECTION

19   no.

IN THE MATTER OF .... A PATIENT

I .... (*full name of person who served the notice*)

of .... (*address*)

HEREBY CERTIFY as follows:

(1)   I served the above-named patient with a notice in the form annexed.[2]

(2)   I delivered it to (him)/(her) personally at .... (*address*) and left it with (him)/(her).

(3)   The date I delivered it was .... (*date*)

SIGNED ....

DATE ....

1 Court of Protection Rules 1994 (SI 1994/3046), r 26(1) provides that where a first application is made for the appointment of a receiver for a patient or for an order authorising a person to do any act or carry out any transaction on behalf of a patient without appointing a receiver, the patient shall be notified in such manner as the court or the Public Trustee may direct. Rule 28(1) states that, if the court so directs, a certificate of service showing where, when, how and by whom service was effected shall be filed as soon as practicable after service of a document has been effected in accordance with these Rules.
2 The notice of the first application (Form CP6) is the letter addressed to the patient and signed by an officer of the Court of Protection: see p 300 above.

PRECEDENTS

See Chapter 3 for a precedent for obtaining the client's consent to the disclosure of confidential information for the purpose of assessing capacity (Precedent 1, p 64), and a letter to a GP requesting medical evidence of a client's managerial capacity (Precedent 2, p 65).

1 LETTER TO THE PUBLIC TRUST OFFICE REQUESTING THAT AN ALLEGED PATIENT'S GP SHOULD COMPLETE AND RETURN FORM CP3

Public Trust Office
Enquiries and Applications
Stewart House
24 Kingsway   (*Reference*)
London WC2B 6JX   (*Date*)

Dear Sirs

(*Patient's name, address, and date of birth*)

We act for (*patient's name*) and are of the opinion that (he)/(she) is now incapable, by reason of mental disorder, of managing and administering (his)/(her) property and affairs.

We base our opinion on the following grounds:
(*state reasons why you consider the patient is mentally incapable*)

As far as we are aware, the patient has not executed an enduring power of attorney.

We wish to apply for an order appointing the patient's (*son*) as receiver but are experiencing difficulties in obtaining a completed medical certificate (Form CP3) from (his)/(her) GP. The GP has said that (he)/(she) is not willing to complete such a certificate without first obtaining the patient's consent in writing to the waiver of the professional rules of confidentiality.[1]

In the circumstances, we would be grateful if you could kindly consider exercising your powers under r 73[2] and request a completed CP3 from the GP directly. (His)/(Her) name, address and telephone number are: (*name, address, and telephone number of the alleged patient's GP*).

Yours faithfully

1 General Medical Council, *Professional Conduct and Discipline: Fitness to Practise* (May 1992), para 77: 'Where a patient, or a person properly authorised to act on a patient's behalf, consents to disclosure, information to which the consent refers may be disclosed in accordance with that consent'.
2 Court of Protection Rules 1994 (SI 1994/3046), r 73: 'The court or the Public Trustee may make or cause to be made any other inquiries which it or he may consider necessary or expedient for the proper discharge of their functions under the Act or these Rules'.

2 NOTICE OF INTENTION TO APPLY FOR THE APPOINTMENT OF A RECEIVER[1]

(applicant's address)

(date)

Dear *(relative of the patient)*

I am required to give you notice that I intend to apply to the Court of Protection for (my own appointment)/(the appointment of *(name)*) as receiver for *(patient's name or relationship)*.

A receiver is a person appointed by the court to deal with the day-to-day management of the financial affairs of someone whom the court, after considering medical evidence, believes to be incapable by reason of mental disorder of managing and administering (his)/(her) own property and affairs.

I shall be grateful if you will kindly acknowledge receipt by signing, dating and returning to me the enclosed duplicate copy of this letter.[2]

[*OR*]

I shall be grateful if you will kindly sign, date and return to me the enclosed consent form so that I can send it to the court with all the other papers.[3]

Yours sincerely

(applicant's signature)

1 The Court of Protection Rules 1994 (SI 1994/3046) introduced a new rule whereby an applicant must notify next of kin, etc, of his or her intention to apply for the appointment of a receiver. Rule 27 provides as follows:
'(1) Where an applicant proposes to make an application for the appointment of a receiver or a new receiver, the applicant shall give notice of his intention to—
(a) all relatives of the patient who have the same or a nearer degree of relationship to the patient than the applicant or proposed receiver; and
(b) such other persons who appear to the court to be interested as the court may specify;
unless the court directs that such notification shall be dispensed with.
(2) For the purposes of this rule, notice of intention to make an application is given if the person concerned is notified by letter of the identities of the patient, the applicant and the proposed receiver and what the application is for.'

2 *Ibid*, r 28 provides that:
'(1) If the court so directs, a certificate of service showing where, when, how and by whom service was effected shall be filed as soon as practicable after service of a document has been effected in accordance with these Rules.
(2) The provisions of paragraph (1) of this rule shall apply to the giving of notification under rules 26 and 27 . . . '
3 For a precedent of a form of consent to the appointment of a receiver, see Precedent 3 below.

3 RELATIVE'S CONSENT TO THE APPOINTMENT OF A RECEIVER[1]

COURT OF PROTECTION

IN THE MATTER OF .... A PATIENT

I .... (*relative's full name*)
of ....(*address*)
the .... (*relationship*) .... of the above-named patient
CONSENT
to the appointment of .... (*full name of proposed receiver*)
as receiver in this matter.

SIGNED ....

DATE ....

1 Court of Protection Rules 1994 (SI 1994/3046), r 27 requires an applicant who proposes to apply for the appointment of a receiver or new receiver to notify the patient's next of kin of his or her intention. See, generally, the footnotes to Precedent 2 above: 'Notice of intention to apply for the appointment of a receiver'.

4 SOLICITOR'S LETTER IN SUPPORT OF AN APPLICATION FOR A SHORT ORDER OR DIRECTION[1]

Public Trust Office
Enquiries and Applications
Stewart House
24 Kingsway   (*Reference*)
London WC2B 6JX   (*Date*)

Dear Sirs

Application for a Short Order or Direction[2]
In the matter of (*full name of patient*) (a patient)

We act for (*full name and address, including postcode, of the applicant*).

His wife, (*full name of patient*), suffers from Alzheimer's Disease and is incapable of managing and administering her property and affairs. Until now there has been no need for the Court of Protection or the Public Trust Office to become involved in her affairs.

On (*date*), (*name of deceased*) died leaving the patient a legacy of (*amount under £5000*). The executors are now in a position to pay this legacy, and we would be grateful if the Public Trustee would consider giving a direction, or request the court to make a short order, authorising the applicant to receive and give a valid receipt for the legacy on the patient's behalf.

We enclose:

- an office copy of the will and probate;
- a Medical Certificate (Form CP3) completed by the patient's GP;[3]
- the doctor's fee note for visiting the patient and completing the Medical Certificate;
- a Certificate of Family and Property (Form CP5);[4] and
- a cheque for £100 made payable to 'Public Trust Office' in respect of the commencement fee.[5]

If the Public Trustee or the court is willing to deal with this application by way of a direction or short order, the applicant proposes to open a National Savings Bank Investment Account in the patient's name and would appreciate it if he could also be authorised to operate that account on her behalf.

We would be obliged if the applicant could be reimbursed from the patient's estate for the various out-of-pocket expenses he has incurred in making this application on her behalf. They are:

- the doctor's fee;
- the commencement fee; and
- our costs which, assuming that there are no complications, we estimate will be in the region of £ ...... plus VAT.

We see no reason why the patient should not be notified of the proposed direction or order,[6] although we believe that she would be incapable of understanding any such notification.

Yours faithfully

(signature of firm of solicitors)

---

1 See 'Short procedure', at p 275 above.
2 Court of Protection Rules 1994 (SI 1994/3046), r 9.
3 *Ibid*, r 36.
4 *Ibid*.
5 *Ibid*, r 79: 'A commencement fee shall be payable on any first application for the appointment of a receiver or other originating process in respect of any patient'. The commencement fee of £100 appears in col 2 of the Appendix to the Rules.
6 *Ibid*, r 26(1)(b).

---

5 LETTER TO THE PUBLIC TRUST OFFICE REQUESTING AGREEMENT OF COSTS[1]

Public Trust Office
Protection Division   *(Reference)*
DX: 37965 Kingsway   *(Date)*

Dear Sirs

Request to agree costs
In the matter of *(full name of patient)*, a patient: 19   no.

We enclose a draft bill of costs[2] relating to the application for an order making gifts out of the patient's estate.[3] Receipts for the disbursements are also enclosed.

We would be willing to accept (£750)[4] plus VAT and disbursements by way of costs, and look forward to receiving the court's agreement.[5]

Yours faithfully

(signature of firm of solicitors)

---

1 See, generally, 'Agreed costs' in the section on 'Solicitors' costs' at p 280 above.
2 The draft bill should contain a narrative of the work done, time spent and level of fee-earner involved.
3 Agreed costs should not be sought in respect of any of the five categories of work for which there is already provision for fixed costs. For further details on fixed costs, see p 279.
4 The maximum amount for agreed costs was raised from £750 to £1000 on 1 October 1994. Unlike fixed costs, the limit for agreed costs is not reviewed annually and the current limit is unlikely to be raised in the foreseeable future.
5 The application will be accepted or rejected. It will not be subject to negotiation. The staff at the Public Trust Office are not experienced in costs drafting or negotiation.

CHAPTER 11: LIVING WILLS

INDEX

Text

Precedents

Miscellaneous clauses

LIVING WILLS

TEXT

Definitions[1]

An *advance directive* is a statement, usually in writing, in which a competent person expresses his or her preferences about medical treatment in the event of becoming incapable of making and communicating a treatment decision.

An advance directive may be:

- an *instruction directive* in which the maker gives instructions about the kind of treatment he or she wants (a *request directive*), or does not want (a *refusal directive*);
- a *proxy directive* in which the maker appoints someone else to make and communicate treatment decisions on his or her behalf; or
- a combined instruction and proxy directive.

Advance directives (particularly refusal directives) are commonly known as *living wills*.[2]

---

1 The terms, although not the definitions, are those used by the President's Commission for the Study of Ethical Problems in Medicine and Biomedical and Behavioral Research in its report, *Deciding to Forgo Life-Sustaining Treatment* (US Government Printing Office, Washington DC, 1983).

2 The expression 'living will' was first used by Luis Kutner, a member of the Illinois and Indiana Bars, in his article, 'Due Process of Euthanasia: The Living Will, A Proposal' (1969) 44 *Indiana Law Journal* 539–554. At p 551, he stated: 'Therefore, the suggested solution is that the individual, while fully in control of his faculties and his ability to express himself, indicate to what extent he would consent to treatment. The document indicating such consent may be referred to as "a living will", "a declaration determining the termination of life", "testament permitting death", "declaration for bodily autonomy", "declaration for ending treatment", "body trust" or other similar reference'. Given the alternatives, one can understand how the term 'living will' caught on.

Legal status

Recent court decisions on medical treatment and end-of-life issues have held that, in England and Wales at least, a refusal directive (as distinct from a request directive or a proxy directive) will be valid and enforceable at common law provided that:

- it is clearly established;[1]
- it is applicable in the circumstances;[2]
- the maker was competent when he or she made it;[3]

- the maker was not unduly influenced by anyone else;[4]
- the maker contemplated the situation that eventually arose;[5]
- the maker was aware of the consequences of refusing treatment;[6]
- it does not request any unlawful intervention or omission;[7]
- it does not request treatment which the medical team considers to be clinically inappropriate.[8]

A proxy directive, in which the maker nominates somebody else to make treatment decisions on his or her behalf, is not currently valid or enforceable in English law.[9] It is unlikely, however, that a simple request that a named individual should be consulted before any treatment decision is made would be ignored.[10]

Where a patient is liable to be detained under the Mental Health Act 1983, the contents of any advance directive he or she has made may be overridden by s 63 of that Act, which provides that 'the consent of a patient shall not be required for any medical treatment given to him for the mental disorder from which he is suffering'.[11] The contents of an advance directive may possibly also be overridden by an order under s 47 of the National Assistance Act 1948, which authorises the removal of persons from the premises in which they are residing, without their consent, if such action is in their own interests or if they present a health threat or serious nuisance to others.

Following the celebrated case of the Hillsborough Stadium crush victim, Tony Bland, *Airedale NHS Trust v Bland*,[12] the House of Lords convened a Select Committee on Medical Ethics to consider the ethical, legal and clinical implications of a person's right to withhold consent to life-prolonging treatment, and the position of persons who are no longer able to give or withhold consent. The committee published a report of its findings in February 1994, in which it concluded that it would:

- commend the development of advance directives (but concluded that legislation for advance directives generally is unnecessary);
- recommend that a code of practice on advance directives should be developed;
- not favour the more widespread development of a system of proxy decision making.[13]

In response to the Select Committee's recommendation, the British Medical Association, in conjunction with the medical and nursing Royal Colleges, published a Code of Practice in April 1995.[14]

---

1 'An anticipatory choice, if clearly established and applicable in the circumstances – two major "ifs" – would bind the practitioner': *Re T (Adult: Refusal of Treatment)* [1992] 4 All ER 649, at p 653f, per Lord Donaldson MR.

2 *Ibid.*

3 *Re C (Refusal of Medical Treatment)* [1994] 1 All ER 819.

4 *Re T (Adult: Refusal of Treatment)* [1992] 4 All ER 649, at p 662c–g.

5 'Especial care may be necessary to ensure that the prior refusal of consent is still properly to be regarded as applicable in the circumstances which have subsequently occurred': *Airedale NHS Trust v Bland* [1993] 1 All ER 821, at p 866e, per Lord Goff.

6 'What is required is that the patient knew in broad terms the nature and effect of the procedure to which consent (or refusal) was given': *Re T* (fn 1 above), at p 663f, per Lord Donaldson MR.
7 House of Lords, *Report of the Select Committee on Medical Ethics* (HL 21–I, 1994), para 263.
8 *Ibid.*
9 The House of Lords Select Committee on Medical Ethics, whilst commending in its Report (above) the development of advance directives, was opposed to a more widespread development of a system of proxy decision making: para 271. The Law Commission, however, has proposed that 'it should be possible for a person to execute an enduring power of attorney giving another person the authority to give or refuse consent on his or her behalf to some or all medical treatment in relation to which the donor has become incapacitated': Consultation Paper No 129, p 86.
10 For a precedent appointing alternative persons to be consulted before a treatment decision is made, see Precedent 6 at p 324 below.
11 *B v Croydon Health Authority* [1995] 1 FLR 470. The case of *Re C (Refusal of Medical Treatment)* [1994] 1 All ER 819, in which a schizophrenic was held to be entitled to refuse treatment for gangrene is distinguishable. The gangrene was entirely unconnected with the mental disorder.
12 [1993] 1 All ER 821.
13 House of Lords, *Report of the Select Committee on Medical Ethics* (HL Paper 21-I), p 58.
14 BMA, *Advance Statements about Medical Treatment* (1995). Copies with explanatory notes may be obtained from BMJ Bookshop, Tavistock Square, London WC1H 9JP, priced £5.95.

The purpose of a living will[1]

The underlying philosophy of advance directives is neither the 'right to die', nor the 'right to life', but the 'right to choose'.[2] This freedom of choice is generally known in the medical profession as *autonomy*, and in the legal profession as *the right of self-determination*.

> 'Prima facie every adult has the right and capacity to decide whether or not he will accept medical treatment, even if a refusal may risk permanent injury to his health or even lead to premature death. Furthermore, it matters not whether the reasons for the refusal were rational or irrational, unknown or even non-existent. This is so notwithstanding the very strong public interest in preserving the life and health of all citizens.'[3]

> 'The same principle applies where a patient's refusal to give his consent has been expressed at an earlier date, before he became unconscious or otherwise incapable of communicating it.'[4]

A patient who is no longer competent, or never was competent in the first place, is unable to exercise this right of self-determination, and in such cases an application must be made to the High Court for a declaration authorising whatever course of action it considers to be in the patient's 'best interests'.[5] The evaluation of best interests is not entirely paternalistic because it, too, is subject to another basic right, 'the right to be respected'.[6]

The purpose of living wills can be summarised as follows:

- They enhance autonomy and, in theory, extend it to the end of the patient's life.
- They can rebut, or endorse, the presumption of consent. 'There is without doubt a very strong presumption in favour of a course of action which will prolong life, but it is not irrebuttable'.[7]
- They are probably the best evidence of a patient's wishes.[8]

- They can safeguard the dignity and privacy of an incapacitated patient against unwanted or unwarranted treatment. Recent advances in medical science have made it possible to prolong life through the use of artificial procedures. In some cases, this can result in a precarious or burdensome existence, without providing anything medically necessary or beneficial for the patient.[9]
- They could be a catalyst for improved communication between patients and their GP, family and friends, on treatment options at the end of life.[10]
- They could reduce health care costs. In its *Declaration on Euthanasia* (1980), the Roman Catholic Church acknowledged that 'a desire not to impose excessive expense on the family or the community' is a legitimate reason for deciding to forgo life-sustaining treatment in certain circumstances.[11]
- They enable an individual to plan for possible future incapacitation.[12] In this respect, their function is similar to that of an enduring power of attorney although for medical, rather than financial, purposes.
- They relieve others (both the medical team and the patient's family) of the responsibility of having to make a decision without any predetermined guidelines to go by, and thereby increase confidence in end-of-life decision-making.[13]

---

1 For a more extensive discussion, see Denzil Lush, 'The Purposes of A Living Will', *EAGLE Journal*, vol 1, issue 6 (June/July 1993), pp 4–8.
2 *Re T (Adult: Refusal of Treatment)* [1992] 4 All ER 649, at p 652f, per Lord Donaldson MR.
3 *Ibid*, at p 664a, per Lord Donaldson MR.
4 *Airedale NHS Trust v Bland* [1993] 1 All ER 821, at p 866e, per Lord Goff.
5 *Re T* (fn 2 above), at p 663h.
6 *Airedale NHS Trust v Bland* (fn 4 above), at p 848c–d, per Butler-Sloss LJ.
7 *Re J (A Minor) (Wardship: Medical Treatment)* [1990] 3 All ER 930, at p 938, per Lord Donaldson of Lymington MR.
8 *Cruzan v Director, Missouri Department of Health* (1990) 497 US 261, (1990) 110 S Ct 2841, United States Supreme Court.
9 '[A mentally incompetent patient] has the right to be respected. Consequently he has a right to avoid unnecessary humiliation and degrading invasion of his body for no good purpose': *Airedale NHS Trust v Bland* (fn 4 above), at p 848c, per Butler-Sloss LJ.
10 The United States Presidential Commission which reported in March 1983 regarded the potential for initiating dialogue between doctors and patients as the greatest advantage of the first wave of Natural Death Acts.
11 Sacred Congregation for the Doctrine of the Faith, *Declaration on Euthanasia*, 5 May 1980, published by the Catholic Truth Society, London, p 9.
12 See, generally, George J. Alexander, *Writing a Living Will* (Praeger, 1988), Chapter 2, 'The Need to Plan'.
13 See, generally, Linda Emanuel and Ezekiel Emanuel, 'The Medical Directive: A New Comprehensive Advance Care Document', *Journal of the American Medical Association*, vol 261, no 22 (9 June 1989), p 3289.

The market for living wills[1]

Living wills are increasingly becoming a regular part of the incapacity and end-of-life 'package', along with enduring powers of attorney and conventional wills.[2] There is evidence of a growing public demand for them,[3] particularly among the elderly.[4] It has been said that clients who have completed a living will generally find them reassuring; that they feel a greater sense of control over treatment they can eventually expect to receive; that they are less afraid of dying; and that they are less anxious about being utterly helpless at the end of life.[5]

---

1 The author was first asked to draft an advance directive for a client in 1984. In 1988, after Age Concern issued a press release to coincide with the publication of its working party report, *The Living Will: Consent to Treatment at the End of Life*, he received requests for a living will from four clients. In 1989, another seven were drawn up, and from 1990 onwards – when other members of the firm became more actively involved in the preparation of advance directives – there has been a steady average of between 30 and 40 per year, peaking at 46 following the launch of the Terrence Higgins Trust Living Will in September 1992 and the press coverage of the Tony Bland case a few months later. By 31 July 1995 the firm had prepared advance directives for more than 200 clients. 61% of these clients are female, and 39% male, which is entirely consistent with the gender breakdown of the British population aged 65 and over. Five of the clients who have made a living will are doctors. Several of the living wills have become operative, and so far there have been no problems regarding the implementation of the makers' wishes. An experiment, briefly tried in 1992, was to abandon the use of any precedent and, after discussion with the clients, encourage them to write their own living will. The experiment was abandoned because the handwritten statements prepared by the clients themselves usually requested an unlawful intervention.

2 In 1990, during the Gulf War, US forces in the Middle East were encouraged, as service personnel always are during hostilities, to write a will. For the first time in history, they were also advised to complete a durable power of attorney and an advance directive: George Annas, 'The Health Care Proxy and the Living Will', *The New England Journal of Medicine*, vol 324, no 17 (25 April 1991), p 1212.

3 The Terrence Higgins Trust launched its *Living Will* in September 1992, and 15,000 copies of the first edition were distributed during the following eighteen months. It is now in its second edition, and already more than 5000 copies have been distributed. Most of the requests for the Terrence Higgins Trust Living Will come, not from people with HIV or AIDS, but from the elderly.

4 *Yours*, a popular magazine for the over 60s, published the results of a survey on end-of-life issues in its September 1994 issue. More than 2000 people, with an average age of 69.5, responded to a questionnaire. 84% said that everyone should make a living will, although only 13% had actually made one.

5 M. Henderson, 'Beyond the Living Will' (1990) 30 *Gerontologist*, 480–485. See, also, John La Puma, David Orentlicher and Robert Moss, 'Advance Directives on Admission: Clinical Implications of the Patient Self-Determination Act of 1990', *Journal of the American Medical Association*, vol 266, no 3 (17 July 1991), p 402.

The lawyer's role

The Code of Practice on Advance Statements about Medical Treatment published by the BMA in April 1995 was principally designed to encourage health care professionals to assist their patients in drafting advance statements. Nevertheless, it could be argued that there is also a role for lawyers in:

- informing and educating existing and potential clients about advance directives;[1]
- drafting and otherwise assisting in the preparation of living wills;
- advising on their legal status;

- assessing whether a client is competent to make one;
- liaising, wherever necessary, with medical professionals to ensure that a directive is realistic and suited to the sort of circumstances which are likely to arise;
- providing strongroom facilities for the storage of the original, and photocopying facilities for reproducing the required number of copies;
- ensuring that the client's GP has a copy of the document with instructions to place it on the client's medical record;[2]
- reminding the client of the need to review an advance directive at regular intervals (perhaps annually), or whenever there is any major change of circumstances;
- record-keeping;
- intervening, if necessary, to ensure that an advance directive is honoured.

---

1 The BMA has received complaints through the Advertising Standards Authority that some firms of solicitors have been advertising living wills guaranteeing non-treatment for anybody who completes one.

2 For a specimen letter to a client's GP enclosing a copy of his or her advance directive, see Precedent 7 at p 325 below.

Drafting a living will[1]

The drafting of a living will is very much a client-orientated exercise, because it deals with intensely individual moral choices. In this respect, any standard precedent should be regarded as merely a framework on which to base a more individualised document.

Insofar as there is any formal order of contents, the structure of a living will is usually as follows:

(1) **Commencement**. A description of the document; the date; and the full name and address, and possibly the date of birth, of the maker. In addition, if it is considered necessary, the document could begin with an address, for example: 'To my doctor, my family, and all others whom it may concern'.[2]

(2) **Incapacity**. A statement that the directive will only come into effect 'if I am no longer capable of making and communicating a treatment decision', and perhaps some indication as to who should decide whether the maker is no longer capable.

(3) **Triggering condition**. A description of any terminal illness or other condition which will trigger off a particular course of action or inaction. For example, 'if I become terminally ill and there is no likelihood that I will regain the ability to make a treatment decision for myself', or 'if I have dementia, and I am doubly incontinent, unable to recognise people, unable to speak intelligibly, and incapable of washing, feeding and dressing myself, and I also have an illness or condition which, if it were left untreated, would probably be the cause of my death'.[3]

(4)   **Unacceptable treatment**. This can be expressed generally, for example, 'I do not wish to be kept alive by medical treatment. I wish medical treatment to be limited to keeping me comfortable and free from pain, and I refuse all other medical treatment'.[4] Alternatively, unacceptable treatment could be described specifically in terms of discrete medical or surgical interventions, for example any one or more of the following: 'cardiopulmonary resuscitation; mechanical breathing; artificial nutrition and hydration; major surgery; kidney dialysis; chemotherapy; minor surgery; invasive diagnostic tests; blood or blood products; antibiotics; simple diagnostic tests; and pain medication'.[5]

(5)   **Acceptable treatment**. There are two types of acceptable treatment: 'basic care', such as comfort care and direct oral feeding, the acceptance of which is obligatory; and any other form of treatment, the acceptance of which is, within reason, optional. The Law Commission has recommended that an advance refusal of treatment should not preclude the provision of 'basic care', namely care to maintain bodily cleanliness and to alleviate severe pain, as well as the provision of direct oral nutrition and hydration.[6]

(6)   **Other wishes and statements**. Examples might include the maker's 'values history';[7] a request that someone should be given the opportunity to be present before or when the maker dies;[8] organ donation;[9] the extent to which the maker is willing to participate in therapeutic or non-therapeutic research; a severability clause;[10] if it is appropriate, a clause stating what effect the directive will have during the pregnancy of a female of child-bearing age;[11] or a statement to the effect that the maker has discussed his or her wishes with a particular, named doctor.

(7)   **Proxy**. The name(s) and address(es) of any person(s) whom the maker wishes to be consulted before any treatment decision is made.[12]

(8)   **Signature and attestation clause**.

- Do not be overly concerned that the document might fail to foresee every possible eventuality. This is one of the basic defects of advance directives generally.[13]
- Try to be as general as possible. Only refer to specific diseases and disorders if the maker has actually been diagnosed as having that specific disease or disorder, or has an hereditary predisposition to a particular condition, and is aware of the course the illness is likely to take. By being too specific, you might fail to pinpoint the disorder that eventually develops. For example, if a living will expressly refers to Alzheimer's Disease, it may not be clear whether the same instructions would apply if the maker were suffering from, say, Multi-Infarct Dementia. Make sure, if you are listing a series of specific interventions, that they do not contradict each other; or suggest unusual patterns of medical practice;[14] or detract from the client's overall treatment objectives.
- Bear in mind the medical viability of what is being drafted. If you have any doubts, contact the client's GP.
- Do not let the maker authorise any act or omission which is or may be unlawful. If you do, it would be sensible to include a severability clause in the living will.[15]

There are currently no rules about the number or eligibility of witnesses, but it is suggested that one independent witness (perhaps the lawyer who drafts the document for the client) should be sufficient.

A copy of the executed living will should be sent to the client's GP with a request that it be filed and marked on the client's medical record. For a precedent of a letter registering a living will with a GP, see Precedent 7 at p 325 below.

---

1 For a more in-depth analysis of drafting advance directives, see Denzil Lush, 'Drafting a Living Will', *EAGLE Journal*, vol 2, issue 2 (October/November 1993), pp 4–9; and Nancy M.P. King, *Making Sense of Advance Directives* (Kluwer Academic Publishers, 1991).

2 See Clause 1 at p 328 below.

3 The maker may wish to refuse treatment at a much earlier stage, for example, 'if I am suffering from the early stages of dementia, and also have a physical illness which, if it were left untreated, would probably be the cause of my death'.

4 Terrence Higgins Trust, *Living Will* (2nd edition, 1994).

5 Linda L. Emanuel and Ezekiel J. Emanuel, 'The Medical Directive: A New Comprehensive Advance Care Document', *Journal of the American Medical Association*, vol 261, no 22 (9 June 1989), pp 3288–3293. For a criticism of this technique, see Allan S. Brett, 'Limitations of Listing Specific Medical Interventions in Advance Directives', *Journal of the American Medical Association*, vol 266, no 6 (14 August 1991), pp 825–828.

6 Law Commission Report No 231, *Mental Incapacity* (HMSO, March 1995), para 5.34, and draft Mental Incapacity Bill, clauses 9(7)(a) and 8. Note that the definition of 'basic care' in para 2.3 of the BMA's Code of Practice, *Advance Statements about Medical Treatment*, is slightly different.

7 A 'values history' is a personal statement of views which the maker considers relevant to his or her instructions. See Clause 19 at p 335 below.

8 See Clause 14 at p 332 below.

9 There are arguments for and against including an organ donation clause in an advance directive. The arguments in favour are that: combining the two is likely to stimulate discussions on both issues; it makes the doctor's task much easier if he or she needs to raise the question of organ donation with the donor's nearest relatives; and it relieves the relatives themselves of having to make such a decision at a time of stress and bereavement. The arguments against include the suggestion that the main reason why many people do not complete a donor card is that they are worried that the doctors 'might do something to me before I'm really dead', and that combining a living will and a donor card could exacerbate this concern and deter people from signing either document.

10 For a severability clause, see Clause 16 at p 333 below.

11 For example, the living will drawn up by Chris Grant Docker of the Voluntary Euthanasia Society of Scotland gives these alternatives: (a) 'This Living Will is to be temporarily overruled if I am pregnant and, to a reasonable degree of medical certainty, the foetus may develop to the point of live birth'; or (b) 'My advance refusal of treatment, as stated in this document, is to be carried out even if I am pregnant and carrying a viable foetus, and even if this means that the foetus will not develop to the point of a live birth'.

12 See Precedent 6 at p 324 below.

13 Nancy M.P. King, *Making Sense of Advance Directives* (Kluwer Academic Publishers, 1991), p 109.

14 For example: 'in the context of advanced dementia, he selected blood transfusions, but rejected invasive diagnostic procedures such as upper gastrointestinal endoscopy. If that patient developed upper gastrointestinal bleeding, we would be asked to administer transfusions, while avoiding an endoscopic procedure that might not only be diagnostic but also therapeutic . . . It is absurd to dissociate the two interventions by replacing blood losses but not performing a simple procedure to stop the bleeding': Allan S. Brett, *op cit*, p 826.

15 See Clause 16 at p 333 below.

Proposed legislation

In its report on *Mental Incapacity*, published 1 March 1995, the Law Commission recommended that advance refusals of treatment should form part of its overall strategy to reform the law on mental incapacity and to ensure that actions are taken in the best interests of a person without capacity.[1] It defines 'advance refusal of treatment' as 'a refusal by a person who has attained the age of eighteen and has the necessary capacity of any medical, surgical or dental treatment or other procedure, being a refusal intended to have effect at any subsequent time when he may be without capacity to give or refuse his consent', but an advance refusal cannot preclude the provision of 'basic care' for the person who made it. 'Basic care' means care to maintain bodily cleanliness and to alleviate severe pain, and the provision of direct oral nutrition and hydration.[2]

On 16 January 1996, the Lord Chancellor, Lord Mackay of Clashfern, announced that 'the Government has decided not to legislate on the basis of the Law Commission's proposals in their current form and ... proposes to issue a consultation paper on mental incapacity in due course'.

---

1 Law Commission Report No 231, *Mental Incapacity* (HMSO, 1995, £21.85), paras 5.1–5.39, and draft Mental Incapacity Bill, cl 9.
2 *Ibid*, para 5.34, and draft Bill, cls 9(7)(a) and 8. The British Medical Association, in its Code of Practice, *Advance Statements about Medical Treatment*, at para 2.3 defines 'basic care' as meaning 'those procedures essential to keep an individual comfortable. The administration of medication or the performance of any procedure which is solely or primarily designed to provide comfort to the patient or to alleviate that person's pain, symptoms or distress are facets of basic care'.

PRECEDENTS

1 LIVING WILL: REFUSAL DIRECTIVE[1]

THIS LIVING WILL is made on ....

by me   ....

of   ....

         ....

born on ....

I WISH these instructions to be acted upon if two registered medical practitioners are of the opinion that I am no longer capable of making[2] and communicating[3] a treatment decision AND that I am:

- unconscious, and it is unlikely that I shall ever regain consciousness; or
- suffering from an incurable or irreversible condition that will result in my death within a relatively short time; or
- so severely disabled, physically or mentally, that I shall be totally dependent on others for the rest of my life.

I REFUSE[4] any medical or surgical treatment if:

- its burdens and risks outweigh its potential benefits;[5] or
- it involves any research or experimentation which is likely to be of little or no therapeutic value to me;[6] or
- it will needlessly prolong my life or postpone the actual moment of my death.

I CONSENT to being fed orally,[7] and to any treatment that may:

- safeguard my dignity; or
- make me more comfortable; or
- relieve pain and suffering;

even though such treatment might unintentionally precipitate my death.[8]

SIGNED by me in the presence of: ....

---

1 This precedent was originally published, with a full commentary, in *EAGLE Journal*, vol 2, issue 3 (December 1993/January 1994), pp 4–7.

2 For capacity to make a treatment decision, see, inter alia, Chapter 15 of the Code of Practice issued pursuant to the Mental Health Act 1983, s 118; and *Re C (Adult: Refusal of Medical Treatment)* [1994] 1 All ER 819, at p 824.

3 It is important to remember that some people, although mentally capable of making a treatment decision, are physically or mentally incapable of communicating the decision they have made. They might, for example, be deaf and dumb, or suffering from aphasia. In its report *Mental Incapacity*, the Law Commission has recommended that legislation should provide that a person is without capacity if at the material time he or she is: (1) unable by reason of mental instability to make a decision on the matter in question; or (2) unable to communicate a decision on that matter because he or she is unconscious or for any other reason: Law Com No 231 (HMSO, 1995), para 3.14, and draft Mental Incapacity Bill, cl 2(1). It also recommends that a person should not be regarded as unable to communicate his or her decision unless all practicable steps to enable him or her to do so have been taken without success: *ibid*, para 3.21 and draft Bill, cl 2(5).

4. 'Prima facie every adult has the right and capacity to decide whether or not he will accept medical treatment, even if a refusal may risk permanent injury to his health or even lead to premature death. Furthermore, it matters not whether the reasons for the refusal were rational or irrational, unknown or even non-existent': *Re T (Adult: Refusal of Treatment)* [1992] 4 All ER 649, at p 664a, per Lord Donaldson MR.

'The same principle applies where the patient's refusal to give his consent has been expressed at an earlier date, before he became unconscious or otherwise incapable of communicating it': *Airedale NHS Trust v Bland* [1993] 1 All ER 821, at p 866e, per Lord Goff.

5 In its *Declaration on Euthanasia* (Catholic Truth Society, 1980), the Roman Catholic Church permits an individual to refuse medical treatment which is disproportionate to the results that can reasonably be expected. Proportionality in the use of remedies involves weighing (a) the type of treatment, its complexity, the risks involved, and the cost, with (b) the likely results, taking into account the state of the patient and his or her physical, mental, moral, and financial resources.

6 The *Declaration of Helsinki*, originally produced by the World Medical Association in 1964, distinguishes between 'therapeutic research', in which medical experimentation is combined with professional care for the patient, and 'non-therapeutic reasearch', in which the principal objective is the advancement of medical knowledge.

7 In para 5.34 of its report *Mental Incapacity* (Law Com No 231) (HMSO, 1995), the Law Commission recommended that an advance refusal of treatment should not preclude the provision of 'basic care', namely care to maintain bodily cleanliness and to alleviate severe pain, as well as the provision of direct oral nutrition and hydration.

8 It is unlawful for a doctor to administer a drug to a patient in order to bring about his or her death, even though this course of action is prompted by a humanitarian desire to end the patient's suffering: *R v Cox* (unreported, 18 September 1992, per Ognall J at Winchester Crown Court). However, 'it is an established rule that a doctor may, when caring for a patient who is, for example, dying of cancer, lawfully administer painkilling drugs despite the fact that he knows that an incidental effect of that application will be to abbreviate the patient's life. Such a decision may properly be made as part of the care of the living patient, in his best interests; and, on this basis, the treatment will be lawful. Moreover, where the doctor's treatment is lawful, the patient's death will be regarded in law as exclusively caused by the injury or disease to which his condition is attributable': *Airedale NHS Trust v Bland* [1993] 1 All ER 821, at p 868h, per Lord Goff.

2 LIVING WILL IN WHICH THE MAKER DEFINES AN INTOLERABLE CONDITION

THIS LIVING WILL is made on ....
by me ....
of...
born on ....

(1)   If two registered medical practitioners are of the opinion that I am no longer capable of making and communicating a medical treatment decision, and that I am suffering from an intolerable condition, as defined below:

- I REFUSE any medical treatment which is designed simply to keep me alive; but
- I CONSENT to being fed orally, and to any treatment that may relieve my pain and suffering, even though it might unintentionally shorten my life.

(2)   An intolerable condition is one in which I will almost certainly spend the rest of my life:

- being mentally incapable of making or communicating a treatment decision for myself; or
- in constant, unremitting pain; or
- in a coma; or
- with severe disfigurement to my face or head; or
- permanently confined to bed.

(3)   An intolerable condition is also one in which I will suffer from any [two or more] of the following disabilities for the rest of my life:

- unable to communicate sensibly;
- unable to recognise my family and friends;
- unable to feed, dress and wash myself;
- unable to control my bladder and bowel;
- (*specify any other disabilities which the maker believes would make his or her life intolerable*).

SIGNED by me in the presence of: ....

3 LIVING WILL: ANY SUPERVENING ILLNESS IS NOT TO BE ACTIVELY TREATED

THIS LIVING WILL is made on...

by me ....

of ....

....

born on ....

(1)   I HAVE been diagnosed as suffering from........................ (*state diagnosis*), and I am fully aware of:

- the course the illness may take;
- the extent to which its symptoms can and cannot be alleviated by medical treatment and nursing care; and
- the consequences of refusing treatment.

(2)   I WANT these instructions to be implemented if I am no longer capable of making and communicating a decision about my health care.

(3)   IF I sustain an injury, or suffer from any separate illness, condition or disease, which, if it were left untreated, would probably be the cause of my death:

- I REFUSE any active treatment of that injury, illness, condition or disease
- BUT I CONSENT to being fed orally, and to any treatment which may relieve pain or be considered necessary for the health, safety and protection of others.

(4)   IF, for any reason, these instructions are not clear or not applicable in the circumstances, I WOULD LIKE my .... (*state relationship, if any*)

Name: ....

Address: ....

....

Telephone: ....

to be consulted before any irrevocable decision is made about my health care.

SIGNED by me in the presence of:...

4 LIVING WILL: MAXIMUM TREATMENT[1]

THIS LIVING WILL is made on ....

by me   ....

of   ....

           ....

born on   ....

(1)   IF I am no longer capable of making and communicating a decision about my health care, I WISH to be kept alive for as long as reasonably possible using any form of treatment available, regardless of:

- my condition;
- the prognosis;
- the cost – provided I have sufficient resources to pay for such treatment.

(2)   I CONSENT to any medical, surgical or nursing treatment or care that may:

- save or sustain my life;
- make me more comfortable;
- relieve pain and suffering;
- be necessary for the health, safety or protection of others.

(3)   I AGREE to take part in any therapeutic or non-therapeutic research or experiment, provided that:

- it does not involve any substantial risk to my health;
- it does not defeat my overall objective to remain alive for as long as I reasonably can.

(4)   I DO NOT REQUIRE anyone who is responsible for my care to:

- do anything unlawful;[2]
- give me any treatment they regard as futile;
- do anything they consider to be clinically inappropriate;[3]
- act otherwise than a responsible and competent body of relevant professional opinion would act.[4]

SIGNED by me in the presence of: ....

---

1 See, generally, Marshall B. Kapp, 'Response to the Living Will Furor: Directives for Maximum Care', *The American Journal of Medicine*, vol 72, pp 855–859 (June 1982).

     More ethical problems are created by a request directive, such as this precedent – in which the patient requests specific interventions – than a refusal directive. See, generally, Allan S. Brett and Laurence B. McCollough, 'When Patients Request Specific Interventions: Defining the Limits of the Physician's Obligation', *The New England Journal of Medicine*, vol 315, no 21 (20 November 1986), pp 1347–1351.

2 See House of Lords, *Report of the Select Committee on Medical Ethics* (HMSO, 1994), vol 1, para 263: 'We commend the development of advance directives . . . We emphasise however that they should not contain requests for any unlawful intervention or omission; nor can they require treatment to be given which the health-care team judge is not clinically appropriate.'
3 *Ibid.*
4 'A doctor is not guilty of negligence if he has acted in accordance with a practice accepted as proper by a responsible body of medical men skilled in that particular art': *Bolam v Friern Hospital Management Committee* [1957] 2 All ER 118, at p 121, per McNair J.

5 LIVING WILL: TREATMENT PREFERENCES[1]

THIS LIVING WILL is made on ....
by me ....
of ....
....
born on ....

IF I AM UNABLE TO MAKE DECISIONS FOR MYSELF, AND:

(1) IF I AM CRITICALLY ILL, in other words, very ill but not terminally ill, and my condition could improve with medical treatment:

- I want to be hospitalised.
- I want to go into intensive care.
- I want to be resuscitated if my heart stops.
- I want to have surgery.
- I want to be put on a breathing machine.

(2) IF I AM TERMINALLY ILL, in other words, dying and my condition cannot be improved by medical treatment, no matter what is done:

- I want to be hospitalised.
- I want my family to decide whether I should go into intensive care after they have discussed the matter with my doctor.
- I want my doctor to decide whether to resuscitate me if my heart stops.
- I want my family to decide whether I should have surgery after they have discussed the matter with my doctor.
- I want my family to decide whether I should be put on a breathing machine after they have discussed the matter with my doctor.

(3) IF I AM IN AN IRREVERSIBLE COMA, and it is unlikely that I shall ever regain consciousness:

- I want to be hospitalised.
- I want my family to decide whether I should go into intensive care after they have discussed the matter with my doctor.

- I want my doctor to decide whether to resuscitate me if my heart stops.
- I want my family to decide whether I have surgery after they have discussed the matter with my doctor.
- I do not want to be put on a breathing machine.
- I want my family to decide whether I should be fed through a tube after they have discussed the matter with my doctor.

SIGNED by me in the presence of: ....

---

1 This precedent is based on the 'Sample Statement of Patient's Preferences', which appeared as an appendix to Marion Danis et al 'A Prospective Study of Advance Directives for Life-Sustaining Care', *The New England Journal of Medicine*, 28 March 1991, pp 882–887. The authors, who mainly came from the Departments of Medicine and Epidemiology at the University of North Carolina, carried out a market research study over a two-year period during which they interviewed 126 competent residents of a nursing home and 49 family members of incompetent patients to determine their treatment preferences.

---

6 PEOPLE TO BE CONSULTED BEFORE A TREATMENT DECISION IS MADE[1]

THIS ADVANCE STATEMENT is made on ....
by me   ....
of   ....
        ....
born on ....

IF I AM NO LONGER CAPABLE OF MAKING AND COMMUNICATING A DECISION ABOUT MY HEALTH CARE

I would like the following person to be consulted before any decision about my treatment or care is made:

Relationship, if any: ....
Full name: ....
Address: ....
                ....
Telephone (home): ....
Telephone (work): ....

If that person is not reasonably available, or is incapacitated, or is unwilling to be consulted, I would like the following person to be consulted instead:

Relationship, if any: ....
Full name: ....
Address: ....
  ....
Telephone (home): ....
Telephone (work): ....

SIGNED by me in the presence of: ....

---

1 The legal status of a 'proxy' decision-maker for medical treatment is unclear, and at para 298 of its Report published in 1994, the House of Lords Select Committee on Medical Ethics specifically stated that 'we do not favour the more widespread development of a system of proxy decision-making'. This precedent does not appoint proxies as such, but merely people whom the patient wishes to be consulted before any treatment decision is made.

7 LETTER REGISTERING A LIVING WILL WITH A CLIENT'S GP

(Date)

Dear Dr *(GP's name)*,

(Full name, address, and date of birth of client)

I am enclosing a photocopy of the living will recently signed by your patient, *(client's name)*, who is also one of my clients.

Please would you:

- acknowledge receipt by signing and dating the duplicate copy of this letter, and returning it to me in the enclosed pre-paid envelope;
- ensure that the living will is placed in *(client's)* medical records and is clearly visible;
- bring it to the attention of the authorities if (he)/(she) is hospitalised.

The original document is being held for safe custody in our strongroom, and a copy has been retained by *(client)* (and (his)/(her) family)/(and the person in charge of the (residential care home)/(nursing home) where (he)/(she) resides). (He)/(She) has been advised to review the document at regular intervals and whenever there is a major change in (his)/(her) personal circumstances.

If, for any reason, you consider that the instructions could be inapplicable in the situation which is likely to arise in (his)/(her) case, please would you let (him)/(her) and me know as soon as possible so that we can consider amending the document accordingly.

Yours sincerely

Enclosures:

- Copy living will
- Duplicate copy of this letter
- Pre-paid envelope

8 LIVING WILL CARD
   ## FOR CARRYING IN A WALLET OR PURSE[1]

front

LIVING WILL

I ....
Address ....
.... born on ....
have made a Living Will which says that, if I am likely to be severely incapacitated for the rest of my life, any treatment I receive should be limited to relieving pain and keeping me comfortable, and I refuse all other treatment.

back

My GP ....
Address ....
Telephone ....
has a copy of the Living Will.

In an emergency, please contact my ....
Name ....
Address ....
Telephone ....
who also has a copy of the Living Will.

1 Various organisations, notably the Voluntary Euthanasia Society and the Voluntary Euthanasia Society of Scotland, supply medical alert cards drawing attention to the fact that an individual has made an advance directive. It is understood that most Jehovah's Witnesses carry cards (renewable annually) relating to their refusal to consent to the transfusion of blood or blood products.

MISCELLANEOUS CLAUSES

1 ADDRESS[1]

TO MY FAMILY, MY FRIENDS AND THOSE WHO ARE RESPONSIBLE
FOR MY MEDICAL CARE

---

1 In the United States, living wills are often prefaced by an address to someone. For example, the
recommended form of terminal care document in the State of Vermont is addressed: 'To my
family, my physician, my lawyer, my clergyman. To any medical facility in whose care I happen
to be. To any individual who may become responsible for my health, welfare or affairs'. An
address of this kind serves little useful purpose. On the other hand, it does no harm, provided
that it is not intended as a substitute for dialogue between the maker of the living will, during
his or her lifetime, and the people to whom it is addressed.

---

2 AGE-RELATED INSTRUCTIONS

I do not wish to be resuscitated if:

- I suffer a cardiac arrest; and
- I am aged (*90*) or over.

3 ATTESTATION CLAUSE[1]

I CERTIFY that (*maker's name*) signed this Living Will in my presence. To the best
of my knowledge, I am not currently entitled to any part of (his)/(her) estate under
(his)/(her) Will, or the law relating to intestacy, or by right of survivorship.

---

1 Currently there are no rules in English law as to who can and cannot witness an advance
directive. One witness is probably sufficient, unless the living will is executed by somebody else
in the presence of and at the direction of the maker, in which case it would be preferable for
the execution to be attested by two independent witnesses. American statutes usually provide
that the following persons cannot witness a living will:
- a relative by blood, marriage or adoption;
- anyone who stands to inherit any part of the maker's estate at the time of execution of the
directive;
- anyone who, at the time when the directive is executed, may have a claim under the
equivalent of the Inheritance (Provision for Family and Dependants) Act 1975;
- anyone who has been appointed as a health-care proxy, and his or her partner;
- a health-care provider, or any employee of a health-care provider;

- the operator of a residential care home or nursing home;
- anyone who is responsible for financing the maker's health-care.

It would probably be wise to adhere to similar guidelines or safeguards in the UK.

4 CHEMOTHERAPY AND RADIOTHERAPY

If I have incurable cancer, and there is no likelihood that my condition will improve, and any further chemotherapy and radiotherapy will merely extend my life for a little longer, I direct that all chemotherapy and radiotherapy be withheld or discontinued, unless it is absolutely essential to alleviate pain and distress.

5 COMPETENCE[1]

I understand the nature and effect of this living will and am [emotionally and][2] mentally competent to make it.

1 Most American living wills contain a statement of this nature. Strictly speaking, it is unnecessary. A person is presumed to be *mentally competent* until the contrary is proved: *Attorney-General v Parnther* (1792) 3 Bro CC 441, at p 443.
2 Emotional competence is almost impossible to evaluate. It probably means that the maker is not suffering from depression after, say, the death of a spouse or receiving an unfavourable prognosis.

6 CONSCIENTIOUS OBJECTION[1]

Any doctor or nurse who is unwilling to comply with these wishes should take reasonable steps as soon as possible to transfer the responsibility for my care to another doctor or nurse who is willing to comply with these wishes.

1 In the Code of Practice on Advance Statements about Medical Treatment issued by the BMA, it is suggested that health professionals are entitled to have their personal and moral beliefs respected, and that they should not be pressurised into acting contrary to those beliefs. However, the *sanctity of life* argument should not be imposed on those for whom it has no meaning. Health professionals with a conscientious objection to limiting treatment at a patient's request should make their views clear when the patient initially raises the matter. If a health professional is involved in the management of a case and cannot, for reasons of conscience, accede to the patient's request for limitation of treatment, the management of that patient should be passed to a colleague.

7 DECISION-MAKING

Any treatment decision made on my behalf should be made:

- in accordance with my own wishes; but if for any reason they are not known, or not clear, or not applicable in the circumstances,
- in the way that (*name*) believes I would have made the decision myself, having regard to: (a) my ascertainable past and present wishes and feelings; (b) whether there is any alternative to the proposed treatment which is more conservative or less intrusive or less restrictive; and (c) any other factors which I might be expected to consider if able to do so, including the likely effect of the treatment on my life expectancy, health, happiness, freedom and dignity; failing which,
- in my best interests.

8 DEMENTIA[1]

IF I AM SUFFERING FROM MILD DEMENTIA, for example:

I am able to have meaningful conversations, but I am forgetful, and have a poor short-term memory.

I am able to carry out most routine daily activities, such as housework, dressing, eating, bathing and using the toilet.

I have bladder and bowel control.

I am able to live at home with someone caring for me for a few hours each day.

My instructions are as follows: (*specify instructions*)

IF I AM SUFFERING FROM MODERATE DEMENTIA, for example:

I am not always able to recognise family and friends.

I can engage in conversation, but may not always make sense.

I need help with my daily routines.

I may still have bladder and bowel control.

I could possibly live at home with someone caring for me throughout the day, but probably should be in a residential care home or nursing home.

My instructions are as follows: (*specify instructions*)

IF I AM SUFFERING FROM SEVERE DEMENTIA, for example:

I cannot recognise my family and friends.

I am unable to have a meaningful conversation.

I am unable to carry out any routine daily activities.

I cannot feed myself.

I no longer have bladder and bowel control.
I need to be cared for day and night.

My instructions are as follows: (*specify instructions*)

---

1 These descriptions of mild, moderate and severe dementia are taken from the *Living Will* produced by the Centre for Bioethics, University of Toronto, Canada.

---

9 DIABETES

I am a diabetic.

I do not wish to be treated if my blood sugar level rises above (25) mm/vol and continues for (10) days, and if I am at risk of losing my sight.

I am aware that in future I may have circulatory and other problems which could involve a decision about major surgery.

I refuse to undergo any major surgery, such as the amputation of a limb, even though such refusal may jeopardise my life.[1]

---

1 This precedent is based on an example of a specific directive published by Dying with Dignity, Toronto, Canada, and emphasises the need for a living will to be drawn up in liaison with the client's medical practitioner (see Clause 10 below).

---

10 DISCUSSION WITH DOCTOR[1]

I have discussed this living will with my GP

(*Name*) ....
(*Address*) ....
(*Telephone*) ....

---

1 It is not essential to the validity of a living will that the maker has discussed its contents with his or her doctor. However, discussions with the doctor, both before and after the completion of an advance directive, are strongly recommended. The patient can offer information to the doctor about his or her treatment preferences, obtain information from the doctor about the various medical issues that may need to be addressed, and ascertain whether the doctor would be willing to honour the patient's wishes.

   If, at a later stage, there is any dispute as to whether the decisions are 'clearly established' and 'applicable in the circumstances', evidence of discussions with the doctor is likely to assist in establishing that the maker was fully aware of the consequences of the decisions he or she has made.

11 FEEDING

I (consent to)/(refuse) enteral feeding (through the gastro-intestinal tract with the aid of a naso-gastric tube).[1]

I (consent to)/(refuse) parenteral nutrition (the intravenous provision of carbohydrate, fat and proteins).[2]

---

1 For further information, see the entry on 'enteral feeding' in C.W.H. Havard (ed), *Black's Medical Dictionary* (36th edition, A & C Black, 1990).

2 For further information, see the entry on 'parenteral nutrition' in *Black's Medical Dictionary* (above).

---

12 ORGAN DONATION

If brain stem death has occurred, and any part of my body is needed for the treatment of others, I consent to being kept on a ventilator for no more than (*24 hours*) in order to preserve the part(s) for transplantation.[1]

---

1 This is often referred to as 'interventional' or 'elective' ventilation. Currently, it is unlawful, but the Law Commission has recommended that the Secretary of State may make an order providing for the carrying out of a procedure in relation to a person without capacity to consent if the procedure, although not carried out for the benefit of that person, will not cause him or her significant harm and will be of significant benefit to others: Law Com No 231 (HMSO, 1995), para 6.26, and draft Mental Incapacity Bill, cl 10(4).

---

13 PLACE OF DEATH

If it is practicable in the circumstances, I would rather die at home than in a hospital, hospice, or nursing home.

14 PRESENCE OF RELATIVE OR FRIEND[1]

If my death is imminent I would like:

(*Name*)   ....
(*Address*)   ....
(*Telephone*)   ....

to be contacted and given the chance to be with me before I die.

1 The Terrence Higgins Trust Living Will (1st edition, 1992) contains a similar request, which goes further by asking for any refusal instructions to be disregarded until the specified person can be called to the patient's bedside.

15 REVOCATION OF EARLIER WISHES

These wishes supersede any earlier written or spoken statements about my health care.

16 SEVERABILITY CLAUSES[1]

If any part of this living will is unlawful, invalid or unenforceable, it can be severed from the parts that are lawful, valid and enforceable.

1 'The general rule is that, where you cannot sever the illegal from the legal part of a covenant, the contract is altogether void; but where you can sever them, whether the illegality be created by statute or by the common law, you may reject the bad part and retain the good': *Pickering v Ilfracombe Railway Co* (1868) LR 3 CP 235, at p 250, per Willes J.

17 SPECIFIC INTERVENTIONS[1]

(*Describe the clinical situations in which these instructions are to apply*)

I [DO NOT] WANT:[2]

- Cardiopulmonary resuscitation
- Mechanical breathing
- Artificial nutrition and hydration
- Majory surgery
- Kidney dialysis
- Chemotherapy
- Minor surgery
- Radiotherapy
- Invasive diagnostic tests
- Blood or blood products
- Antibiotics
- Simple diagnostic tests
- Pain medications, even if they dull consciousness and indirectly shorten my life

1 This list of specific interventions is taken from 'The Medical Directive: A New Comprehensive Advance Care Document', by Linda L. Emanuel and Ezekiel J. Emanuel, which appeared in the *Journal of the American Medical Association*, vol 261, No 22 (9 June 1989), p 3290. The Medical Directive has been circulated in England and Wales by Law Pack Publishing Ltd. For a detailed criticism of the specific intervention approach, see Allan S. Brett, 'Limitations of Listing Specific Medical Interventions in Advance Directives', *Journal of the American Medical Association*, 14 August 1991, vol 266, No 6, pp 825–828.

2 The Medical Directive provides two further options: 'I am undecided', and 'I want a trial. If no clear improvement, stop treatment'. The request for a trial intervention is inapplicable in the case of cardiopulmonary resuscitation; major surgery; minor surgery; invasive diagnostic tests; and simple diagnostic tests.

18 STROKE[1]

If I am suffering from a mild stroke, for example:

I have mild paralysis on one side of my body.
I can walk unaided, or with a stick or frame.
I am able to have meaningful conversations, but might have speech difficulties.
I can carry out most routine daily activities, such as work, household tasks, dressing, eating, bathing and using the toilet.
I have bowel and bladder control.
I could live at home with someone caring for me for a few hours each day.

My instructions are:

If I am suffering from a moderate stroke, for example:

I have moderate paralysis on one side of my body.
I am unable to walk and need a wheelchair.
I can carry out conversations, but might not always make sense.
I need help with routine daily activities.
I may have bowel and bladder control.
I could live at home with someone caring for me throughout the daytime; otherwise I would probably need to live in a residential care home or nursing home.

My instructions are:

If I am suffering from a severe stroke, for example:

I have severe paralysis on one side of the body.
I am unable to walk, and need to be in a chair or in bed.
I am unable to have meaningful conversations.
I am unable to carry out routine daily activities.
I may need to be fed through a tube.
I do not have control over my bowel or bladder.
I could live at home with someone caring for me all day and night; otherwise I would probably need to be cared for in a nursing home.

My instructions are as follows: (*specify instructions*)

---

1 These descriptions of mild, moderate and severe strokes are taken from the *Living Will* produced by the Centre for Bioethics, University of Toronto, Canada.

---

19 VALUES HISTORY[1]

I am not afraid of death but I am afraid of having no control over my bodily and mental functions until I die [because . . .][2]

[OR]

What I fear most is . . .

---

1 Values histories express the individual's underlying beliefs, fears and aims. They are increasingly recognised as providing important guidelines to those who are involved in making treatment decisions on behalf of an incapacitated adult.

2 The Voluntary Euthanasia Society of Scotland, 17 Hart Street, Edinburgh EH1 3RN produces a living will in which the maker is invited to complete a values history statement.

CHAPTER 12: FUNERAL PLANNING

INDEX

Text

Checklists

Precedents

Will clauses

FUNERAL PLANNING

TEXT

Introduction

Funeral planning is treated as a discrete subject in this book. Its purpose is to identify and resolve in advance some of the problems that can arise at or after a funeral. In this respect it is more proactive than merely recording a client's funeral wishes in a will, although ascertaining those wishes is often likely to be the first stage in the process. Elderly clients may also require advice on such matters as setting aside finances for their funeral; pre-payment schemes; eligibility for a funeral payment from the Social Fund; reserving a grave space; the suitability of the material, design and wording of a proposed memorial; and complaints procedures if they are dissatisfied with the services provided by a funeral director.

In view of soaring funeral costs, the aggressive marketing of pre-payment plans, the imposition of greater restrictions on Social Fund funeral payments, and tougher guidelines on memorial designs and inscriptions, there is a growing need for professional legal advice on all aspects of funeral planning.

Funeral instructions in wills

There are two schools of thought as to whether funeral wishes should be included in a will. On the one hand, it is argued that:

- the purpose of a will is to appoint an executor and dispose of the estate. Funeral wishes are not essential to this purpose;
- funeral instructions are not legally binding. A testator or testatrix cannot oust the executor's rights and duties regarding the disposal of the body;[1]
- the will might not be found until after the funeral has taken place;
- the testator or testatrix might have a change of mind about some of the details. It would be pointless, and unnecessarily expensive, to have to make a codicil or even a new will for something relatively unimportant;
- it is better to record funeral instructions in a separate letter or memorandum which can be kept with the will; although, presumably, the argument that the will might not be discovered until it is too late would apply equally as cogently to any letter or memorandum;
- for some bereaved people, arranging the funeral is an important part of the grieving process, and it might be inconsiderate to deny them that opportunity. After all, for whose benefit is the funeral?
- a final reason why many lawyers, banks or professional will-writers prefer not to raise such matters is purely psychological. Until recently, any discussion about death, bereavement and funeral arrangements was strictly taboo.[2]

There are, however, a number of reasons why funeral wishes should be included in a will, for instance:

- they require a testator or testatrix to think about the practical arrangements that need to be made immediately after his or her death. Sometimes this exercise enables a person to anticipate and resolve some of the difficulties that can arise, for example, acquiring the right to be buried or to have one's ashes interred in the churchyard of a particular parish;[3]
- they relieve others of having to make decisions at a time of distress;
- although the executors are legally responsible for the disposal of the body, they are not necessarily members of the deceased's family or even beneficiaries under his or her will. Solicitors and banks are obvious examples;
- in some cases, the testator or testatrix may have no friends or relatives who are in a position to organise the funeral;
- there is less likelihood of friction among the executors, surviving relatives and beneficiaries. This is a particularly important consideration where the deceased had a step-family,[4] or was one of an unmarried couple;
- even though the funeral wishes of the deceased are not legally binding, they are usually honoured;[5]
- expenditure can be formally authorised. Otherwise, the executors' obligation is to incur reasonable funeral expenses reflecting the deceased's social status;[6]
- there is no empirical evidence to suggest that funeral wishes are changed more often than any other part of a will. If anything, they tend to be the most durable contents of a will;
- modern funerals – and maybe modern wills – can be very bland. They need to be personalised.[7]

An increasing number of wills now include funeral wishes. One hundred and seventy-five wills were proved in the Exeter District Probate Registry during the first two weeks of January 1968. Only thirty-two (18.25%) contained funeral instructions. Twenty-five years later, during the fortnight from 8 May to 21 May 1983, 235 wills were proved in the same office which had since become a sub-registry. Seventy-one (30.25%) included funeral directions. In both samples, roughly 10% of the wills were written or typed on printed forms, none of which suggested that funeral wishes could be included in the will. The adjusted percentages of wills prepared professionally by solicitors and banks indicate that, whereas in 1968 only one in five of the wills proved contained funeral directions, in 1993 the ratio was one in three.

In the 1983 sample, the timespan between the date of executing the will and the date of death varied between forty years at one extreme to the same number of hours at the other. The average was 6.5 years. The average age for making one's last will was 75, and the average age at death was 81.5. Of the seventy-one people who had expressed their wishes, fifty-nine chose to be cremated, eleven to be buried, and one wished to donate her body to an anatomy school. The funeral wishes appeared at the beginning of thirty-eight of the wills, and at the end of the other thirty-three. These statistics have their limitations, notably the sample sizes and the fact that the wills examined were prepared predominantly in one county – Devon.[8]

1 *Williams v Williams* (1882) 20 ChD 659.
2 Philippe Aries, *The Hour of Our Death* (Penguin Books, 1987), chapter 12.
3 See 'Burial in an Anglican churchyard', at p 342 below.
4 *Re St Mary, Berrow* (1994) 3 Ecc LJ 188.
5 *Re Grandison (Deceased)* (1989) *The Times*, July 10.
6 *Rees v Hughes* [1946] 1 KB 517.
7 Tony Walter, *Funerals – And How to Improve Them* (Hodder & Stoughton, 1990).
8 This survey was conducted by the author and the results were originally published in *The Legal Executive Journal*, November 1993, pp 46–47.

Burial in a local authority cemetery

Local authorities have a mandatory duty to cause the body of anyone who has died or been found dead in their area to be buried or cremated, if no suitable arrangements for the disposal of the body have been made by anyone else.[1] They also have a discretion to arrange for the burial or cremation of the body of anyone who, immediately before their death, was living in Part III accommodation.[2] In either case, the expenses incurred may be recovered from the deceased's estate or from anyone who, for the purposes of the National Assistance Act 1948, was liable to maintain the deceased.

The Local Authorities' Cemeteries Order 1977[3] empowers a burial authority[4] to grant the following rights to any person, subject to any terms and conditions it thinks proper:

- the exclusive right of burial (which, for these purposes, includes the interment of cremated human remains)[5] in any grave or grave space;[6]
- the right to construct a walled grave or vault together with the exclusive right of burial therein;
- the right to one or more burials in any grave or grave space which is not subject to any exclusive right of burial;
- the right to place and maintain, or to put any additional inscription on, a tombstone or other memorial on the grave space, grave or vault in respect of which the burial right subsists.

No body can be buried, and no cremated human remains can be interred or scattered, in or over any grave or vault in which an exclusive right of burial subsists, except by the owner of that right or with his or her consent in writing.[7] An exclusive right of burial may be assigned by the owner.[8]

The rights are granted for the period specified in the grant. This period commences on the date of the grant and cannot exceed one hundred years,[9] except in the case of graves maintained by the Commonwealth War Graves Commission.[10] The burial authority can extend the period of any grant, subject to any modification of its terms or conditions as it may think fit, for up to one hundred years from the date on which the extension is granted.[11]

The cost of acquiring exclusive rights of burial varies from one burial authority to another and may vary from cemetery to cemetery within the area covered by the authority. It can even vary within a cemetery itself. The national average is £291 for seventy-two years.[12] By contrast, the cost of acquiring a burial plot in Highgate Cemetery, London is said to range from £2200 to £6850 for a term of seventy years. Some local authorities (eg London Boroughs of Hackney, Haringey and Tower Hamlets) have no cemetery space left, and residents are compelled to purchase space outside their local authority area.

Note that:

- some cemeteries charge an optional maintenance fee;
- the cost of burial rights is often doubled (or even trebled) in respect of non-residents;[13]
- some cemeteries impose restrictions on the type of memorial that can be erected;
- the cost of acquiring a burial plot does not include the cost of digging the grave.

---

1 Public Health (Control of Disease) Act 1984, s 46(1).

2 *Ibid*, s 46(2).

3 Local Authority Cemeteries Order 1977 (SI 1977/204), Art 10(1).

4 Under the Local Government Act 1972, s 214, the burial authorities responsible for the acquisition, maintenance and control of public cemeteries are district councils; London borough councils; the Common Council of the City of London; parish councils; parish meetings in parishes which have no parish council; and community councils in Wales.

5 Local Authority Cemeteries Order 1977, Art 2(2).

6 For a specimen grant of exclusive right of burial in a local authority cemetery, see Precedent 2 at p 359 below.

7 Local Authorities Cemeteries Order 1977, Art 10(6). See also *Reed v Madon* [1989] 2 All ER 431.

8 For a specimen assignment of exclusive right of burial in a local authority cemetery, see Precedent 1 at p 358 below.

9 *Ibid*, Art 10(2).

10 *Ibid*, Art 20(4).

11 *Ibid*, Art 10(4).

12 Nicholas Albery, Gil Elliot and Joseph Elliot (eds), *The Natural Death Handbook* (Virgin Books, 1993), p 167.

13 See Social Security Advisory Committee's Report on Funeral Payments, Cmnd 2858 (HMSO, May 1995, £5.90), paras 17 and 18.

Burial in an Anglican churchyard

(1) Common law rights

The following people have a right to be buried in the churchyard or other burial ground of a parish, provided there is still room, and provided that the churchyard or burial ground has not been wholly closed for burials by an Order in Council:[1]

- everyone who lives in the parish;
- everyone who dies in the parish;

- everyone whose name is on the electoral roll of the parish (even though they do not live in the parish);[2]
- everyone who, although not resident in the parish, occupies land in the parish and pays rates or, presumably, council tax.[3]

This right extends to the burial of their cremated remains,[4] and applies irrespective of whether the deceased was a member of the Church of England or the Church in Wales,[5] and regardless of whether they were even Christian.

The personal representatives or relatives of any parishioner or person dying within the parish also have the right to require that the burial shall take place in the churchyard either without any service at all or with a Christian (though non-Anglican) service conducted by a person of their own choosing: for example, a minister of another denomination.[6]

Parishioners have no right to be buried in any particular part of the graveyard and, unless a space has been specifically reserved by faculty, it is within the incumbent's discretion to choose the location.[7]

Non-parishioners have no right of burial in the churchyard or other burial ground of the parish without the incumbent's consent. In deciding whether to give consent, the incumbent is required to obtain and take into account the views of the parochial church council.[8] Incumbents are advised to grant such permission sparingly because it infringes the rights of parishioners for whose interment the churchyard or burial ground is primarily intended,[9] and consent is only likely to be given where there is sufficient space for further interments. Such consent usually commands a suitable fee, although incumbents are advised to avoid giving the impression that permission will automatically be given in return for a substantial payment.[10]

(2) Rights attainable by faculty

The following rights should be acquired by a faculty granted by the Chancellor of the Diocese:

- burial in the church itself;[11]
- burial in a particular place in the churchyard or burial ground.[12] In the absence of such a faculty, the incumbent may choose the location;
- burial of someone who is not a parishioner;
- the erection of a tombstone or memorial. In practice, the incumbent's consent is usually sufficient but, if the incumbent refuses to grant permission, the person wishing to erect the tombstone or memorial may petition for a faculty;
- the removal of a corpse or cremated remains from an existing grave or vault for re-interment elsewhere.[13] Although the Chancellor has a discretion in such matters, it will only be exercised in exceptional circumstances and not as a matter of course. The purpose of interment is that the deceased's remains should be laid to rest once and for all.[14]

(3) Erection of monuments

The right of burial does not confer the right to erect a tombstone. Strictly speaking, a monument cannot be erected in a churchyard unless a faculty has been granted by the Chancellor of the Diocese. In practice, the faculty jurisdiction is not enforced to this extent, and the Chancellors have delegated to incumbents the authority to grant permission for the erection of an ordinary, uncontroversial tombstone.[15] Although the procedures vary from one diocese to another, the best advice to any client who intends to place a monument in a parish churchyard is as follows.

- Defer any decision on design or wording of the memorial until at least six months after the death.
- Don't place an order with the stonemason until permission has been granted for the proposed memorial.
- Obtain advice from the incumbent about suitable stones, appropriate designs, and the composition of the inscription. The advice given should generally accord with the local Diocesan Regulations, which are largely based on the recommendations made in *The Churchyards Handbook*.[16]
- Ask the monumental mason to draw a sketch of the proposed design, with the inscription properly set out in the style of lettering to be used, and to provide full particulars of the material, dimensions and proposed foundation work.
- Submit the sketch and proposals to the incumbent for his or her approval.[17]
- If the incumbent approves the proposed memorial, obtain written permission for its erection. An incumbent cannot bind his or her successor,[18] so, if the client is making plans well in advance of his or her death, it would be better to petition for a faculty.[19]
- If the incumbent refuses to grant permission for the proposed memorial, consult the Diocesan Advisory Committee or the archdeacon.
- Consider petitioning for a faculty. The appropriate form (Form FJ5) can be obtained from the Diocesan Registrar.
- Only when permission has been granted by the incumbent or a faculty should instructions be given to the monumental mason.

The rules on the kind of memorial that is acceptable or unacceptable in parish churchyards have become increasingly strict during the last few years. Petitions have recently been refused for: the word 'toodle' (meaning 'goodbye') to be included in an inscription;[20] gold lettering on a headstone;[21] a reference in the epitaph to any relationship other than that of husband and wife, or parent and child;[22] a black granite headstone;[23] a porcelain portrait of the deceased in the corner of the headstone;[24] a sandstone kerbstone;[25] and a reference in the inscription to 'a devoted and much loved dad and grandad'.[26] Although the decision of a Diocesan Chancellor is binding only on the churchyards within his jurisdiction, it is likely to be of persuasive force elsewhere.[27]

---

1 See, generally, E. Garth Moore and Timothy Briden, *Moore's Introduction to English Canon Law* (2nd edition, Mowbray, 1985), pp 97–99. For Wales, see *The Constitution of the Church in Wales*, vol II, 'The Canons and the Rules and Regulations'.
2 Church of England (Miscellaneous Provisions) Measure 1976.

3 Such a person is a *parishioner*: Moore and Briden, *op cit*, p 39.

4 Church of England (Miscellaneous Provisions) Measure 1992, s 3.

5 See, generally, the Welsh Church (Burial Grounds) Act 1945, and the rules made by the Representative Body in 1946 in pursuance of s 4(2) of that Act.

6 Burial Laws Amendment Act 1880, s 6.

7 The incumbent's decision is final. A diocesan Consistory Court will not interfere unless the incumbent's discretion has been exercised in some improper way, or if relevant or material considerations have been disregarded: *In re Marks (deceased)* [1994] TLR 532 (Chester Consistory Court), per Lomas Ch.

8 Church of England (Miscellaneous Provisions) Measure 1976, s 6(2). See also *Re St John the Baptist, Werrington* (1992) 2 Ecc LJ 319.

9 Peter Burman and Henry Stapleton, *The Churchyards Handbook* (3rd edition, Church House Publishing, 1988), p 57.

10 *Ibid*, p 58. In *The Churchyards Handbook* (2nd edition, 1976), at p 18, the authors suggested, for example, 'a sum equal to twice the fees payable on the burial of a parishioner'.

11 Burial in a church or other place of public worship constructed in an urban area since 1848 is prohibited by statute: Public Health Act 1848, s 83. In *Re St Margaret's, Eartham* [1981] 1 WLR 1129, the Dean of Arches suggested that, where burial within the walls of or underneath any church is still permissible, a faculty would only be granted nowadays where the deceased had performed outstanding service to church, country or mankind.

12 A grave space cannot be reserved for a particular person for longer than one hundred years: Faculty Jurisdiction Measure 1964 (no 5), s 8.

13 A licence from the Home Office is also required unless the body is to be removed from one consecrated place of burial to another by a faculty granted for that purpose: Burial Act 1857, s 25. See, generally, David A. Smale, *Davies' Law of Burial, Cremation and Exhumation* (6th edition, Shaw & Sons, 1993), chapter 11.

14 *Re Edward William Knight (Deceased)* (1994) 3 Ecc LJ 257 (Chester Consistory Court), per Lomas Ch.

15 *Re Woldingham Churchyard* [1957] 2 All ER 323.

16 Peter Burman and Henry Stapleton, *The Churchyards Handbook* (3rd edition, Church House Publishing, 1988), App I.

17 For a suggested form of application to the incumbent for permission to erect a memorial, see Precedent 3 at p 359 below.

18 *Re St Luke's, Holbeach Hurn* [1990] 2 All ER 749.

19 The form of Petition for Faculty (Form FJ5) can be obtained from the Diocesan Registrar. The contents of the petition will be similar to the contents of the application to the incumbent, see Precedent 3 at p 359 below.

20 *Re Christ Church, Ainsworth* (1992) Ecc LJ 321 (Manchester Consistory Court), per Spafford Ch.

21 *Re St Chad's, Bishop's Tachbrook* (1993) 3 Ecc LJ 60 (Coventry Consistory Court).

22 In *Re St Mark's, Haydock (No 2)* [1981] 1 WLR 1167, Liverpool Consistory Court held that a woman with whom the deceased had been living at the time of his death should not be named on the headstone. However, in *Re St Mary, Sheviock* (1993) 3 Ecc LJ 62, Boydell Ch in Truro Consistory Court granted a faculty for the inscription to include a reference to the deceased's brother in the exceptional circumstances where the a young man had been killed in a car crash in which his brother had been seriously injured.

23 *Re St Anne, Clifton* (1993) 3 Ecc LJ 117 (Manchester Consistory Court).

24 *Ibid*.

25 *Re Eunice Elizabeth Posnett (Deceased)* (1994) 3 Ecc LJ 255 (Chester Consistory Court).

26 *In re Holy Trinity, Freckleton* [1994] TLR 493, (1994) 3 Ecc LJ 350 (Blackburn Consistory Court).

27 *Ibid*, per Bullimore Ch. For a report of subsequent proceedings in which the petitioners sought to exhume the remains of their devoted and much loved dad and grandad from the churchyard and to transfer them to a municipal cemetery, see (1994) 3 Ecc LJ 429.

Pre-paid funeral schemes

There are currently half-a-dozen schemes in Britain which allow an individual to pay for his or her funeral in advance. The purchaser is usually required to select one of three options:

- a lower-range plan, with a simple coffin and no limousine;
- a middle-range plan, which includes an oak-veneered coffin and one limousine;
- a top-range plan, which provides a solid hardwood coffin and two limousines.

Payment is generally made in a single lump sum, although most of the companies operating these schemes allow the purchaser to pay by instalments, which attract a commercial rate of interest, over a one-year, two-year or five-year period.

The market leader, and the scheme endorsed by Age Concern, is Chosen Heritage, based at East Grinstead, and part of the Great Southern Group. At the time of writing (September 1995), Chosen Heritage offered four plans: *Sovereign* at £2700; *Popular* at £1030; *Economy* at £920; and *Basic* at £695.[1] These prices exclude disbursements such as church fees, flowers, crematorium or cemetery fees, doctors' fees, obituary notices, etc. So, in the case of a standard cremation, roughly £300 should be added to the cost of the plan itself. Chosen Heritage's former middle-range and top-of-the-range plans, which have recently been superseded, were considered to be the best buys in their respective classes in a *Which?* report on funerals published in February 1992, although there have been several price rises since the report was issued. *Which?* regarded the *Standard Way* plan provided by Golden Charter, which represents over 1200 independent funeral directors, as the best buy in the lower range. Other pre-payment schemes are operated by The Dignity Plan, which recently merged with Chosen Heritage to form Funeral Plans Limited; the Perfect Assurance Funeral Trust; and the Co-op, which runs two schemes – one through the CRS and the other through the CWS.

(1) Advantages

The main advantages of pre-paid funeral schemes are as follows.

- The customer can shop around during his or her lifetime for the best package available.
- Bereaved people – especially the elderly – are often in no fit state to shop around when dealing with a death.[2]
- Relatives are relieved of the responsibility of having to make all the funeral arrangements.
- The schemes are guaranteed against inflationary increases in the cost of a funeral.
- Relatives are not presented with the funeral account while they are still in mourning.
- It provides some people with peace of mind, and maybe even a sense of dignity and self-esteem, to know that their funeral has already been paid for.
- They alleviate concern over the possibility of having a pauper's funeral. The

author knows of at least one elderly woman on income support, who has been abandoned by her nephews and nieces because they are afraid that, if they have any contact with her, they might be under an obligation to pay for her funeral when she dies.

- Like funeral instructions in wills, they provide an opportunity to anticipate, and maybe resolve, some of the practical difficulties that can arise after a death: for example, the preferred location for a burial or the interment of ashes.

(2) Disadvantages[3]

The disadvantages of funeral pre-payment schemes largely depend on the terms of the scheme itself, but may include the following points.

- It has been suggested that they are a means whereby large chains of funeral directors can increase basic funeral costs in excess of the normally inflationary trends.[4]
- Pre-payment schemes are really only suitable for cremation, and are primarily concerned with the quality of the coffin and the number of vehicles in the cortege.
- The price paid is slightly higher than the price that would be currently payable for a funeral of comparable quality.
- Where a member has been paying by instalments, the company may require any outstanding instalments to be paid prior to the funeral.
- There could be problems in obtaining a full refund if the member changes his or her mind. There will almost certainly be a cancellation fee.
- The family will be tied to a particular firm or chain of funeral directors.
- It is possible that the selected funeral directors could cease trading during the member's lifetime.
- Disbursements are not usually covered. Crematorium fees, doctors' fees and the minister's fees rose by 69% from £164 in April 1990 to £278 in April 1995, while the Retail Prices Index rose by only 17% during the same period.[5]
- Most schemes only cover deaths in England, Wales and the Scottish mainland. If the member travels abroad regularly, it would be worth checking that his or her medical insurance includes appropriate repatriation arrangements.
- If a member moves to another part of the country, it may be difficult to find a local undertaker who participates in the scheme.
- The executor or next-of-kin who organises the funeral might not be aware of the pre-payment. Anyone who enters into such a scheme should be advised to inform their relatives or prospective executors, and to leave details of the plan in or with their will.[6]
- Entry into a pre-paid funeral scheme could, in theory, fall foul of the notional capital rules for means-tested benefits.[7] In practice, the lump sum payment will only be treated as notional capital if the claimant's significant operative purpose[8] was to secure entitlement, or greater entitlement, to means-tested benefits.
- Most pre-payment scheme members choose the cheapest, simplest funeral. This can sometimes cause difficulties. Bereaved relatives might prefer more dignified rites of passage. For example, they might like the opportunity to view the body in a chapel of rest, or they may feel the need for a church service. Any potential customer should check to see whether it is possible to upgrade the plan during

his or her lifetime, or whether the family can upgrade the plan on his or her death.

(3) Funeral insurance

An alternative, which may be worth considering, is funeral insurance. Several insurance companies and friendly societies market schemes to cover funeral expenses, whereby, in return for a fixed regular premium there will be a guaranteed minimum payout on death. Generally, no medical examination is required, but there is usually a maximum age of entry into such a scheme.[9] These schemes are essentially a gamble based on how long the policyholder lives. There is a cross-over point – usually after seven or eight years – at which the amount paid in premiums exceeds the amount paid out on death.[10]

---

1 There are discounts of £80, £35, £25 and £15 respectively for persons aged 60 and over.
2 The Office of Fair Trading's report in 1989 found that only 3% of the people surveyed actually shopped around for funeral services.
3 See, generally, the *Which?* report, 'Finding the right funeral director', February 1995, pp 26–29, at p 28. Apparently, the Office of Fair Trading is investigating the pre-paid funeral industry following concerns about the management of funds, and poor regulation within the industry. The Consumers' Association shares these concerns.
4 Nicholas Albery, Gil Elliot and Joseph Elliot, *The Natural Death Handbook* (Virgin Books, 1993), pp 161–163.
5 The Social Security Advisory Committee, in its report on Social Fund funeral payments, Cmnd 2858, (HMSO, May 1995), at paras 24 and 25, notes that between 1985 and 1995 the fees for the two doctors' certificates went up from £33.60 to £64, and the minister's fee has risen from £27 in 1991 to £55 in 1995.
6 See Clause 1 at p 361 below.
7 Income Support (General) Regulations 1987 (SI 1987/1967), reg 51; Family Credit (General) Regulations 1987 (SI 1987/1973), reg 34.
8 *R(SB) 40/85.*
9 See, generally, the *Which?* report, 'Report on funerals', February 1992, p 114. The funeral insurance schemes mentioned, although not evaluated in the report, are operated by: Ambassador Life; City of Glasgow Friendly Society; CIS; Sun Life; The Ideal Benefit Society; Tunbridge Wells Equitable Friendly Society; and the UK Civil Service Benefit Society (for public sector employees).
10 See the *Which?* report, 'Finding the right funeral director', February 1995, p 28.

Social Fund funeral payments

Social Fund funeral payments were introduced in April 1987 to replace the contributory death grant, which had stood at £30 for many years, and the regulated single payment for those in receipt of supplementary benefit. Approximately 94,000 claims were made in 1993/94, of which 72,000 were successful.[1] Expenditure on funeral payments rose from £30 million in 1990/91 to £61 million in 1993/94, and the average award increased from £612 to £873 during the same period.[2] In an attempt to curb this expenditure and put downward pressure on the spiralling cost of funerals, in April 1994 the Department of Social Security tightened up the criteria for entitlement to a Social Fund funeral payment.[3] It also proposed a ceiling of £875 on the amount to which any claimant may be entitled. In March 1995, the Social Security Advisory Committee recommended that the DSS should not proceed with the proposed ceiling because, in many parts of the country, it would be entirely inadequate to pay for the full cost of a simple dignified funeral.[4] Instead, a ceiling of £500 on the funeral director's fees was imposed by regulations which came into force on 5 June 1995.[5]

Deciding whether a funeral payment can be made from the Social Fund is a four-step process. The adjudication officer must:

- first, establish whether the claimant is entitled, and whether it is reasonable in the circumstances for him or her, to accept responsibility for the cost of the funeral;
- secondly, decide what items of expenditure can be allowed and what expenses should be disallowed;
- thirdly, deduct from the potential award any assets in the deceased's estate; and
- finally, find out how much capital the claimant has. If it exceeds a specified limit, the claimant is expected to meet the costs of the funeral from the excess.

(1) Conditions of entitlement

To be entitled to a funeral payment from the Social Fund, all four of the following conditions must be satisfied:[6]

- at the date of claim, the claimant, or his or her partner, must be in receipt of one or more of the following *qualifying benefits*: income support, family credit, disability working allowance, housing benefit, or council tax benefit; and
- the claimant must not only accept responsibility for the cost of the funeral but also satisfy *the responsible person test*; and
- the funeral must take place in the UK; and
- the claim must be made within *three months* of the date of the funeral.

The purpose of the responsible person test is to establish who is the most appropriate person to accept responsibility for the funeral costs. Normally, it will be the surviving partner or, failing whom, a close relative.[7] A person who was closely acquainted with the deceased may accept responsibility where there is no surviving partner and it is reasonable that they, rather than a close relative, should do so.

In deciding whether it is reasonable for someone other than the deceased's partner to assume responsibility for the funeral expenses, the adjudication officer has to apply two tests.[8] First, where there are other close relatives who could take responsibility for the funeral costs, he or she must consider the nature and extent of the contact each of them had with the deceased.[9] Secondly, if another close relative was as closely acquainted with the deceased as the claimant, and is not in receipt of any of the qualifying benefits *or* has capital in excess of the capital disregard for a funeral payment, the adjudication officer will decide that it is not reasonable for the claimant to accept responsibility for the funeral costs.

Example

Eileen died leaving three daughters, Jackie, Pamela and Brenda, each of whom had regularly visited her once a week. Jackie is on income support. Pamela receives family credit. Brenda does not receive any of the qualifying benefits, and has savings of £1500. Pamela assumes responsibility for Eileen's funeral and claims a payment from the Social Fund. The adjudication officer decides that a funeral payment cannot be made because it is not deemed reasonable that Pamela should assume responsibility for the cost of her mother's funeral.

(2) Allowable expenses

The 1995 Regulations imposed a ceiling of £500 on the funeral director's fees. These include:

- the collection of the deceased within the UK and transporting the body to the funeral director's premises or to a place of rest over a total distance of up to 50 miles;
- a simple veneered coffin and plain robe;
- the care of the deceased prior to the funeral;
- transport by a vehicle for the coffin and bearers and one additional vehicle, for a total distance of up to 50 miles; and
- necessary funeral director's services and staff.

In addition to covering the funeral director's fees up to £500, a Social Fund funeral payment will also include an amount sufficient to meet:

- in the case of an interment, the necessary costs of a new or re-opened grave and of the interment;
- in the case of cremation: the cremation fee; the cost of the two doctors' certificates; and any doctor's fee for the removal of a pace-maker;
- the cost of necessary documentation;[10]
- the minister's fee;
- any additional expenses arising from a requirement of the religious faith of the deceased, but not in excess of £75;
- the organist's fee;
- the cost of a floral tribute from the responsible person, but not in excess of £25;
- the reasonable expenses of one return journey within the UK for the responsible person either for arranging or attending the funeral;
- the reasonable cost of transport in excess of 50 miles.

Example

Alan's funeral cost £1100. His widow, Betty, claimed a Social Fund funeral payment. The undertaker's fees came to £600; £25 was paid for an obituary notice in the local paper (which is not 'necessary documentation'); and Betty spent £100 on flowers. The Social Fund funeral payment came to £900 (ie £1100 less the disallowed excess of £100 in respect of the funeral director's fee; less £25 for the obituary notice; less the disallowed excess of £75 for the flowers).

(3) Deductions from an award of a funeral payment

The following amounts must be deducted from an award of a funeral payment:[11]

- the deceased's assets which are available to the family without probate or letters of administration having been granted;
- any lump sum due to the claimant or a member of the family on the death under an insurance policy, occupational pension scheme, or burial club or any analogous arrangement;
- any contributions received from a charity or from relatives of the deceased or the claimant (although these contributions must first be set off against 'disallowable' funeral expenses such as obituary notices, a headstone, refreshments for the mourners, or extra cars or flowers);
- a war pensioner's funeral grant.

Example
John's funeral cost £1150. His widow, Florrie, claimed a Social Fund funeral payment. She received £600 from an insurance policy on John's death. The funeral payment is limited to £550, being the cost of the funeral less the lump sum due under the policy.

(4) Effect of the claimant's capital

Finally, any capital possessed by the claimant, or his or her partner, must be taken into account if it exceeds £500, where both the claimant and his or her partner are under the age of 60, or £1000 where the claimant or his or her partner is aged 60 or over.[12] The excess capital must be applied towards the funeral costs, and a payment from the Social Fund will only be made to cover any shortfall. Certain capital assets, such as the claimant's home and personal possessions, can be disregarded.[13]

Example
Ethel, aged 75, has savings of £1750. Her late husband's funeral cost £875, all of which is allowable expenditure. She has to pay £750 towards the cost of the funeral. The Social Fund will pay the remaining £125.

---

1 *Social Security Statistics 1994* (HMSO, 1994), Table A4.02. The number of appeals to a Social Security Appeal Tribunal against an adjudication officer's award or refusal to award a funeral payment in 1993/94 was 528, of which 107 (20%) were successful: *ibid*, Table H4.02.
2 *Ibid*, Table A4.02.
3 Social Fund Maternity and Funeral Expenses (General) Amendment Regulations 1994 (SI 1994/506).
4 The Report of the Social Security Advisory Committee can be found in Command Paper Cmnd 2858 (HMSO, May 1995, £5.90).
5 The Social Fund Maternity and Funeral Expenses (General) Amendment Regulations 1995 (SI 1995/1229).
6 Social Fund Maternity and Funeral Expenses (General) Regulations 1987 (SI 1987/481), reg 7(1).

7 'Close relative' means a parent, parent-in-law, son, son-in-law, daughter, daughter-in-law, step-parent, stepson, stepson-in-law, stepdaughter, stepdaughter-in-law, brother, brother-in-law, sister or sister-in-law: Social Fund Maternity and Funeral Expenses (General) Regulations 1987, reg 3(1), as substituted by the 1995 regulations.

8 It may be worth advising clients to make a will specifically naming the person responsible for arranging the funeral.

9 Regulation 7(3)(1A) of the 1987 Regulations, as substituted by the 1995 Regulations. For an evidential statement in a will or memorandum to the effect that one relative has had closer contact than another, see Clause 6 at p 364 below.

10 Necessary documentation does not include obituary notices in newspapers: *R(SB) 46/84*; *CSB 552/1984*.

11 Social Fund Maternity and Funeral Expenses (General) Regulations 1987 (SI 1987/481), reg 8.

12 *Ibid*, reg 9(1).

13 The list of capital disregards in Income Support (General) Regulations 1987 (SI 1987/1967), Sch 10 applies for the purpose of assessing the capital of a person claiming a funeral payment: Social Fund Maternity and Funeral Expenses (General) Regulations 1987 (SI 1987/481), reg 9(2)(b).

Complaints procedures[1]

The National Association of Funeral Directors (NAFD), which claims to represent approximately 80% of funeral directors, has issued a code of practice recommending the following complaints procedures.[2]

- First, the funeral director should be informed of the complaint.
- The complainant may refer the matter to the local Trading Standards Department or Citizens' Advice Bureau.
- The NAFD provides a conciliation service to deal with any complaints against its members which are not already the subject of legal proceedings.[3]
- The NAFD also provides an arbitration scheme whereby the judgment of an independent arbitrator will be binding on both the complainant and the funeral director.

If the funeral director is a member of the Funeral Planning Council[4] or Funeral Standards Council,[5] a complaint can be made to the Funeral Ombudsman Scheme which was set up in 1994.[6] This scheme is free and compensation can be awarded up to a maximum of £50,000.

A complainant can, of course, seek redress in the county court or High Court. Like all businesses which supply goods, funeral directors should ensure that the goods they supply fit their description and are of satisfactory quality. Similarly, like all businesses which provide services, funeral directors have a duty to carry out their service with reasonable skill and care.

1 See, generally, *Which?*, December 1993, p 7, and the *Which?* report, 'Finding the right funeral director', February 1995, pp 26–29. The Consumers' Association is highly critical of the NAFD's Code of Practice.

2 For criticisms of the NAFD's complaints procedures, see Nicholas Albery, Gil Elliot and Joseph Elliot, *The Natural Death Handbook* (Virgin Books, 1993), p 203.

3 Problems may be referred to The National Secretary, National Association of Funeral Directors, 618 Warwick Road, Solihull, West Midlands B91 1AA (tel 0121 711 1343).

4 Funeral Planning Council, Melville House, 70 Drymen Road, Bearsden, Glasgow, G61 2RP.
5 Funeral Standards Council, 30 North Road, Cardiff CF1 3DY (tel 01222 382046).
6 Funeral Ombudsman Scheme, 31 Southampton Row, London WC1B 5HJ (tel 0171 430 1112).

CHECKLISTS

1 LETTERS OF CONDOLENCE[1]

Ideally, a letter of sympathy or condolence should be handwritten, although if it is sent on behalf of a firm, typescript is acceptable. A letter from a firm should be in impeccable business style without being too rigid or unnecessarily formal. It should be well drafted, and balanced aesthetically on the page.[2]

A standard letter of condolence usually contains the following seven points, although a brief letter could adequately consist of points 1, 2, 3 and 7.

(1) Acknowledge the loss

- Don't feel embarrassed about acknowledging your shock or dismay.
- Mention the deceased by name.
- Say how you got to hear about the death.

(2) Express your sympathy

- Express your sorrow sincerely.
- Let the grieving person know that you can relate to their anguish.
- Don't be embarrassed to use the word 'died' or 'death', and don't feel that you have to ignore the actual cause of death.

(3) Note the special qualities of the deceased

- Acknowledge the characteristics you most admired in the deceased.
- They could be specific attributes, for example, a good sense of humour, or a love of sports.
- They could be personality traits, such as courage, bravery, leadership, or decisiveness.
- They could relate to public service, or religious devotion.
- The purpose is to remind the bereaved that the deceased was appreciated by others.
- If you didn't know the deceased personally, you may prefer to comment on any of their qualities you had heard about.

(4) Recount a memory about the deceased

- Recall a brief, but memorable, anecdote or two.
- Don't feel shy about recalling humorous incidents.

(5) Note the special qualities of the bereaved[3]

- After a death, strong feelings of inadequacy or guilt surface.[4]
- Reassure them. Remind them of their personal strengths and qualities, for example, resilience, optimism, courage.

- A kind remark made by the deceased about the survivor(s) can be particularly helpful.

(6) Offer assistance

- Don't be afraid to be specific. For example, help might be needed with organising the funeral itself, household chores, running errands, shopping, making phone calls, help with correspondence, help with transport, even 'house-sitting' during the funeral.
- If you make a promise, follow it through.

(7) Close with a thoughtful word or phrase.

---

1 This checklist is based on the recommendations made by Leonard M. Zunin and Hilary Stanton Zunin in *The Art of Condolence* (Harper Perennial, 1991), pp 36–38.

2 *Ibid*, pp 124–129.

3 The severing of the bond between husband and wife typically catapults the survivor into psychological disorientation, out of which he or she must try and redefine himself or herself as an individual. For the surviving spouse, the burden of being solely responsible (for finances, the house, the garden, the car, etc) is often overwhelming. In addition to the fear that they might not be able to cope with everyday tasks, those who have lost their partner may experience a dread of inadequacy, loneliness and social isolation which emerges early in bereavement. For those who are still employed or self-employed, the workplace can either be a supportive environment, or it can actually reinforce the suppression of grief. If the spouse died as a result of a long terminal illness, the survivor may have begun to grieve before the death itself. In older age, with limited financial or social resources and failing health, the surviving partner may see only a deteriorating, difficult and painful future.

4 W. Dewi Rees and Sylvia G. Lutkins, 'Mortality of Bereavement', *British Medical Journal*, 7 October 1967, pp 13–16, recorded that 13.7% of widowers die within the first six months of their wife's death; 5.9% during the second six months; and 4.9% in the following twelve months. See, generally, M. Stroebe, W. Stroebe and R. Hansson (eds), *Handbook of Bereavement Theory, Research and Intervention* (Cambridge University Press, 1993).

---

2 REGISTERING A DEATH

(1) Are you a 'qualified informant'?

1.1 Where the death occurred in a house, the following people are qualified to give information regarding the death:[1]

(a) any relative of the deceased present at the death or in attendance during his or her last illness;

(b) any other relative of the deceased residing or being in the sub-district where the death occurred;

(c) any person present at the death;

(d) the occupier of the house if he or she knew of the happening of the death;

(e) any inmate of the house who knew of the happening of the death;

(f) the person causing the disposal of the body.[2]

1.2 Where the death occurred elsewhere than in a house, or a body is found and no information is available as to the place of death, the following people are qualified to give information regarding the death:[3]

    (a) any relative of the deceased who has knowledge of any of the particulars required to be registered concerning the death;

    (b) any person present at the death;

    (c) any person finding or taking charge of the body;

    (d) any person causing the disposal of the body.

(2) Find out which register office covers the place where the death occurred

2.1 Ring the register office that seems the most likely to cover the place where the death occurred.

2.2 Find out:

    (a) the address of the right office for registering the death;

    (b) its opening hours;

    (c) whether an appointment is necessary;

    (d) what the current fee is for a copy of the 'death certificate'.

(3) Watch out for the time-limits

3.1 If the death has not been reported to the Coroner:

    (a) it must be registered within five days;[4] or

    (b) if, within five days of the death, a qualified informant has sent a notification of the death to the registrar together with the appropriate written notice of the signing of the medical certificate of the cause of death, the time-limit for the actual registration of death may be extended to fourteen days.[5]

3.2 If the death has been reported to the Coroner:

    (a) no registration can take place until the Coroner has issued a certificate;

    (b) the Coroner may, on request, issue a letter recording the fact of the death which can be used to get the administration of the estate under way.

(4) Attend the register office

4.1 Take with you:

    (a) the doctor's certificate (Medical Certificate of Cause of Death);

    (b) the deceased's medical card;

    (c) the deceased's birth certificate if it is available. Although it is not essential to produce the birth certificate, it may help you to supply some of the information which has to be inserted in the register.

4.2 Give the registrar the following details about the deceased:[6]

  (a) date of death;
  (b) place of death;
  (c) name and surname;
  (d) sex;
  (e) maiden surname (if the deceased was a married woman);
  (f) date of birth;
  (g) place of birth;
  (h) occupation;
  (i) usual address.

4.3 The registrar will also need the following information about you, the informant:

  (a) name and surname;
  (b) qualification;
  (c) usual address.

4.3 Check that the registrar has recorded all the details correctly. It is very difficult to alter a register entry once it has been made.

4.4 Sign the register. The registrar will hand you a pen which contains the prescribed colour ink.

4.5 Obtain from the registrar:

  (a) the certificate for burial or cremation (a green certificate), which should be handed to the funeral director as soon as possible;
  (b) the Certificate of Registration of Death, which needs to be sent to the Department of Social Security;
  (c) as many copies as are needed of the 'Death Certificate' (Certified Copy of Entry of Death). A fee is chargeable for each copy.

---

1 Births and Deaths Registration Act 1953, s 16(2).
2 A solicitor registering a death is usually a qualified informant by virtue of causing the body to be buried or cremated.
3 Births and Deaths Registration Act 1953, s 17(2).
4 *Ibid*, s 16(3) and 17(3).
5 *Ibid*, s 18.
6 Registration of Births and Deaths Regulations 1987 (SI 1987/2088), reg 39 and Sch 2.

PRECEDENTS

1 GRANT OF EXCLUSIVE RIGHT OF BURIAL IN A LOCAL AUTHORITY CEMETERY[1]

BY VIRTUE of the powers conferred by the Local Authorities' Cemeteries Order 1977 on burial authorities constituted under the Local Government Act 1972 the (*name of Council*) ('the Council') acting as a burial authority constituted under the said Act, in consideration of the sum of (*amount in words*) pounds (£   ) paid to the Council by (*full name of grantee*) of (*address of grantee*) ('the Grantee') HEREBY GRANTS to the Grantee the exclusive right of burial in the Grave Space numbered (*number*) on the plan of (*name of cemetery*) Cemetery (being a cemetery provided and maintained by the Council) and the right of placing a monument, tablet or gravestone on the said grave TO HOLD the same unto the Grantee and (his)/(her) successors in title for the term of (*number of years*) years from the date hereof for the purpose of burial Subject to the provisions of the said Order and to the orders, bye-laws and regulations for the time being in force with regard to the management, regulation and control of the said cemetery.

It is hereby certified that the transaction hereby effected does not form part of a larger transaction or of a series of transactions in respect of which the amount or value or the aggregate amount or value of the consideration exceeds (*threshold*) thousand pounds.

IN WITNESS WHEREOF the Council has executed these presents as a deed this   day of   19   .

THE COMMON SEAL of (*name of Council*) was affixed to this deed in the presence of:

_____

1 See, generally, 'Burial in a local authority cemetery' at p 341 above. This precedent is an adaptation of the suggested form of grant of burial rights which appears in the Schedule to the Cemeteries Clauses Act 1847. Section 42 of that Act provides that: 'The grant of the exclusive right of burial in any part of the cemetery, either in perpetuity or for a limited time, and of the right of one or more burials therein, or of placing therein any monument, tablet or gravestone may be made in the form in the Schedule to this Act, or the like effect'.

_____

2 ASSIGNMENT OF EXCLUSIVE RIGHT OF BURIAL IN A LOCAL AUTHORITY CEMETERY[1]

I (*full name of assignor*) of (*address of assignor*) in consideration of the sum of (*amount in words*) pounds (£   ) paid to me by (*full name of assignee*) of (*address of assignee*) ('the Assignee') HEREBY ASSIGN to the Assignee the exclusive right of burial in (*name of cemetery*) Cemetery in the grave space numbered (*number*) on the plan of the said Cemetery which was granted to me (*or, as the case may be, a predecessor in title*) for (*number of years*) years by (*name of burial authority*) by a deed of grant dated (*date*) and all my estate, title and interest therein TO HOLD the same unto the Assignee for the remainder of the said period Subject to the conditions on which I held the same immediately before the execution hereof.

It is hereby certified that the transaction hereby effected does not form part of a larger transaction or of a series of transactions in respect of which the amount or value or the aggregate amount or value of the consideration exceeds (*threshold*) thousand pounds.

AS WITNESS my hand this   day of   19   .

Executed as a deed by
(*full name of assignor*)
in the presence of:

---

1 See, generally, 'Burial in a local authority cemetery' at p 341 above. This precedent has been adapted from the suggested form of assignment in the Schedule to the Cemeteries Clauses Act 1847 and modified in respect of cemeteries provided by local authorities under the Local Government Act 1972 and the Local Authorities' Cemeteries Order 1977 (SI 1977/204).

---

3 APPLICATION TO THE INCUMBENT FOR PERMISSION TO ERECT A MEMORIAL IN A CHURCHYARD[1]

To the Reverend (*name of incumbent*)
Parish of (*name*)
Diocese of (*name*)

APPLICATION FOR PERMISSION TO ERECT A MEMORIAL

I (*full name of applicant*) of (*address*) APPLY for permission to erect a memorial in (*name of parish*) Churchyard at the grave of (*full name of deceased*) who died on (*date*).

(1)   A sketch of the proposed design is attached.
(2)   The proposed dimensions are (*height*) high,[2] measured from the surface of the ground, (*width*) wide,[3] and (*thickness*) thick.[4]

(3)   The proposed material is (*describe the colour and material*) with a (*describe the finish, eg non-reflecting*) finish.[5]

(4)   The proposed inscription is:[6]

           (*set out the proposed lettering, layout and wording*)[7]

SIGNED ....

DATE   ....

---

1 See, generally, 'Erection of monuments' at p 344 above. 'Every application to erect a memorial, or place anything whatsoever, or to do any works in the churchyard should be made in writing to the incumbent, in the first instance, with a full description for the proposed work': Peter Burman and Henry Stapleton, *The Churchyards Handbook* (3rd edition, Church House Publishing, 1988) p 170. Each diocese has its own regulations on memorials, but most are based on recommendations in *The Churchyards Handbook*, which appear in the following footnotes.

2 The recommended height is a minimum of 2 ft 6 in (750 mm) and a maximum of 4 ft (120 mm).

3 The recommended width is a minimum of 1 ft 8 in (500 mm) and a maximum of 3 ft (900 mm).

4 The recommended thickness is a maximum of 6 in (150 mm) and a minimum of 3 in (75 mm), except in the case of slate memorials, which may be thinner but no less than 1.5 in (38 mm) thick.

5 'All memorials should be made of natural stone with no reflecting finish, or of hardwood. Stones traditionally used in local buildings, or stones closely similar to them in colour or texture, are to be preferred. Black, blue or red granites are not generally permitted, nor granites darker than Rustenburg grey, nor white marble, synthetic stone or plastic': *The Churchyards Handbook*, p 171.

6 'Inscriptions must be simple and reverent, and may include felicitous quotations from literary sources. Inscriptions should be incised, or in relief, and may be painted. Plastic or other inserted lettering should not be permitted. Additions may be made to an inscription at a later date following a subsequent interment in the same grave or for other suitable reason. However, any such alteration must be separately approved. The lettering, layout and wording must be consistent with the original inscription': *ibid*, pp 171–172.

7 'An epitaph is a public document, and not a cosy one at that. Nicknames or pet-names ("Mum", "Dad", "Ginger") inscribed in stone would carry overtones of the dog cemetery unsuitable for the resting place of Christian men and women': *ibid*, p 106. See also: *Re Christ Church, Ainsworth* (1992) Ecc LJ 321; *Re St Mary, Sheviock* (1993) 3 Ecc LJ 62; and *Re Holy Trinity, Freckleton* [1994] TLR 493; (1995) 3 Ecc LJ 350.

WILL CLAUSES

1 PRE-PAYMENT SCHEMES[1]

I have already paid for my funeral under a pre-payment agreement with (*name of company, eg Golden Charter, Chosen Heritage, etc*) dated (*date*) and numbered (*number*).

I have nominated (*name and address of funeral directors*) to be my funeral directors.

If (*my wife, husband, children, or as the case may be*) wish(es) to upgrade the plan I have selected, and it is possible to do so, I authorise the additional expenditure incurred to be paid out of my estate.

---

1 See, generally, 'Pre-paid funeral schemes' at p 346 above.

---

2 DONATION OF BODY FOR MEDICAL EDUCATION OR RESEARCH[1]

I request that my body be made available to (*name of medical school*) or, failing which,[2] any other medical school willing to accept it, for the purposes of medical education or research, and that it should eventually be cremated.[3]

---

1 A request that one's body be used for *anatomical examination*, which is defined as meaning 'the examination by dissection of a body for the purposes of teaching or studying, or researching into, morphology', is governed by Anatomy Act 1984, s 4. Any client who wishes to donate their body in this way should be advised to contact the medical school in question, or alternatively HM Inspector of Anatomy, Department of Health, Wellington House, 133–155 Waterloo Road, London SE1 8UG (tel 0171 072 4342).

2 Not all bodies that are donated for anatomical examination are accepted. Generally speaking, medical schools will only accept bodies which are unautopsied, non-cancerous, and within easy reach of the school. For an illuminating account of the origins of the Anatomy Act 1832, see Ruth Richardson, *Death, Dissection and the Destitute* (Penguin Books, 1988).

3 The authority to carry out an anatomical examination expires at the end of the 'statutory period', which is defined as 'three years (or such other period as the Secretary of State may from time to time prescribe) beginning with the date of the deceased's death': Anatomy Act 1984, s 4(8) and (10).

3 ORGAN OR TISSUE DONATION[1]

I would like any part of my body which may be of use to others to be made available for treatment or transplantation.

[OR]

I would like my (corneas)[2]/(eyes)/(heart)/(kidneys)/(liver)/(lungs)/(pancreas) to be used for transplantation.

For the avoidance of doubt, I do not want my body or any part of it to be used for the purposes of medical education or research.[3]

---

1 'If any person, either in writing at any time or orally in the presence of two witnesses during his last illness has expressed a request that his body or any specified part of his body be used after his death for therapeutic purposes or for purposes of medical education or research, the person lawfully in possession of his body after his death may, unless he has reason to believe that the request was subsequently withdrawn, authorise the removal from the body of any part, or as the case may be the specified part, for use in accordance with the request': Human Tissue Act 1961, s 1(1). For a detailed discussion of the problems in interpreting this section, see Ian Kennedy and Andrew Grubb, *Medical Law: Text and Materials* (Butterworths, 1989), p 1022 *et seq.*

2 The Corneal Tissue Act 1986 permits for therapeutic purposes and purposes of medical education or research the removal of eyes or parts of eyes by persons who are not medically qualified, subject to appropriate safeguards.

3 Note that Human Tissue Act 1961, s 1(1) authorises the removal of any part, or any specified part, of the body for therapeutic purposes *or* for the purposes of medical education or research. The testator/testatrix may prefer to limit the request to therapeutic purposes alone.

---

4 BURIAL

I wish to be buried wherever may be most convenient.

I wish to be buried in (*name and address of cemetery*) in the grave space numbered (*number*) which was granted to me (*or, as the case may be*) by (*name of burial authority*) in a deed dated (*date*).[1]

I wish to be buried in (*name of parish*) churchyard in the grave space reserved to me by a faculty granted on (*date*) by the Diocesan Court of (*name of diocese*).[2]

I wish to be buried beside my (wife)/(husband) if (she)/(he) dies before me.

(I would like) a headstone with a suitably worded inscription to be placed on my grave and I request my (*family*)/(*executors*) to obtain the church authorities' approval of the proposed design, dimensions, material and inscription before commissioning the monumental mason to carve the stone.[3]

I wish to be buried at sea.[4]

1 For further details on the acquisition of exclusive rights of burial in a local authority cemetery, see, generally, 'Burial in a local authority cemetery' at p 341 above, and Precedents 1 and 2 above.

2 See, generally, 'Rights attainable by faculty' at p 343 above.

3 See, generally, 'Erection of monuments' at p 344 above.

4 The legal requirements for the burial of a body at sea are discussed in David A. Smale (ed), *Davies' Law of Burial, Cremation and Exhumation* (6th edition, 1993), pp 55–57, and the practical considerations are discussed by Nicholas Albery, Gil Elliot and Joseph Elliot in *The Natural Death Handbook* (Virgin Books, 1993), pp 142–143. The Coroner must be informed. An application for a licence under the Food and Environment Protection Act 1985 (as amended by the Environmental Protection Act 1990) should be made to the local Fisheries Officer of the Ministry of Agriculture, Fisheries and Food. There are very few places around the coast where sea burials are permitted. For an entertaining account of how a burial at sea can go disastrously wrong, see the Scottish case *Herron v Diack and Newlands* 1973 SLT (Sh Ct) 27.

5 CREMATION[1]

I wish to be cremated at (*name of crematorium*) Crematorium.

I would like my ashes to be (buried)/(scattered) in the grounds of (*name of crematorium*) Crematorium.[2]

I would like a suitably worded entry to be placed in the Book of Remembrance at the Crematorium.

I would like my ashes to be (buried) in (*name of parish*) churchyard or burial ground and request that my (executors)/(family) seek advice from the (rector)/(vicar) before commissioning or erecting any memorial tablet.[3]

I would like my ashes to be (buried)/(scattered) by (*name*) at whatever spot (he)/(she) wishes.

I do not want to be cremated.[4]

I would like my ashes to be (buried)/(scattered) at sea.[5]

1 There are currently between 430,000 and 440,000 cremations in Great Britain each year: approximately 70% of the total number of deaths. As at 1 January 1993, there were 226 crematoria in the UK: 194 operated by municipal authorities and 32 operated by private companies. For a directory of crematoria, see David A. Smale (ed), *Davies' Law of Burial, Cremation and Exhumation* (6th edition, 1993), Appendix I. In the last few decades, the Roman Catholic Church has modified its attitude towards cremation, and its current doctrine is as follows: 'The Church recommends that the pious custom of burial be retained; but it does not forbid cremation, unless this is chosen for reasons which are contrary to Christian teaching': The Code of Canon Law 1983, Canon 1176(3).

2 After a cremation, the ashes must be given into the charge of the person who applied for the cremation. In *Re Korda* (1958) *The Times*, April 23, a claim by a son for the delivery of his father's ashes was dismissed on a summons taken out by the father's executors. In the absence of any special arrangements for their disposal, the ashes must be retained by the cremation authority and either interred or scattered in a burial ground or in land adjoining the crematorium reserved for the burial of ashes.

3 See, generally, 'Burial in an Anglican churchyard' at p 341 above. The rights of burial in an Anglican churchyard or burial ground also apply to the burial of cremated remains: Church of England (Miscellaneous Provisions) Measure 1992, s 3.

4 Regulation 4 of the Cremation Regulations 1930 (SR&O 1930/1016), which prohibited the cremation of a person who had left a written direction not to be cremated, was revoked by the Cremation Regulations 1965 (SI 1965/1146), reg 7(a).

5 An application should be made to the local fisheries officer of the Ministry of Agriculture, Fisheries and Food for a licence under the Food and Environment Protection Act 1985 (as amended by the Environmental Protection Act 1990) if cremated remains are to be buried at sea. If cremated remains are merely to be scattered at sea, there is no need to obtain such a licence, although it may be sensible to contact the local fisheries officer for further information and advice.

6 THE FUNERAL

(I would like) (*name and address of funeral directors*) to be my funeral directors.

(I would like) a notice recording the date and place of my death and the time, date and place of my funeral to be inserted in (*name of newspaper, journal, etc*).

(I would like) my funeral service to be held at (*location*).

(I would like) my funeral service to be conducted in accordance with the (rites)/(usages) of (*name of faith or denomination*).

I do not want any religious formalities at my funeral.[1]

(I would like) the following readings: (*specify the passages to be read*).

(I would like) the following hymns: (*give the first line of the hymn, its number in a named hymn book, and the name of the tune*).

(I would like) family flowers only.[2]

(I would like) donations, if desired, to be made to (*charity, cause or purpose*).

(I would like) my funeral to be as simple as possible.

(I would like) (*name of person*) to make all the [other] arrangements for my funeral[3] [because in recent years I have had much closer contact with (him)/(her) than with my other children].[4]

I authorise the expenses incurred in carrying out these wishes to be paid out of my estate.[5]

1 The British Humanist Association, 14 Lamb's Conduit Passage, London WC1R 4RH, has published a booklet, *Funerals without God*, giving advice on how to conduct a non-religious funeral.

2 Nicholas Albery, Gil Elliot and Joseph Elliot in *The Natural Death Handbook* (Virgin Books, 1993), p 144, suggest 'one flower each'. The testator or testatrix could ask family and friends not to buy flowers but to bring one flower each, preferably from their garden, and to place it on the coffin.

3 The court would probably not interfere with the responsible person's decision, at the suit of a

near relative or even the executor(s), unless it could be shown that the discretion conferred on the responsible person has been exercised dishonestly, capriciously or wantonly: *Re Grandison (Deceased)* (1989) *The Times*, July 10.

4 In deciding whether to award a Social Fund funeral payment, an adjudication officer has to consider whether it is reasonable for a person to accept responsibility for meeting the expenses of a funeral having regard to the nature and extent of that person's contact with the deceased: Social Fund Maternity and Funeral Expenses (General) Regulations 1987 (SI 1987/481), reg 7(3)(1A), as amended by the Social Fund Maternity and Funeral Expenses (General) Amendment Regulations 1995 (SI 1995/1229). See, generally, 'Social Fund funeral payments' at p 348 above.

5 As against a creditor, executors are allowed to incur only funeral expenses which are reasonably necessary according to the circumstances and to the deceased's position in life: *Hancock v Podmore* (1830) 1 B & Ad 260; *Bisset v Antrobus* (1831) 4 Sim 512; *Reeves v Ward* (1835) 1 Hodg 300; *Yardley v Arnold* (1842) Car & M 434, NP. Even where a person dies with considerable assets, unreasonable funeral expenses may be disallowed on the grounds of extravagance: *Stacpoole v Stacpoole* (1816) 4 Dow 209, where the deceased's estate came to more than £31,000, and the funeral cost £1200, it was held that £200 was sufficient for the funeral, and the excess was disallowed.

---

7 LEGACY FOR THE MAINTENANCE OF A GRAVE IN A CHURCHYARD[1]

I GIVE the sum of (*amount in words*) pounds (£   )[2] free of tax to the (*name of diocese*) Diocesan Board of Finance ('the Board') upon trust to pay the income to the (Parochial Church Council)/(incumbent) of the Parish of (*name of parish*) in the County of (*name of county*) and Diocese of (*name of diocese*) for the maintenance of the church and churchyard of the parish so long as the grave of (*name of deceased*) is kept in good order and repair.

I DIRECT that a certificate signed every (three) years by the Rural Dean that the grave of (*name of deceased*) is kept in good order and repair shall be sufficient evidence and that any question as to the breach of this condition shall be finally decided by the Rural Dean.

I FURTHER DIRECT that if the Rural Dean decides that this condition has been breached, then on receiving notice of his or her decision the Board will hold the sum and the investments representing it and the income from it for the general purposes of the Board.

---

1 A legacy for the maintenance of a particular tomb may be valid as a trust of imperfect obligation provided that it is limited to the perpetuity period. The only way in which a testator can ensure that a perpetual trust of this kind is valid is: (a) to apply the gift for the whole of the churchyard in which the grave is located; or (b) to leave the legacy to a charity with a gift over to another charity if the grave is not kept in good order and repair. It is important, however, to ensure that no actual trust is imposed on the first charity to keep up the tomb. See, generally, David A. Smale (ed), *Davies' Law of Burial and Cremation* (6th edition, Shaw & Sons, 1993), chapter 8, 'Gifts for the Maintenance of Monuments, Memorials, Graves or Tombstones'. This precedent is based on the recommendations contained in Appendix IIIf of Peter Burman and Henry Stapleton, *The Churchyards Handbook* (3rd edition, Church House Publishing, 1988).

2 The sum given should provide sufficient income to keep the specified grave in order.

CHAPTER 13: WILLS

INDEX

Text

Precedents

Clauses

WILLS

TEXT

Introduction

There are some extremely good will precedent books in circulation[1] and there would be little point in repeating material which is already adequately covered in the specialist texts. Although this chapter contains several standard wills and clauses, the precedents tend to concentrate one or two aspects of will drafting for the elderly which may not have received a great deal of attention elsewhere. Some complement various other topics considered in this book, such as gifts, disability issues, and sharing residential accommodation. There are also a few precedents relating to the estate planning problems that can arise when there is a second or subsequent marriage in later life.

---

1 For example, *Butterworths Wills, Probate and Administration Service* (looseleaf updated work) and *The Encyclopedia of Forms and Precedents* (5th edition, Butterworths, 1992), vol 42, both of which contain useful contributions by Gordon Ashton on wills for incapacitated beneficiaries; *Williams on Wills* (6th edition, Butterworths, 1987, plus supplement); D.T. Davies, *Will Precedents and Inheritance Tax* (4th edition, Butterworths, 1991); D.M. Pettit, *The Will Draftsman's Handbook* (6th edition, Longman, 1990); *Practical Will Precedents* (looseleaf, Longman); *Parker's Modern Will Precedents* (2nd edition, Butterworths, 1987), E.F. George and A. George, *Brighouse's Precedents of Wills and Life Transfers* (11th edition, Sweet & Maxwell, 1986), etc.

Statistics

About 570,000 people die each year in England and Wales. No formal steps are taken to wind up the deceased's affairs in respect of more than half of these deaths. Often the estate is too small to justify any action, but there must be a considerable number of deaths where no grant of representation is obtained because the deceased's assets pass automatically to a surviving joint tenant.

In 1994, the Principal Registry and District Probate Registries issued 252,249 grants of representation.[1] These included 186,566 probates (74% of the total number of grants, but only 33% of the total number of deaths) and 10,904 grants of letters of administration with the will annexed. There were 54,860 grants of letters of administration (22% of the total number of grants, but only 9% of the total number of deaths). In view of the considerable number of estates where no grant is issued, it would be impossible to say with any degree of accuracy how many people die testate or intestate, but at a rough guess about 40% die testate.

The following trends seem to be emerging.

- More people are dying testate. The proportion of grants involving a will (probate and letters of administration with the will annexed) increased from 73% in 1986 to 78% in 1994, and the grants of letters of administration on intestacy fell commensurately from 27% to 22% during the same period.[2]
- During the last few years, the number of personal applications has steadily increased. Throughout the 1980s, the percentage of grants extracted by solicitors and those extracted personally remained constant at 80% and 20% respectively. By 1994, however, the number of personal applications had risen to 26%.
- There has also been a significant increase in the number of wills deposited for safe custody in the Principal Registry at Somerset House. 15,247 wills were lodged in 1994: 56% more than in 1993 (9776).[3] This may reflect the growing number of wills being prepared by professional will-writers who are unable to provide the storage facilities that solicitors and banks can offer.
- The wills currently prepared by solicitors and banks are considerably lengthier than the wills they prepared twenty-five years ago before word-processors came onto the scene.[4] Generally speaking, the additional verbiage is attributable to an indiscriminate use of administrative provisions, although on the positive side there are clearly more 'gifts over' to insure against the possibility that a beneficiary might predecease the testator. It is to be hoped that if the Standard Provisions of the Society of Trust and Estate Practitioners[5] are adopted on a widespread basis, wills will revert to a more manageable length, concentrate on the dispositive provisions, and be easier for testators to understand.

---

1 Lord Chancellor's Department, *Judicial Statistics Annual Report 1994*, Cmnd 2891 (HMSO, 1995, £14.90), p 59.
2 Lord Chancellor's Department, *Judicial Statistics Annual Report 1987*, Cmnd 428 (HMSO, 1988, £9.60), Table 5.1.
3 Lord Chancellor's Department, *Judicial Statistics Annual Report 1994*, Cmnd 2891 (HMSO, 1995, £14.90), p 58. The system for the voluntary deposit of wills in the Principal Registry of the Family Division was originally set up by the Supreme Court of Judicature (Consolidation) Act 1925, s 172, now replaced by the Supreme Court Act 1981, s 126. See also the Wills (Deposit for Safe Custody) Regulations 1978 (SI 1978/1724). The system will ultimately be replaced by provisions for the voluntary deposit and registration of wills contained in the Administration of Justice Act 1982, ss 23–26 (which are not yet in force). It is also possible for a testator or his agent personally to deliver a will at any Probate Registry in England and Wales. The Principal Registry of the Family Division produces a leaflet, 'I want to deposit my will for safe-keeping', copies of which may be obtained from the Record Keeper's Department, Principal Registry of the Family Division, Somerset House, Strand, London WC2R 1LP (tel 0171 936 7000).
4 In June 1993 the author carried out a survey in the Exeter Sub-registry which involved examining 175 wills proved during one fortnight in 1968, and 235 wills proved during one fortnight in 1993. The results were originally published in *The Legal Executive Journal*, November 1993, pp 46–47, and are further discussed in Chapter 12, see 'Funeral instructions in wills' at p 339 above. There was a discernible difference between the relatively brief wills proved in 1968 and the lengthier wills proved in 1993. There was also a noticeable deterioration in the quality of paper used in recent years.
5 See Clause 24 at p 403 below.

The will-drafting market

In October 1994, *Which?* published a report on will-making services.[1] The Consumers' Association arranged for wills to be drawn up by fifty separate organisations: thirty-one solicitors' firms; ten banks and building societies; six specialist will-writers; and three insurance companies. On closer scrutiny, five of the wills prepared by solicitors were rated as poor, six good, and twenty reasonable. Of the ten wills prepared by banks and building societies, two were considered poor, three were good, and the others reasonable. Of the six wills prepared by will-writers, four were poor and two reasonable; and of the three commissioned from insurance companies, two were reasonable and the other one never materialised (it was simply a 'soft sell' exercise for insurance-related products generally).

The cost varied considerably. The price (including VAT) of a single will prepared by a solicitor ranged from £23.50 to £117.50 in Scotland, and from £35.25 to £88.12 in England and Wales. The cost of wills prepared by a bank ranged from £29.25 for a single will and £40.95 for mirror image wills (Ulster Bank) to £58.75 for a single will prepared by Barclays Bank, the Midland Bank and the National Westminster Bank. Professional will-writers charged within a range of £40 and £58.75.

According to *Which?* the advantages and disadvantages of the different sectors of the will-drafting market were as follows.

	Advantages	Disadvantages
Solicitors	Professional expertise. The possibility of obtaining a refund and compensation via the Solicitors' Complaints Bureau.	The level of service and quality can vary significantly. There is no sure-fire way of picking a good firm.
Banks/Building Societies	The ability to complain to the Banking/Building Societies Ombudsman.	Most insist on being appointed as executors.
Will Writers	The representative is normally willing to visit you at home outside working hours. Alternatively, the matter can be dealt with by post.	Anybody can set up as a will-writer. No proper channels for complaints. No protection if the firm goes bust.
Insurance Companies	The representative will normally visit you at home outside normal working hours.	They may try to sell life insurance and other investments.

Some of the above observations may appear naive, but it is undeniable that what the average consumer – or testator – expects is:

- expert knowledge;
- freedom of choice in the appointment of executors;
- recognised channels for complaints;
- indemnity cover;
- secure storage facilities;[2]
- home visits or interviews outside normal office hours;
- less emphasis on the cross-selling of other services or products; and
- an inexpensive, but nevertheless professional, service.

It is estimated that currently 74% of wills are drawn up by solicitors or legal executives; 6% by will-writers; 5% by banks; and the remaining 15% are home-made or written or typed on a printed form.[3]

---

1 'Where there's a will', *Which?*, October 1994, pp 48–53. *Which?* published a similar report, 'Making your will', in June 1991. Without derogating from the findings in these *Which?* reports, the Consumers' Association has a vested interest in that it produces *Make Your Will: A Practical Guide to Making Your Own Will: An Action Pack from Which?*, which was first published in January 1989. According to Gallup, the percentage of people who had drawn up their own will was 11% in 1991, and this had risen to 15% in 1994.

2 *Which?* advised its readers of the scheme whereby they can deposit their will for £1 at Somerset House. For further information on the deposit of wills with the court, see footnote 3 at p 370 above.

3 Source: The Law Society, *Wills & Probate: Beating the Competition*: notes for the one-day conferences held in May and June 1994. This information was attributed to Gallup polls conducted in 1991 and 1994. In 1991, only 31% of adults had made a will. The 1994 poll showed no material change. The percentage of wills drawn up by solicitors decreased from 77% in 1991 to 74% in 1994, whereas the percentage of home-made wills increased from 11% to 15% during the same period.

Elderly infirm clients

Testamentary capacity is examined in detail in Chapter 3. If the testator lacks capacity, an application could be made to the Court of Protection for an authorised person to execute a statutory will on his behalf. Such applications are discussed separately in Chapter 14. This section summarises a few practical points that may need to be considered when acting for infirm elderly clients.

In *Kenward v Adams* (1975)[1], Templeman J laid down what he described as 'the golden if tactless rule': namely, that 'when a solicitor is drawing up a will for an aged testator or one who has been seriously ill, it should be witnessed or approved by a medical practitioner, who ought to record his examination of the testator and his findings ... Other precautions were that if there was an earlier will it should be examined and any proposed alterations should be discussed with the testator'. He reiterated this rule in *Re Simpson*.

Re Simpson (Deceased): Schaniel v Simpson (1977)[2]

Mr Simpson, who suffered from Parkinson's Disease, made a will in July 1973 leaving legacies to the children of his first marriage, legacies to his second wife and their daughter, half the residue to their daughter, and the other half to his wife for life. His condition subsequently deteriorated. On 19 September 1973, another solicitor was sent for and within 24 hours Mr Simpson executed a new will leaving a small legacy to the daughter and the residue to his wife. He died within a week.

HELD, by Templeman J – the testator did not know or approve the September will and was acting under the influence of his wife. The judge repeated his warning in *Kenward v Adams* and added that, wherever possible, in cases of borderline capacity it is preferable that the testator be seen by a solicitor who knows him.[3]

Principle 12.04 in The Law Society's *Guide to the Professional Conduct of Solicitors*[4] states that: 'a solicitor must not accept instructions where he or she suspects that those instructions have been given by a client under duress or undue influence'. The commentary goes on to advise that: 'if a solicitor suspects that the client's instructions infringe this Principle, either the client must be seen alone in order that the solicitor can be satisfied that the instructions were freely given, or the solicitor must refuse to act. Particular care may need to be taken where clients are elderly or otherwise vulnerable to pressure from others'.[5]

Principle 12.05 provides that 'where instructions are received not from a client but from a third party purporting to represent that client, a solicitor should obtain written instructions from the client that he or she wishes the solicitor to act. In any case of doubt the solicitor should see the client or take other appropriate steps to confirm instructions'. The commentary to Principle 12.05 states that 'in relation to the preparation of wills, especially where the client may be elderly, it is important to obtain enough information about the client's circumstances to be able properly to act for the client. When asked to prepare a will on the basis of written instructions alone, a solicitor should always consider carefully whether these are sufficient or whether the solicitor should see the client to discuss the instructions'. Principle 12.10 would also have been relevant in *Re Simpson*. It states that 'a solicitor must not accept instructions to act in a matter where another solicitor is acting for the client in the same matter until the first retainer has been determined'.[6]

It may be worth noting that Scottish law recognises a concept known as 'facility and circumvention'. It arises where an elderly person suffers a degree of mental deterioration which, although it does not technically amount to incapacity, leaves him or her vulnerable to exploitation by others. 'In effect the concept is a sliding scale, merging at one end into insanity (where the mental element is everything) and at the other undue influence'.[7] There is authority for this concept in English law although, surprisingly, the issue does not appear to have been considered by the courts since *Ingram v Wyatt* (1828).[8]

---

1 (1975) *The Times*, November 29. The full, albeit extremely brief, report of this case is on p 42 above.

2 (1977) 121 Sol Jo 224.

3 The desirability that an elderly, infirm testatrix should be seen by a solicitor who knows her was also stressed by Lord Merrivale P in *Re Belliss: Polson v Parrott* (1929) 141 LT 245.

4 Sixth edition, 1993. Note also Principle 15.08, which provides that 'where a client intends to make a gift inter vivos or by will to his or her solicitor, or to the solicitor's partner, or a member of staff or to the families of any of them and the gift is of a significant amount, either in itself or having regard to the size of the client's estate and the reasonable expectations of prospective beneficiaries, the solicitor must advise the client to be independently advised as to that gift and if the client declines, must refuse to act'.

5 Note that *Home Life, A Code of Practice for Residential Care* (Centre for Policy on Ageing, 1984), para 2.6.1, states that 'proprietors and staff should not, except in the most extreme emergency, act as witnesses to any resident's will. In no circumstances should the proprietor or any member of staff become an executor of a resident's will'.

6 For the procedure on contacting another solicitor's client, see The Law Society, *The Guide to the Professional Conduct of Solicitors* (6th edition, 1993), Principle 12.10.

7 D.R. Macdonald, *An Introduction to the Scots Law of Succession* (W. Green & Son, 1990), p 82. In *Ross v Gosselin's Executors* 1926 SC 325, Lord President Clyde distinguished the doctrines of facility/circumvention and undue influence as follows: 'The essence of undue influence is that a person who has assumed or taken a position of quasi-fiduciary responsibility in relation to the affairs of another, allows his own self-interest to deflect the advice or guidance he gives in his own favour. On the other hand, the essence of circumvention and facility is that a person practises on the debility of another whose individuality is impaired by infirmity or age, and moulds the inclinations of the latter to his own profit'.

8 *Ingram v Wyatt* (1828) 1 Hagg Ecc 384, Prerogative Court of Canterbury.

Negligence and delay

In 1958, the Supreme Court of California held that a disappointed beneficiary could recover damages for negligence from the lawyer who had drawn up the will.[1] In October 1965, in an article in the *Law Quarterly Review*, this and a similar case[2] were discussed by REM, who presciently asked, 'is it beyond the bounds of possibility that the doctrine of *Biakanja v Irving* and *Lucas v Hamm* will find expression in England within a decade or two?' It wasn't, and it did, and the judge who introduced the doctrine was REM himself, the Vice-Chancellor, Sir Robert Megarry.

Ross v Caunters (1979)[3]

William Philp of Liskeard, Cornwall instructed his solicitors, Caunters, to draw up a will. He wanted to leave various personal chattels and a quarter of his residuary estate to his sister-in-law, Mrs Eileen Ross. He executed the will on 3 July 1974 in the presence of Isaac Ross (Eileen's husband) and another witness. Caunters had omitted to forewarn him of the effect of the Wills Act 1837, s 15, which says that a gift to a witness or his or her spouse is void. Mr Philp died in March 1976 aged 83. His net estate came to £22,500. Eileen Ross sued the solicitors for negligence.

HELD, by Sir Robert Megarry – 'a solicitor who is instructed by his client to carry out a transaction that will confer a benefit on an identified third party owes a duty of care towards that third party in carrying out that transaction, in that the third party is a person within his direct contemplation as someone who is likely to be so closely and directly affected by his acts or omissions that he can reasonably foresee that the third party is likely to be injured by those acts or omissions'.

The 'reasonable contemplation' principle applied in *Ross v Caunters* had its origins in the judgment of Lord Wilberforce in *Anns v London Borough of Merton* (1977)[4] and was subsequently applied in *Smith v Claremont Haynes & Co.*[5]

Smith v Claremont Haynes & Co (1991)[6]

Joan Irene Smith lived in Newhaven, East Sussex. In December 1983, she executed a will appointing the Midland Bank Trust Company to be her executor. She gave a legacy of £500 to her brother Thomas, and left the rest of her estate to charities – mainly animal charities. She made no mention of her uncle, Leonard Smith, or his wife, Evelyn. In fact, they seem to have had very little contact with her until she was diagnosed as suffering from leukaemia and admitted to hospital in December 1987. While she was in hospital, Joan decided to update her will and leave something to Leonard and Evelyn. Her solicitor came to see her on 19 January 1988, but didn't visit her again until 22 February 1988. By then she was far too ill to see anyone, and she died three days later. The 1983 will was admitted to probate, and her net estate amounted to £154,000. Leonard and Evelyn sued her solicitors for the loss of their would-be windfall.

HELD, by Judge Barnett QC, sitting as a deputy judge of the Queen's Bench Division – where a solicitor had the essence of an intended will expressed or made known to him by a person he knew to be an intended testator, and where he might reasonably be expected to be aware of the element of urgency in the preparation of the will by reason of the state of the intended testator's health, then he was liable in negligence when his failure to act promptly deprived two intended beneficiaries of their expectancies under the intended will.

In the meantime, however, in *Murphy v Brentwood District Council*,[7] the House of Lords concluded that *Anns* had been wrongly decided, overruled it, and narrowed any claim for economic loss to one sustained through an assumption of responsibility – in accordance with its earlier decision in *Hedley Byrne*.[8] This left open the question whether *Ross v Caunters*, which had been decided on the basis of *Anns*, was still good law.[9] The matter was eventually resolved by a majority decision of the House of Lords in *White v Jones*.

White v Jones (1995)[10]

Arthur Barratt, 78, lived in Birmingham. In January 1986, his wife died. On 4 March 1986, following a quarrel about her estate, he executed a will in which he disinherited his two daughters, Carole and Pauline. He decided instead to leave his estate to Carole's former husband and their two children, Mandy and Maxine. In June 1986, Arthur and his daughters were reconciled, and on 17 July 1986, he wrote to his solicitors, Philip Baker King & Co with instructions for the preparation of a new will. Mr Jones, the legal executive handling the case, did nothing until 16 August 1986 when he dictated an internal memo. Meanwhile, Arthur went on holiday to Weston-super-Mare where he fell and banged his head. Shortly after returning home, he had a heart attack and on 14 September 1986 he died leaving an estate of just under £30,000. The new will had not been drawn up. Carole and Pauline sued the solicitors and the legal executive. Turner J dismissed the claim in negligence. The Court of Appeal reversed the judge's decision and held that the daughters were entitled to recover in negligence: [1993] 3 WLR 730.

HELD, by a 3:2 majority in the House of Lords, dismissing the appeal of the defendant legal executive and firm – solicitors who undertake to perform services for a client are liable to the client for failure to exercise due care and skill in relation to the performance of those services not only in contract but also in negligence under the principle in *Hedley Byrne & Co Ltd v Heller & Partners Ltd* [1964] AC 465 on the basis of an assumption of responsibility.

1 *Biakanja v Irving* (1958) 320 P 2d 16.

2 *Lucas v Hamm* (1961) 364 P 2d 685.

3 [1979] 3 All ER 580.

4 [1977] 2 WLR 1024, [1977] 2 All ER 492.

5 *Ross v Caunters* was not followed by the Supreme Court of Victoria in *Seale v Parry* (1982) VR 1993, on the basis that, since the testator is free to alter or revoke his will at any stage during his lifetime, the solicitor, who is after all merely his agent, cannot be held liable for failing to achieve what the testator is not required to do himself.

6 [1991] TLR 409. The facts of this case are described by David Chatterton in 'Wills Without Delay', *The Law Society's Gazette*, 13 November 1991, pp 17 and 18.

7 [1990] 3 WLR 414, [1990] 2 All ER 908.

8 *Hedley Byrne & Co Ltd v Heller & Partners Ltd* [1964] AC 465.

9 See, for example, Hugh Evans, 'Is Ross v Caunters Still Good Law?', *Professional Negligence*, September 1991, pp 137–141.

10 (1995) *The Times*, February 17.

Legal aid[1]

Legal aid[2] is only available for making a will on behalf of a person who satisfies the financial criteria for eligibility[3] and is also:

- aged 70 or over; or
- disabled; or
- the parent of a disabled person and wishes to provide for him or her in the will.[4]

For this purpose, 'disabled' means:

- blind or partially sighted;[5] or
- deaf or hard of hearing; or
- dumb;[6] or
- suffering from 'mental disorder' as defined in the Mental Health Act 1983;[7] or
- having a substantial and permanent handicap caused by illness, injury or congenital deformity.[8]

1 See, generally, Legal Advice and Assistance (Scope) Regulations 1989 (SI 1989/550), reg 4. The regulation also provides that legal aid is available for a single parent who wishes to make a will appointing a guardian for the child or children. A less formal, but equally effective, method of appointing guardians is possible under the Children Act 1989, s 5(5). Note that, 'A solicitor is under a duty to consider and advise the client on the availability of legal aid where the client might be entitled to assistance under the Legal Aid Act 1988': The Law Society, *The Guide to the Professional Conduct of Solicitors* (6th edition, 1993), Principle 5.01. Failure to advise clients of

their rights under the Legal Aid Act 1988 can amount to unbefitting conduct and may also lead to a claim in negligence against a solicitor for breach of duty owed to the client: *ibid*, Commentary 4. Legally aided clients must be treated in the same way as privately funded clients, and the same standards of care apply: *ibid*, Commentary 6.

2 Green Form plus Form GF4.

3 'It may be thought that a person who is financially eligible for green form legal advice would not need to make a will, but that is not so. The testator may qualify through receipt of income support yet still own a house . . . and there is then a substantial asset to be disposed of': Gordon Ashton, *Elderly People and the Law* (Butterworths, 1995), p 364.

4 See, generally, the contributions by Gordon Ashton in *Butterworths Wills, Probate and Administration Service* (looseleaf updated work), Division A1; and *The Encyclopedia of Forms and Precedents* (5th edition, Butterworths, 1992), vol 42, Part 6.

5 For a discussion of some of the practical difficulties arising when a blind or partially sighted person executes a will, see the footnotes to Clause 27 at p 405 below.

6 For a recommended procedure for dealing with dysphasic patients, see Dr Pam Enderby, 'The Testamentary Capacity of Dysphasic Patients' (1994) *Medico-Legal Journal*, vol 62, Part 2, pp 79–80.

7 'Mental disorder' means 'mental illness, arrested or incomplete development of mind, psychopathic disorder and any other disorder or disability of mind': Mental Health Act 1983, s 1(2). A testator may suffer from a mental disorder without it affecting his testamentary capacity: see, generally, Chapters 3 and 14. In such a case, it is recommended that a registered medical practitioner should sign a certificate stating that the client has testamentary capacity despite the fact that he or she is suffering from mental disorder. It is also recommended that the medical practitioner should be one of the witnesses when the will is executed: *Kenward v Adams* (1975) *The Times*, November 29.

8 For a discussion of some of the practical difficulties which can arise when a person is physically incapable of signing a will, see the footnotes to Clause 26 at p 404 below.

PRECEDENTS

1 WILL LEAVING THE ENTIRE ESTATE TO THE SPOUSE, FAILING WHOM, TO THE CHILDREN

THIS IS THE LAST WILL of me (*full name of testator/testatrix*) of (*address*)

(1)   I REVOKE all my former wills and testamentary dispositions.

(2)   I WISH to be cremated.[1]

(3)   IF (she)/(he) survives me by [seven] days[2] I GIVE my estate to my (wife)/ (husband) (*full name*) AND APPOINT (her)/(him) to be the sole executor of this will, but if (she)/(he) does not so survive me, the following provisions will apply.

(4)   I APPOINT (*full name*) of (*address*) and (*full name*) of (*address*) ('my trustees') to be the executors and trustees of this will.

(5)   I GIVE my estate to my trustees on trust to:
    (a)   sell or postpone the sale for as long as they think fit;
    (b)   pay my debts, funeral and testamentary expenses; and
    (c)   hold what remains ('my residuary estate') as follows.

(6)   MY TRUSTEES will hold my residuary estate on trust for my children who survive me, and if more than one in equal shares.

(7)   IF any child of mine dies before me leaving a child or children living at my death, such child or children shall take, and if more than one in equal shares, on attaining the age of (18), the share of my residuary estate which his, her or their parent would have taken if he or she had survived me.

(8)   THE STANDARD PROVISIONS of the Society of Trust and Estate Practitioners (1st edition) apply to the trusts of my residuary estate.[3]

DATED (*date*)

SIGNED by (*full name of testator/ testatrix*) in our joint presence and then by us in (his)/(her) presence:

---

1 For more detailed funeral instructions, see Chapter 12.
2 See footnotes to Clause 1 at p 390 below.
3 See footnotes to Clause 24 at p 403 below.

2 WILL OF WIDOW: ONE HALF OF THE ESTATE TO HER LATE HUSBAND'S FAMILY AND THE OTHER HALF TO HER OWN FAMILY[1]

THIS IS THE LAST WILL of me (*full name*) of (*address*)

(1)   I REVOKE all my former wills and testamentary dispositions.

(2)   I WISH to be cremated.

(3)   I APPOINT (*full name*) of (*address*) and (*full name*) of (*address*) ('my trustees') to be the executors and trustees of this will.

(4)   I GIVE [the rest of][2] my estate to my trustees on trust to:
   (a)   sell or postpone the sale for as long as they think fit;
   (b)   pay my debts, funeral and testamentary expenses; and
   (c)   hold what remains ('my residuary estate') as follows.

(5)   MY TRUSTEES will divide my residuary estate into two equal shares, namely 'the (*late husband's surname*) Fund' and 'the (*testatrix's former surname*) Fund' and, if the trusts of either share completely fail, that share will accrue and be added to the other share and will be held on the trusts affecting it.

(6)   MY TRUSTEES will hold the (*late husband's surname*) Fund for my late husband's (children)/(brothers and sisters) [*or as the case may be*] namely (*full names*) who survive me, and if more than one in equal shares, but if any of them dies before me leaving a child or children living at my death, such child or children will take, and if more than one in equal shares [when they attain the age of (*age*)] the share of the (*late husband's surname*) Fund that his, her or their parent would have taken if he or she had survived me.

(7)   MY TRUSTEES will hold the (*testatrix's former surname*) Fund for my (children)/(brothers and sisters) [*or as the case may be*] namely (*full names*) who survive me, and if more than one in equal shares, but if any of them dies before me leaving a child or children living at my death such child or children will take, and if more than one in equal shares [when they attain the age of (*age*)] the share of the (*testatrix's former surname*) Fund that his, her or their parent would have taken if he or she had survived me.

(8)   (*Administrative provisions*)[3]

DATED (*date*)

SIGNED by (*full name of testatrix*) in our
joint presence and then by us in her presence:

---

1 This precedent could be appropriate in two situations: first, where the couple were childless and the wife leaves one-half of the estate to her side of the family and the other half to her late husband's side of the family; and, secondly, where the couple were married in later life and had no children of that marriage but either or both of them had children of a former marriage.

2 The words in brackets are only necessary if this clause has been preceded by legacies, etc.

3 For example: charging clause for trustee, if appropriate; exclusion of rules of apportionment; investment clause; powers of advancement, etc.

---

3 WILL OF WIDOW: EVERYTHING TO GO TO HER ONLY DAUGHTER

THIS IS THE LAST WILL of me (*full name*) of (*address*)

(1)   I REVOKE all my former wills and testamentary dispositions.

(2)   I WISH to be cremated.

(3)   I GIVE all my estate to my daughter (*full name*) AND I APPOINT her to be the sole executrix of this will, but if she dies before me the following provisions will apply.

(4)   I APPOINT (*full name*) of (*address*) and (*full name*) of (*address*) ('my trustees') to be the executors and trustees of this will.

(5)   I GIVE my estate to my trustees on trust to:
     (a)   sell or postpone the sale for as long as they think fit;
     (b)   pay my debts, funeral and testamentary expenses; and
     (c)   hold what remains ('my residuary estate') on the following trusts.

(6)   MY TRUSTEES will hold my residuary estate for my daughter's children who survive me and attain the age of (18) and if more than one in equal shares.

(7)   IF none of my daughter's children survives me and attains the age of (18), my trustees will hold my residuary estate for (my brothers and sisters) (*full names*) who survive me, and if more than one in equal shares, but if any of them die before me leaving a child or children living at my death such child or children will take, and if more than one in equal shares, the share of my residuary estate that his, her or their parent would have taken if he or she had survived me.

(8)   (*Administrative provisions*)

DATED (*date*)

SIGNED by (*full name*) in our joint
presence and then by us in her presence:

4 WILL OF MARRIED MAN WHOSE WIFE IS SUFFERING FROM DEMENTIA[1]

THIS IS THE LAST WILL of me (*full name*) of (*address*)

(1) I REVOKE all my former wills and testamentary dispositions.

(2) I WISH to be cremated.

(3) I APPOINT (*full name*) of (*address*) and (*full name*) of (*address*) ('my trustees') to be the executors and trustees of this will.

(4) I GIVE my estate to my trustees on trust to:
  (a) sell or postpone the sale for as long as they think fit;
  (b) pay my debts, funeral expenses and testamentary expenses; and
  (c) hold the residue ('my residuary estate') on the following trusts.

(5) DURING the lifetime of my wife (*full name*):
  (a) my trustees may apply the income of my residuary estate for the maintenance or benefit of such of the following people ('the beneficiaries'), namely my wife, children and grandchildren, as they in their absolute discretion decide;
  (b) my trustees have complete discretion as to how much of the income (if any at all) they apply for the maintenance or benefit of any one or more of the beneficiaries;
  (c) or during the period of 21 years from the date of my death (whichever is shorter), my trustees may accumulate any income which has not been applied for the maintenance or benefit of the beneficiaries and such accumulations may be added to the capital of my residuary estate;
  (d) my trustees may pay or apply any accumulations of income from past years as if those accumulations were the income of the present year;
  (e) (*Specific powers and administrative provisions, if any*).[2]

(6) AFTER the death of my wife my trustees shall hold my residuary estate for my children who survive me, and if more than one in equal shares, but if any of them predeceases me leaving a child or children living at my death such child or children shall take, and if more than one in equal shares, on attaining the age of (18), the share of my residuary estate that his, her or their parent would have taken if he or she had survived me.

(7) (*General administrative provisions*).[3]

DATED (*date*)

SIGNED by (*full name*)
in our joint presence and
then by us in his presence:

1 See, generally, the contributions by Gordon Ashton on 'Wills – Providing for Disabled Beneficiaries', in *Butterworths Wills, Probate and Administration Service* (looseleaf updated work) Division A1, and 'Incapacitated Beneficiaries', in *The Encyclopedia of Forms and Precedents* (5th edition, Butterworths, 1992) vol 42, Part 6.

2 For example: power to advance capital for specified purposes for the benefit of a person without capacity (Clause 19 below); or power to advance capital provided it does not jeopardise means-tested benefits (Clause 20 below); or power to raise capital to pay for the funeral of a person without capacity (Clause 21 below); or a charging clause authorising payment for professional services performed on behalf of a person without capacity (Clause 22 below).

3 For a precedent incorporating the Standard Provisions of the Society of Trusts and Estate Practitioners, see Precedent 24 at p 403 below.

5 WILL MAKING ALTERNATIVE PROVISION FOR THE TESTATOR'S WIDOW DEPENDING ON WHETHER SHE HAS THE CAPACITY TO MANAGE HER PROPERTY AND AFFAIRS AT THE TIME OF THE TESTATOR'S DEATH[1]

THIS IS THE LAST WILL of me *(full name)* of *(address)*

(1)　I REVOKE all my former wills and testamentary dispositions.

(2)　I WISH to be cremated.

(3)　IF at the time of my death my wife is capable of managing and administering her property and affairs, Schedule 1 will apply.

(4)　IF at the time of my death my wife is incapable, by reason of mental disorder, of managing and administering her property and affairs, Schedule 2 will apply.

(5)　IF my wife predeceases me, Schedule 3 will apply.

(6)　Schedule 4 will apply (in any event)/(to the trusts in Schedules 2 and 3).

(7)　IT will be presumed that my wife is capable of managing and administering her property and affairs unless at the time of my death:
　　(a)　a receiver [or manager][2] has been appointed by the Court of Protection to manage and administer her property and financial affairs; or
　　(b)　an enduring [or continuing][3] power of attorney created by her has been registered, and the Court of Protection is satisfied, after considering medical evidence, that she is without capacity to manage and administer her property and affairs.

SCHEDULE 1

I GIVE my estate to my wife absolutely AND I APPOINT her to be my sole executrix.

SCHEDULE 2

(1)   I APPOINT (*name*) of (*address*) and (*name*) of (*address*) ('my trustees') to be the executors and trustees of this will.

(*Set out the provisions which are to apply if the testator's wife is without capacity. Instead of paying or transferring assets to her receiver [manager], or attorney, the testator may prefer to create a discretionary trust or give the trustees power to pay or transfer the assets to the trustees of another settlement*)[4]

SCHEDULE 3

(1)   I APPOINT (*name*) of (*address*) and (*name*) of (*address*) ('my trustees') to be the executors and trustees of this will.

(*Set out the trusts which apply if the testator's wife predeceases him*).

SCHEDULE 4

(*Set out the trustees' powers and any other administrative provisions*)

DATED (*date*)

SIGNED by (*full name*) in our
joint presence and then by us
in his presence:

---

1 A similar format (for community care planning purposes) could be used to make alternative provision for the testator's widow depending on whether she is or would have been, but for any temporary absence, living in a residential care home or nursing home at the time of the testator's death.

2 In its report *Mental Incapacity* published on 1 March 1995 (Law Com No 231), the Law Commission has proposed that a newly constituted Court of Protection should have the power to appoint a 'manager' to be responsible for making decisions (including decisions concerning property and affairs) on behalf of a person without capacity to make such decisions: draft Mental Incapacity Bill, cl 24. Clause 23 of the draft Bill empowers the new Court of Protection to make a declaration on 'the capacity of a person to make a particular decision or decisions on particular matters'.

3 In its report *Mental Incapacity* (above), the Law Commission has proposed the repeal of the Enduring Powers of Attorney Act 1985 and the creation of a new type of power of attorney to be known as a 'continuing power of attorney'.

4 See, generally, the contributions by Gordon Ashton on 'Wills – Providing for Disabled Beneficiaries', Division A1 in *Butterworths Wills, Probate and Administration Service* (looseleaf updated work), and 'Incapacitated Beneficiaries', in *The Encyclopedia of Forms and Precedents* (5th edition, Butterworths, 1992), vol 42, Part 6. See also Precedent 4 at p 381 above.

6 WILL LEAVING THE RESIDUARY ESTATE TO CHARITIES[1]

THIS IS THE LAST WILL of me *(full name)* of *(address)*

(1) I REVOKE all my former wills and testamentary dispositions.

(2) I WISH to be cremated.

(3) I APPOINT *(full name)* of *(address)* and *(full name)* of *(address)* ('my trustees') to be the executors and trustees of this will.

(4) I GIVE my estate to my trustees on trust to:
  (a) sell or postpone the sale for as long as they think fit;
  (b) pay my debts, funeral and testamentary expenses; and
  (c) hold the residue ('my residuary estate') as follows.

(5) MY TRUSTEES will hold my residuary estate for the following charities in the following shares:[2]
  (a) *(percentage)* % for *(name of charity)* of *(registered address)* registered number *(number)*;
  (b) *(percentage)* % for *(name of charity)* of *(registered address)* registered number *(number)*;
  (c) *(percentage)* % for *(name of charity)* of *(registered address)* registered number *(number)*, etc.

 (6) (a) The receipt of the legacy officer, treasurer or any other authorised officer of the above charities will be a sufficient discharge to my trustees, who need not thereafter be concerned to see how the legacy is applied.[3]
  (b) Unless I have stated that the legacy should be used for a specific purpose, the legacy can be used for the general purposes of the charity.
  (c) If any of the charities has changed its name or amalgamated with another charity my trustees will give effect to the legacy by paying it to the charity in its changed name or to the charity with which it has amalgamated.
  (d) If any of the charities has ceased to exist before my death or never did exist in the first place,[4] my trustees will give effect to the legacy by paying it to any charity or charities of their choice whose objects appear to them most closely to fulfil the objects I had intended to benefit.

(7) *(Administrative provisions)*.[5]

DATED *(date)*

SIGNED by *(full name)*
in our joint presence and then
by us in (his)/(her) presence:

1 See, generally, *Williams on Wills* (6th edition, Butterworths, 1987), chapter 101, 'Charities'.

2 In *Re Recher's Will Trusts, National Westminster Bank Ltd v National Anti-Vivisection Society Ltd* [1971] 3 All ER 401, at p 412a, Brightman J said that it is a professional adviser's most elementary duty not only to get the name right but to confirm that the association is still in existence when the will is made and not to rely on possibly inaccurate information supplied by the client.

3 'The prudent conveyancer provides that the receipt of the treasurer or other proper officer of the recipient society for a legacy to the society shall be a sufficient discharge to executors. If it were not so, the executors could only get a valid discharge by obtaining a receipt from every member': *Leahy v Attorney-General for New South Wales* [1959] AC 457, at p 477, per Viscount Simonds.

4 See, generally, *Re Harwood* [1936] Ch 285.

5 Or, 'The Standard Provisions of the Society of Trust and Estate Practitioners (1st edition) shall apply': see Precedent 24 at p 403 below.

7 WILL OF MARRIED MAN: RESIDUE TO WIFE FOR LIFE, REDUCIBLE ON REMARRIAGE

THIS IS THE LAST WILL of me *(full name)* of *(address)*

(1)   I REVOKE all my former wills and testamentary dispositions.

(2)   I WISH to be cremated.

(3)   I APPOINT *(full name)* of *(address)* and *(full name)* of *(address)* ('my trustees') to be the executors and trustees of this will.

(4)   I GIVE all my personal chattels as defined by statute to my wife *(full name)* absolutely.

(5)   I GIVE the rest of my estate to my trustees on trust to:
(a)   sell or postpone the sale for as long as they think fit;
(b)   pay my debts, funeral and testamentary expenses; and
(c)   hold the residue ('my residuary estate') on the following trusts.

(6)   MY TRUSTEES will pay the income from my residuary estate to my wife until she remarries.

(7)   AFTER the remarriage of my wife my trustees will pay her (one-half) of the income of my residuary estate until her death.

(8)   SUBJECT to the above, my trustees will hold my residuary estate for my children who survive me, and if more than one in equal shares.

(9)   IF any of my children dies before me leaving a child or children living at my death, such child or children will take, and if more than one in equal shares, on attaining the age of (18), the share of my residuary estate that his, her or their parent would have taken if he or she had survived me.

(10)   (*Administrative provisions*).

DATED (*date*)

SIGNED by (*full name*)
in our joint presence and
then by us in his presence:

8 SECOND OR SUBSEQUENT MARRIAGE IN LATER LIFE: CONTRACT WAIVING SUCCESSION RIGHTS[1]

THIS MARRIAGE CONTRACT is made on..
BETWEEN 'the parties' (1)..
of..(*the man*)
and (2) ....
of..(*the woman*)

WHEREAS

1.   Recitals
1.1   The parties intend to marry each other on (*date*).
1.2   Both are domiciled in England and Wales.
1.3   Both have children from their former marriages.
1.4   Each wishes to ensure that after his or her death his or her children will inherit his or her estate, and that the surviving spouse will have no claim on the deceased spouse's estate.
1.5   Each has fully disclosed to the other full details of his or her present and anticipated income, earning capacity, property and other financial resources and his or her present and anticipated financial needs, obligations and responsibilities.[2]
1.6   Each has received independent legal advice on his or her rights and duties in the absence of this contract, and the way in which those rights and duties may be affected or extinguished by this contract.[3]
1.7   Each is entering into this contract freely and voluntarily, without pressure of any kind being exerted by the other or anyone else.[4]
1.8   Neither is exploiting a dominant position in order to secure an unreasonable advantage over the other.
1.9   They intend this contract to be legally binding on them to the fullest extent permissible under the laws of England and Wales.

NOW IT IS AGREED as follows:

2. Freedom of disposition

The parties acknowledge that each of them has the right to dispose freely of his or her estate whether by lifetime gifts, settlements, nominations or by testamentary dispositions in favour of such persons, at such times, and on such terms and conditions as he or she may think fit, without being under any obligation to make reasonable financial provision for the other party.[5]

3. No claims against the other's estate[6]

The parties covenant with each other that unless, because of an important change of circumstances which was either unforeseen or overlooked when this contract was made,[7] failure to apply to the court will result in severe hardship, the survivor of them will not:

3.1　apply to the court for financial provision from the deceased party's estate;

3.2　challenge the validity of the deceased party's will or any gift, settlement, nomination or other disposition made by the deceased party during his or her lifetime; or

3.3　challenge the validity and enforceability of this contract.

4. Savings

Nothing in this contract constitutes a waiver, surrender or release of the right of either party to:

4.1　receive assets from the other during their joint lives;

4.2　inherit under the other's will, or intestacy, or a combination of his or her will and intestacy;

4.3　any property which accrues to him or her by right of survivorship;

4.4　benefit financially in any other way as a result of the other's death;

4.5　disclaim any benefit arising on the other's death;

4.6　assign or enter into a deed of variation in respect of any benefit arising on the other's death.

5. Severability[8]

If the court finds that any provision of this contract is illegal, invalid or otherwise unenforceable, such provision may be severed from this contract without affecting any of the other provisions.

SIGNED as a deed by (*the man*)
and delivered in the presence of:

SIGNED as a deed by (*the woman*)
and delivered in the presence of:

1 The status of marriage contracts or antenuptial agreements in England and Wales is not entirely clear because no legislation directly governs their validity and enforceability. However, the position is probably clearer than is generally imagined. Matrimonial Causes Act 1973, s 25(1) imposes a duty on the court, when deciding whether and how to exercise its powers to make an order for ancillary relief in matrimonial proceedings, to have regard to 'all the circumstances of the case', including 'the conduct of each of the parties, if that conduct is such that it would in the opinion of the court be inequitable to disregard it': *ibid*, s 25(2)(g). In *Sabbagh v Sabbagh* [1985] FLR 29, at p 37, it was held that a marriage contract made in Brazil should be considered 'in all the circumstances of the case'. Similarly, the Inheritance (Provision for Family and Dependants) Act 1975, s 3(1)(g) requires the court to have regard to 'any other matter, including the conduct of the applicant or any other person, which in the circumstances of the case the court may consider relevant'. The decision of the Court of Appeal in *Edgar v Edgar* [1980] 3 All ER 887, although it concerned a separation agreement, would probably also apply to a marriage contract. Ormrod LJ held that the court would not enforce an agreement where there had been any of the following irregularities: 'undue pressure by one side; exploitation of a dominant position to secure an unreasonable advantage; inadequate knowledge; possibly, bad legal advice; or an important change of circumstances overlooked at the time of making the agreement'. He did not intend this list to be exhaustive, and went on to say that 'formal agreements, properly and fairly arrived at, with competent legal advice, should not be displaced unless there are good and substantial reasons for concluding that an injustice will be done by holding the parties to the terms of their agreement': [1980] 3 All ER 887, at p 893c. This precedent does not address the question of divorce and concentrates solely on succession rights. For a more detailed discussion, see Denzil Lush, 'Marriage Contracts and Older People', *EAGLE Journal*, vol 2, Issue 6, June/July 1994, pp 4–7.

2 Alexander Lindey, the American authority on antenuptial agreements, suggests that 'in order to protect the validity and enforceability of any agreement, complete disclosures of all material facts should be made. At a minimum, the disclosures should include the property, assets and expectancies of the respective parties, and their intentions and expectations regarding the relationship': *Lindey on Separation Agreements and Antenuptial Contracts* (Matthew Bender & Co Inc, New York, 1991), chapter 95-1.

3 In May 1991, The Law Society's Family Law Committee published a memorandum on *Maintenance and Capital Provision on Divorce* in which it recommended that legislation be introduced to make marriage contracts enforceable. At para 3.43, it recommended that 'marriage contracts should only be enforceable if the parties have both received independent legal advice before signing it. This advice could take the form of a financial planning package explaining the different methods available for owning property and the taxation implications etc'. Although nothing as yet has come of these proposals, the Committee's recommendations on independent legal advice can be regarded as a matter of current good practice.

4 See, generally, *Zamet v Hyman* [1961] 1 WLR 1442. Morris Zamet was a 79-year-old widower. Bluma Schonberg was a widow aged 71. Three days before their wedding in August 1955, Morris took Bluma to his solicitor's office where she signed an agreement relinquishing her rights under the Inheritance (Family Provision) Act 1938 and the Intestates' Estates Act 1952. In return, she would receive a lump sum of £600 on Morris's death. He died intestate in July 1958, leaving an estate of approximately £10,000. His children produced the marriage contract and submitted that Bluma's entitlement as the surviving spouse was limited to £600. The Court of Appeal held that the onus was on the children to prove that Bluma had fully understood the nature and effect of the transaction and that she had entered into the contract of her own free will. As they had failed to discharge this burden, the contract was not binding.

5 Inheritance (Provision for Family and Dependants) Act 1975, s 1(2)(a) provides that for a surviving spouse 'reasonable financial provision' means 'such financial provision as it would be reasonable in all the circumstances of the case for a husband or wife to receive, whether or not that provision is required for his or her maintenance'.

6 In *Hyman v Hyman* [1929] AC 601, at p 608, the Lord Chancellor, Lord Hailsham, held that parties cannot validly make an agreement '(1) not to invoke the jurisdiction of the court, or (2) to control the powers of the court when its jurisdiction is invoked'. If, as is usually the case, a marriage contract includes such terms, it should also contain a severability clause to prevent the entire agreement being declared null and void. See footnote 8 below.

7 In *Edgar v Edgar* [1980] 3 All ER 887, at p 893c, Ormrod LJ said that the court would not enforce an agreement where there had been 'an important change of circumstances, unforeseen or overlooked at the time of making the agreement'.

8 See footnote 6 above. 'The general rule is that, where you cannot sever the illegal from the legal part of a covenant, the contract is altogether void; but where you can sever them, whether the illegality be created by statute or by the common law, you may reject the bad part and retain the good': *Pickering v Ilfracombe Railway Co* [1868] LR 3 CP 235, at p 250, per Willes J. This is sometimes referred to as 'the blue pencil rule'.

CLAUSES

1 GENERAL SURVIVORSHIP CLAUSE[1]

ANYONE who does not survive me by (14 days)[2] will be deemed to have died before me for all the purposes of this will.

---

1 According to the Law Commission 'it is the current practice to incorporate a survivorship clause into wills': Law Commission Report No 187, *Distribution on Intestacy* (HMSO, 1989), para 57. The Scottish Law Commission, however, found that only about 8% of testators included such a provision, and that the usual survivorship period was one month: Scot Law Com No 124, *Report on Succession* (HMSO, 1990), p 64.
2 The Law Commission, *op cit*, para 57 states: 'We consider that an appropriate length for such a survivorship clause is 14 days. Any longer might lead to unacceptable delays in the administration of estates'. Sections 2-104 and 2-601 of the Uniform Probate Code (USA) provide for a survivorship period of 120 hours.

---

2 APPOINTMENT OF SOLICITORS' FIRM AS EXECUTORS AND TRUSTEES

(a) I APPOINT as the executors and trustees of this will the partners at the date of my death in the firm of solicitors known as (*name of firm*) of (*address*) or the firm which at that date has succeeded to and carries on its practice.[1]

(b) I EXPRESS the wish that two and only two such partners shall prove this will and act initially in its trusts.[2]

(c) THE following words have the following meanings:
  (i) 'firm' means an unincorporated partnership of solicitors or an incorporated practice recognised by The Law Society;[3]
  (ii) 'partners' includes solicitors who are the directors or members of or the beneficial owners of shares in an incorporated practice recognised by The Law Society;
  (iii) 'my trustees' means the executors and trustees of this will whether original, substituted or added.

(d) MY TRUSTEES may charge and be paid for all the work done by them or the firm in obtaining probate, administering my estate and acting as a trustee, including work which could have been done by a person who is not a solicitor.[4]

(e) I APPROVE the firm's current terms and conditions of business AND DECLARE that my trustees may be remunerated in accordance with the firm's scale of fees current at the date of my death as varied from time to time during the course of administering my estate and the trusts arising under this will.[5]

(f) ANY powers given to trustees (whether in this will or any codicil to it or by the general law) may be exercised by my trustees regardless of whether a grant of representation to my estate has been obtained or whether the administration of my estate has been finalised.

---

1 This subclause is loosely based on the form of appointment drafted by R.T. Oerton and approved by the court in *Re Horgan* [1969] 3 All ER 1570. See, generally, Mr Oerton's comments in *Butterworths Wills, Probate and Administration Service* (looseleaf), of which he is the editor, at A3024. For arrangements on the death of a sole practitioner, see The Law Society, *The Guide to the Professional Conduct of Solicitors* (6th edition, 1993), Principle 3.04.

2 There is no need for the non-proving executors to be named in the oath for executors: *Practice Direction* [1990] 2 All ER 576. Similarly, it is not necessary for notice to be given to them or the firm on their behalf: Non-Contentious Probate Rules 1987, r 27(1A), added by the Non-Contentious Probate (Amendment) Rules 1991.

3 See, generally, the Solicitors' Incorporated Practice Rules 1988, which appear in The Law Society, *The Guide to the Professional Conduct of Solicitors* (6th edition, 1993), pp 98–109.

4 The basic rule that a trustee should act without remuneration is part of the wider principle that trustees must not profit from their trust. Although a will or trust instrument may authorise the payment of remuneration to a trustee, such charging clauses are strictly construed, so if a solicitor–trustee is authorised to make 'professional charges', he will not be allowed to charge for time and trouble expended otherwise than in his position as a solicitor. Trustees may recover their legitimate out-of-pocket expenses, wherever their employment is justified, and the proper costs of litigation: Trustee Act 1925, s 30(2).

5 There is, as yet, no Practice Rule requiring solicitors to provide information about executorship and trusteeship costs, but a failure to provide such information could be construed as 'inadequate professional services' on the grounds that there has been a 'failure by the solicitor to advise the client or keep the client fully informed, or other lack of communication': see, generally, The Law Society, *The Guide to the Professional Conduct of Solicitors* (6th edition, 1993), p 745. In any event, it is good practice, and certainly good public relations, to supply costs information from the outset.

---

3 WISH THAT A PARTICULAR FIRM OF SOLICITORS SHOULD BE EMPLOYED[1]

I WISH my trustees[2] to employ (*name and address of firm*) as their solicitors.

---

1 'Executors appointed under a will are free to choose any solicitor to act in the administration, notwithstanding that the testator may have expressed a wish in the will that a particular firm be used. There is no duty imposed on the solicitor instructed to act to notify the firm named in the will': The Law Society, *The Guide to the Professional Conduct of Solicitors* (6th edition, 1993) Principle 12.10, Commentary 4.

2 It is assumed that the expression 'my trustees' has already been defined.

4 GIFT OF FAMILY PHOTOGRAPHS

(a) I GIVE free of tax all my photographs including moving pictures, prints, slides and negatives [and my photograph albums] to *(full name)* and *(full name)* to be divided between them as they agree.

(b) IF both of them wish to retain any photograph of which there is currently no copy I DIRECT my trustees to acquire a copy at the expense of my residuary estate and to distribute the original and the copy in such manner as they in their absolute discretion think fit.

(c) WITHOUT imposing any binding trust or legal obligation IT IS MY WISH that these photographs shall remain in the family.

5 GIFT OF CLOTHES, JEWELLERY, ETC[1]

I GIVE to (my daughter) *(full name)* free of tax [any of the following items that have not already been disposed of in this will or any codicil to it]:

(a)   my clothes, furs and footwear;

(b)   my jewellery including rings, necklaces, earrings, brooches, pendants, bracelets and watches;[2] and

(c)   other paraphernalia such as my bags, brushes, combs, mirrors, perfumes and scent bottles.

---

1 Although the traditional precedent – 'all my clothes, jewellery and items of personal use or adornment' – is perfectly adequate, it may be helpful to clarify the extent of the intended gift by the use of a more extensive definition. The definition of 'jewellery' is an adaptation of Precedent 29 on p 176 of D.T. Davies's excellent book *Will Precedents and Inheritance Tax* (4th edition, Butterworths, 1991).

2 In *Allen v Allen* (1729) Mos 112, it was held that a watch is not 'jewellery'.

---

6 DIRECTIONS REGARDING PETS[1]

I DIRECT my trustees within a period of (two months) from the date of my death:

(a)   to find a suitable home for any pet I own at the time of my death;

(b)   to pay in respect of each pet a legacy of £ ...... (free of tax) to the person (including any of my trustees) or charity acquiring the pet;

(c)   if they are unable to find a suitable home for any pet, to arrange for it to be put to sleep;

(d)   to pay from my residuary estate the expenditure they incur in carrying out these directions.

7 PECUNIARY LEGACY TO GRANDCHILDREN[1]

I GIVE the sum of £ .... free of tax to each of my grandchildren living at my death

[OR]

I GIVE the sum of £...... free of tax to be divided equally among my grandchildren living at my death

[and the receipt of the parent or guardian of any grandchild who is under the age of 18 will be a sufficient discharge to my trustees].[2]

1 Elderly people quite often leave a reasonably small, immediate legacy to their grandchildren, whether or not larger funds are held in trust for them until they reach a specified age. For many children, the loss of a grandparent is their first encounter with death and is quite a traumatic experience.

2 In the absence of any directions in the will authorising a parent to give a receipt on a minor's behalf, neither the minor nor his or her parents can give a valid receipt for a legacy without leave of the court. The personal representatives may, however, discharge themselves by: (a) exercising the power conferred on them by Administration of Estates Act 1925, s 42, and appointing trustees to hold the money or property for the minor; (b) exercising the power conferred on them by Administration of Estates Act 1925, s 41 (as amended) and appropriating any part of the deceased's property towards the minor's interest, although the consent of the parent, guardian or the court is required; or (c) paying the legacy into court: Trustee Act 1925, s 63, as amended by Administration of Justice Act 1965, s 36(4).

8 PECUNIARY LEGACY TO THE MANAGEMENT OR STAFF OF A RESIDENTIAL CARE HOME OR NURSING HOME[1]

I GIVE the sum of £ ...... free of tax to (*full name of owner or member of staff*) whether or not (he)/(she) is still (the owner of)/(employed at) (*name of residential care home or nursing home*) at the time of my death and whether or not I am still residing in that home at the time of my death.

1 *Home Life: A Code of Practice for Residential Care* (Centre for Policy on Ageing, 1984), para 2.6.1 states that: 'Adult residents should be encouraged tactfully, by their relatives or sponsors, to make a will prior to admission to the home. For those who do not do so, then information about where independent advice and assistance can be obtained should be made available, not only to the resident but, where necessary, to his relatives or sponsors as well. Because it is essential that the advice and assistance given is seen to be independent, it is important that residents are not referred, for instance, to the proprietor's own solicitor. Proprietors and staff should not, except in the most extreme emergency, act as witnesses to any resident's will. In no circumstances should the proprietor or any member of staff become an executor of a resident's will'. *Home Life*, para 2.6.2, considers gifts made during the resident's lifetime but is silent on the question of legacies given by residents to the proprietor or staff. The Law Society, *The Guide to the Professional Conduct of Solicitors* (6th edition, 1993) Principle 12.04 states, that 'a solicitor must not accept instructions where he or she suspects that those instructions have been given by a client under duress or undue influence'. Note also the Commentary to Principle 12.05, which suggests that 'when asked to prepare a will on the basis of written instructions alone, a solicitor should always consider carefully whether these are sufficient or whether the solicitor should see the client to discuss the instructions'.

9 GRANNY ANNEXE: ABSOLUTE GIFT OF THE ELDERLY PERSON'S INTEREST IN THE PROPERTY[1]

I GIVE [free of tax] to *(name(s))* my share of the proceeds of sale of property known as *(address)*.

1 In '"Living-in Relatives": Some Legal Consequences', *The Law Society's Gazette*, 14 September 1983, p 2203, Godfrey Gypps recommended that: 'careful thought should be given to the position on the parent's death. Unless a joint tenancy is created the parent's interest will pass into his or her estate whence, if there are other children, it may not pass solely to the couple unless the parent's will so provides. This has caused practical problems known to the writer where a couple have found themselves obliged to sell the home at an inconvenient time in order to put money into the estate for the benefit of other beneficiaries. The parent should be advised accordingly, and such arrangements as are appropriate made in the will, or perhaps the trust instrument, for the greater safety of the couple. It may be fair for the parent's share to pass to the couple and not to the other children, who will have been freed from anxiety over the parent by reason of the couple having had the inconvenience (as it would usually be) of having the parent live with them. The net effect should be that they take the parent's beneficial interest in the property as their share of the estate, or if not are given a sensible period of time to buy it out if they wish'.

10 GRANNY ANNEXE: RELEASE OF DEBT WHERE AN ELDERLY PERSON HAS LENT MONEY FOR THE PURCHASE OF A HOUSE OR THE CONSTRUCTION OF A GRANNY ANNEXE[1]

I LENT (*names of daughter and son-in-law, or as the case may be*) the sum of £ ...... to enable them to (buy)/(build an extension to) (*address*).

I RELEASE them or the survivor of them or their personal representatives [free of tax] from such part of that debt, including interest, as is still outstanding at the time of my death [BUT I DIRECT that the sum of money hereby released shall be brought into hotchpot when ascertaining their share of my residuary estate].

I DECLARE that any security for the debt will be discharged at the expense of my residuary estate.

---

1 Godfrey Gypps, in '"Living-in Relatives" Some Legal Consequences', *The Law Society's Gazette*, 14 September 1983, p 2203, refers to the situation in which an elderly parent has lent money to a couple with whom he or she lives to enable them to acquire or extend the residential property in which they all live. He makes the following observations: 'On the parent's death the balance outstanding of the loan will fall into his or her estate and pass to the beneficiaries thereunder. Consideration should be given to this when drafting the parent's will if there are other beneficiaries. A failure to do so might leave the couple in difficulties in raising money quickly to repay all or part of the loan. Depending upon the circumstances, a sensible course might be for the will to "forgive" the loan or direct the executors to accept repayment by affordable instalments over a period of time, or for the charge document to cater for the position on death to the same effect'.

11 GRANNY ANNEXE: DECLARATION THAT THE ELDERLY PERSON'S CONTRIBUTION WAS A GIFT, NOT A LOAN

I DECLARE for the avoidance of doubt that the money I paid for the construction of a granny (flat at)/(extension to) (*address*) was a gift to (*name(s) of owner(s) of the property*) and not a loan and that it does not have to be repaid to my estate [or brought into hotchpot when assessing the share of my residuary estate to which (he is)/(she is)/(they are) entitled].

12 GRANNY ANNEXE: OPTION TO PURCHASE THE ELDERLY PERSON'S INTEREST IN THE PROPERTY[1]

(1) IN (*year*) I paid £ ...... towards the construction of an extension to (*address*) ('the property') and [by a declaration of trust dated (*date*) the registered proprietor(s) (*name(s) of registered proprietor(s)*) declared that] I am entitled to (*percentage*) of the proceeds of sale of the property ('my share').

(2) I GIVE:
- (a) my share to my trustees on trust for sale; and
- (b) to (*registered proprietor(s)*) the option to purchase my share at the price and on the terms and conditions stated below.

(3) THE purchase price will be:
- (a) the sum that my share bears to the open market value of the whole of the property with vacant possession at the date of my death; LESS
- (b) (15)%.[2]

(4) FROM the date of my death:
- (a) within (4) weeks the property will be valued by a professionally qualified valuer appointed by my trustees;
- (b) within (8) weeks my trustees will give written notice of this option to (*registered proprietor(s)*);
- (c) within (12) weeks (*registered proprietor(s)*) will give written notice to my trustees of (his)/(her)/(their) intention to exercise this option; and
- (d) within (26) weeks (*registered proprietor(s)*) will complete the purchase of my share.[3]

(5) MY TRUSTEES have power:
- (a) to compromise on the purchase price if there is more than one valuation of the property and the valuations conflict;
- (b) to reduce or extend any of the above time-limits if, having regard to all the circumstances, they consider that it would be reasonable to do so;
- (c) to enforce their trust for sale at any time after the expiration of a period of (26) weeks from the date of my death.

(6) MY RESIDUARY ESTATE will pay:
- (a) the costs of any valuation obtained by my trustees;
- (b) the legal costs and disbursements of transferring my share to (*registered proprietor(s)*) including the legal costs and disbursements reasonably incurred by (*registered proprietor(s)*);
- (c) any inheritance tax payable because the purchase price is less than the open market value.

(7) THIS OPTION:
- (a) is personal to (*registered proprietor(s)*) and may not be exercised by anyone else;
- (b) may be exercised by (*registered proprietor(s)*) even though ((he)/(she) is one of my trustees)/(they are my trustees);
- (c) will lapse if it has not been exercised within (12) weeks from my death or such later period as my trustees consider reasonable having regard to all the circumstances.

(8) SUBJECT to the above my trustees will hold my share [as part of my residuary estate].

1 In '"Living-in Relatives": Some Legal Consequences', *The Law Society's Gazette*, 14 September 1983, p 2203, Godfrey Gypps discusses the effect of the parent's death in the context of a granny annexe arrangement. He suggests that 'it may be fair for the parent's share to pass to the couple and not to other children, who will have been freed from anxiety over the parent by reason of the couple having had the inconvenience (as it would usually be) of having the parent living with them. The net effect should be that they take the parent's beneficial interest in the property as their share of the estate, or if not they are given a sensible period of time to buy it out if they wish'.

2 In *Wight v CIR Lands Tribunal* (1982) 264 EG 935, it was held that for capital transfer tax purposes the discount for joint ownership of residential property held by beneficial tenants in common in equal shares should be 15% rather than the 10% which had been customary since the earlier decision in *Cust v CIR* (1917) 91 EG 11. The method of valuing a share of jointly owned property was considered by the Court of Appeal – for income support purposes, although possibly the decision would also apply to local authority community care funding – in *Chief Adjudication Officer v Palfrey and Others* (judgments handed down on 8 February 1995).

3 If desired, provision could be made that the co-owner will not be required to complete the purchase until his or her share of the testator's residuary estate had been distributed.

13 HOUSE SETTLED ON WIDOW(ER) FOR LIFE UNDER THE SETTLED LAND ACT 1925[1]

(1) I APPOINT my trustees[2] to be trustees for the purpose of the Settled Land Act 1925.

(2) I GIVE my property known as (*address*) or failing which the property that is my principal residence at the time of my death ('the property') to my (husband)/(wife) (*full name of spouse*) for (his)/(her) life.

(3) MY (husband)/(wife) will be responsible for:
(a) paying all the outgoings on the property;
(b) keeping the property in reasonable repair, decoration and condition;[3]
(c) keeping the property insured to its full reinstatement value with an insurance company of which my trustees approve; and
(d) complying with the covenants and conditions to which the property is subject.

(4) CAPITAL money may be invested or applied (with my trustees' consent) in any investment authorised by my will in respect of my residuary estate, including the purchase of land outside England and Wales.[4]

(5) AFTER the death of my (husband)/(wife) I GIVE the property or the capital representing it to (*full names*).

1 This clause may be considered appropriate where the testator or testatrix wishes to give the surviving spouse a life interest, but is anxious to ensure that the survivor will not be at the mercy of trustees for sale. As tenant for life, the surviving spouse has all the powers of trustees for sale and can direct the application of the proceeds of sale towards the purchase of another property.

2 It is assumed that the expression 'my trustees' has already been defined.

3 See *Re Cartwright* (1889) 41 ChD 532.

4 'Capital money . . . shall not be applied in the purchase of land out of England and Wales unless the settlement expressly authorises the same': Settled Land Act 1925, s 73(2).

14 LIFE INTEREST IN (A SHARE OF) A HOUSE AND ITS PROCEEDS OF SALE[1]

(1) I GIVE my [share of the] property known as (*address*) or failing which my principal residence at the time of death[2] to my trustees on trust for sale.

(2) ANY residential property subject to these trusts is referred to as 'the property', and the property and any cash or investments representing it are referred to as 'the property fund'.

(3) MY TRUSTEES may invest the property fund in whatever investments they think fit and may purchase and improve any replacement property or a share in any replacement property for (*name*) to live in.[3]

(4) DURING my (husband's)/(wife's) (lifetime)/(widowhood) my trustees will permit (him)/(her) to live in the property rent-free provided that (he)/(she):
(a) pays the outgoings;
(b) keeps it in reasonable repair and condition;
(c) keeps it insured to its full reinstatement value; and
(d) complies with the covenants and conditions to which it is subject.

(5) DURING my (husband's)/(wife's) (lifetime)/(widowhood) my trustees will pay (him)/(her) the income from the property fund.

(6) AFTER the (death)/(remarriage) of my (husband)/(wife) my trustees will hold the property fund for (*names*).

1 This precedent gives the beneficiary a life interest in a fund which may or may not include a dwelling-house in which the beneficiary has residence rights. It assumes that the life-tenant is the surviving spouse, and prima facie there should be no inheritance tax payable on the testator's death in respect of this gift. Consideration will need to be given to any mortgage or charge on the property. It is considered preferable not to deal with the contents of the house in a clause of this nature, but to deal with them separately.

2 This wording is designed to overcome the problem of abatement.

3 On its own, a power to invest does not authorise the trustees to acquire residential property for the occupation of the testator's family. Because the property produces no income it is not an investment: *Re Power* [1947] Ch 572. The Law Reform Committee, at para 3.5 of its 23rd Report, Cmnd 8733 (HMSO, 1982), on the powers and duties of trustees, suggested that 'legislation is required to reverse the decision in *Re Power*'.

15 TRUSTEES TO GRANT A LEASE OF THE TESTATOR'S HOUSE TO THE SURVIVING SPOUSE[1]

(1) I GIVE my property known as (*address*) or failing which my principal residence at the time of my death ('the property') to my trustees on trust to grant a lease of the property to my (wife)/(husband) at a nominal rent.

(2) THE LEASE shall be for such a term of years and shall contain such terms and conditions as my trustees shall in their absolute discretion think fit.

(3) SUBJECT to the above my trustees shall transfer the property subject to the lease to my (daughter)/(son) (*name*).

---

1 Although this clause may be advantageous for community care planning purposes, the inheritance tax consequences are unclear.

---

16 GIFTS MADE AFTER THE DATE OF THE WILL ARE TO BE BROUGHT INTO ACCOUNT[1]

(1) When calculating the share of my residuary estate to which any beneficiary is entitled he or she shall bring into account every gift of money or property I have made to him or her since (*the date of this will, or as the case may be*) which exceeded £ ...... in value at the time of the gift.

(2) The figure to be brought into account shall be the value of the money or property at the time of the gift rather than (i) the extent to which it exceeded £ ...... at that time, or (ii) its value immediately before my death, or (iii) its value immediately before the date on which my residuary estate is distributed.

---

1 The purpose of this clause is to equalise the benefits which the testator's children receive during his lifetime and those conferred on them by the will. See, generally, the chapter on hotchpot clauses in *Williams on Wills* (6th edition, Butterworths, 1987), chapter 99.

---

17 SECOND OR SUBSEQUENT MARRIAGE IN LATER LIFE: THE SLICE SYSTEM

(1) MY TRUSTEES will pay or transfer to my wife (*name*) absolutely:
(a) (75)% of the first (£100,000) of my residuary estate; and
(b) (25)% of my residuary estate so far as it exceeds (£100,000).

(2) SUBJECT to the above my trustees will hold the remainder of my residuary estate on trust to pay the income from it to my wife during her lifetime.

(3)   AFTER the death of my wife my trustees will hold the remainder of my residuary estate (both the capital and income) for my children (*names*) who survive me and if more than one in equal shares.

18 SECOND OR SUBSEQUENT MARRIAGE IN LATER LIFE: PROVISION FOR SPOUSE ACCORDING TO THE DURATION OF THE MARRIAGE

(1)   MY TRUSTEES will pay or transfer to my wife absolutely (5)% of my residuary estate for each complete year that has elapsed between the date of our marriage, namely (*date*), and the date of my death [up to a maximum of (50)% of my residuary estate].

(2)   SUBJECT to the above my trustees will hold my residuary estate on trust to pay the income from it to my wife during her lifetime.

(3)   AFTER the death of my wife my trustees will hold the capital and income of my residuary estate on trust for my children (*names*) who survive me and if more than one in equal shares.

(4)   IF any child of mine dies before me leaving a child or children living at my death, such child or children shall take, and if more than one in equal shares [on attaining the age of (18)], the share of my residuary estate that his, her or their parent would have taken if he or she had survived me.

19 POWER TO ADVANCE CAPITAL FOR SPECIFIED PURPOSES FOR THE BENEFIT OF A PERSON WITHOUT CAPACITY[1]

My trustees may raise capital from my residuary estate and apply it for the benefit of (*person without capacity*) in such manner, at such times and on such terms and conditions as they think fit, and without prejudice to the generality of the foregoing they may raise and apply capital for the purpose of:

(a)   altering or adapting any residential accommodation in which (*person without capacity*) normally resides or is likely to reside;

(b)   purchasing or hiring aids and appliances for (*person without capacity*) or the persons with whom (he)/(she) resides;

(c)   providing domestic assistance for (*person without capacity*) or the person or persons with whom (he)/(she) resides;

(d)   providing transport, including the purchase of any vehicle, appropriate to (his)/(her) needs;

(e)   paying for holidays for (*person without capacity*) and any person accompanying (him)/(her) on holiday;

(f)   paying for holidays for any person who cares for (*person without capacity*) on a day-to-day basis.

1 See, generally, the contributions by Gordon Ashton on 'Wills – Providing for Disabled Beneficiaries' in *Butterworths Wills, Probate and Administration Service*, Division A1, and 'Incapacitated Beneficiaries', in *The Encyclopaedia of Forms and Precedents* (5th edition, Butterworths, 1992), vol 42, Part 6.

20 POWER TO ADVANCE CAPITAL PROVIDED IT DOES NOT JEOPARDISE MEANS-TESTED BENEFITS[1]

My trustees may from time to time raise capital from my residuary estate and pay it to or apply it for the benefit of (*name*) in such manner as they in their absolute discretion think fit, provided that any capital sum they raise shall not for the time being cause or result in a loss to (*name*) of State benefits or local authority funding.

[*OR*]

My trustees may from time to time raise capital from my residuary estate and apply it for the benefit of (*name*) by paying for goods or services which are not otherwise provided by the National Health Service, State benefits or local authority funding.

1 Care should be taken when giving trustees a discretionary power to advance capital to a beneficiary, as the existence of such a power could jeopardise the beneficiary's entitlement to local authority funding or income-related benefits. See, generally, the section contributed by Gordon Ashton in *Butterworths Wills, Probate and Administration Service*, at para A1/511.

21 POWER TO RAISE CAPITAL TO PAY FOR THE FUNERAL OF A PERSON WITHOUT CAPACITY[1]

My trustees may during (*name's*) lifetime[2] or as soon as practicable after (his)/(her) death pay from the capital [or income] of my residuary estate such sum as they in their absolute discretion think fit towards the cost of (his)/(her) funeral.

1 Where a testator has left his estate in trust for an incapacitated beneficiary, it may be useful to extend the trustees' discretionary powers to enable them to raise capital to meet the costs of the beneficiary's funeral. See, generally, Division A1, edited by Gordon Ashton, in *Butterworths Wills, Probate and Administration Service*.

2 For pre-paid funeral plans, see Chapter 12 at p 346 above.

22 CHARGING CLAUSE AUTHORISING PAYMENT FOR PROFESSIONAL SERVICES CARRIED OUT ON BEHALF OF A PERSON WITHOUT CAPACITY[1]

I DIRECT my trustees to visit (*person without capacity*) from time to time as occasion requires; to make any enquiries or arrangements they consider necessary or expedient for (his)/(her) welfare; to employ any other suitable person to make such visits, enquiries and arrangements; and to charge and be paid for these services out of the capital of my residuary estate.

---

1 The basic rule that a trustee should act without remuneration is part of the wider principle that trustees must not profit from their trust. Although a will or trust instrument may authorise the payment of remuneration to a trustee, such charging clauses are strictly construed, so if a solicitor–trustee is authorised to make 'professional charges', he will not be allowed to charge for time and trouble expended otherwise than in his position as a solicitor. Trustees may recover their legitimate out-of-pocket expenses wherever their employment is justified and the proper costs of litigation: Trustee Act 1925, s 30(2). This precedent assumes that there is a discretionary or life-interest trust for the benefit of a person without capacity, and authorises a professional trustee to visit the beneficiary from time to time and to make any arrangements necessary for the beneficiary's welfare.

---

23 CLAUSE AUTHORISING A RECEIPT TO BE GIVEN ON BEHALF OF A PERSON WITHOUT CAPACITY[1]

Any payment which would otherwise be made to a person without capacity may be made to his or her attorney or receiver [or any person authorised by the Court of Protection or the Public Trustee to receive such payment].[2]

Any payment [not exceeding £1000] which would otherwise be made to a person without capacity for whom nobody has been formally appointed to act may be made to any person who my trustees reasonably believe is acting on behalf of and in the best interests of the person without capacity.[3]

The receipt of the person receiving the payment shall be a sufficient discharge to my trustees who shall not afterwards be concerned to see how it is applied.

---

1 This clause is based loosely on the recommendations of the Law Commission that there should be: (a) a general authority to act reasonably and in the best interests of a person without capacity; and (b) a scheme enabling payments which would otherwise be made to a person without capacity to be made instead to a person acting on his or her behalf: Law Commission Report No 231, *Mental Incapacity* (HMSO, 1995), Part IV.

2 For example, a person authorised by a short order or direction given under the Court of Protection Rules 1994 (SI 1994/3046) (see p 275 above).

3 It is suggested that in the receipt itself, any such recipient should, inter alia, state that he or she: (a) understands the obligation to apply the money in the best interests of the person without capacity; (b) is aware that civil or criminal liability may be incurred if the money is misapplied; and (c) is not aware of any other person who has authority to receive the money: Law Commission, *op cit*, para 4.16.

24 INCORPORATION OF STANDARD ADMINISTRATIVE PROVISIONS

The standard provisions of the Society of Trust and Estate Practitioners (1st edition) apply.[1]

1 The Society of Trust and Estate Practitioners was launched in 1991, and its standard provisions (1st edition) were published by Sweet & Maxwell in November 1992. The Society's aim is to incorporate these administrative provisions in wills and settlements in order to simplify and shorten the documents. The standard provisions are in plain English and can be understood by the layman with comparative ease. A copy of the standard provisions with a commentary should be supplied to and approved by the testator or testatrix before he or she executes the will.

25 STATEMENT EXPLAINING WHY THE TESTATOR HAS NOT MADE (GREATER) PROVISION FOR THE SURVIVING SPOUSE[1]

I HAVE NOT MADE (any)/(greater) provision in my will for my (wife)/ (husband) (*name of spouse*) because:

- We were married on (*date*).[2] Ours is my (second)/(subsequent) marriage and my (wife's)/(husband's) (second)/(subsequent) marriage. Each of us has children by a former marriage. When we married we agreed that each of us would leave his or her estate to our respective children [and that neither of us would pursue any claim against the other's estate].[3]
- I am satisfied that (he)/(she) has adequate resources to enable (him)/(her) to live comfortably for the rest of (his)/(her) life.
- If I had left my estate to (him)/(her) absolutely my family might be disinherited and (his)/(her) family might be unfairly enriched.
- I consider that I have already made reasonable provision for (him)/(her) during my lifetime.
- The property we hold as joint tenants will automatically pass to (him)/(her) by right of survivorship.
- I inherited most of my assets from my former (husband)/(wife) and it was (his)/ (her) wish that on my death such assets should pass to our children.

1 When a testator or testatrix does not make reasonable financial provision for a person who could apply to the court for an order under the Inheritance (Provision for Family and Dependants) Act 1975, he or she should be invited to make a written statement explaining the reasons why. In some cases, it may be advisable not to include such a statement in the will itself, because when representation is granted the will becomes a document of public record: see *Re Hall's Estate* [1943] 2 All ER 159.

Inheritance (Family Provision) Act 1938, s 1(7), now repealed, required the court to 'have regard to the deceased's reasons, so far as ascertainable, for making the disposition made by his will, if any, or from refraining from disposing by will of his estate or part of his estate, or for not making any provision, or any further provision, as the case may be, for a dependant'. The Inheritance (Provision for Family and Dependants) Act 1975 does not specifically require the court to consider the deceased's reasons, although they could be considered under s 3(1)(g) which provides that the court shall have regard to 'any other matter, including the conduct of the applicant or any other person, which in the circumstances of the case the court may consider relevant'.

Section 21 of the 1975 Act says that: 'In any proceedings under this Act a statement made by the deceased, whether orally or in a document or otherwise, shall be admissible under section 2 of the Civil Evidence Act 1968 as evidence of any fact stated therein in the like manner as if the statement were a statement falling within section 2(1) of that Act; and any reference in that Act to a statement admissible, or given or proposed to be given, in evidence under section 2 thereof or to the admissibility or the giving in evidence of a statement by virtue of that section or to any statement falling within section 2(1) of that Act shall be construed accordingly'.

2 Inheritance (Provision for Family and Dependants) Act 1975, s 3(2)(a) requires the court to have regard to 'the age of the applicant and the duration of the marriage'.

3 In *Hyman v Hyman* [1929] AC 601, at p 608, Lord Hailsham LC held that parties cannot validly make an agreement '(1) not to invoke the jurisdiction of the court, or (2) to control the powers of the court when its jurisdiction is invoked'. In *Zamet v Hyman* [1961] 1 WLR 1442, the question whether parties can 'contract out' of the family provision legislation was left open. See, generally, the footnotes to Precedent 8 at pp 388–389 above.

---

26 ATTESTATION CLAUSE WHERE THE TESTATOR IS PHYSICALLY INCAPABLE OF SIGNING[1]

The (testator)/(testatrix) is unable to write because (he)/(she) is suffering from (*disability*).[2] This will was read (by)/(to) the (testator)/(testatrix), who confirmed that (he)/(she) fully knew, understood and approved its contents,[3] and then signed by (*name of person signing*) in the (testator's)/(testatrix's) presence and by (his)/(her) direction[4] and in our presence, and by us in the presence of the (testator)/(testatrix), (*name of person signing*), and each other.

---

1 If the testator is suffering from an illness which restricts him to looking in one direction, care must be taken to ensure that the person signing the will on his behalf and the two witnesses are within the testator's line of vision, otherwise it may be difficult to establish that they were in his presence: *In the Goods of Killick* (1864) 3 Swab & Trist; *Brown v Skirrow* [1902] P 3. A person may be mentally present despite the administration of a drug such as morphia: *Re Chalcraft* [1948] 1 All ER 700.

2 Note that, provided the testator satisfies the criteria for financial eligibility, Green Form Legal Aid is available for making a will for a person suffering from a disability: Legal Advice and Assistance (Scope) Regulations 1989 (SI 1989/550), reg 4. See, generally, the section on legal aid at p 376 above.

3 The presumption that a testator knows and approves the contents of his will does not apply where another person signs the will on his behalf and at his direction. Rule 13 of the Non-Contentious Probate Rules 1987 (SI 1987/2024) provides that 'before admitting to proof a will which appears to have been signed by a blind or illiterate testator or by another person by direction of the testator, or which for any other reason raises doubt as to the testator having had knowledge of the contents of the will at the time of its execution, the registrar shall satisfy himself that the testator had such knowledge'. Rule 16 provides that 'a registrar may require an affidavit from any person he may think fit for the purpose of satisfying himself as to any of the matters referred to in [rule 13] and in any such affidavit sworn by an attesting witness or other person present at the time of the execution of a will the deponent shall depose as to the manner in which the will was executed'. For a recommended procedure for dealing with dysphasic patients, see Dr Pam Enderby, 'The Testamentary Capacity of Dysphasic Patients' (1994) *Medico-Legal Journal*, vol 62, Part 2, p 70, at pp 79–80.

4 'No will shall be valid unless —
  (a) it is in writing, and signed by the testator, or by some other person in his presence and by his direction; and
  (b) it appears that the testator intended by his signature to give effect to the will; and
  (c) the signature is made or acknowledged by the testator in the presence of two or more witnesses present at the same time; and
  (d) each witness either:
    (i) attests and signs the will; or
    (ii) acknowledges his signature in the presence of the testator (but not necessarily in the presence of any other witness), but no form of attestation shall be necessary.'

(Wills Act 1837, s 9, as substituted by the Administration of Justice Act 1982, s 17).

---

27 ATTESTATION CLAUSE WHERE THE TESTATOR IS BLIND OR PARTIALLY SIGHTED[1]

The (testator)/(testatrix) is (blind)/(partially sighted).[2]

This will was read to (him)/(her) by (*name of person reading*) in our presence.

The (testator)/(testatrix) confirmed that (he)/(she) knew and approved its contents.[3]

It was then signed by the (testator)/(testatrix) in our presence[4] and subsequently by us in (his)/(her) presence.

[OR]

It was then signed in by (*name of person signing*) in our presence and in the presence and by the direction of the (testator)/(testatrix), and subsequently by us in the presence of the (testator)/(testatrix), (*name of person signing*) and each other.

1 The Royal National Institute for the Blind (RNIB) produces a guide for professional advisers on *Will-making for Blind People*. It suggests that solicitors can do a great deal to help visually impaired people by producing documents which are clear and easy to read. For example:
- Use a larger than average type size whenever possible: 14-point or 16-point are ideal.
- Use a plain typeface such as Helvetica or Univers.
- Medium or bold type is better for people with poor sight, and ensures that photocopies are clear.
- Never print text in capital letters. They are difficult to read even if your vision is normal.
- Solid blocks of text are particularly daunting for visually impaired readers. Use short paragraphs wherever possible, and put extra spacing between lines of type and between paragraphs.

Although it would be perfectly legal, the RNIB does not recommend a will in braille, as it could so easily be altered and the meaning changed. If, however, a client would like a braille copy or draft of his or her will, the RNIB can arrange it.

2 Note that, provided the testator satisfies the criteria for financial eligibility, Green Form Legal Aid is available for making a will for a person who is blind or partially sighted: Legal Advice and Assistance (Scope) Regulations 1989 (SI 1989/550), reg 4. See, generally, the section on legal aid at p 376 above.

3 Rule 13 of the Non-Contentious Probate Rules 1987 (SI 1987/2024) (L 10)) states that 'before admitting to proof a will which appears to have been signed by a blind or illiterate testator or by another person by direction of the testator, or which for any other reason raises doubt as to the testator having had knowledge of the contents of the will at the time of its execution, the registrar shall satisfy himself that the testator had such knowledge'.

4 A blind person cannot witness a will, even though it is executed by the testator in his or her presence. ' "Witness" means in regard to things audible, one who has the faculty of hearing, and in regard to things visible, one who has the faculty of seeing. The signing of a will is a visible matter. Therefore I think that a will is not signed "in the presence of" a blind person, nor is a blind person a witness for the purposes of [Wills Act 1837, s 9]': *In the Estate of Charles Gibson (Deceased)* [1949] P 434, at p 437, per Pearce J.

28 MEMORANDUM OF WISHES WHERE A BENEFICIARY UNDER A DISCRETIONARY TRUST IS IN RECEIPT OF INCOME SUPPORT[1]

To the trustees of my will dated (*date*)

MEMORANDUM OF WISHES

My daughter (*name*) is currently receiving income support.

If I left [a share of] my residuary estate to her absolutely, her capital would exceed the prescribed limit (currently £8000) and she would no longer be entitled to income support.[2] So, instead, I have left [her share of] my estate to you to hold on a discretionary trust for her benefit.[3]

Although you have an unfettered discretion as to how her legacy should be applied, it is my wish that, if she is still in receipt of income-related benefits at the time of my death, you should consider how the legacy can be applied to her best advantage without affecting her entitlement to benefit.[4]

SIGNED *(testator's signature)*

DATE *(date)*

---

1 Although this precedent relates specifically to income support, the same principle would apply in respect of other income-related benefits, for example family credit, disability working allowance, housing benefit and council tax benefit.

2 Social Security Contributions and Benefits Act 1992, s 134(1); Income Support (General) Regulations 1987 (SI 1987/1967), reg 45.

3 For a discussion about the treatment of discretionary trusts for income support purposes, see, generally, the footnotes to regs 42 and 46 of the Income Support (General) Regulations 1987 (SI 1987/1967) in the current issue of John Mesher and Penny Wood, *Income Related Benefits: The Legislation* (Sweet & Maxwell, annual).

4 For example, acquiring assets which are disregarded under Sch 10 to the Income Support (General) Regulations 1987 (SI 1987/1967).

CHAPTER 14: STATUTORY WILLS

INDEX

Text

Case examples

Checklists

Precedents

STATUTORY WILLS

TEXT

The jurisdiction

A *statutory will*[1] is a will executed by an *authorised person*[2] on behalf of a *patient*[3] pursuant to an order of the Court of Protection. The court acquired this jurisdiction in 1969;[4] a logical extension of the powers it had been granted in 1925 to order the settlement of a patient's property during his or her lifetime.[5] Before 1970, the court was often asked to order the execution of a revocable settlement under which the patient took a life interest, in order to fill the lacuna caused by the inability of the patient to execute a will.[6] The statutory will jurisdiction is exercised in the first instance by the Master or an assistant master, with a right of appeal to a judge of the Chancery Division.[7]

The legislation governing the making of statutory wills can be found in the Mental Health Act 1983. Section 96 contains the empowering provisions, and s 97 contains a number of supplementary provisions. Section 96 provides:

> '(1) . . . the judge shall have power to make such orders or give such directions or authorities for—
>
> . . .
>
> (e) the execution for the patient of a will making any provision (whether by way of disposing of property or exercising a power or otherwise) which could be made by a will executed by the patient if he were not mentally disordered;
>
> . . .
>
> (4) The power of the judge to make or give an order, direction or authority for the execution of a will for a patient—
> (a) shall not be exercisable at any time when the patient is a minor, and
> (b) shall not be exercised unless the judge has reason to believe that the patient is incapable of making a valid will for himself.'

The law, practice and procedure relating to statutory wills can be found in:

- Part VII of the Mental Health Act 1983;[8]
- the Court of Protection Rules 1994;[9]
- PN9 and PN9A, the two Procedure Notes issued by the Court of Protection;[10]
- Practice Directions;[11]
- reported decisions;[12]
- Heywood & Massey's *Court of Protection Practice*;[13] and
- Atkin's *Court Forms*.[14]

The decisions summarised later on in this chapter illustrate some of the reasons why it may be advisable to apply to the court for an order authorising the execution of a statutory will:

- marriage, or any other major change in the patient's status or circumstances;[15]
- ademption of a legacy in the patient's existing will;[16]
- any major change in the personal circumstances of the beneficiaries, or any major change in the patient's relationship with them;[17]
- where the patient's existing will, or the law relating to intestacy, fails to make provision for a person or organisation for whom the patient 'might be expected to provide' if he or she were not mentally disordered;[18] and
- tax planning. The right of everyone 'if he can, to arrange his affairs so that the tax attaching under the appropriate Acts is less than it otherwise would be'[19] is not confined to those who are mentally capable of arranging their affairs in the most tax-efficient manner. Indeed, one of the principal reasons for conferring the statutory will jurisdiction on the court in the first place was to facilitate tax planning, even though such an exercise is not directly for the benefit of the patient but for the greater advantage of his or her family.[20]

The Court of Protection makes approximately 250 orders for the execution of a statutory will each year, half of which are made without an attended hearing.

---

1 The term 'statutory will' is colloquial and is not found in either the Mental Health Act 1983 or the Court of Protection Rules 1994.

2 Mental Health Act 1983, s 97(1).

3 *Ibid*, s 94(2) defines 'patient' as a person who is 'incapable, by reason of mental disorder, of managing and administering his property and affairs'. For a detailed discussion of the meaning of this definition, see 'Capacity to manage and administer one's property and affairs', at p 48 above.

4 Administration of Justice Act 1969, s 17.

5 Law of Property Act 1925, s 171.

6 See, generally, Christopher Sherrin, 'Statutory Wills Under the Mental Health Act 1959' [1984] Fam Law 135–138.

7 Mental Health Act 1983, s 105(1).

8 Part VII of the Act comprises ss 93–113 inclusive. The sections most pertinent to statutory wills are ss 96 and 97.

9 SI 1994/3046.

10 PN9A was originally issued in November 1987 in response to applications for the execution of a statutory will on behalf of the donor of a registered enduring power of attorney.

11 For example, the Practice Direction issued by the Master on 15 August 1984: [1984] 1 WLR 1171, [1984] 3 All ER 128.

12 See 'The patient' at p 413 below.

13 12th edition, 1991, pp 191–196 and 445–446.

14 2nd edition, vol 26 (1992 issue) on Mental Health. See, in particular, paras 71–73 and Forms 150–153.

15 As in *Re Davey (Deceased)* [1981] 1 WLR 164. See the summary of this case at p 423 below.

16 As in *Re D(J)* [1982] Ch 237, [1982] 2 WLR 373. See the summary of this case at p 424 below.

17 As in *Re HMF* [1976] Ch 33, [1975] 3 WLR 395, where the patient began to take a renewed interest in her two nephews with whom she had previously lost contact. See the summary of this case at p 423 below.

18 As in *Re C (Spinster and Mental Patient)* [1991] 3 All ER 866. See the summary of this case at p 425 below.

19 *IRC v Duke of Westminster* [1936] AC 1, per Lord Tomlin.

20 Christopher Sherrin, *op cit*, p 135.

The patient[1]

The Court of Protection can only order the execution of a statutory will on behalf of someone who is:

- aged 18 or over;[2] and
- suffering from mental disorder;[3] and
- incapable, by reason of mental disorder, of managing and administering his or her property and affairs;[4] and
- incapable of making a valid will for himself or herself.[5]

The court can order the execution of a statutory will on behalf of the donor of an enduring power of attorney, provided that he or she satisfies the above criteria.[6] The court can also order the execution of a statutory will on behalf of someone who has neither a receiver nor an attorney, provided that he or she satisfies the above criteria.

---

1 A 'patient' is a person whom a judge, after considering medical evidence, considers to be 'incapable, by reason of mental disorder, of managing and administering his property and affairs': Mental Health Act 1983, s 94(2).

2 Mental Health Act 1983, s 96(4)(a). The court can, however, order the settlement of property belonging to a patient who is a minor: *ibid*, s 96(1)(d).

3 'Mental disorder' means 'mental illness, arrested or incomplete development of mind, psychopathic disorder and any other disorder or disability of mind': Mental Health Act 1983, s 1(2).

4 The court would have no jurisdiction if the incapacity were due to any cause other than mental disorder, for example alcohol or drug dependence: see Mental Health Act 1983, s 1(3).

5 Mental Health Act 1983, s 96(4)(b).

6 There is no provision in the Enduring Powers of Attorney Act 1985 for the execution of a statutory will on behalf of the donor of an EPA. Any such application must be made under Mental Health Act 1983, s 96(1)(e).

Medical evidence

The criteria for testamentary capacity and the capacity to manage and administer one's property and affairs are not the same and, despite the appointment of a receiver or the registration of an enduring power of attorney, a patient or donor may be perfectly capable of making a valid will for himself or herself. For this reason, it is recommended that medical evidence of both types of capacity be obtained before preparing the affidavit and other documentation required to support an application to the Court of Protection for an order authorising the execution of a statutory will.[1]

The court requires recent, primary evidence[2] from a registered medical practitioner stating whether an individual is:

- incapable, by reason of mental disorder, of managing his or her property and affairs; and
- incapable of making a valid will for himself or herself.

The best and simplest way of providing evidence of an individual's managerial capacity is to ask his or her doctor to complete and sign the printed Medical Certificate (Form CP3) issued by the Court of Protection.[3] Even if a receiver has been appointed, and a medical certificate was submitted to the court before the appointment was made, it is good practice to obtain a restatement of the patient's managerial incapacity in an up-to-date CP3. The need for proper medical certification applies *a fortiori* in the case of a registered enduring power of attorney. An EPA is registrable when the attorney has reason to believe that the donor is or 'is becoming' mentally incapable, and the fact that it is registered with the court is not for this purpose sufficient evidence that the donor is incapable, by reason of mental disorder, of managing and administering his or her property and affairs.

Medical evidence of the individual's testamentary capacity can be included in the 'Additional Comments' section of the CP3, or set out in a separate letter or certificate.[4]

A registered medical practitioner who is asked to complete Form CP3 and to express an opinion on an individual's testamentary capacity should, ideally, know:

- the individual whose capacity he or she is assessing;
- something about that individual's property and affairs;[5]
- something about that individual's testamentary history and intentions;[6]
- what the Court of Protection is, and the circumstances in which it can authorise the execution of a statutory will on behalf of a patient;
- something about mental disorder;
- how to assess whether a person is incapable, by reason of mental disorder, of managing and administering his or her property and affairs;[7]
- how to assess whether a person has testamentary capacity.

The quality of the medical evidence generally – although not always – reflects the quality of the information supplied to the doctor by the instructing solicitor.

In most cases, if properly instructed, a GP should be able to express an opinion on his or her patient's managerial capacity or testamentary capacity. However, if the patient is in hospital it is recommended that an opinion as to testamentary capacity be obtained from a consultant.[8]

The medical evidence may establish that a person is:

- incapable, by reason of mental disorder, of managing and administering his or her property and affairs; but
- capable of making a valid will for himself or herself.

In this case, the person's solicitor should send the original medical evidence to the Court of Protection and request further directions. It is likely that the court will authorise the solicitor to receive instructions for the preparation of a will from the patient in person. The will is then drafted, approved and engrossed, and, if the patient is in a hospital or mental nursing home, the court usually requires the consultant who provided the evidence of testamentary capacity, or the medical practitioner in charge of the patient's treatment to be one of the attesting witnesses.

If the patient is not in a hospital or mental nursing home, his or her GP should, if possible, be a witness.[9]

The court stresses that the final responsibility rests upon the solicitor who takes the instructions to satisfy himself or herself that the patient has testamentary capacity, (a) when the instructions for the preparation of the will are taken, and (b) when the will is executed.[10]

If the medical evidence establishes that a person lacks both managerial and testamentary capacity, the solicitor should consider obtaining a second opinion if there is any doubt in his or her mind as to the weight of the evidence. If there is no doubt that a patient lacks both managerial and testamentary capacity, a formal application for a statutory will would be necessary.

---

1 For a precedent of a letter from a solicitor to a GP requesting evidence of a client's managerial capacity and testamentary capacity, see Precedent 2, Chapter 3 at p 65 above.

2 The original certificate or letter signed by the doctor who has assessed the patient's capacity, not a photocopy.

3 Form CP3 is reproduced in Chapter 10 at p 289.

4 A precedent of a letter to a registered medical practitioner requesting an assessment of testamentary capacity appears in Chapter 3 at p 65.

5 It is accepted that the disclosure of confidential information about a person's property and affairs raises an ethical dilemma. Ideally, the consent of the alleged patient should be obtained wherever possible. For a form of consent, see Precedent 1, Chapter 3 at p 64 above. On the question of confidentiality generally, see The Law Society, *The Guide to the Professional Conduct of Solicitors* (6th edition, 1993), Chapter 16.

6 See footnote 5 above. There is judicial authority to suggest that the doctor must be aware of the contents of any previous will and the proposed changes to it: *Kenward v Adams* (1975) *The Times*, November 29, per Templeman J. See the report of this case in Chapter 3 at p 42.

7 The doctor should be given a copy of the Court of Protection's *Notes to Accompany Certificate of Incapacity* (Form CP3), which were prepared in consultation with the Royal College of Psychiatrists and the BMA.

8 See Court of Protection Procedure Note PN5, *Procedure for the Execution of Testamentary Documents*.

9 Form PN5.

10 *Ibid.*

The applicant

An application for an order for the execution of a statutory will can only be made by a person who has *locus standi* under r 20 of the Court of Protection Rules 1994, namely:[1]

- the receiver for the patient;[2]
- any person who has made an application for the appointment of a receiver which has not yet been determined;
- any person who, under any known will of the patient or under his or her intestacy, may become entitled to any property of the patient or any interest in it;[3]

- any person for whom the patient might be expected to provide if he or she were not mentally disordered;[4]
- an attorney acting under a registered enduring power of attorney;
- any other person whom the court or Public Trustee may authorise to make it.

Identifying the client is generally not a problem in statutory will proceedings.[5] If the applicant is personally interested in the application or if there is any other reason for having the patient's interests separately represented, the court will direct that the patient be represented by the Official Solicitor.[6] The solicitor who has carriage of the proceedings is, therefore, generally the solicitor for the applicant, even although he or she may have acted for the patient in the past and may continue to do so in the future.

---

1 SI 1994/3046. Rule 20 also applies to applications for the settlement or gift of a patient's property.
2 The applicant is usually the receiver. If, however, the receiver is not the applicant, he or she should be given notice of the hearing of the application: Court of Protection Rules 1994 (SI 1994/3046), r 21(2).
3 For example, a beneficiary under an existing will whose legacy has adeemed: see *Re D(J)* [1982] Ch 237, summarised at p 424 below.
4 As a result of the decision of Hoffmann J in *Re C* [1991] 3 All ER 866, this category would include a charity for whom the patient might be expected to provide.
5 See, generally, Chapter 2, 'Who is the Client?'.
6 Court of Protection Rules 1994 (SI 1994/3046), r 15.

The application

The following documents should be sent to The Registrar, Court of Protection, Stewart House, 24 Kingsway, London WC2B 6JX, or via the Document Exchange to DX 37965 Kingsway:

- General Form of Application (Form CP9) in duplicate;[1]
- an affidavit in support of the application, plus exhibits;[2]
- the original medical evidence (not a copy) that the person is incapable, by reason of mental disorder, of managing and administering his or her property and affairs (Form CP3);[3]
- the original medical evidence (not a copy) that the person is incapable of making a valid will for himself or herself;
- a copy (not the original) of the person's existing will, if any;[4]
- a draft of the proposed statutory will in duplicate;[5]
- consent(s) to act signed by the person(s) to be appointed as executor(s) of the proposed statutory will.[6]

The affidavit must substantiate the need for a statutory will, and should include the following information:

- the applicant's *locus standi* to make the application;[7]
- the patient's domicile;[8]

- whether the patient owns any immovable property outside England and Wales;[9]
- details about the patient's family by way of a 'family tree' showing the relationship between the patient and other members of his or her family. Full names and dates of birth, or current ages, should be stated where known;[10]
- particulars of the patient's current capital assets, with up-to-date valuations;[11]
- particulars of the patient's current income and expenditure;
- a statement of the patient's present and anticipated needs, and his or her general circumstances;[12]
- full details of the patient's general health at present and in the future (if these details have not already been provided in the Medical Certificate Form CP3);
- if no existing will for the patient is produced, details of the enquiries made to establish whether or not the patient has already made a will.

The following matters could be raised separately in an accompanying letter when lodging the papers with the court:

- whether, and why, the application is urgent;[13]
- whether, and why, formal notification of the application should not be given to an interested party;[14]
- who is likely to be attending the hearing (the applicant; the applicant's solicitor; a London agent; perhaps even the patient in person);[15]
- whether, in view of travelling arrangements, a hearing in the morning or the afternoon would be preferable.

A cheque made payable to 'Public Trust Office' for the transaction fee of £100 should be sent with the application.

---

1 See Precedent 1 at p 432 below.

2 For a precedent of an affidavit in support of an application for a statutory will, see Precedent 2 at p 433 below.

3 Form CP3 is reproduced in Chapter 10 at p 289.

4 The court can order the production of any testamentary document executed by a patient: Court of Protection Rules 1994 (SI 1994/3046), r 72.

5 For the form of commencement preferred by the court, see Precedent 3 at p 434 below. For the form of testimonium and attestation clause preferred by the court, see Precedent 4 at p 435 below.

6 For the form of consent preferred by the court, see Precedent 5 at p 435 below.

7 Court of Protection Rules 1994 (SI 1994/3046), r 20.

8 Mental Health Act 1983, s 97(4).

9 *Ibid.*

10 Procedure Note PN9.

11 *Ibid.*

12 *Ibid.*

13 In cases of extreme urgency, a phone call to the registrar (tel: 0171 269 7352) or registrar's assistant (tel: 0171 269 7208) is advisable.

14 For the rules on notification of other parties, see Court of Protection Rules 1994, rr 21 and 40. See also, *Re Davey (Deceased)* [1980] 3 All ER 342, and *Re B* [1987] 2 All ER 475.

15 Court of Protection Rules 1994, r 78 and Appendix.

The hearing

When the court receives an application for the execution of a statutory will on behalf of a patient, it will:

- fix a date and time for the hearing,[1] unless it considers that the application can properly be dealt with without a hearing. It might do so, for example, if an application were made for the execution of a codicil to the patient's will appointing a new executor, and there is no dispute as to the suitability of the proposed executor;
- return the duplicate copy of the application form to the applicant's solicitors, duly endorsed with the date and time of the hearing;[2]
- raise preliminary enquiries arising out of the application or suggest any amendments to the draft of the proposed statutory will;
- ask the Official Solicitor if he is willing to act as solicitor for the patient;[3]
- require that the receiver, if he or she is not the applicant, be joined in or given notice of the application;[4]
- determine who else ought to be joined in the proceedings.[5] Although the court has a general discretion concerning joinder and notification, it must be exercised in relation to the circumstances of each individual case. In the normal course of events, all persons who may be materially and adversely affected should be notified;[6]
- direct the applicant's solicitor to send copies of all the relevant documentation to the Official Solicitor and to all other parties joined in the proceedings.

Notice of a hearing must be given not less than two clear days before the date fixed for the hearing.[7] In practice, unless the matter is urgent, the hearing usually takes place about six weeks after the court receives the application. If the application relates merely to minor, non-contentious alterations or additions to the patient's will, the application may be agreed between the Official Solicitor and the applicant's solicitor, and the hearing may then be cancelled.[8]

The application is heard in chambers[9] in the offices of the Court of Protection at Stewart House, Kingsway, London WC2, before the Master or an assistant master. However, if the Master or assistant master refers the proceedings to a judge,[10] the hearing will be in the Royal Courts of Justice in the Strand. The court may determine who is entitled to attend the hearing.[11] Where two or more persons at the hearing are represented by the same legal representative, the court may, if it thinks fit, require any of them to be separately represented.[12]

Over the last twenty-five years, case-law has established a number of guidelines to assist the court in exercising its statutory will jurisdiction.

- The court must seek to make the will which the actual patient, acting reasonably, would have made if notionally restored to full capacity, memory and foresight.[13]
- It is to be assumed that the patient is having a brief lucid interval at the time when the will is made.[14]
- During the lucid interval, the patient has a full knowledge of the past, and a full

realisation that as soon as the will is executed he or she will relapse into the actual mental state that previously existed, with the prognosis as it actually is.[15]

- It is the actual patient who has to be considered, and not a hypothetical patient. One is not concerned with 'the patient on the Clapham omnibus'.[16]
- During the hypothetical lucid interval, the patient is to be envisaged as being advised by competent solicitors. The patient is not to be treated as bound to accept the imaginary legal advice that is given to him or her, but is to be treated as doing what he or she does either because of the advice or in spite of it, and not without having had it.[17]
- In all normal cases, the patient is to be envisaged as taking a broad brush to the claims on his or her bounty, rather than an accountant's pen.[18]
- The court must assume that the patient is a normal decent person, acting in accordance with contemporary standards of morality.[19]
- In considering how the patient's estate should be distributed, the court should have regard to all the circumstances, including the patient's relations with his or her family, the services which have been rendered by strangers, and the size of his or her fortune.[20]
- In dividing the patient's estate between private individuals and charities, there is no reason why the individuals should share in the fiscal advantages which the law gives to charities.[21]
- Where the patient would otherwise die intestate, special reasons are required for departing from the rules for distribution on intestacy.[22] For example, in *Re C* (1991)[23] where the patient was intestate and had no surviving spouse, issue, parents, or brothers and sisters, there was a suggestion that her estate might be divided equally between the paternal and maternal branches of her family. Her father had been one of eleven siblings; her mother one of two.
- On appeal, the judge has a complete discretion to consider the matter at large, and is in no way fettered by any decision of the Master or an assistant master.[24]

---

1 Court of Protection Rules 1994 (SI 1994/3046), r 10.

2 *Ibid*, r 10(2).

3 *Ibid*, r 15.

4 *Ibid*, r 21(2).

5 *Ibid*, rr 21 and 40.

6 See the cases summarised at pp 423–426: *Re HMF* [1976] Ch 33; *Re Davey (Deceased)* [1981] 1 WLR 164; and *Re B* [1987] 2 All ER 475.

7 Court of Protection Rules 1994 (SI 1994/3046), r 21(5)(b).

8 *Ibid*, r 10(1).

9 *Ibid*, r 39(1).

10 *Ibid*, r 42.

11 *Ibid*, r 40.

12 *Ibid*, r 41.

13 *Re D(J)* [1982] 2 All ER 37, at p 43e, per Sir Robert Megarry V-C.

14 *Ibid*, at p 42h.

15 *Ibid*, at p 42h. This proposition emerges from the judgment of Cross J in *Re WJGL* [1965] 3 All ER 865, at pp 871–872; [1966] Ch 135, at pp 144–145.

16 *Re D(J)* [1982] 2 All ER 37, at p 43a.

17 *Ibid*, at p 43f–h.

18 *Ibid*, at p 43h–i.

19 *Re C (Spinster and Mental Patient)* [1991] 3 All ER 866, at p 870c, per Hoffmann J.
20 *Ibid*, at p 870h.
21 *Ibid*, at p 871d.
22 *Ibid*, at p 872c.
23 *Ibid*.
24 *Re D(J)* [1982] 2 All ER 37, at p 45j, per Sir Robert Megarry V-C.

Execution of a statutory will

Section 97(1) of the Mental Health Act 1983 states that a statutory will must be:

- expressed to be signed by the patient acting by the *authorised person* (usually the receiver);
- signed by the authorised person with the name of the patient, and with his or her own name, in the presence of two or more witnesses present at the same time;
- attested and subscribed by those witnesses in the presence of the authorised person; and
- sealed with the official seal of the Court of Protection.[1]

As the authorised person is signing the statutory will on the patient's behalf and is not a witness as such, he or she will not be barred from benefiting under the will by virtue of the Wills Act 1837, s 15 (gifts to an attesting witness, or to his or her wife or husband, to be void). However, no beneficiary named in the statutory will, nor his or her spouse, should act as a witness.[2]

After the statutory will has been signed and witnessed, it must be sent to the Court of Protection for sealing. After the court has sealed it, the statutory will is returned to the applicant's solicitor, and the solicitor is usually required to sign an undertaking to hold the will in safe custody for the rest of the patient's lifetime.[3]

1 For a precedent of the testimonium and attestation clause, see Precedent 4 at p 435 below.
2 Mental Health Act 1983, s 97(2) states that: 'The Wills Act 1837 shall have effect in relation to any such will as if it were signed by the patient by his own hand, except that [s 9 of that Act shall not apply]'.
3 For the form of 'Receipt and Undertaking for Safe Custody of a Patient's Will' (Form CP12), see Precedent 6 at p 436 below.

Effect of a statutory will

A statutory will generally has the same effect as if the patient were capable of making a valid will, and the will had been made by him or her personally and had been executed in the manner required by the Wills Act 1837.[1] So, for example:

- if it declares an intention to revoke all former wills and codicils, it will revoke all former wills and codicils,[2] regardless of whether the court was aware of their existence when it ordered the execution of a statutory will;

- it will be revoked if the patient gets married, unless it was expressed to be made in expectation of that marriage;[3]
- if it contains a devise or bequest to a child or remoter descendant of the patient, and the intended beneficiary dies before the patient leaving issue who are alive at the patient's death, then, unless a contrary intention appears in the statutory will, the devise or bequest will take effect as a devise or bequest to such issue;[4]
- a gift to, or to the spouse of, a person who attests the execution of the statutory will by the authorised person will be utterly null and void.[5]

A statutory will is ineffective insofar as it disposes of any immovable property outside England and Wales.[6] This is because, under the rules of private international law, the capacity to make a will disposing of immovable property is determined by the *lex situs*.

Capacity to make a will disposing of movable property is, under private international law, determined by the *lex domicilii*. Accordingly, if, when the statutory will is executed, the patient is domiciled outside England and Wales, the will would also be ineffective to deal with any movable property, unless under his or her *lex domicilii*, any question of capacity would fall to be determined in accordance with the law of England and Wales.

---

1 Mental Health Act 1983, s 97(3).
2 Wills Act 1837, s 20.
3 *Ibid*, s 18 (as amended).
4 *Ibid*, s 33 (as amended).
5 *Ibid*, s 15.
6 Mental Health Act 1983, s 97(4)(a).

Safe custody

The receivership order usually contains directions for the safe custody of any existing will 'during the lifetime of the patient'. By arrangement with The Law Society, where solicitors have prepared a will, it is the practice to allow them to retain it for safe custody:[1] otherwise, the receivership order will require the will to be deposited at the bank with which the receivership account is held.

Where a patient makes a new will or codicil (if he or she has testamentary capacity, and the prior approval of the court is obtained), or if a statutory will is executed, the old will must not be destroyed but remain in safe custody as before. The envelope containing the old will must be endorsed with a note to the effect that a new will or codicil was executed on a particular date.[2] Whoever holds the will for safe custody is required to give a receipt and undertaking in Form CP12.[3] If the patient recovers, the order determining the proceedings will contain a direction for the will to be delivered up to him or her.[4]

On the patient's death, the will should be released to his or her personal representatives, without the need for any direction from the Public Trustee or the

Court of Protection. However, if the will is held for safe custody subject to the directions of the court without the limitation 'during the lifetime of the patient', a Certified Copy of Entry of Death (a death certificate) should be sent to the court along with a request for an authority to hand over the will.[5]

1 Norman Whitehorn, *Court of Protection Handbook* (9th edition, Longman, 1991), p 71.

2 Procedure Note PN5, *Procedure for the Execution of Testamentary Documents* (November 1987).

3 Form CP12 is reproduced below: see Precedent 6 at p 436.

4 Court of Protection Rules 1994 (SI 1994/3046), r 76(1).

5 Procedure Note PN3, *Procedure on Death of Patient.*

Costs[1]

Legal aid is not available for Court of Protection proceedings.

There is no provision for *fixed costs* in respect of an application for a statutory will.

On a hearing before the Master or an assistant master, the costs of all parties are normally ordered to be taxed and paid out of the patient's estate on the indemnity basis. The same principles do not necessarily apply on appeal.[2]

Taxation may not be necessary where the application for a statutory will is made by a solicitor/attorney acting under an enduring power which contains a professional charging clause: the presumption being that the donor authorised the solicitor's reasonable costs before becoming mentally incapacitated.

Taxation may also be unnecessary in the case of *agreed costs*. If the solicitor's bill for costs incurred in connection with the application does not exceed £1000[3] excluding VAT and disbursements, the solicitor may lodge a narrative bill with a summary of the work done, time spent and category of fee-earner involvement, together with receipts for any disbursements, and suggest a figure which he or she is prepared to accept by way of costs. If the bill appears to be reasonable, the amount sought will be agreed by the court.

1 See, generally, Court of Protection Rules 1994 (SI 1994/3046), Part XIX: rr 87–92.

2 The question of costs was considered at length by Sir Robert Megarry V-C, in *Re D(J)* [1982] Ch 237, [1982] 2 WLR 373.

3 The maximum level for agreed costs is changed periodically, although far less regularly than the annual amendments to the levels of fixed costs.

CASE EXAMPLES

There have been relatively few reported decisions on statutory wills, but those which have been published are of major importance in terms of policy, practice and procedure.

Re HMF (1975)[1]

HMF made a will in 1960 in which she gave her residuary estate to two named charities in equal shares. In 1969, she became a 'patient'. In 1975, when she no longer had testamentary capacity, she began to take an interest in her two nephews, and expressed a wish to make a new will in their favour. The nephews applied to the Court of Protection for an order authorising the execution of a statutory will, and the question arose as to whether the two charities (who were unaware of their entitlement under the 1960 will) should be joined as respondents to the application.

HELD, by Goulding J – the charities should be joined in the proceedings. The desire to maintain the confidentiality of a living patient's affairs had to give way to the necessity for the court to act fairly in exercising its powers. Furthermore, the charities might be able to show that the patient had a particular interest in their objectives and activities, or that she had some sort of moral obligation towards them.

---

1 [1976] Ch 33, [1975] 3 WLR 395, [1975] 2 All ER 795.

Re Davey (Deceased) (1980)[1]

Olive St Barbe was a 92-year-old spinster. In June 1979, when she was suffering from dementia, she moved into a private nursing home in Kensington. On 30 October 1979, at Fulham Register Office, she married Wallace Davey, who was 48 and lived and worked in the nursing home. The Court of Protection was informed of the circumstances, and on 18 December 1979, the Official Solicitor was appointed as her receiver. On 21 December 1979, the Official Solicitor executed a statutory will on her behalf which had the effect of reinstating an earlier will that had been revoked by her marriage. She died on 27 December 1979 leaving an estate of £56,698. The Deputy Master had ordered the execution of the statutory will without giving notice to Mr Davey for four reasons: (1) in view of Olive's age and poor health the matter was urgent; (2) if she died the bulk of her estate would pass to her husband on her intestacy; (3) the marriage was apparently clandestine; and (4) Mr Davey could apply for a further statutory will in his favour or, if Olive died, he could apply for an order under the Inheritance (Provision for

Family and Dependants) Act 1975. Mr Davey appealed against the order contending that the Deputy Master had exercised his discretion wrongly by not giving him notice; that he should not have taken into account the possibility of an application under the 1975 Act; and that the validity of the marriage should have been assumed.

HELD, by Fox J – what are now rr 21 and 40 of the Court of Protection Rules 1994 give the court a discretion as to whom notice of proceedings should be given. In normal circumstances, the court would generally insist on joining anyone who would be adversely affected by the application, but in an emergency the position might be different, and the court had to balance various factors, including the possibility of an application under the 1975 Act, in order to reach a just conclusion. The Deputy Master's order offered the widest opportunities for a full investigation of the matter at a later stage and, therefore, the best prospect of a just result in the end. The judge also held that the circumstances of the marriage were highly suspicious, and that it was unreal to say that the court should have proceeded on the basis that the marriage was necessarily valid.

---

1 [1981] 1 WLR 164, [1980] 3 All ER 342.

Re D(J) (1982)[1]

The patient was a widow born in 1901. In 1962, she made a will leaving her house and its contents to her daughter, A, and the rest of her estate to her five children equally. In 1973, the house was sold, and the legacy adeemed; and the patient subsequently lost testamentary capacity. A and her sister R (the receiver) applied to the court for a statutory will to compensate A for the adeemed legacy. The patient's estate was worth about £50,000, and the Deputy Master ordered that a statutory will be executed giving A a legacy of £10,000 and leaving the residue to the patient's five children in equal shares. A wasn't happy about this order, because her mother's house had been sold for £22,000. A and R appealed.

HELD, by Sir Robert Megarry V-C – on an appeal from a decision of the Master or an assistant master (under what is now s 105 of the Mental Health Act 1983), the judge has a complete discretion to consider the matter at large, unfettered by the decision of the Court of Protection. The importance of this judgment lies in the Vice-Chancellor's statement of five principles which should guide the court when deciding what provisions to insert in a statutory will.

- It is to be assumed that the patient is having a brief lucid interval at the time when the will is made.
- It is to be assumed that during the lucid interval the patient has a full knowledge of the past, and a full realisation that as soon as the will is executed he or she will relapse into the actual mental state that previously existed, with the prognosis as it actually is.
- It is the actual patient who has to be considered and not a hypothetical patient. One is not concerned with the patient on the Clapham omnibus.

- During the hypothetical lucid interval, the patient is to be envisaged as being advised by competent solicitors.
- In all normal cases, the patient is to be envisaged as taking a broad brush to the claims on his bounty, rather than an accountant's pen.

Applying those principles, the Vice-Chancellor concluded that A ought to be given a legacy of £15,000 and the residue should be divided equally between the five children.

---

1 [1982] Ch 237, [1982] 2 WLR 373, [1982] 2 All ER 37.

Re B (Court of Protection) (Notice of Proceedings) (1987)[1]

In 1977, B's husband executed a codicil in which he gave her a power of appointment in favour of his two nephews, P and E, and their issue. In default of appointment, the estate would go to P alone. The husband died, and B became a 'patient'. Her receiver, Sir David Napley, applied to the Court of Protection for an order under s 96(1)(k) of the Mental Health Act 1983 to 'exercise any power vested in the patient, whether beneficially or as guardian or trustee or otherwise'. Sir David did not want to give P and E formal notification of the application because he had reason to believe that the application would be bitterly contested, and that P and E would indulge in a great deal of mutual mud-slinging. The Master referred the application to the judge.

HELD, by Millett J – under what are now rr 21 and 40 of the Court of Protection Rules 1994, the court has a discretion as to who should be notified of proceedings. In exercising this discretion, the court should have regard to two considerations: (1) that all relevant material and arguments are before the court; and (2) that all persons materially and adversely affected should be given the opportunity of putting forward their case, and that this could only be overridden in the most exceptional circumstances. In this case, the circumstances were not exceptional, and P and E should be informed of the application.

---

1 [1987] 1 WLR 552, [1987] 2 All ER 475, [1987] 2 FLR 155.

Re C (Spinster and Mental Patient) (1991)[1]

C, aged 75, had been born with severe brain damage and had lived in the same hospital just outside London since she was 10. She was an only child and had inherited from her parents an estate which was worth £1,600,000. Very few, if any, of her numerous distant cousins knew of her existence. In May 1989, the Official Solicitor, acting on behalf of her receiver, the Public Trustee, applied to the Court of Protection for an order to execute a statutory will and also to make an immediate gift of £500,000 to the League of Friends of the hospital in which she lived. This is the first reported decision on the execution of a statutory will on behalf of a person who never had testamentary capacity in the first place. It is also an endorsement of the tendency throughout the 1980s of the Court of Protection to make provision for mental health charities in some statutory wills.

HELD, by Hoffmann J – the court had jurisdiction to make lifetime gifts and authorise the execution of a statutory will on the assumption that the patient is a normal decent person who acts in accordance with contemporary standards of morality. Accordingly, if she were not mentally incapacitated, C would feel a moral obligation to show recognition to the community in which she had spent most of her life by making gifts and leaving legacies to the hospital and voluntary mental health charities. A person in C's position would have wished to benefit other people who suffered from mental illness, rather than wider or different charitable purposes, and, because people tend to prefer local and familiar causes to those which are more general and remote, she would have wished primarily to benefit mentally handicapped people at the hospital or within the area which the hospital serves. As she had derived her fortune from being a child of a family, she would also be expected to recognise the interests and needs of her family. Accordingly, the court ordered immediate gifts to both the family and charities connected with the hospital, and ordered that a statutory will be executed in which the patient divided her residuary estate equally between charity and her family. The distribution to her family would be based on the rules of intestacy.

1 [1991] 3 All ER 866, [1992] 1 FLR 51.

Re S (1994)[1]

In *Re S*, Ferris J said:

> 'I think it would be unfortunate if *Re C* were taken as a firm model of the form of dispositions to be made in circumstances of this kind, even in closely similar circumstances. This is not an area in which judicial precedent really has any weight and it seems to me that there is as much scope for somewhat differing results to be arrived at in different cases as there is for different individuals who are of full capacity but in similar personal and economic circumstances to make substantially different dispositions of their estate.'

In this case, the judge ordered that an estate of £1,100,000 be split 25% to charity and 75% to the patient's family.

1 Unreported, 16 March 1994.

CHECKLISTS

1 CONSIDERATIONS PRELIMINARY TO AN APPLICATION FOR A STATUTORY WILL

(1) Where did the idea of applying for a statutory will come from?

- The patient himself or herself
- The receiver or attorney
- Someone else who has an interest in the outcome
- The solicitor

(2) Locate the patient's existing will (if any)

- If a bank, solicitor, or anyone else who is holding the patient's existing will refuses to release it, inform the Court of Protection. The court has power to order production of any testamentary document executed by a patient, r 72 of the Court of Protection Rules 1994.

(3) Why is a statutory will needed?

- The patient has got married, and his or her existing will has been revoked as a consequence.
- The patient has sold or disposed of property which he or she had specifically bequeathed to someone in his or her existing will.
- The circumstances of one or more of the beneficiaries has changed. For example:
  - death;
  - bankruptcy;
  - marriage;
  - childbirth;
  - separation or divorce;
  - the patient has lost contact with beneficiaries in his or her existing will;
  - the patient and beneficiaries have fallen out.
- Tax planning.
- The patient does not have a will, and the intestacy laws do not make provision or adequate provision for a person or charity for whom the patient might have been expected to provide if he or she had testamentary capacity.

(4) Wherever possible, obtain the patient's or donor's consent to the disclosure of his or her existing will and any other confidential information relating to his or her property and affairs.

(5) Does the patient lack capacity?

- Two distinct types of capacity need to be considered:
    (1) whether, by reason of mental disorder, the patient is incapable of managing and administering his or her property and affairs; and
    (2) whether the patient is capable of making a valid will for himself or herself.
- If the patient is not in hospital, write to his or her GP asking for medical evidence of both types of capacity. Precedent 2 in Chapter 3 gives some ideas on the contents of such a letter. (If the patient is in hospital, obtain the evidence of both types of capacity from a consultant.)
    - Send the doctor a copy of Court of Protection Form CP3 (Medical Certificate).
    - Send the doctor a copy of the 'Notes to accompany Certificate of Incapacity' which were prepared by the court in consultation with the Royal College of Psychiatrists and the British Medical Association.
    - (Provided that the requisite consent has been obtained from the patient/donor or the court), tell the doctor about the patient's property and affairs. After all, how can a doctor assess the patient's capacity to manage his or her property and affairs unless the doctor knows something about the property and affairs that the patient has to manage?
    - Tell the doctor about the function of the Court of Protection and its jurisdiction to authorise the execution of a statutory will on behalf of a patient.
    - Tell the doctor about the legal criteria for testamentary capacity. Explain, in clear terms that a person who is not legally qualified can understand, the tests in *Banks v Goodfellow* (1870).
    - Let the doctor know about the patient's testamentary history, and tell him or her the reason why it is necessary to apply to the court for a statutory will.
    - If the doctor feels that he or she is not qualified to assess the patient's capacity, give him or her the opportunity to say so, and to recommend another registered medical practitioner who might be better qualified to assess both types of capacity.
    - Give the doctor some indication as to what a reasonable fee might be in these circumstances.
    - Let the doctor know whether the application for a statutory will is likely to be contested.
- Read the medical report or certificate on the patient's testamentary and managerial capacity. Do you agree with the doctor's assessment? If you disagree, consider obtaining a second – specialist – opinion.

(6) Is the patient incapable of managing his or her affairs, but capable of making a valid will?

If the medical evidence establishes that the patient is incapable, by reason of mental disorder, of managing and administering his or her property and affairs, but is perfectly capable of making a valid will for himself or herself:

- Send the original medical evidence (not a photocopy) to the Court of Protection.
- Ask the court for further directions, and a copy of its procedure note PN5.
- The court will probably authorise the patient's solicitor to take will instructions from the patient in person, and require that the doctor who gave evidence that the patient has testamentary capacity should be one of the witnesses to the will.

2 APPLYING FOR A STATUTORY WILL

(1) Write to the Court of Protection and obtain the application forms

The court will send you:

- Procedure Notes PN9 and PN9A.
- Medical Certificate, Form CP3.
- notes to accompany the Medical Certificate.
- a General Form of Application (Form CP9) in duplicate.

(2) Obtain medical evidence of the patient's incapacity (a) to manage and administer his or her property and affairs, and (b) to make a valid will for himself or herself

- This is considered in greater detail in the preceding checklist on 'Considerations preliminary to an application for a statutory will'.
- If the patient lacks both types of capacity, a formal application to the Court of Protection will be necessary.

(3) Obtain the following information

- The full names, addresses and dates of birth, of every member of the patient's family (within reason).
- An up-to-date valuation of all the patient's assets.
- Up-to-date details of the patient's income, including pensions and State benefits.
- Details of the patient's current outgoings, such as income tax, and nursing home or residential care home fees.

(4) Draft the proposed statutory will

- It is sensible to draft the proposed statutory will before drafting the affidavit in support of the application. You will need to refer to the will in the affidavit.

- Bear in mind the principle that the court will seek to make the will which the actual patient, acting reasonably and with competent legal advice, would make if he or she were notionally restored to full capacity, memory and understanding.
- Make sure that the commencement of the will conforms to the court's requirements. See Precedent 3 at p 434 below.
- Make sure that the testimonium and attestation clause conform to the court's requirements. See Precedent 4 at p 434 below.

(5) Obtain consents to act from the proposed executors and trustees

- See Precedent 5 at p 435 below.

(6) Draft the affidavit in support of the application

- An example of an affidavit in support of an application for a statutory will appears as Precedent 2 at p 433 below.
- Make sure that the standard heading is used.
- The affidavit should:
  - state the *locus standi* of the applicant. Those who are entitled to make such an application are listed in r 20 of the Court of Protection Rules 1994;
  - state where the patient is domiciled;
  - state whether the patient owns any immovable property outside England and Wales;
  - substantiate the need for a statutory will.
- Refer to the exhibits. There are likely to be at least three, and possibly as many as nine or ten, namely:
  - medical evidence that the patient is incapable, by reason of mental disorder, of managing and administering his or her property and affairs;
  - medical evidence that the patient is incapable of making a valid will for himself or herself;
  - a 'family tree' setting out the patient's family background;
  - an up-to-date statement of the patient's capital assets;
  - an up-to-date statement of the patient's income;
  - an up-to-date statement of the patient's outgoings;
  - the patient's existing will (if any);
  - the draft of the proposed statutory will;
  - the consents of the proposed executors and trustees.
- Make sure that the affidavit conforms with the requirements of the Practice Direction issued by the Master on 15 August 1984, noting in particular:
  - Marking. At the top right hand corner, and also on the backsheet, there must be written in clear permanent dark blue or black marking: (1) the name of the person on whose behalf it is filed; (2) the initials and surname of the deponent; (3) the number of the affidavit in relation to the deponent; and (4) the date when sworn;
  - Binding. Affidavits must not be bound with thick plastic strips or anything else which would hamper filing;

- Exhibits. Where space allows, the first page of every exhibit should be marked in the same way as the affidavit to which it is an exhibit. Exhibits must not be bound up with, or otherwise attached to, the affidavit itself.

(7) Draft the application itself (Form CP9)

- A specimen application appears at p 432 below.
- Remember, particularly if the application is made on behalf of the donor of a registered enduring power, that the court's statutory will jurisdiction is conferred in s 96(1)(e) of the Mental Health Act 1983.

(8) Send all the relevant documentation (in particular, the draft affidavit and draft statutory will) to the applicant for approval or amendment

(9) Arrange for the applicant to be sworn to the affidavit

- Make sure that all the exhibits are present and correctly marked.
- Make sure that the details in the top right hand corner of the front page, and on the backsheet, are properly completed.

(10) Before sending the papers to the Court of Protection, make sure that you retain complete photocopies of all the documentation

- You will, almost certainly, be required by the court to serve copies of the papers on the Official Solicitor.
- You may be required to serve copies of the papers on various relatives or others who may be interested in the application.

(11) Lodge the application with the Court of Protection

The following documents should be sent to The Registrar, Court of Protection, Stewart House, 24 Kingsway, London WC2B 6JX, or via the Document Exchange to DX 37965 Kingsway:

- the application (duly dated and signed) in duplicate;
- the affidavit and exhibits;
- an extra copy of the draft of the proposed statutory will;
- the original Medical Certificate, Form CP3;
- the original medical evidence that the patient lacks testamentary capacity;
- a cheque for the transaction fee of £100 made payable to the 'Public Trust Office'.

(12) Don't serve the papers on anyone else until you are instructed to do so by the court

- Once he or she has received the application, the Registrar will advise you of:
  - the date and time of the hearing;
  - the names of any other parties who are to be served with copies of the application.

PRECEDENTS

A precedent letter requesting medical evidence from a GP is included in Chapter 3 as Precedent 2.

1 APPLICATION TO THE COURT OF PROTECTION FOR AN ORDER AUTHORISING THE EXECUTION OF A STATUTORY WILL[1]

COURT OF PROTECTION
19   no

IN THE MATTER OF .... A PATIENT

I .... (*full name of applicant*) ....
of .... (*address of applicant*) ....
the receiver in this matter [*or*, having made an application for the appointment of a receiver which has not yet been determined] [*or*, being a person who under the patient's will (or intestacy) may become entitled to any property of the patient or any interest in it] [*or*, being a person for whom the patient might be expected to provide if (he)/(she) were not mentally disordered] [*or*, the attorney acting under a registered enduring power of attorney][2]

apply to the Court of Protection for an order that:

pursuant to section 96(1)(e) of the Mental Health Act 1983, I [*or*, the receiver in this matter] [*or*, some other proper person]

be authorised to execute for the patient a statutory will in the terms of the draft accompanying this application or in such other terms as the court may think fit.

AND that the costs of and incidental to this application may be provided for out of the patient's estate

and for any directions which are necessary as a result of this application.

Applicant's signature   ....
Date   ....

OR Solicitors for the applicant   ....
of   ....

---

1 This form is based on the Court of Protection's 'General Form of Application' Printed Form CP9 (Form B in the Schedule to the Court of Protection Rules 1994 (SI 1994/3046)).
2 The applicant is required to state his or her standing under r 20 of the Court of Protection Rules 1994 (SI 1994/3046).

2 AFFIDAVIT IN SUPPORT OF AN APPLICATION FOR A STATUTORY WILL

Filed on behalf of:
Deponent:
No of affidavit:
Date sworn:

COURT OF PROTECTION
19   no
IN THE MATTER OF   A PATIENT

I...

of...

MAKE OATH and say as follows:

(1)   I am the receiver in this matter and was appointed receiver by an Order dated (*date*).

(2)   This affidavit is in support of my application for an order to execute a statutory will for the patient pursuant to s 96(1)(e) of the Mental Health Act 1983.

(3)   'Exhibit 1' is a medical certificate in Form CP3 in which the patient's GP has expressed the opinion that the patient is incapable, by reason of mental disorder, of managing and administering (his)/(her) property and affairs.

(4)   'Exhibit 2' is a report dated (*date*) in which the patient's GP has expressed the opinion that the patient is incapable of making a valid will for (himself)/(herself).

(5)   The patient is domiciled in England and Wales, and owns no immovable property outside England and Wales.

(6)   The patient was born on (*date*) and is a (*marital status*).

(7)   I am the patient's (*state the relationship of the applicant to the patient*).

(8)   'Exhibit 3' is a 'family tree' showing the relationship between the patient and the other members of (his)/(her) family, naming the members of the family and giving their dates of birth or current ages, where known to me.

(9)   'Exhibit 4' is a copy of the last will executed by the patient on (*date*).

(10) In clause (*number*) of the will the patient has left (his)/(her) residuary estate to 'such of my nephews and nieces as shall survive me and if more than one in equal shares between them'.

(11) The patient's niece (*name*) died on (*date*) and was survived by her three children, namely (*names*). Under the terms of the patient's present will the share of the residuary estate to which (*name of deceased niece*) would have been entitled if she had survived the patient will now be divided equally between the patient's other nephews and nieces if they survive the patient. I am sure that this is not what the patient would have intended or wished, and I believe that, if (he)/(she) were mentally capable of doing so, the patient would execute a codicil or new will to ensure that (*deceased niece's*) children inherit their late mother's share of the estate.

(12) 'Exhibit 5' is a draft of the proposed statutory will. Its terms replicate the present will except that it is now proposed that, if any of the patient's

nephews or nieces predecease (him)/(her), the share of the residuary estate to which they would have been entitled will be held in trust for their children who survive the patient and attain the age of 18 years, and if more than one in equal shares. The inclusion of this provision means that it is possible that a minor could become entitled to a share of the patient's residuary estate, and accordingly it will be necessary to appoint more than one trustee. It is proposed that (*name of proposed executor and trustee*) be appointed, and (his)/(her) consent to act is exhibited as 'Exhibit 6'.

(13) 'Exhibit 7' is a statement of the patient's current capital assets.

(14) 'Exhibit 8' is a statement of the patient's current income, both before and after the deduction of tax.

(15) The patient's only outgoings are the fees for (his)/(her) accommodation, board and personal care at (*name and address of residential care home*). The present fees are £ ...... per week, and the fees are generally reviewed in (*month*) each year.

(16) The terms of the proposed statutory will have no inheritance tax implications.

SWORN &c

3 STATUTORY WILL: COMMENCEMENT

THIS IS THE LAST WILL of me .... (*full name of Patient*) ....
of .... (*Patient's address*) ....
acting by .... (*authorised person's full name*) ....
the person authorised in that behalf by an Order dated the .... day of
.... 19.. made under the Mental Health Act 1983.

I HEREBY REVOKE all former Wills and Codicils made by me and declare this to be my last Will.

(*Insert the contents of the statutory will in numbered paragraphs and conclude with the testimonium and attestation clause in Precedent 4*)

4 STATUTORY WILL: TESTIMONIUM AND ATTESTATION CLAUSE[1]

IN WITNESS whereof this Will is signed by me (*full name of Patient*) acting by (*full name of authorised person*) pursuant to the said Order this .... day of .... 19..

SIGNED by the said (*full name of Patient*)
by the said (*full name of authorised person*)
and by the said (*full name of authorised person*) with (his)/(her) own name pursuant to
the said Order in our presence and attested by
us in the presence of the said (*full name of authorised person*)

(*Names and addresses of the **two or more** witnesses*)[2]

SEALED with the official seal of the
Court of Protection this   day
of   19..[3]

---

1 The attestation clause must comply with the execution requirements contained in the Mental Health Act 1983, s 97(1).
2 *Ibid*, s 97(1)(a).
3 *Ibid*, s 97(1)(c).

---

5 STATUTORY WILL: CONSENT OF PROPOSED EXECUTOR OR TRUSTEE TO ACT[1]

COURT OF PROTECTION

IN THE MATTER OF   A PATIENT

I .... (*full name of proposed executor/trustee*) ....
of .... (*address of proposed executor/trustee*) ....
CONSENT to acting as an executor and trustee of the patient's will.

SIGNED ....

DATED ....

I .... (*full name of person certifying the above signature*) ....
of .... (*address*) ....
CERTIFY that the signature written above is that of the person giving the consent.

SIGNED ....

DATED ....

1 This form is based on the Court of Protection's printed Form CP14A.

6 RECEIPT AND UNDERTAKING FOR SAFE CUSTODY OF A PATIENT'S WILL[1]

COURT OF PROTECTION   No

IN THE MATTER OF   (A PATIENT)

WE HEREBY ACKNOWLEDGE the receipt of the articles and documents mentioned in the Schedule hereto which are deposited with us in the name of the above-named Patient to be held for safe custody.

AND WE UNDERTAKE not to part with the same during (his)/(her) lifetime without the directions under seal of the Court of Protection.

SCHEDULE

	FOR OFFICIAL USE ONLY
INSERT DETAILS OF INVESTMENT, ETC, IN THIS COLUMN LEAVING DOUBLE SPACING BETWEEN EACH ENTRY	(Changes in investments, etc, to be noted in pencil only.)

THE TITLE AND ADDRESS OF THE BANK, THE DATE, AND THE SIGNATURE OF THE PROPER OFFICER OF THE BANK SHOULD BE PLACED IMMEDIATELY BELOW THE LAST ENTRY, SO THAT ADDITIONS MAY BE MADE AS NECESSARY.

DATED   19   .

TO THE COURT OF PROTECTION

1 This precedent is based on Form CP12, or Form no 11 in Heywood & Massey, *Court of Protection Practice* (12th edition, Sweet & Maxwell, 1991), pp 396, 397.

INDEX